21世纪英语专业系列教材

A Textbook on English-Chinese Translation

英汉翻译教程

（第二版）

杨士焯　编著

图书在版编目(CIP)数据

英汉翻译教程/杨士焯编著. —2 版. —北京:北京大学出版社,2011.3
 (21 世纪英语专业系列教材)
 ISBN 978-7-301-11277-9

Ⅰ. ①英… Ⅱ. ①杨… Ⅲ. ①英汉－翻译－高等学校－教材 Ⅳ. ①H315.9

中国版本图书馆 CIP 数据核字(2011)第 024030 号

| 书　　　　名：英汉翻译教程(第二版)
| 著作责任者：杨士焯　编著
| 责 任 编 辑：李　颖
| 标 准 书 号：ISBN 978-7-301-11277-9/H·2761
| 出 版 发 行：北京大学出版社
| 地　　　　址：北京市海淀区成府路 205 号　100871
| 网　　　　址：http://www.pup.cn　电子信箱：evalee1770@sina.com
| 电　　　　话：邮购部 62752015　发行部 62750672　编辑部 62754382　出版部 62754962
| 印 刷 者：北京鑫海金澳胶印有限公司
| 经 销 者：新华书店
| 787 毫米×1092 毫米　16 开本　18.5 印张　450 千字
| 2006 年 9 月第 1 版
| 2011 年 3 月第 2 版　2020 年 5 月第 9 次印刷(总第 14 次印刷)
| 定　　　　价：38.00 元

未经许可,不得以任何方式复制或抄袭本书之部分或全部内容。
版权所有,侵权必究
举报电话：(010)62752024　电子信箱：fd@pup.pku.edu.cn

第二版前言

本教程从拿到初版样书的那一刻起，修订增补的工作就从未间断过。书中出现的各种问题，小至标点符号、拼写错误，大至立论是否得当、译文是否正确等，无时不在作者心中萦绕盘桓。凡有错误，皆恨不得立马改之为快！作者上课或科研甚至闲暇之时，不忘用心于广搜博览，故当出版社通知计划再版时，手头增补资料已是现成，唯花数日拼装而已。再版除补缺补漏外，还对部分章节加以改写，务必使新读者一览而收全功之效，使老读者温故而知新。

感谢国内十几所院校的看重，这本教程或作为英语专业本科和研究生的英汉翻译教材，或作为考研的必备参考书。我和这其中一些院校的师生（如东北师范大学傅兴涛同学）多有交流，他们的支持和信息反馈让我感到我不是一个人在战斗。

感谢厦门大学英语系本科生、研究生和校选课的同学们，他们是这本教材是否符合学以致用的最直接检验者和反馈者。书中不少错误和问题就是在他们的质疑和探讨下得到更正的。

感谢我的历届研究生，如徐琴、彭宇航、郑琳、黄玮、李懿、刘丹、吕杭蔚等，他们对其中部分章节，尤其"数字和倍数的翻译"一节反复打磨，使之臻于完善。

最后我希望这个第二版能将错误减到最少，而使读者受益最多。诚如是，吾愿足矣！

前　言

　　英汉翻译教学,首先是教材建设问题。所谓工欲善其事,必先利其器。一本教材的编写适当与否,直接影响到在此教材模式培养下的学生,真正马虎不得。本书编著者多年从事英语专业三年级翻译教学工作,深刻意识到翻译教学的基础在于词句的锤炼锻造。大部分翻译实施的层面其实就是在词句上,而且比较好把握。有了词句翻译的技能训练,才能过渡到句群、段落翻译,并且学会从整体上把握语篇。这其实是一个连续体,并不是矛盾的。

　　本教程的创作思路是这样的:首先介绍翻译的基本知识、翻译的方法论,使学生头脑中对翻译形成初步认识。接着我们从翻译的理解角度出发,详细论述词法和句法上的翻译疑难问题,使学生意识到翻译学习的过程,就是深化认识英语语言的过程,错误理解导致错误翻译。在"翻译的技巧篇",我们介绍了翻译的基本技法,并对时下流行的一些技巧,加以删繁就简,重新整合。在"翻译的文采篇",作者采用一种全新的编排法,精心罗致了许多精彩佳译,以展示翻译的魅力和中文的神奇,使学生认识到翻译不但是技巧,也是艺术。"翻译的文化篇"则从文化的角度论述原语文化和译语文化对译文的双重影响,使学生意识到文化和意识形态因素也是引起译文在各种程度上有别于原文的关键因素。在"翻译的语篇类型篇",我们介绍本科学生基本应掌握的翻译语篇类型,使之对以前学习到的翻译知识和技巧等得以综合运用。考虑到学生即将面临的英语八级考试中的英汉翻译,我们专章分析了英语八级英汉翻译。本书最后的"翻译写作篇"目的在强调翻译是一种写作,应注重写作能力的培养,并据此提出"翻译写作学"的概念。

　　纵观全书,自认有四大特色:1. 例证丰富。全书收集、筛选精美佳译1600句、85篇短文、篇章。学习者可以从精彩译文中直接感悟翻译。本书的雏形原本就是《英汉语句佳译撷萃》。2. 文中论述部分言简意赅,非常适合教师课堂讲授和临场发挥,丰富的例句、例文省却教师不少抄写工夫。3. 本书采纳了许多非翻译教程类的翻译著述编排法,有述有论,许多译文都附有详细评析,它将译者的用心、所使用的译巧加以精心剖析,务必使学习者知其所以然。4. 书中相当部分章节是作者历年科研、创作成果(论文、译作等)的有机融入和总成,作者的治学观点得以充分体现,并借此以提高本教材的学术价值。

　　当然,本作者深知,一部教程的编写,所赖绝非作者一人之力,它是对前人成果的吸收、继承和创新的结果。由此我要感谢所有使本书的编撰获益良多的各位前辈和同行。尽管我在文中和参考书目中都尽可能标出受益于他们的地方,仍恐有挂一漏万之憾,特表歉意。

　　在此我要感谢林纪熹、叶子南、马红军、孙万彪、苏福忠、陈廷祐、冯树鉴、黄邦杰、林相周、李运兴、毛荣贵、思果、许渊冲等专家学者,这其中大部分我是只拜读其书而无缘结识其人。从他们的书中我学习了很多东西,非常敬佩他们的翻译研究的学养,恨不能集他们之长于一身,而解见贤思齐之渴。

感谢厦门大学连淑能教授,我于1997年从连教授那里接手英语系英汉翻译教学工作,长期使用连教授编写的《英译汉教程》,边教边学,揣摩浸润,获益良多。连教授非常关心这本教材的编写,并亲自帮助审阅校改,纠错多多,提出了许多可贵的意见建议,深表铭谢。

感谢我的硕士导师,浙江大学郭建中教授,是他带我进入了翻译研究和教学的一片天地。毕业多年以来,郭建中教授对我一如既往地奖掖扶持,耐心未尝稍减。书中引用的先生的一些重要的翻译理论观点和论述给本书增色不少。先生俯允的佳序也使拙书赖以自壮。

感谢厦门大学外文学院副院长傅似逸教授,承蒙她的热情推荐,我得以和北京大学出版社取得联系。

我的研究生朱玉敏、黄阿仙、辜莹莹和李梅红帮助校对了全书,朱玉敏协助整理了"数字和倍数的翻译"一节,在此一并感谢。

最后感谢北京大学出版社的游冠辉编辑和李颖编辑,感谢他们的辛勤工作。

杨士焯

厦门大学外文学院英语系

2006年9月10日

szyang@xmu.edu.cn

序

近年来，国内外翻译研究蓬勃发展，高等学校的翻译教学也越来越受到重视。最近，教育部批准复旦大学、广东外语外贸大学和河北师范学院设立翻译专业，这是翻译学科成熟的标志。

翻译课历来是外语专业高年级学生的必修课。《高等学校英语专业英语教学大纲》的"教学原则"中明确规定："在注意听、说、读、写、译各项技能全面发展的同时，更应该突出说、写、译能力的培养。"说、写、译，都是涉及英语的应用能力，而其中的"译"更是涉及到汉、英两种语言的运用能力。学外语、教外语的人都普遍认为，翻译能力的高低，是一个人外语水平综合能力的体现。因此，外语专业重视翻译课的教学，自不待言。越来越多的业内外人士也都认识到，懂外语不一定就能搞翻译。因此，翻译课的重要性，就不言而喻了。而要上好翻译课，教材是至关重要的。

据不完全统计，从1980至2005年，出版的各种翻译教材就有上百种。那么，杨士焯的这本《英汉翻译教程》是否仅仅在同类翻译教材中多了一本呢？

我从头至尾通读了这本教程，认为整本教材的内容编排，有显著的不同于同类教材的特点。编著者在绪论篇中介绍了翻译的基本知识、翻译方法和翻译过程后，全书分为理解篇、技巧篇、文采篇、文化篇、语篇类型篇、八级英译汉试卷评析篇和翻译写作篇。其中的文采篇、语篇类型篇和翻译写作篇等更是别具特色。下面我把本教程的特色作一个简要的介绍：

1. 教材紧密结合大学英语专业本科学生实际，紧扣教学大纲和英语专业四、八级对翻译课的要求。由于编著者多年从事英语本科翻译教学，了解本科学生水平和学习翻译的难点，因此教材深浅程度适中，能适应多种类型高校的英语专业本科学生使用。

2. 教材从对翻译的认识入手，介绍了翻译的基本理论和知识、翻译方法和翻译过程。由于编著者长期从事翻译研究，深得翻译理论精髓，并择善介绍给本科学生。同时，在后面的各章中，编著者把当代有代表性的翻译理论，如纽马克的语言学翻译理论、文化学派的操纵理论、温努蒂的异化理论等，都能自然地融合进对例句和篇章的分析讲解之中，使理论与实践密切结合。

3. 强调英语语言基本功的训练。因为编著者一直在英语本科翻译教学的第一线工作，深知学生的英语语言和基本功水平。因此，编著者从对英语的理解入手，提高学生的英语理解水平。第二章"翻译的理解篇"的内容，也与一般的翻译教科书不同。本教程特别强调学生英语理解的难点。在词汇理解方面，编著者编排了专有名词先天性歧义、普通名词先天性歧义、普通词语结合后产生的歧义和普通词语与专业术语的词义混淆等内容。在句法方面，编著者讨论了英语相似句、怪异句、修饰结构疑难句等问题。这些也往往是一般翻译教科书编者所忽略的。

4. 在第三章的"翻译技巧篇"，编著者安排的内容和讨论翻译技巧的角度也与众不同。编著者特别强调拆译——不仅是长句的拆译，而且还有短句的拆译，可谓抓住了英汉句法差异的根本和英汉翻译技巧的根本。这些安排，必然是出于编著者自己的翻译实践和翻译教学的经验所致。

5. "文采篇"中，讨论了英译汉中中国古代诗文典籍词语、句法及四字格词组的运用。就我所知，在编著此书之前，编著者曾广泛搜集有关例句，编写了《英汉语句佳译撷萃》，这次择其精华，编进了本教程，其中"钱钟书古文译法赏析"、"四字格词组翻译欣赏"、"巧译英语意美、音美、形美"和"电影名称佳译"等，更是不可多得的材料，对学生提高翻译能力有很大的作用。但编著者也指出了翻译中不宜滥用四字组成语的问题。

6. 编著者在"翻译的语篇类型篇"一章中，讨论了报纸杂志语篇、文学语篇和科技语篇的翻译。应该说，在此章的内容安排上，表现了编著者对本科翻译教学十分现实的态度。在第二节"文学语篇的翻译"中，只涉及了散文和小说的翻译，而没有讨论诗歌和戏剧的翻译。讨论的方法是给出同一语篇几种不同的译文，供学生比较、揣摩，从中体会翻译的真谛。

7. 全书编写密切结合英语本科对学生翻译能力要求的实际，辟出专章，分析了专业英语八级英译汉试卷，给学生准备八级考试以实际的帮助。

8. 编著者不回避现在大学生的汉语使用水平低下的问题，特别强调了亟须提高学生中文水平的问题。因此，教程中最后一章的"翻译写作篇"，就特别能切中要害。编著者提出的这个观点，可谓是"翻译是再创作"和"翻译是重写"观点的发展和创新。

此外，全书例句丰富，精彩例句俯拾皆是。这儿仅举数例，以见一斑。

People who value their privileges above their principle soon lose both.

重利轻义，利义皆失。

It was just growing dark, as she shut the garden gate.

关上院门时，已是暮色苍茫了。

Without industry and frugality nothing will do and with them everything.

不勤不俭，一事无成；又勤又俭，事事亨通。

特别需要一提的是，编著者除平时精心搜集例句外，不少材料是从自己译作中选出来的译文。例如，编著者曾参与笔者主持的《麦克米伦百科全书》的翻译，教程中的不少例句就选自编著者自己的译文。

教程也提供了大量、多样的练习，教师和学生均可根据需要选择使用。

当然，这么一部内容宏富的教材，不可能白璧无瑕。例如，第一章对理论的解释尚可通俗些，个别正文例句与练习有重复等。瑕不掩瑜，尽管这是一句套话，但对本教程来说，则应该是符合事实的评价。

杨士焯老师是我第一次带的两位硕士生之一。大学本科毕业后，他分配在厦门海关工作。在一般人眼里，海关工作是一个"美差"。但他放弃优厚的待遇，离开家乡，来杭州大学攻读硕士学位。这足以看出其对翻译的爱好和对学问的追求。因此，他以优异的成绩获得硕士学位,也就毫不奇怪了。1990年毕业后,回家乡厦门大学任教,对专业一如既往地孜孜以求,一步一个脚印,教学、翻译、研究,三管齐下,刻苦努力,成绩斐然。尽管他毕业多年,但我们之间一直保持着师生的情谊和学术上的联系。我们曾数度合作,完成多项翻译任务,也经常交流文章和研究心得。当他通过 E-mail 发给我这本教程初稿,并希望我能为之作序时,我欣然命笔。因为,看到自己学生在学业上作出的成绩,真比自己取得的成绩更高兴!因为,只有"青出于蓝而胜于蓝",社会才会发展,人类才会进步。是为序。

郭建中
2006年6月6日于杭州

目　　录

第一章　翻译的基本知识篇 …………………………………………………… (1)
- 第一节　翻译的类型 ………………………………………………………… (1)
- 第二节　东西方学者论翻译 ………………………………………………… (2)
- 第三节　翻译的方法 ………………………………………………………… (4)
- 第四节　翻译的过程 ………………………………………………………… (7)

第二章　翻译的理解篇 …………………………………………………………… (10)
- 第一节　理解与词汇研究 …………………………………………………… (10)
- 第二节　理解与句法分析 …………………………………………………… (18)

第三章　翻译的技巧篇 …………………………………………………………… (40)
- 第一节　拆译 ………………………………………………………………… (41)
- 第二节　转换 ………………………………………………………………… (47)
- 第三节　精简与增补 ………………………………………………………… (52)
- 第四节　实译与虚译 ………………………………………………………… (59)
- 第五节　褒译与贬译 ………………………………………………………… (62)
- 第六节　倒译与顺译 ………………………………………………………… (65)
- 第七节　反译 ………………………………………………………………… (70)
- 第八节　被动式的翻译 ……………………………………………………… (75)
- 第九节　数字和倍数的翻译 ………………………………………………… (79)

第四章　翻译的文采篇 …………………………………………………………… (89)
- 第一节　巧用中国古代诗文典籍词语、句法 ……………………………… (90)
- 第二节　巧用汉语四字格词语 ……………………………………………… (99)
- 第三节　巧用汉语习惯语 …………………………………………………… (115)
- 第四节　巧译英语意美、音美、形美 ……………………………………… (133)
- 第五节　巧译电影片名 ……………………………………………………… (140)

第五章　翻译的文化篇 …………………………………………………………… (146)
- 第一节　文化差异与表达差异 ……………………………………………… (146)
- 第二节　直译、归译与译语文化因素的介入 ……………………………… (147)
- 第三节　英汉亲属词称谓的文化差异性及汉译处理 ……………………… (152)
- 第四节　翻译的意识形态影响 ……………………………………………… (155)

第六章　翻译的语篇 ……………………………………………………………… (157)
- 第一节　报刊语篇的翻译 …………………………………………………… (157)

第二节　文学语篇的翻译 ································ (165)
　　第三节　科技语篇翻译 ···································· (204)
第七章　八级英译汉试卷评析篇 ································ (224)
　　第一节　简介 ·· (224)
　　第二节　试卷评析 ·· (225)
　　第三节　亟待加强的几个问题 ······························ (233)
第八章　翻译写作篇 ··· (238)
　　第一节　汉语的表达优势和行文特点 ··················· (238)
　　第二节　翻译写作论 ·· (240)
　　第三节　译文写作的格式规范 ···························· (242)
　　第四节　译文修改 ·· (244)
练习答案 ··· (246)
参考书目 ··· (282)

第一章　翻译的基本知识篇

第一节　翻译的类型

根据语言学家罗曼·雅可布逊(Roman Jakobson)(1959/1966：233)论述，翻译可以分成三种类型：

语内翻译(intralingual translation, an interpretation of verbal signs by means of other signs in the same language)，是指同一语言中用一些语言符号解释另一些语言符号，如古文翻译成现代文。

语际翻译(interlingual translation, an interpretation of verbal signs by means of some other language)，是指两种语言之间的翻译，即用另一种语言的语符来解释一种语言的语符，这就是人们通常所指的"翻译"，如英汉翻译。

符际翻译(intersemiotic translation, an interpretation of verbal signs by means of non-verbal sign system)，是指通过非语言的符号系统解释语言符号，或用语言符号解释非语言符号，如把语言符号用图画、手势、数学、电影或音乐来表达。

罗曼·雅可布逊的这三种类型的划分具有重要的意义。他使我们认识了广义和狭义的翻译概念。雅可布逊首次提出了翻译中的对等概念。在语内翻译中，是用一个语符单位替代另一个语符单位，对一个词的翻译可以选用同义词或者迂回表达法。但同义词不可能是完全对等的词，而改换说法会使原意有增减。同样，在语际翻译中，符号与符号之间一般也没有完全的对等关系。人们通常不是用一种语言的语符替代另一种语言中的单个的符号，而是替代"更大的单位"，即"信息"(message)，是用信息替代信息。也就是说，在语际翻译中，我们所关注的不仅是符号与符号之间的对应(即逐词对应)，而且也关注符号和符号组合的对等。翻译所涉及的是两种不同语符的对等信息。但双语符之间不存在完全对等的关系，对等关系存在于符号所承载的信息。因此，语际翻译不是符号翻译，而是信息转换(李文革，2004)。符际翻译的内容更是广泛多样，把语言符号转换为其他形式，如图画、电影、电视或音乐，其改编的幅度可能更大，常会涉及情节、内容、人物等的较大更改。雅可布逊对翻译的三种分类，表明他对语言概念的观点，即语言概念是广泛的和无所不包的。这三种类型的翻译，几乎包括了一切语言(和非语言)的交际活动。

翻译的定义虽然广泛，但当我们说"翻译"时，自然是指"语际翻译"。而中文"翻译"一词词义丰富，基本可以涵盖英文的四种表达形式，表达四种不同的含义：

translating (翻译过程)：进行翻译的过程，是活动而不是有形的物体；

a translation（译作）：翻译过程的产品，即译语语篇；
translation（翻译）：一个抽象概念，包括翻译过程和该过程的产品。
translator（译者）：翻译过程的执行者，译作的制作者。

在用中文表达时，我们或许可以用"翻译"一言以蔽之，但在用英文表述时，就要注意使用不同的词语。

第二节 东西方学者论翻译

翻译是把一种语言文字所表达的意义用另一种语言文字表达出来，具体说来，就是"换易言语使相解也"（[唐]贾公彦《义疏》）。翻译的定义是开放性的，而不是排斥性的。其目的不是要给翻译套上"紧箍咒"，或给出一个十全十美的定义，而是通过各家对翻译概念的论述，来展现翻译的特性和本质。

一、西方翻译家、翻译理论家观点

语文学观点

The translation should give a complete transcript of the idea of the original work.

The style and manner of writing should be of the same character with that of the original.

The translation should have all the ease of original composition. (Tytler, 1790)

Translation should produce a version which may be read with as much pleasure as the original, and yet remain faithful to its spirit, sense and style. (Federov, 1953)

Translation, the surmounting of the obstacles, is made possible by an equivalence of thought that lies behind its different verbal expressions. (Savory, 1959)

Translation is a pane of glass through which we look at the work of art. (Mounin, 1963)

语言学观点

Translation is "an interpretation of verbal signs by means of some other language" (Jakobson, 1959).

Translation is "the replacement of textual material in one language (SL) by equivalent textual material in another language (TL)" (Catford, 1965).

Translating consists in reproducing in the receptor language the closest natural equivalent of the source-language message, first in terms of meaning and secondly in terms of style. (Nida, 1969/1982)

Translation is the replacement of a representation of a text in one language by a representation of an equivalent text in a second language. (Meetham and Hudson, 1972)

Translation is the expression in another language (or target language) of what has been expressed in another, source language, preserving semantic and stylistic equivalences. (Dubois, 1973)

Translation is the "transfer of 'meaning' from one set of language signs to another set of language signs" (Lawendowski, 1978).

功能理论观点

Translation is the production of a functional target text maintaining a relationship with a given source text that is specified according to the intended or demanded function of the target text. (Nord, 1991)

Translation is a written communication in a second language having the same meaning as the written communication in a first language. (www.wordreference.com)

二、中国翻译家、翻译理论家学者观点

严复：信、达、雅

译事三难：信、达、雅。求其信，已大难矣。顾信矣不达，虽译犹不译也，则达尚焉。……易曰修辞立诚。子曰辞达而已。又曰言之无文，行之不远。三者乃文章正轨，亦即为译事楷模。故信达而外，求其尔雅。（严复：《天演论》序言）

(Translation has to do three difficult things: to be faithful, expressive, and elegant. It is difficult enough to be faithful to the original, and yet if a translation is not expressive, it is tantamount to having no translation. Hence expressiveness should be required too.

The Book of Changes says that the first requisite of rhetoric is truthfulness; Confucius says that expressiveness is all that matters in language. He adds that if one's language lacks grace, it won't go far. These three qualities then are the criterion of good writing and, I believe, of good translation too. Hence besides faithfulness and expressiveness I also aim at elegance.)

鲁迅：信、顺

凡是翻译，必须兼顾两面，一则当然力求其易解，一则保存原作的丰姿。（《翻译论集》）

林语堂：忠实标准、通顺标准、美的标准

翻译是一种艺术。……翻译的艺术所依赖的：第一是译者对于原文文字上及内容上透彻的了解，第二是译者有相当的国文程度，能写清顺畅达的中文，第三是译事上的训练，译者对于翻译标准及手术的问题有相当的见解。（《翻译论集》）

朱生豪论翻译

朱生豪在谈到翻译莎士比亚的宗旨时说："第一，求于最大可能之范围内，保存原作之神韵；必不得已而求其次，亦必以明白晓畅之字句，忠实传达原文之意趣；而于逐字逐句对照式之硬译，则未敢赞同。凡遇原文中与中国语法不合之处，往往再四咀嚼，不惜全部更易原文之结构，务使作者之命意豁然呈露，不为晦涩之字句所掩蔽。每译一段竟，必先自拟为

读者,查阅译文中有无暧昧不明之处。又必自拟为舞台上之演员,审辨语调之是否顺口,音节之是否调和。一字一句之未惬,往往苦思累日。"(《翻译论集》)

傅雷:重神似不重形似

译文必须为纯粹之中文。

任何作品,不精读四、五遍决不动笔,是为译事基本法门。第一要将原作(连同思想、感情、气氛、情调等等)化为我有,方能谈到迻译。(《论文学翻译书》)

钱钟书:化境

一国文字和另一国文字之间必然有差距,译者的理解和文风跟原作品的内容和形式之间也不会没有距离……翻译总是以原作的那一国语文为出发点而以译成的这一国语文为到达点。从最初出发以至终竟到达,这是很艰辛的历程。一路上颠顿风尘,遭遇风险,不免有所遗失或受些损伤。因此译文总有失真和走样的地方,在意义或口吻上违背或不很贴合原文。

文学翻译的最高理想可以说是"化"。把作品从一国文字转变成另一国文字,既能不因语文习惯的差异而露出生硬牵强的痕迹,又能完全保存原作的风味,那就算得入于"化境"。(《翻译论集》)

第三节 翻译的方法

一、直译与意译、异化与归化

翻译活动始终受到二分法的制约,这反映出了翻译的本质特征。它们体现在直译与意译、异化与归化等对子上。它们都是翻译的对立统一的方法论,对翻译实践有极大的指导意义。英国翻译理论家西奥多·塞弗瑞(1957:49)曾列举出著名的翻译六对原则:

1. A translation must give the words of the original.
   译文必须保留原文的措辞。
   A translation must give the ideas of the original.
   译文必须传达原文的思想。
2. A translation should read like an original work.
   译文读起来应该像原创作品。
   A translation should read like a translation.
   译文读起来应该像译文。
3. A translation should reflect the style of the original.
   译文应该反映原文的风格。
   A translation should possess the style of the translator.
   译文应该具有译者的风格。
4. A translation should read as a contemporary of the original.
   译文读起来应该像原文同时代的作品。

A translation should read as a contemporary of the translator.

译文读起来应该像译者同时代的作品。

5. A translation may add to or omit from the original.

译文可以对原文有所增减。

A translation may never add to or omit from the original.

译文不能对原文有所增减。

6. A translation of verse should be in prose.

诗歌应当译成散文。

A translation of verse should be in verse.

诗歌应当译成诗歌。

以上这六对原则基本可以延伸或归纳到直译与意译、异化与归化的对子里去，它们是对立统一的结合体。历来的翻译实践和论述基本离不开这一点，虽然各家对这些概念的定义会有不同，乃至发展创新，但基本大同小异。郭建中教授在总结了历来无数的定义和概念的争议后，重新作了非常全面而系统的界定(2004：211)：

直译(literal translation)：译文的语言表达形式，在目的语规范容许的范围内，基本上遵循源语表达的形式，而又忠实于原文的意思。

意译(free translation)：译文的语言表达形式，完全遵循目的语的规范而不考虑源语的表达形式，但又忠于原文的意思。

异化(foreignization)：在译文中保留源语的文化观念和价值观，特别是保留原文的比喻、形象和民族地方色彩等。

归化(domestication)：在译文中把源语中的文化观念和价值观，用目的语中的文化观念和价值观来替代，特别是把原文的比喻、形象和民族地方色彩等用相应的目的语中的比喻、形象和民族地方色彩来替代。

本着把事情简单化的思想，我以为，这两对方法是有重叠和互补的地方。首先，直译包含意译，直译是原文形式和内容兼具，而意译则一般顾及内容。直译和异化一致，直译既然遵循源语表达的形式，而又忠实于原文的意思，不就把原文的比喻、形象和民族地方色彩等传递过去了吗？倒是意译和归化不能混为一谈：意译是只传其意，而归化则是把原文的比喻、形象和民族地方色彩等用相应的目的语中的比喻、形象和民族地方色彩来替代。例如"kill two birds with one stone"，译成"一石二鸟"是直译、异化；译成"一箭双雕"是归化，而不只是意译；译成"一举两得"或"一下做成两件事"才是意译。可以说异化、归化也是从形式上看文化，看翻译。如果把这两个对子整合，可以称之为异化、归化和意化，或**直译**、**归译(换译)**和**意译**。再者，采用异化、归化和意化，或直译、归译(换译)和意译，必须根据翻译的目的、译者的方式取向、译文语言的容许度和读者的接受能力来决定的，否则同样的原文可以衍生出各种不同译法的译文。

Birds of a feather flock together.（归译：物以类聚，人以群分。）

（直译：同毛鸟，飞一道。）

Laugh off one's head.（归译：笑掉大牙；捧腹大笑。）

（直译：笑掉脑袋。）

At sixes and sevens.（归译：颠三倒四；乱七八糟。）

（直译：颠六倒七；六七相杂。）

Neither fish nor fowls.（归译：不伦不类；不三不四；非驴非马。）

（直译：既非鱼，又非禽；非鱼非禽。）

按照辜正坤(2003:371)的论述，上面的译文都各具千秋。成语"物以类聚，人以群分"道出了这条成语的核心思想或称深层结构，对不懂外语者和一般娱乐性读者层来说，无疑是较受欢迎的，符合一般读者的习惯性审美趣味，且形式简洁，成语味浓，但直译"同毛鸟，飞一道"的好处在于译文"鸟"、"道"在押韵修辞这一层次上和原文的修辞结构"feather"、"together"功能对等。其二，从译文文字上可以明显地看出其内涵义。其三，它输入了外国人特有的表现法：我们以"物""人"作喻，而他们却用"鸟"来作喻，这就增加了本国语言文化的表达方式。

二、语义翻译与交际翻译

英国翻译理论家纽马克的语义与交际翻译则是从现代语言学的角度来论述形式与内容的关系。他把**语义翻译**（semantic translation）定义为在目的语的语义和句法结构尽可能容许的情况下，译出原文确切的上下文意义(1981:47)。它用于翻译所有那些原创的语篇，诸如文学、哲学、宗教、政治或人类学的语篇。这种表达性语篇的形式和内容一样重要，或者形式和内容密切结合因而无法分离。语义翻译试图再现原作精确的风格和格调：词语中的思维过程（表达形式）和交际翻译中词语后面的意图同样重要。语义翻译是以作者为中心的，为了保留作者的个性语言，译者不仅需要特别关注语篇的每一个词语，而且关注组合这些词语的句法，关注语篇特有的强调和节奏。对译者来说，他无权改进或更正源语篇。原来的词汇或语篇结构、句子长度、词位置等应尽量保留。下面这个法、英、中对照翻译典型地体现了语义翻译的特征：

Car la France n'est pas seule! Elle n'est pas seule! Elle n'est pas seule!（法）

For France is not alone! She is not alone! She is not alone!（英）

因为法国并不孤单！她不孤单！她不孤单！（中）

在这里，三个不同语种的语句序列、结构、语气基本相同。如果英译文写成："For remember this, France does not stand alone! She is not isolated."，或中译文写成："因为法国并不孤单！她有国际支持，她并不孤立。"表达虽然丰富了，但原句的结构模式变化了，原文的气势也就走样了。概而言之，语义翻译要求译文尽可能在词法、句法及至语气上都逼似原作，求得语义结构的对等或贴切。很明显，语义翻译是纽马克翻译理论的基础，它集中反映了纽马克对翻译中准确的重要性的关注。

交际翻译（communicative translation）是试图使读者阅读译文所得到的效果尽可能接近原文读者阅读原文得到的效果(1981:39)。

交际翻译应用于所有那些内容或信息比形式更重要的语篇。这就是那些所谓"普通的"语篇，他们构成译者日常工作的大部分。与语义翻译不同，交际翻译只面对译文读者，它关注作者意图，而不是作者的思维过程，它试图更能适应读者，使原作文化内容更能让读者接受。这不意味着译者非得忽略源语语篇的形式，相反，源语仍然是译者工作的基础。

如果在语义翻译中不准确总是错的话，那么，在交际翻译中，译者某种程度的干预总会出现。为了使信息内容尽可能为读者接受，呼唤效果尽可能强，纽马克认为：

译者有权去改正或改进文章的逻辑，用优美的或至少是功能良好的、符合句法的结构去取代笨拙的结构;删除晦涩的字句;消除重复和赘述;排除某个模棱两可的词句中不太可能的释义;修改并澄清难懂的行话(将松散的类属词削减至比较具体的成分),并将个人习语中的怪异词句,即语言的任意运用给予规范化。进一步说,译者有权改正论据错误和疏忽,一般是在脚注里加以说明。所有这些更正和改进在语义翻译中通常是不可接受的(1981:42)。

交际翻译出来的语篇比较易读、清楚、简洁和自然,使读者感觉它正是为他们而写。比起语义翻译出来的语篇更为地道。交际翻译与语义翻译的基本区别在下面例子中一目了然,在翻译这些语句上,交际翻译远远胜过语义翻译。

正确使用交际翻译的例句:
(a) *Défense de marcher sur le gazon*(法)
交际翻译:Keep off the grass(英)
　　　　勿踏草坪(中)
语义翻译:Walking on the turf is forbidden.(英)
　　　　或 It is forbidden to walk on the turf(英)
　　　　在草坪上走是禁止的(中)
(b) *Frisch angerstrichen*!(德)
交际翻译:Wet paint!(英)
　　　　油漆未干,请勿触摸!(中)
语义翻译:Recently painted!(英)
　　　　刚刷了油漆!(中)

从以上例句看出,在具有交流、警示意义的祈使句中,使用交际翻译的效果更佳。它其实就是寻找出译入语中的相应习惯语对译,而不是如语义翻译那样,如实地译出原文的内容乃至词、句子的语义结构。

第四节　翻译的过程

翻译的过程,最通俗地讲,是一个从理解到表达的过程。从翻译的语言学角度上讲,翻译的过程是一个解码和重编码的过程。其模式如下:

根据美国翻译理论家尤金·奈达的论述(1969:484),翻译需要经过三个步骤:(1) 分析,就是从语法和语义两个方面对原文的表层结构、原文的信息进行分析;(2) 传译,就是译者在脑子里把经过分析的信息从源语传译成目的语;(3) 重构,就是把传递过来的信息重新加以组织,最后形成译文。

英国翻译理论家罗杰·贝尔则描述了一个全面而略显复杂的翻译过程图(1991:21):

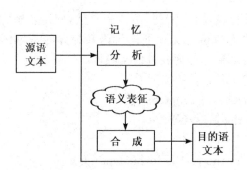

这一模式表明,源语文本向目的语文本的转化是通过发生在记忆中的几个过程来实现的:(1) 把源语文本分析成普遍的(不依赖任何特定语言)的语义表征(semantic representation);然后(2) 将该语义表征合成,构建目的语文本。在分析阶段,它包含句法分析、语义分析和语用分析。在合成阶段,它包含语用合成、语义合成和句法合成。句法分析就是语篇解读。语义分析是识别出施动者、过程、目标。语用分析是对语义所承担的交际功能进行分析,包括主述结构和语域分析。语义表征是一个抽象、普遍的概念和关系集,代表所译小句的全部思想。它包含句法、语义和语用信息。语义表征是对原文句子进行三向分析的结果,也是我们翻译时对一个新句子进行三向合成的基础。翻译不是把语言 A 的句子译成语言 B 中的句子。而是把语言 A 小句拆解成它的语义表征,以此为基础,在另一种语言里建立另一个可替换它的小句。在语用合成阶段,它要考虑如何处理原文的目的,如何处理原文本的主述结构,如何处理原文的风格。在语义合成阶段,创造出一些结构来承载命题内容并提出一个令人满意的命题,在此基础上进入句法合成,构成目的语语篇的符号串。总结起来可以为三大步骤:(1) 对源语语篇的分析;(2) 解读语篇时读者所能累积的全部认识;(3) 新目的语语篇的合成。

另一位英国翻译理论家巴希·海提姆则把译者在翻译工作中所遇到的各种基本问题按翻译过程归纳为以下几条(1991:20):

1. 对源语语篇的理解
(a) 从语法上分析语篇(语法和词汇)
(b) 能理解专业知识
(c) 能理解意想意义

2. 意义的迁移
(a) 传递词汇意义
(b) 传递语法意义
(c) 传递修辞意义,包括为潜在的读者提供隐含意义或可推导的意义

3. 对目标语语篇的评价
(a) 可读性

(b) 遵循目标语通用的话语规范
(c) 判断为达到具体目的的翻译的充分性

这告诉我们,译者应具备源语和目标语两种语言能力,深刻理解原文,以意义为中心进行转换翻译。在翻译的过程中,既要注意到读者,也要考虑到具体语篇和翻译目的。翻译过程虽然各家论述皆有不同,但总结起来,不外乎是"一个从理解到表达的过程"。

 本章推荐阅读书目

郭建中. 科普与科幻翻译[M]. 北京:中国对外翻译出版公司,2004.
罗新璋. 翻译论集[C]. 北京:商务印书馆,1984.
杨士焯. 英汉翻译写作学[M]. 北京:中国对外翻译出版公司,2012.
Bell, R. *Translation and Translating: Theory and Practice* [M]. London: Longman, 1991.
Newmark, P. *Approaches to Translation* [M]. Oxford: Pergamon, 1981.

第二章 翻译的理解篇

第一节 理解与词汇研究

英语一词多义与翻译中的望文生义

翻译是涉及至少两种语言的操作。本科英语专业学生一般在研修英汉翻译课之前就已接受两年英语专业基础课学习,他们已比较系统地掌握英语基本语法知识,其听、说、读、写能力已基本达到能表达、交流的要求,并已顺利通过全国英语专业四级考试。但是,这样的成绩还并不足以证明学习者已没有语言问题,翻译学习仍离不开语言基本功的锤炼。具有一定语言知识的人往往认为在英语词汇及语法结构的理解方面问题不大,好像困难仅仅在于汉语表达方面。其实,翻译能不能过关,主要决定于英汉两种语言水平的高低和实际经验的多少。掌握一些翻译技巧,只不过有助于扩大思路、提高熟练程度、使语句更加生色而已。不打好英汉两种语言的扎实基础,翻译是搞不好的。因此,本篇着重从理解的角度论述翻译中的词法与语法问题。

翻译时不仅要考虑到中英文的语篇、语体是否对等,还要照顾到具体词语的正确理解和传译,因为词是构筑词组、句子、段落和篇章最基本最具体的单位。翻译中的错误,大多表现在词语方面。英语词语讲究一词多义,越是普通常用的词,其在词典中的义项就越多。有些词,由于各方面的原因,翻译者很难把握其真切的含义,即使是有一定英语学习基础的人也常常免不了误判词义,影响到译文内容的精确性。这种一词多义可概括成以下几个方面:(1) 专有名词先天性歧义;(2) 普通词语先天性歧义;(3) 普通词语结合后产生新义;(4) 普通词语与专业术语的词义混淆。导致望文生义的主要原因是疏忽大意,未能根据上下文语境正确选择词义。

一、专有名词先天性歧义

英语专有名词,尤其是地名专有名词,在这方面表现得特别突出。由于篇幅关系,恕无法引出所述全文,但这并不意味着编著者在割离上下文情况下分析译例。

[1] A succulent desert cactus, ... native to tropical and subtropical *America*. (*The Macmillan Encyclopedia*,简称 ME)

译文:一种多汁沙漠仙人掌,……原产美洲热带、亚热带地区。

评析:此句中的"America"不能译为"美国",这里涉及普通历史、地理常识。事实上,

"America"和"American"严格来说应作"美洲"和"美洲的"解,现在则更多地用来指称"美国",即"the United States of America"(美利坚合众国)。因此此词应在一定的上下文中注意区分,否则就造成上义词与下义词关系的混淆。例中的"America"应为自然地理概念,而非行政概念。

[2] The first permanent *Anglo-American* settlement was established in 1821. （ME）

译文:第一个永久英裔美洲人定居点建立于1821年。

评析:本词皆可解作"英裔美洲人"或"英裔美国人",根据上下文判断,得克萨斯1821年成为开发地,直到1845年才加入联邦,成为美国第28州。因此,"英裔美国人"是以后的事。

[3] There are now 35 in *England*, eight in Scotland, two in Northern Ireland and one in Wales. （ME）

译文:现在在英格兰有35所,苏格兰有8所,北爱尔兰有2所,威尔士有1所。

评析:"England"常泛指"英国"。而"英国"和"英格兰"是两个不同的概念,"英国"之谓有其历史由来,它的英文全称是"the United Kingdom of Great Britain and Northern Ireland",简称UK,即联合王国。其中英格兰历来势力最大,主宰大不列颠事务,故转而代表全国。如今约定俗成,只好将就,但翻译时务必弄清其具体所指。本句曾请几个学生翻译,就有人将"England"翻译成"英国",结果和后面的"苏格兰"、"北爱尔兰"和"威尔士"造成概念上的混淆。在本句中,"England"只宜译成"英格兰",它和"苏格兰"、"北爱尔兰"和"威尔士"等构成英国(UK)整体。

[4] The majority of the population is of *Indian* and mixed descent, with minorities of African descent, *East Indians*, and others. （ME）

译文:居民以印第安人和混血人为主,有少数非洲后裔、东印度人等。

评析:根据《牛津高阶英汉双解词典》(第四版,1997),Indian 指:1. (native or inhabitant) of the Republic of India 印度共和国的(土著或居民);印度的;印度人。2. ＝American Indian,美洲印第安人。而 East Indian,根据《英汉大词典》,意为"东印度人",是旧时西方使用的一个含糊和不确切的名称,一般指印度、印度支那半岛、马来半岛和马来群岛等。这些带有浓厚历史地理色彩的词语极易造成混乱。解决的办法唯有了解历史和地理,详加考证,否则极易出错。

二、普通词语先天性歧义

普通词语的一词多义是英语中极其普遍的现象。这些多义词主要来自下面几个方面:原始意义与引申意义(如,"candidate"从原始意义"穿白衣服的人"到引申意义"候选人");普遍意义与特殊意义(如,"case"从"事例、实例"这一普遍意义到"病例"和"案件"两个特殊意义);抽象意义与具体意义(如,"beauty"表示"美貌"这种抽象意义到"美人"这一实体);字面意义与比喻意义(如,"cool"的字面意义为"凉的"比喻为"不热情的、冷淡的")。(汪榕培、李冬,1983)现举数例阐述之:

[5] *Maurice Sendak*, US *artist*, best known for his illustrations of children's books... （ME）

译文:莫里斯·森达克,美国画家,以在儿童书籍中画插图最为出名。

评析:根据《牛津高阶英汉双解词典》(第四版,1997),"artist"指 "person who practises any of the fine arts, esp. painting"(美术家)。但许多人都把它理解为"艺术家",因为"art"

一词更常用来表示"艺术",泛指绘画、雕塑、音乐、舞蹈、文学等,它还指技术、技艺、技巧等。在本例句中仍以"美术家"或"画家"更为准确。

[6] A small abscess at the root of an eyelash. Styes, which commonly occur *in crops*, are usually treated with warm compresses to drain the pus. (ME)

译文:睫毛根部的小脓肿。一般是<u>成群出现</u>,常以热敷排脓的方法治疗。

评析:英文斜体部分很容易译成"农业上普遍见于庄稼物",说明该词被理解为"庄稼"的诱惑力极强,且孤立地看并无错误。解决的办法就是联系上下文来置疑,因为在这里出现"庄稼"是不合逻辑的。

[7] Translations of French romances, Latin *histories*, and saints' lives were part of the saga tradition...(ME)

译文:法国传奇故事、拉丁<u>历史剧</u>和使徒列传等翻译作品也属于萨迦传说的一部分。

评析:此句英文斜体部分有"历史剧"的义项,但不少学生常习惯翻译成"历史"。

[8] Nyalas are *shy* and nocturnal, inhabiting dense undergrowth...(ME)

译文:林羚<u>易受惊</u>,夜间活动,居住在稠密的下层灌丛中……

评析:此句英文斜体部分极易译成"害羞",这主要涉及词的搭配问题。但人们常常拘泥于基本义而难以在译文中考虑词义是否搭配。

[9] If the skin has become thoroughly wet or one has perspired a great deal, *sunscreens* should be applied as often as every 30 to 60 minutes to maintain a reasonably high degree of effectiveness.

误译:如皮肤已完全潮润,或大量排汗,则应每隔30分钟或60分钟使用<u>遮阳屏幕</u>,以保证适当的高效。

改译:如果浑身湿透,或者大量排汗,应每隔30分钟到60分钟涂用一次<u>防晒油</u>,以保持理想的防晒效果。(《翻译批评散论》,132)

评析:误译中的"遮阳屏幕"令人费解,"sunscreens"确有"遮阳帘"和"遮阳板"一类的含义,但它还有"防晒油"的含义。因其多义,导致误解。

[10] Clark in "Handle with Care": A bittersweet *case* of double identities.

误译:《小心翼翼》,主角克拉克,这是一部集好人和坏蛋于一身的啼笑因缘<u>片</u>。

改译:《小心翼翼》中的克拉克——一个具有双重身份、令人又爱又恨的<u>角色</u>。

评析:原文中的"case"是多义词,冒号后的成分显然用来说明主语 Clark 是怎样一个人。"case"在这里是指"an extraordinary character",即指具有某一特点的人。可惜这词义太偏,如果原文是"man"或"person",怎么会引起这样的麻烦?

[11] I have been to Edinburgh just for two days, and my brothers have followed *in the train of my trip*.

误译:我到达爱丁堡刚刚两天,我的兄弟们就乘坐我旅行的<u>火车接踵而至</u>。

改译:我到达爱丁堡刚刚两天,我的兄弟们就<u>循着我的行踪</u>到来了。(《译事余墨》,51)

评析:英文句子有点蹩脚,是那种不够地道却又从语法上找不到什么毛病的句子。问题出在"train"这个词上。从词源上讲,"train"的意思更接近"a succession or series of things"(一列或一溜东西)。火车不就是一串车厢和车头组成的东西吗?这个误译是因为对"train"这个词了解不够细致所致。"in the train of"意为"接着"、"继……之后"。可以说,这个词确实令人迷惑,上下文也起了误导作用。

三、普通词语结合后产生新义

根据陆国强(1999:20),以名词为中心的语义结构可分为两种:一种是自由词组,另一种是固定词组。自由词组可以随意组合,见词知意。固定词组具有习语性,是在语言发展过程中约定俗成的。这一类词组多半表示转义,带有隐喻性,其表达方式形象生动。英语中由形容词+名词(短语)合成的结构在转译成汉语时不受词性的制约,也多半不能用对等模式来移植,如"white elephant"(无用而累赘的东西)、"fond dream"(美梦)、"happy medium"(中庸之道;折中办法)、"narrow escape"(九死一生)、"proud flesh"(伤口愈合后凸现出来的疤)等。下面从《麦克米伦百科全书》译文中摘出的例句有力地说明了这个问题。

[12] He ... was prominent in the *ragged schools* movement.(ME)
  误译:他以破衣学校运动而闻名。
  改译:他在推动贫民免费学校运动中表现出色。
评析:"ragged school"在英国历史中指"贫民儿童免费学校"。译者不可凭词的表面结构去直译。在英文中"ragged school"经过了几次词义的引申转义:穿破衣者→贫民→无钱读书→为他们设立学校→提供免费教育。

[13] An indoor game for two or four players that originated in England in the late 19th century from *real tennis*.(ME)
  原译:一种两人或四人参加的室内运动,19世纪末起源于英格兰,由真正的网球发展而来。
评析:原文斜体部分应译成"庭院网球"、"室内网球",也有词典译成"纯网球"。有的译者把"real"和"tennis"割裂开,当作普通形容词处理,结果译成了"真正的网球"。

[14] The houses were built of *dry stone* with stone slabs for furniture, all very well preserved.(ME)
  原译:房子由干石头建成,以石板为家具,一切保存完好。
评析:何谓"干石头"?经查阅词典方知,它在建筑上指的是"由石头干砌而成",即无浆砌成的石墙(of a stone wall built without mortar)(*Oxford Advanced Learner's English-Chinese Dictionary*,1997)。若照直翻译成"干石头",岂不叫人伤透脑筋!

[15] The Greek grave stelae were usually inscribed and ornamented with *relief sculptures* of the dead.(ME)
  译文:希腊墓碑通常刻有或装饰着死者的浮雕像。
评析:"relief"作为名词,既指"减轻或解除",也指"浮雕或凸现"。受思维定式影响,较常用的词义会首先干扰人们的选择,如果不查阅工具书,人们简直无法想到它的确切含义。

四、普通词语与专业术语的词义混淆

普通词语与专业术语也常易造成混淆。许多专业术语一般是普通词语引申而来的,即先有普通词语,后衍生出专业术语词义,如先有"mouse"(老鼠),后有"mouse"(鼠标),这是因为普通词语和专业术语因隐喻关系而产生的。

[16] This difference, known as the *comma* of Pythagoras, can be compensated in several ways.(ME)

原译：这个音差,称为毕达哥逗号,能够以几种方法弥补。

评析:"comma"一词的普通词义是逗号,但其音乐专业术语的词义却是"音差",在涉及音乐的条目中,它的释义只能是第二个。

[17] A method of comprising music using all 12 notes of the chromatic *scale* equally, invented by Arnold Schoenberg in the 1920s. (ME)

译文:20世纪20年代作曲家勋伯格所创立的作曲法,即平等使用半音音阶中的所有12个音。

评析:"scale"作为普通词语表示"阶层",作为音乐专业术语意为"音阶",在翻译中译者应充分意识到专业术语与普通词语的差别。又如,"function"一词指"功能"、"官能",在数学中指"函数"。这类词,我们称之为"半技术词"(李鲁、李霄翔,2000),排列如下:

A 组(特点:科技词义单一),如:

单词	普通词义	科技词义
reading	阅读;读物	读数
mouse	老鼠	鼠标
impotence	衰弱;无力	阳痿
civil	民事/民用的	土木

B 组(特点:科技词义多样,因专业而异),如:

(a) dog　普通词义:狗

　　　　机械:车床的夹头;止动器

　　　　电子:无线电测向器

　　　　船舶:水密门夹扣

　　　　天文:大犬座;小犬座

　　　　气象:雾虹;(预示有雨的)小雨云

(b) base　普通词义:基础;底部

　　　　化工:碱;盐基

　　　　药学:主剂

　　　　纺织:固色剂;媒染剂

　　　　数学:底边,基线;基数

　　　　建筑:垫板,脚板

　　　　军事:基地

(c) rectify　普通词义:纠正;整顿

　　　　数学:(曲线)求长;从切

　　　　化工:精馏;提纯

　　　　机械:调整,拨准(仪表)

　　　　焊接:直流探伤

　　　　电气电子:整流;检波

五、典型词语的翻译

1. poor 的几个译法:

[18] In my *poor* opinion, you should let her go.

鄙意你应当放她走。

[19] Other media closer to the scene dismissed Carter as a *poor* loser.
对此事比较了解的其他报纸认为,卡特是一个输不起的人。

[20] She took me in her cabin and told me that she was a *poor* sailor and always went to bed immediately on getting on the boat.
她把我带到她房间内,并告诉我说,她有晕船的毛病,所以总是一上船就上床睡觉。

[21] Nor was he in the slightest disturbed by the outcries of wealthy alumni whose sons were forced to leave the college because they were *poor* students.
尽管那些由于孩子学习成绩太差被勒令退学的有钱的老校友大叫大嚷,他一点也不为所动。

[22] The Department of Justice was reluctant to bring *poor* cases into court.
司法部不愿意把没有把握打赢的官司拿到法庭上去。

2. (un) sophisticated 的几个译法:

[23] Mark is a smart and *sophisticated* young man.
马克是一个聪明老成的年轻人。

[24] He was not amused by Pitt's *unsophisticated* sense of humour.
他对皮特那种不到家的幽默感到难受。

[25] They enjoyed every bit of the Communists' simple, *unsophisticated* hospitality.
他们处处受到共产党的淳朴、真心诚意的款待。

六、语境下的词语翻译

在翻译中,我们可从词典中寻找词语的对等意思,但词典给我们的常常是其基本义,或对号入座式的释义,无法直接用在译文中,应该根据语境来确定这句话或词语应该怎么说。叶子南(2003:52)在这个问题上有很好的论述。

[26] The United States exhibits the *qualities* of an individual going through a nervous breakdown.
原译:美国表现了患神经衰弱症病人的特征。
改译:美国表现了患神经衰弱症病人的症状。

评析:"qualities"应转译成与病有关的词语,如"症状"。

[27] Because of this *explosive* progress, today's machines are millions of times more powerful than their crude ancestors.
原译:有了这种爆炸性的进步,今天的机器比起原始期的机器不知强了好几百万倍。
改译:有了这种突飞猛进的进步,今天的机器比起原始期的机器不知强了好几百万倍。

评析:"explosive"被译成"爆炸性的",比较生硬,"突飞猛进的进步"则考虑到语境。

[28] He is always *politically incorrect*.
原译:他总是政治上不够正确。
改译:他讲话总是不合时宜。

评析：这是美国英语特有的表达法，只能从社会、文化大环境中理解词义。

[29] That was not a very *happy* remark.

原译：那可不是一个十分高兴的讲话。

改译：那么说很不得体。

评析：常用词有时会有不常用的意思，译者会想当然地选用一个词的常用意思，而忽略该词的不常用意思。"happy"在这里应是"suitable"的意思。

[30] He *complained of* slight chest pains.

原译：他抱怨说有点胸痛。

改译：他说胸有些痛。

评析："抱怨"一词用在这里有点生硬，其实就是"述说"，但词典一般都注为"抱怨"。译者完全被原词语所束缚。

[31] Enjoy the *luxury* of doing good.

以行善为乐。

评析："luxury"如果译成该词的常见词语（奢侈、奢华）则无法准确传达其义，必须以中文思维去阐释，找出中文本身原有的说法。同样例子还有："give in to the luxury of tears" 应译为"痛哭一场"。

[32] That is the bedroom I *shared* with Tom.

原译：那是我和汤姆分享的卧室。

改译：那是我和汤姆的卧室。

评析："分享"一词被用得太滥，改译才是中国话。这些都是固步原文词语语义所致，照词典硬译，就很别扭。

[33] The friendship Nancy and I *shared* with Kay is one of the *legacies* of my government service.

原译：我和南希与凯的友谊是我为政府服务的遗产之一。

改译：我和南希与凯的友谊是当年我为政府服务的一个收获。

评析：在译文中，"shared"不必译出来，译文已经包含这个意思了。"legacies"一词常译成"遗产"，但它还指"lasting result"，应将其意思融入句子中去。

[34] Roosevelt launched into a vast but *impressionistic* description of his plans for a world liberated from the fear of Nazi Germany.

误译：罗斯福对摆脱了纳粹德国恐怖的世界的计划作了广泛而印象主义的描绘。

改译：罗斯福滔滔不绝、大而化之地描绘了他为摆脱了纳粹德国恐怖的世界所制定的蓝图。

评析：这里的"impressionistic"，在英汉词典中解释为"印象主义的"，若是照此释义将非常生硬、不确切。其实英语里"impressionistic"的释义是"giving only a general impression"（只给一个总的印象），因此，应该灵活理解这个词义。

[35] He did not hesitate in choosing the path of wilderness whenever his convictions, *in the context* of situation he faced, seemed to demand the choice.

凡是他经过审时度势，自信看来需要选择冷僻的道路的话，就毫不犹豫地选择这条道路。

评析："context"意为"上下文"、"文章的前后关系"。"in the context of"＝"根据上下

文、从前后关系看"。如果这样译,原文的意思出不来。其实,"context"的英语释义还有:"the whole situation", "background", or "environment relevant to a particular event", "personality,"等等。因此,"in the context of situation he faced"＝从自己面临的形势考虑。

[36] A month later the Free French Committee in Algiers *challenged* the right of the Lebanese to act in this one-sided manner.

一个月以后,在阿尔及尔的自由法国委员会<u>不承认</u>黎巴嫩有权采取这样的片面行动。

评析:"challenge"＝挑战、责难、反驳。在翻译这句话时直接采用这些词语都很生硬勉强。在英语词典中,"challenge"＝"to make objection to";"defy"。

[37] By the winter of 1942 their resistance to the Nazi terror had become only a *shadow*.

译文一:到了1942年冬季,他们对于纳粹恐怖统治的抵抗已经<u>名存实亡</u>了。

译文二:到了1942年冬季,他们对于纳粹恐怖统治的抵抗只是一个<u>泡影</u>。

评析:"shadow"一般都译成"影子"。"shadow"的英文释义是"something unsubstantial or unreal"。

[38] The announcement was in a sense of *anticlimax*, since it implicitly recognized the failure of their plan.

这个声明真是<u>大煞风景</u>,因为它等于承认他们的计划已经失败了。

评析:"anticlimax"在英汉词典中的释义是"突降法"、"虎头蛇尾",都用不上。这个词的英语释义是"sudden fall from something noble, serious, important, sensible, etc". 大致等于"好事突然变坏"的意思。

从词汇学的角度来看,一词多义(无论是普通词义还是科技词义)的选择,主要涉及到词语的搭配、上下文语境。如果从这一方面考虑,也可避免不少误译。解决一词多义和望文生义的矛盾,最根本的是从翻译的语篇(上下文)考虑,准确判断翻译文本的题材、主题思想、立意,进而探明上下句、搭配词语的关系。勤于查阅各种词典,善于质疑。这样,因望文生义而导致的误译必然可以避免。

本节练习

1. 根据词性确定词义

[1] She needs to find somewhere to *live*.
[2] Where do these plates *live*?
[3] Spiders can *live* for several days without food.
[4] We saw a real *live* rattlesnake!
[5] The club has *live* music most nights.
[6] The terminal is *live*.
[7] The show is going out *live*.
[8] Pollution is still very much a *live* issue.

2. 根据上下文搭配确定词义

[9] The price is *running* high.

[10] Hey, your nose is *running*.
[11] My school *runs* a factory.
[12] They *ran* the enemy blockade.
[13] He *ran* across an old friend of his in town yesterday.
[14] The play *ran* 100 nights.
[15] My watch has *run* down.

第二节　理解与句法分析

思维方式与表达方式的差异

语言是思维的工具。这种在同义表达上采取不同句法形式的现象是由于英汉两民族在思维上的差异所造成的。由于英语民族常取"浓缩型"的思维方式，喜欢将众多的信息靠各种手段凝集在一个单位加以思考，因而在表达时往往倾向于取较低的句法单位，便于互相组合聚集成更高一级的结构，从而使得英语结构单位的信息量较高。这种表达方法也符合英语民族表达含蓄的习惯。而汉语民族往往更趋向于把问题层层铺开，用节节短句逐点交代，这种"展开型"的思维方式更利于把事情说清、说透、说明白；再加上汉语无形态变化，注重时序等特点，故而在表达时往往采用较高层次的句法单位（如把英语词转换成汉语的词组；英语词、词组转换成汉语的分句；英语分句转换成汉语的句子；或英语句子转换成汉语的句群），使汉语句子显得较为松散（王寅，1993）。例如：

He sat there and watched them, so changelessly changing, so bright and dark, so grave and gay.

他坐在那儿注视着，觉得眼前的景象，既是始终如一，又是变化多端，既是光彩夺目，又是朦胧黑暗，既是庄严肃穆，又是轻松愉快。

评析：汉语的神韵与气势正是来自这种短促有力、潇潇洒洒、舒展自如、形立而神聚的语句之中。这个译文很能说明这种"浓缩型"思维与"展开型"思维方式的差异。

从表达方式上看，由于英语有众多的形态变化可用来表示各种语法关系，又有十六种时态变化，还有各类连接词语和从句，因而句子结构复杂、纵横交错，叠床架屋。一个英语句子往往以一个主、谓、宾结构作为核心框架，然后以此为结构向外延伸与扩展，附上各种次要结构，构成了一种葡萄型的句式，在短短的主干上挂结着丰硕的葡萄。而汉语无形态变化，因而只有靠语序和虚词来表示各种语法关系，动作的先后顺序与语序对称，即先发生的事先说，后发生的事后说，构成了一种线性横向排列式的结构，某一意义或意群往往靠一系列的线性句法单位逐步加以展开叙述，这就如竹竿子一样，信息内容是一节一节地通下去的，也可称之为"流水型"句式。因而一个英语句子往往要化译为几个汉语句子。

再从英汉语句法对比上看，英语句法可分为两大类：一类是普通句法，即它的行文表达结构符合汉语语言的句法、行文习惯，不太会造成理解上的失误，翻译也较容易。例如，

In September 2006, I studied at Xiamen University.

2006年9月,我在厦门大学学习。

虽然对比下,原句与译句在词序上还是有不同,其基本句法结构仍是一致的,但下列这句的原文则与译文大相径庭:

September 2006 found me studying at Xiamen University.

这句话只能译成上句译文,而决不能生硬地译成"2006年9月发现我在厦门大学学习"。这一类与汉语表达反其道而行的英语句子很让中文读者和译者感到别扭。对译者和读者造成困难的还有英语中的相似句、费解句、修饰结构疑难句及"多枝共干"式结构,它们一起构成了妨碍读者和译者理解和表达的疑难问题。学习翻译,首先必须面对这些难题。

一、相似句

英语中有些句子,看上去非常相似,其实意思大不相同,甚至截然相反。句子理解混淆,则翻译无从下手。我们把这种似是而非的句子,称为相似句或形似句(林纪熹,1982)。概括起来,相似句对翻译的影响主要表现在以下几种类型(根据林纪熹的分类法)。

1. 语序

[1] *Anyhow*, she works. 不管怎样,她总算工作了。

She works *anyhow*. 她马马虎虎地工作。

评析: "anyhow"前后顺序不同居然导致语义差异。原文第二句的"anyhow"表示"随便地"、"杂乱无章地"。

[2] You may *as well* take this. 你还是收下这个的好。

You may take this *as well*. 你可以把这个也收下。

评析: 原句一的"as well"意为"不妨、不碍事,还是……的好"。原句二的"as well"意为"too, in addition"。

[3] His speech was reported *at length* in the newspapers.

他的演讲词在报纸上详细地登载出来。

At length, his speech was reported in the newspapers.

他的演讲词终于在报纸上登载出来。

评析: 原句一的"at length"等于"in great detail"(详细地),在句中修饰"was reported";原句二的"at length"等于"at last",修饰整个句子,是一种句子副词。

[4] He *had made* a box. 他已经做好一个箱子。

He *had* a box *made*. 他叫人做了一个箱子。

评析: 原句二的"had"属于役使法,意思是"叫别人完成某一件事","made"是宾语"box"的补语。

[5] He *foolishly* spoke. 他竟然开口说话,实在很不明智。

He spoke *foolishly*. 他把话讲得很不聪明。

评析: 原句一的"foolishly"修饰整个句子,说明在这个场合,他本不应该发言。原句二的"foolishly"只修饰动词"spoke"。

[6] They saw him *through*. 他们对他帮助到底。

They saw *through* him. 他们看透他的为人。

评析: "to see somebody through"是"鼓励、支持某人做某事一直到底"的意思。"to see through somebody"却是"看穿某人的居心、行径",含贬义。

[7] I hope he will soon *get over it*. 我希望他很快就会忘掉这件事。

I hope he will soon *get it over*. 我希望他很快就会结束这件事。

评析:"to get over something"指"经过某一不愉快经历后恢复常态"或"克服"。"to get it over"中的"over"是个副词,表示"结束、了却一件事"。

[8] *Quite properly* he was punished. 他受处分,理所当然。

He was punished *quite properly*. 他所受的处分恰如其分。

评析:原句一的"quite properly"是"sentence adverb",修饰句子其余部分,几乎等于"It was quite proper that he was punished",说明"punish"这个决定是对的。原句二的"quite properly"修饰"punished"这个动词。

[9] He is *rather a* foolish fellow.

He is *a rather* foolish fellow.

说他是一个愚笨的人<u>更为恰当</u>。

他是一个<u>有点</u>愚笨的人。

评析:原句一中的"rather"修饰"a foolish fellow",原句二中的"rather"只是修饰"foolish"一词。

2. 非限定动词

[10] I remembered *mailing* the letter.

我记得发过那封信。

I remembered *to mail* the letter.

我记得要发信的。

评析:原句一是在"remember"后接动名词,它叙述过去的事,有"remember having done"的含义,原句二在"remember"后接不定式是说未来的事,有"not to forget to do"的含义。

[11] I *regret to say* that you'll be held responsible. 遗憾的很,你要对此负责。

I *regret saying* that you'd be held responsible. 真抱歉,我上次不该对你说,你要对此负责。

评析:"regret"后的不定式表示的动作所发生的时间与"regret"相同。"regret"后的动名词所表示的动作则发生在"regret"以前。原句二等于"I apologize for having said this"。

[12] When he realized what the tune was, he *stopped to listen*.

当他发觉所唱的是什么曲子时,便停下来静听。

When he realized what the tune was, he *stopped listening*.

当他发觉所唱的是什么曲子时,就不再听下去。

评析:"stop"后的不定式是目的状语,说明停下手头正在进行的事,是为了听歌曲。后接动名词时,动名词作"stop"的宾语,它所表示的动作被停止。

[13] They *tried to speak* English. 他们想学着讲英语。

They *tried speaking* English. 他们想用英语试试看。

评析:后接不定式的"try"表示"企图"、"尝试或竭力去做"。后接动名词的"try"表示"用……试试看",所表示的动作只是手段而非目的。原句二中讲英语只是一种选择。

[14] They were *engaged to* carry out an important piece of research.

他们<u>受聘</u>来进行一项重要的研究项目。

They were *engaged in* carrying out an important piece of research.

他们忙于进行一项重要的研究项目。

评析：句一的"engage"是"雇用"的意思，句二的"engage"与介词"in"连用时，则作"参加、忙于"等解释。

3．名词的数

[15] We had better act on their *advice*.
我们最好按照他们的意见办。
We had better act on their *advices*.
我们最好按照他们的通知办。

评析："advice"一般不可数。作复数时，意思为"通知、消息"。

[16] An *old car problem* may arise.
可能会引起历来已久的汽车问题。
An *old cars problem* may arise.
可能引起旧车(处理)的问题。

评析：原句一的"old"修饰"car problem"。原句二的"old cars"是一个单元，限定"problem"，"cars"须用复数。

[17] We were touched by Mary's *confidence*.
玛丽的信任使我们很受感动。
We were touched by Mary's *confidences*.
玛丽吐露出来的秘密使我们很受感动。

评析："confidence"是"信任"；"confidences"是"秘密"。

[18] We asked him to speak from *experience*.
我们请他根据自己的经验发言。
We asked him to speak about his *experiences*.
我们请他谈谈亲身的经历。

评析：句一的"experience"是不可数名词，句二的"experiences"是可数的。性数差异导致意义差别。

[19] She has an *eye* for antique furniture.
她对古代家具具有审美的眼光。
She has *eyes* only for antique furniture.
她只想看看古代家具。

评析："to have an eye for..."是"对……有判断力"，而"to have eyes only for"是"只要此人此物"或"只想看某事某物"。

[20] It is his *manner* that annoys me.
他的举止态度使我很不舒服。
It is his *manners* that annoy me.
他的客套使我很不舒服。

评析："manner"是态度，"manners"表示社交礼仪。例如，He has manners but no manner(他有礼数却没有风度)。

[21] He is *behind time*. 他迟到了。
He is *behind the times*. 他落伍了。

评析：句一的"time"是一固定时间；句二的"the times"是"时代"，"behind the times"是"落后于时代"。

4. 冠词

[22] They are *the pupils* of our school.
　　他们是本校的<u>全体学生</u>。
　　They are *pupils* of our school.
　　他们是本校的<u>一部分学生</u>。

评析：有定冠词的复数名词代表全体，无定冠词的复数名词代表一部分。

[23] His success is *out of question*.
　　他必成功。
　　His success is *out of the question*.
　　他必失败。

评析："out of question＝beyond question"，意为"无疑"；"out of the question＝quite impossible"，意为"绝不可能"。一冠词之差，竟有如此差别的意义。

[24] He is a man of *middle height*. 他身材适中。
　　He is a man of *the middle height*. 他属于中等身材的人。

评析：多了"the"是指某种高矮类型的人。

[25] You should pay more attention to matters *of moment*.
　　你应当更注意<u>重要的</u>事件。
　　You should pay more attention to matters *of the moment*.
　　你应当更注意<u>当前</u>事件。

评析："of moment"的"moment"作"重要、重大"讲，"of the moment"作"此刻、现在"解释，如"men of the moment"（当代要人）。

[26] They *went to sea*. 他们当水手去。
　　They *went to the sea*. 他们到海滨去。

评析："go to sea"表示"做海上工作"，是一种引申的意义。类似的例子还有"go to bed"（睡觉）、"go to school"（上学）、"go to church"（做礼拜）等。

5. 形容词与副词

[27] They made a *practicable* suggestion.
　　他们提出一个<u>可以实施的</u>建议。
　　They made a *practical* suggestion.
　　他们提出一个<u>切合实际的</u>建议。

评析：句一的"practicable suggestion"指"可以实行的建议"，而句二指"根据客观实际提出的建议"。

[28] It has been raining *continually* for two days.
　　<u>断续地</u>下了两天的雨。
　　It has been raining *continuously* for two days.
　　<u>不停地</u>下了两天的雨。

评析："continual＝frequently or closely repeated"，意为"断断续续，间歇的"。"continuous＝without interruption"表示"继续不断的"。

6. 介词

[29] I *swear at* him. 我诅咒他。

I *swear by* him. 我极相信他。

评析："to swear by"有"深信不疑"的意思。

[30] They are very *jealous of* their success.

他们极为珍惜自己的成就。

She was *jealous of* my success.

他妒忌我的成功。

评析：当对别人表示"jealous"时，意为"妒忌"，对自己则为"珍惜、爱惜"。

[31] He *stood up for* them. 他拥护他们。

He *stood up to* them. 他反抗他们。

评析："to stand up for somebody"是"支持某人"，"to stand up to somebody"是"对某人勇敢抵抗"。一词之差，意思截然不同。

[32] He said he wasn't *informed in* these matters.

他说他对这一方面的事不很熟悉。

He said he wasn't *informed of* this matter.

他说没人告诉过他这件事。

评析：句一的"informed"是过去分词转成的形容词，它和后面的"in"并不连在一起。句二的"to be informed of"是一个固定动词词组，意为"to be told"。

[33] He has *gone into* business. 他经商去了。

He has *gone to* business. 他上班去了。

评析："to go into business"是"经商、进商界"，这里的"business"是"生意、商业"，"to go to business"是"上班"。

[34] He was *familiar to* me. 我对他很熟。

He was *familiar with* me. 他对我很随便。

评析："familiar to"等于"known to"，"familiar with"等于"having a fairly good knowledge of"（知道得很清楚）。

[35] They all *fear* him. 他们都怕他。

They all *fear for* him. 他们都为他焦急。

评析："fear"意为"to be frightened of sb./sth."；"fear for"意为"to be worried about sb./sth."，常指为某人或某事的发展担忧。

[36] John *escaped* prison. 约翰险些进了监狱。

John *escaped from* prison. 约翰越狱了。

评析：后面直接接宾语，"escape"之意等于"avoid, elude, not incur"，有"逃过牢狱之灾"之意。"escape from"等于"break out of, get away from"，有"入狱而越狱"之意。

7. 否定词

[37] He has *no more than* ten books.

他只有十本书。

He has *not more than* ten books.

他至多不过十本书。

评析:"no more than"="only"。"not more than"="at most"。

[38] His brother's words are *no truer than* his.
　　他哥哥的话和他的话<u>一样靠不住</u>。
　　His brother's words are *not truer than* his.
　　两兄弟讲话的<u>真实性不相上下</u>。

评析:句一表示两个人都在撒谎。句二表示两个人都讲真话。

[39] I am *no philosopher*. 我<u>不懂哲学</u>。
　　I am *not a philosopher*. 我<u>不是个哲学家</u>。

评析:句一是一种反面衬托法(litotes),不但否定了是哲学家的可能性,而且有自己贬低自己的语气。句二只是平铺直叙一个事实,色彩是中性的。

[40] He is *not a little* afraid of it.
　　他<u>非常</u>害怕。
　　He is *not a bit* afraid of it.
　　他<u>一点也不</u>怕。

评析:"not a little"="much","not a bit"="not at all"

[41] He has *not a little* experience.
　　他很有经验。
　　He has *not the least* experience.
　　他毫无经验。

评析:"not a little"="much"。"not the least"="no"。

[42] I didn't go because I was afraid. 我不是因为怕才去。
　　I didn't go because I was afraid to. 我没去,因为我不敢去。

评析:句一的"didn't"修饰后面整整一个从句"because I was afraid";句二的"didn't"只修饰"go"。

8. 代词

[43] His English is *anything but* correct.
　　他的英语错误百出。
　　His English is *nothing but* correct.
　　他的英语只是不错而已。
　　His English is *all but* correct.
　　他的英语差不多没有错误。

评析:"anything but"="far from, not at all",意为"绝非,并不"。"nothing but"="only",意为"只,不过"。"all but"="almost",意为"差不多"。

[44] *Any one* will do. 随便<u>哪一个</u>都行。
　　Anyone will do. 任何<u>一个人</u>都行。

评析:"any one"指的是东西;"anyone"指的是人。

本节练习一

[1] *Happily* he did not die.

He did not die *happily*.

[2] She *kept the house*.

She *kept house*.

[3] *This is no place* for me to go to.

There is no place for me to go to.

[4] He is a *man of family*.

He is a *family man*.

[5] I had a good talk *to* him yesterday.

I had a good talk *with* him yesterday.

[6] She *swept out* the room.

She *swept out of* the room.

[7] He kept her *company*.

He kept *company* with her.

[8] Is there *any* difficulty in this?

Is there *some* difficulty in this?

[9] You can tell me your opinion *while we eat*.

You can tell me your opinion *while we are eating*.

[10] We are sure *that man is mortal*.

We are sure *that man is dead*.

[11] *It is a pity* you did not go.

It is a mercy you did not go.

[12] I *wish I were* as rich as he.

I *wish to be* as rich as he.

[13] Let us *repair* our house.

Let us *repair to* our house.

[14] He always *interferes in* my business.

He always *interferes with* my business.

[15] We hired the boat *by the hour*.

We hired the boat *for an hour*.

[16] I *shall* have some people come tomorrow.

I *will* have some people come tomorrow.

[17] What is he *about to speak*?

What is he *to speak about*?

[18] He was *looked upon as* a genius.

He was *looked up to as* a genius.

[19] The island is five miles *around*.

The island is five miles *across*.

[20] I *did not notice* him.

I *took no notice of* him.

二、费解句

之所以称为费解句，是因为某些词法、句法不太符合中国读者和译者的思维模式、句法模式，因此便觉其难，理解颇费周折，稍不小心就容易译错（钱歌川，1980）。

[1] One or two of the jewels would never be missed.

失去一两粒宝石是绝不会知道的。

评析："miss"此处的意思是"觉察（什么）不在"。

[2] He has never recovered her loss.

他永含失恃之悲。

评析：这是英语中最容易弄错意思的一种表现法。此处"her loss"="the loss of his mother"，而不是"his mother's loss"，即不是他母亲的损失，而是他失去母亲。

[3] I could do with more leisure time.

要再有一些闲暇就好了。

评析："can do"="be satisfied with"，意为"满足"。在"do"之前用"could"，便有"要能得到就好了"的意思。

[4] The lecturer carried his audience with him.

讲演者博得全场喝彩。

评析："carry"除"搬运"、"携带"外，还有"吸引"的意思。

[5] The wind blows south.

风从南边吹来。

评析：当指风时，意为"从那方向来"，除此之外，则是"朝那方向去"，如"The river flows south"译为"河水向南流去"。

[6] There was no living in the island.

那岛不能居住。

评析："There was no"＋动名词＝"We cannot"＋原形不定式＝"It is impossible＋to do"

[7] You must make good any loss.

有任何损失你必须赔偿。

评析："make good"有"赔偿"之意，又有"实践"之意，如"You must make good a promise"（你必须实践诺言）。

[8] The apples are good and ripe.

那些苹果很成熟了。

评析："good and"，意为"非常"（very）。同类型的表达语还有"nice and"＝"nicely"，"rare and"＝"rarely"。

[9] The smoke betrayed where the dwelling lay.

炊烟起处有人家。

评析：betray除了有"出卖"、"辜负"、"泄露"外，还有"无意中暴露，显示"的含义。

[10] Curses come home to roost.

害人终害己。

评析："roost"原意为"巢"，句子说诅咒回到原来出发的地方，即是反而害了自己。

[11] He was strong in his time.

他在年轻时身体强壮。

评析："in one's time（days）"意为"when he was young"。相反的说法是"in one's age"（在老年）。

[12] He may be drowned for all I care.

就算他会淹死,我也不在乎。

评析："for all I care"＝"I don't care if"。

[13] It is a wise man that never makes mistakes.

智者千虑,必有一失。

评析：这是一句古来的谚语,凡"it is ... that（who）"的构造,都含有"无论怎样……都不免"的意思。

[14] He is ignorant to a proverb.

他的无知是有名的。

评析：所谓"proverb"是指尽人皆知的事,"to a proverb",意为"众所周知"。

[15] The man was generous to a fault.

他过于宽大。

评析："to a fault"意为"过度地,极端地"。

[16] He has to answer to me for the letter.

关于那封信他必须对我负责。

评析："answer for"有"负责"的意思。You will have to answer for your wrongdoings one day. 将来有一天,你会自食其果的。

[17] He identified himself with the masses.

他和群众打成一片。

评析：转程：使自己和群众同一——使自己和群众无区别——使自己和群众打成一片。

[18] I would rather have his room than his company.

我宁愿他不在此。

评析：句中"room"作"余地"解,"company"作"伴侣"解。"his room"指"他的余地"或"他的空间",即空了他,也就是说他不在。

[19] He said nothing to that effect.

他没有说一点含有那种意思的话。

评析："to that effect"中的"effect"相当于"meaning",例如：He wrote to that effect.（他写的大意如此。）The letter is to the effect that...（那信的大意为……）

[20] Eighty poor fellows perished.

不幸有 80 人死亡。

评析："poor"＝"unfortunate","可怜、不幸"。

[21] He did not see the movie out.

他没有看完那部影片。

评析："see...out",意为"看到最后为止"。

[22] We searched him to no purpose.

我们搜查过了他的身上,但毫无所得。

评析: "search a person", 表示搜查一个人的身上看有无违禁品。"to no purpose" = "with no result", 意为"无结果"。

[23] One fine morning he found himself a ruined man.
一朝醒来,自己已经成为一个破产的人了。

评析: "one fine morning"中"fine"一词,实无意义,可以不译。"find oneself", 意为"不知不觉,而自己已变成了"。

[24] Men of millions are possessed with the idea.
百万富翁满脑子都是这种想法。

评析: "men of millions"不可与"millions of men"混同。

[25] It is two years come Christmas.
到今年圣诞时就是两年了。

评析: "come Christmas"的说法,牛津辞典的解释是"including the time from now to Christmas"(包括从现在到圣诞日的时间)。"come Christmas" = "if Christmas comes", 是假设的用法。

[26] All my advice falls flat on him.
他把我的忠告当作耳边风。

评析: "fall flat"意为"终于完全失败,毫无反应,一点效力也没有"。

[27] He got married accepting a leap-year proposal.
他接受女方提出的求婚而结婚了。

评析: 闰年不比常年,闰年提出的求婚,当然也是不平常的,普通总是男方向女方提出求婚,现反过来由女方提出,故云。

[28] It is no proof that one cannot do a thing because one does not like it.
不喜欢做某事,不能证明就做不成。

评析: "it"的真正的主语,不是"that"以下的文句,而是"because"以下的文句。

[29] He doesn't know any better.
他居然有这样笨。

评析: "know better" = "be wiser"。

[30] Much of our morality is customary.
我们大部分道德观念都源于习俗。

评析: "customary"一词非常难译,有人把它译成"都有习惯性"。

[31] He was glad because he wouldn't have to send me away without buying anything.
译文一:他所以高兴是因为他用不着一点东西不买就打发我走。
译文二:他总算能买点什么让我带走,这令他很高兴。

评析: 译文一照原文直译,令人费解。译文二才比较地道。不过译此句需要上下文语境的配合。

[32] In Europe, Heath's name was well known, *if not* a household word.
在欧洲,希思的名字广为人知,也可以说家喻户晓。

评析: 以往把"if not"当成"即使不",其实它的意思等于"perhaps"或"possibly"。因此,"Such a mistake could cost us thousands, if not millions of pounds"应译成"这种失误可能

造成我们几千镑,或许几百万镑的损失"。

[33] It is warm, *not to say* hot.

天气很暖和,<u>甚至有点儿热</u>。

评析:"not to say"的真正意思是"and indeed";or "possibly even"(*The Concise Oxford Dictionary*),或"and almost";or "perhaps even"(*Longman Dictionary of Contemporary English*)。例如:The result is satisfactory, not to say the best one.(这是一个可喜的,也可以说是最为圆满的结果。)The answer is illogical, not to say totally wrong.(答案不合逻辑,甚至是完全错误的。)

[34] Tom *leaped* to his feet, *moving* with surprising agility.

误译:汤姆纵身跳了起来,他来回走动,显得很灵巧,这真使人感到吃惊。

改译:汤姆<u>猛</u>地站了起来,动作异常敏捷。

评析:误译是因为忽略了"leap"和"move"这两个动作同时发生,而非前后关系。

[35] One observer believed Kissinger's genius was an ability to tell nine different stories to nine people, and *keep them all straight*.

误译:有一位观察家认为,基辛格的本事在于能对九个人讲九种不同的话,而且使<u>他们都服服帖帖</u>。

改译:一位观察家认为,基辛格的天才就在于对九个人讲九种不同的话,而且记得<u>清清楚楚</u>。——马红军译文

评析:理解原文的关键在于确定"them"一词的指代,以及"straight"的确切含义。原译者把"them"看成替代"people",这导致译文表达错误。"them"指的是"stories"。

[36] This explosion (of technology) is already freeing vast numbers of people from their traditional bondage to nature, and now at last we have *it* in our power to free mankind once and for all from the fear which is based on want.

误译:(科技)知识的急剧增长正把为数众多的人们从自然界的传统束缚中解放出来,如今我们终于能把这种急剧增长掌握在我们手中,有力量使人类从贫困的恐惧中一劳永逸地解放出来。

改译:科技的迅猛发展将广大人民从自然界的传统束缚中解放出来。如今,我们终于有能力使人类彻底摆脱对贫困的恐惧。——马红军译文

评析:误译将"we have it in our power to free mankind"中的"it"当成指代前面的名词"explosion",译成汉语时做了重复。但从上下文判断,"it"应为一赘词,或代替后面"to free"引导的不定式。

[37] It is so easy now to see the irony of smoking: Children do it to be like adults, *who* smoke but wish *they* didn't.

误译:在今天很容易看出抽烟的讽刺性:孩子们抽烟是为了模仿大人,大人们抽烟却希望孩子们别抽。

改译:如今,吸烟的讽刺意味是显而易见的——孩子们抽烟是为了模仿大人,而<u>吸烟的大人们却后悔自己学会了吸烟</u>。

评析:原文的句法确实很刁,误译在所难免。从上下文看,定语从句中的代词"who"指代"adults",后面的"they"应该和"who"为同一对象。

[38] Any excuse will *do* for a picture of Audrey Herburn.

误译：任何理由都能得到奥黛丽·赫本的一幅画儿。

改译：为了得到奥黛丽·赫本的一张玉照，什么借口都<u>不为过</u>。

评析：误译的问题是译者对"do"这个英语中最常用的行为动词没有吃透。"do"在这里是"管用"、"好使"、"有效"的意思。同样的例子有：He will do for a teacher.（他适宜做个教师。）

[39] I can make nothing of what he says.
　　他说的话我一点也不懂得。

[40] She made light of her illness.
　　没把自己的病放在心上。

[41] She is well-informed for a woman of the old school.
　　她虽接受旧式教育，却见闻广博。

[42] You are not playing the game.
　　你不公平。

[43] The actress has her head turned.
　　那女演员得意忘形。

[44] I am now a little under the weather.
　　我现在有点不舒服。

[45] Somebody will have to break the ice.
　　总有人得先开口说话。

[46] He has come off second best.
　　他失败了。

[47] She was very accommodating.
　　她在待人接物方面做到八面玲珑。

[48] I could not recollect his name to save my life.
　　我怎么也想不起他的名字。

[49] He is lying on his side.
　　他侧身躺着。

[50] Truth lies at the bottom of the decanter.
　　酒后吐真言。

[51] Don't tell him home truths.
　　不要对他讲逆耳的真话。

[52] Jack is a fair-weather friend.
　　杰克是个不能共患难的朋友。

[53] They were killed to a man.
　　他们被杀得片甲不留。

[54] She is very pregnant.
　　她怀孕好几个月了。
　　或：她怀孕好长时间了。

[55] He had words with her.
　　他和她发生口角了。

[56] He was worn out with company.
　　来客太多使他疲于奔命。
[57] It is the man behind the gun that tells.
　　胜败在人而不在武器。
[58] That picture flatters her.
　　那画像实际上美过她本人。
[59] She's the sort of woman who likes to be very much in evidence.
　　她是那种爱出风头的女人。
[60] He is one of the institutions of the place.
　　他是当地知名人士。

本节练习二

[1] He helped himself to the wine.
[2] He knows what it is to have a boy idle.
[3] They that know nothing fear nothing.
[4] What you cannot afford to buy, do without.
[5] I know he meant business.
[6] He begged to be remembered to you.
[7] The lost child was soon identified.
[8] That women are bad drivers is open to question.
[9] It was not that he had plenty of money.
[10] What shall I go in?
[11] He succeeded to a large property.
[12] He measured his length on the floor as soon as he entered the room.
[13] His English leaves nothing to be desired.
[14] Your loss is nothing to mine.
[15] She has been a widow only six months.
[16] He is free with his money.
[17] The persons elected will sit till 31 Dec., 1973.
[18] He changed his condition only a week ago.
[19] My shoes are the worse for wear.
[20] Grandmother has a green thumb.

三、修饰结构疑难句

英语的修饰结构是导致句子复杂，造成理解混乱的基本原因。对修饰结构的理解正误，直接导致译句的表达。这在英汉翻译也是最棘手的问题(林相周，1979)。

[1] The commission of certain acts such as armed attacks, naval blockades, support lent to *armed gangs of terrorists* was considered as a form of aggression.
　　误译：从事某些诸如武装进攻、海上封锁、向恐怖分子的武装集团提供援助等行为，

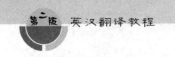

都被认为是一种侵略。

改译：……向武装的恐怖分子集团提供援助……

评析：这句的"armed gangs of terrorists"中，"gangs of terrorists"是个意群，不能拆开；不是"of terrorists"修饰"armed gangs"，而是"armed"修饰"gangs of terrorists"修饰整个词组，所以不能译为"恐怖分子的武装集团"。

［2］ That woman speaks *West of England vulgarism*.

误译：那位妇女讲的是英国粗俗的西部语言。

改译：那位妇女讲的是英国西部俗语。

评析：这句的"West of England"是个意群，修饰"vulgarism"，既不可能是"England"修饰"vulgarism"，更不可能是"of England vulgarism"修饰"West"。

［3］ He played a key role in advising the president how to foil the conspiracy mounted against him *in May of 1971* by seven of his own ministers.

误译：总统于1971年5月粉碎他手下七名部长策划的阴谋时，他的意见起了关键性的作用。

改译：他在告知总统如何粉碎他手下七名部长于1971年5月策划的阴谋方面起了关键性的作用。

评析：这句的状语短语"in May of 1971"前面有"mounted"与"to foil"，但这里的"in May of 1971"不是修饰"to foil"，而是修饰"mounted"，应译为"……1971年5月策划的……"。误译是状语与它所修饰成分的理解偏差造成的。

［4］ South of Tokyo, evidence has emerged of pressures *building up around the earthquake-prone Shizuoka region*.

误译：东京以南，在容易发生地震的静冈地区周围已经出现压力正在集结的迹象。

改译：东京以南，已经出现压力正在容易发生地震的静冈地区周围集结的迹象。

评析：这句的状语短语"around the earthquake-prone Shizuoka region"前面有"has emerged"和"building up"，它不是修饰"has emerged"，而是修饰"building up"，此句也可译为"……已经出现压力正集结在容易发生地震的静冈地区周围"。

［5］ Though they were tortured by the reactionaries, they suffered whatever befell *with fortitude* and fought on heroically.

误译：虽然他们受尽反动派的折磨，但是他们忍受顽强地落在他们身上的一切，继续英勇地进行斗争。

改译：……但是他们坚韧不拔地忍受所遭遇的一切……

评析：这里的状语短语"with fortitude"不是修饰它贴近的"befell"，而是修饰"befell"前面的"suffered"，应译为"他们坚韧不拔地忍受"。这种类型的修饰称为越位修饰。

［6］ It was a tense meeting, but *in typically Arab fashion* the men who had been ready to kill one another in the morning were kissing one another in the evening.

误译：这是一个气氛紧张的会议，但是那些早上准备拼个你死我活的冤家，却在晚上以典型的阿拉伯方式相互亲吻了。

改译：……到了晚上却相互亲吻了，这是典型的阿拉伯风格。

评析：这句的状语短语"in typically Arab fashion"并不修饰"were kissing"，而是修饰"but"引导的整个并列句，所以译成汉语把"这是典型的阿拉伯风格"放在句末。

[7] The task of the revolutionaries is not to regret the outbreak of such just wars or to scare people who are waging war against imperialism *with the danger of thermo-nuclear war*.

误译：革命者的任务绝不是为发生这种战争而感到遗憾，也不是吓唬正在与<u>充满热核战争危险的帝国主义</u>进行斗争的人民。

改译：……也不是去用热核战争的危险吓唬正在与帝国主义进行斗争的人民。

评析：这句的介词短语"with the danger of thermo-nuclear war"不是修饰它前面定语从句里的"imperialism"，而是修饰主句里的"to scare"；定语从句"who are waging war against imperialism"修饰"people"，把"to scare"的宾语同 with 引导的介词短语隔开，所以应译为"……也不是去用热核战争的危险吓唬……人民"。这句是宾语同状语分隔引起的误解，难度极大。

[8] Why does he say nothing about the total *absence* from his list *of poems* about the Malayan liberation struggle going on since 1948?

误译：他的<u>诗单</u>中根本没有关于 1948 年以来一直在进行的马来亚解放斗争，他对此为什么只字不提？

改译：他开列的单子中根本<u>没有</u>关于 1948 年以来一直在进行的马来亚解放斗争的<u>诗歌</u>，他对此为什么只字不提？

评析：这句的定语短语"of poems"很容易被误解为修饰"list"，因为"list of poems"本身也可以成立，但这里的"of poems"却同"absence"有关，中间被"from his list"隔开，而"from his list"也修饰"absence"。这句是定语同其所修饰的词语分隔引起的误解。

[9] There is a school of thought which argues that the announcement prolonged the war and played into the dictator's hands *by driving* their peoples and armies to desperation.

误译：现在有一种看法，认为这个声明拖长了战争，而且有利于独裁者们<u>驱使他们的人民和军队决一死战</u>。

改译：有一种看法认为，该声明将敌国的人民和军队逼上了绝路，从而拖长了战争，反倒帮了独裁者的忙。

评析：误译错误地以为"by driving"只跟"played"，不跟"prolonged"，其实它共同修饰了前面两个动词。

[10] The present crisis in that country is no ordinary economic crisis *which* will pass away in time leaving everything much as it was before.

误译：这个国家当前的危机根本不是一般的经济危机，过些时候就会过去，然后一切和以往一样。

改译一：一般性经济危机过一段时间就会结束，然后一切恢复如初，但该国的这场危机绝非一般性危机。

改译二：这个国家当前的危机根本不是一般的经济危机，它不会过些时候就一切恢复如初。

评析：原译者并未搞清"which"引导的定语从句修饰什么，因此译文的含义和原文相反。改译一虽准确，但较长，改译二则较简洁，意思也明白。

本节练习三

[1] Consumer *goods* are also abundant *of good quality and variety*.

[2] One day a young *woman* was brought to the hospital *with a badly burnt arm*.

[3] Scientists said quite a few years back, an unbreakable *substance* could be found *that would work as well as glass*.

[4] In our work new *contradictions* often arise, *contradictions* which should be handled correctly.

[5] The *objection* is bound to be raised *that such a conception is a complete travesty of the whole idea of philosophy*.

[6] We shall *see* later on, when we travel to other worlds, *that there are stronger and weaker gravities*.

[7] A *list* has been drawn up *of all the verbs taught so far*.

[8] A successful scientist usually directs his attention towards problems *which* he notices *have* no satisfactory explanation.

[9] Every day *news* comes from all over the country *of great success* in one field after another.

[10] So much is art, the art that in common with poetry, drama, painting, and music, *does*, we all know, *enter* into the novel.

四、"多枝共干"式结构

英语句子中有一种结构,常常被错误理解,特别是将它译成汉语时,这种理解错误暴露得更明显,这一切都是由于对修饰语理解偏差引起的。这种英语语言现象,朱光潜将之称为"多枝共干"。林相周(1985:180)将之做了深入阐述。例如"the newly-established nurseries, kindergartens and primary schools",这里的前置定语"newly-established"不但修饰"nurseries",而且也修饰"kindergartens"和"primary schools",译成汉语"新办的托儿所、幼儿园和小学"。然而,就两个或几个前置定语修饰一个名词来说,英汉两种语言并不完全相同。例如,英语"the commercial and cultural districts"译成汉语却为"商业区和文化区",而不能是"商业和文化区",其实原文词组也可以说在"commercial"后面省略了"district",相当于"the commercial district and the cultural district",实际上是说两种不同类型的地区。按照汉语习惯,应在"商业"后面重复"区"字。英语倾向于省略,汉语习惯于重复,这便是两种语言结构中的一个重要差别。因此,翻译这种结构应注意两点:一是词序;一是重复。以下部分例证摘自林相周(1985)。

[1] Young Charles made little progress in *Greek* or *Latin composition*.

　　误译:年轻的查尔斯的希腊文和拉丁文作文进步不大。

　　改译:年轻的查尔斯的希腊文作文和拉丁文作文进步不大。

　　评析:这句中的"Greek"和"Latin"都修饰"composition","composition"用了单数,这是因为前面用了"or"的缘故。

[2] *Intense light* and *heat in the open* contrasted with the *coolness of shaded avenues* and *the interiors of buildings*.

误译：强烈的光线和露天场所的炎热跟林荫道上的凉爽和建筑物内部形成了对比。
改译：露天场所的强烈光线和炎热跟林荫道上和建筑物内部的凉爽形成了对比。

评析：误译在于把定语短语"in the open"看做只修饰"heat"，而忽略了它也修饰"light"；其次，也误把"coolness"看做只受定语短语"of shaded avenues"修饰，而忽略了它也受另一个定语短语"the interiors of buildings"修饰（前面省略了"of"），结果错误地认为"the interiors of buildings"与"coolness"并列。

[3] These documents are detailed with *names*, *dates*, *places* and *full descriptions of the incidents investigated*.

误译：这些文件详细载明了姓名、日期、地点和所调查的事件的全部经过。
改译：这些文件详细载明了所调查的事件中的姓名、日期、地点和全部经过。

评析：这句的定语短语"of the incidents investigated"一共修饰四个名词，即不但修饰"descriptions"，而且修饰"names"，"dates"与"places"，译成汉语应将"所调查的事件中的"放在"姓名"前面。这是名词与定语多枝共干式结构引起的误解。

[4] He received several baskets full of *cards*, *letters* and *telegrams of congratulation* on his birthday.

生日那天他收到好几筐祝贺他生日的名信片、信件和电报。

评析：这句中的后置定语"of congratulation"译成汉语定语必须移前，即它不仅修饰"telegrams"，而且也修饰"cards"和"letters"，所以应将汉语译文"祝贺他生日的"移至所修饰的几个名词中第一个的前面。

[5] As professor of *American and comparative ethnology* at the University of Goteberg, Sweden from 1924 to 1932, he had a marked influence on anthropology in Sweden and Denmark.

1924 到 1932 年，他任瑞典的哥德堡大学美洲人种学和比较人种学的教授，对瑞典和丹麦的人种学产生重大的影响。

评析：这句中的"American and comparative ethnology"相当于"American ethnology and comparative ethnology"，译成汉语必须在"美洲"后面重复"人种学"。又如"engineering and technological education"，不宜译成"工程和工艺技术教育"，应译成"工程教育和工艺技术教育"；"the applied and engineering sciences"也应译成"应用科学和工程科学"。

[6] The *poor health* and *intermittent seizures which had plagued him for a number of years* were his constant tormentors during the ensuing five years of his life.

误译：身体衰弱和折磨了他多年的时愈时发的疾病，在他一生的最后五年中常常使他极感痛苦。
改译：折磨他多年的身体衰弱和时愈时发的疾病……

评析：这句的定语从句"which had plagued him for a number of years"不但修饰"intermittent seizures"，而且修饰"poor health"，译成汉语应将"折磨他多年的"放在"身体衰弱"前面。这是名词与定语多枝共干式结构引起的误解。

[7] It is the working people in the capitalist countries who bear the unemployment, heavy taxation and reduced standard of living *which these aggressive wars entail*.

误译：是资本主义国家的劳动人民忍受失业、苛捐杂税和这些侵略战争所带来的下降的生活水平。

改译:……忍受这些侵略战争所带来的失业、苛捐杂税和下降的生活水平。

评析:这句的定语从句"which these aggressive wars entail"一共修饰三个名词,即不但修饰"reduced standard of living",而且修饰"unemployment"与"heavy taxation",译成汉语应将"侵略战争所带来的"放在"失业"前面。(名词与定语多枝共干式结构引起的误解)

[8] The development of *labour* and *national liberation movements* shows…

误译:劳工与民族解放运动的发展表明……

改译:劳工运动与民族解放运动……

评析:这句的"labour"不是与"movements"并列,而是用作定语,和"national liberation"一样,修饰"movements",译成汉语应在"劳工"后面加上"运动"。(名词与定语多枝共干式结构引起的误解)

[9] The Chinese Revolution *produced* a substantial quantitative change and soon *led to* a qualitative change *in the world relationship of forces*.

误译:中国革命产生了巨大的量变,不久对世界力量的对比引起了质变。

改译:中国革命对世界力量的对比产生了巨大的量变,不久引起了质变。

评析:这句的状语短语"in the world relationship of forces"不但修饰"led",而且修饰"produced",译成汉语"对世界力量的对比"应放在"产生"前面。(动词与状语多枝共干式结构引起的误解)

[10] Few people even *knew* of the existence of this painting *until it was shown at an exhibition in 1937* and *bought shortly afterwards by the museum*.

误译:在1937年画展展出以前,没有多少人甚至知道有这幅画,不久以后被博物馆收购。

改译:在1937年画展展出和接着不久为博物馆收购以前,甚至没有多少人知道有这幅画。

评析:这句的"bought shortly afterwards by the museum"不能误解为与"knew"平行,事实上,它前面省略"until it was",是个状语从句,连同"until it was shown at an exhibition in 1937"共同修饰动词"knew",应译为"在……展出和……收购以前……"。(动词与状语多枝共干式结构引起的误解)

[11] It *is now strictly true* that scarce a fly or mosquito can be seen in the town and *cholera and smallpox are no more*.

误译:城市里几乎看不见什么苍蝇和蚊子,这是千真万确的,而且霍乱和天花已经绝迹。

改译:城市里几乎看不见什么苍蝇和蚊子,霍乱和天花已经绝迹,这是千真万确的。

评析:这句的"cholera and smallpox are no more"前面省略了"that",它不是与主句"It is now strictly true"并列,而是与"that scarce a fly or mosquito can be seen in the town"并列,这两个"that"引导的名词从句,都用作主语,但在句首由it引导,译成汉语应将"这是千真万确的"放在句末。(两个主语共有一个动词)

[12] *The U.S. government waged* the "dirty war" in Korea with 200,000 and *lost*.

误译:美国政府在朝鲜进行过一场"肮脏的战争",死了二十万人。

改译:美国政府曾用二十万军队在朝鲜进行过一场"肮脏的战争",结果输了。

36

评析：这句的"lost"是并列句里的谓语动词，它的主语是"the U. S. government"，它与主句的谓语动词"waged"并列。（两个动词共有一个主语）

[13] They always think of *advancing*, *looking after* their own *interests*.

误译：他们总是考虑<u>前进</u>，关心他们自己的<u>利益</u>。

改译：他们总是考虑<u>增进和维护</u>他们自己的<u>利益</u>。

评析：这句的动名词"advancing"不作"前进"解，而是作"增进"解，与动名词"looking after"共有一个宾语"interests"，所以译为"……考虑增进和关心他们自己的利益"。（动词与宾语多枝共干式结构引起的误解）

[14] It *is as if some vision of Shelly's had come true* and *selfishness had been banished from the world*.

误译：好像雪莱的某种理想已经实现，而自私自利已经从世界上消除。

改译：<u>好像</u>……实现，<u>好像</u>自私自利已经从世界上消除。

评析：这句的"selfishness"前面省略了"as if"，与"as if some vision of Shelly's had come true"一起作"is"的表语，译成汉语要重复"好像"。（一个动词接两个表语引起的误解）

五、晦涩长句理解与翻译

在翻译中，原文难度大、句子繁复、作者表达晦涩和作品的文化背景复杂等因素，使得翻译极其艰难。运用简明的语法法则，梳理长句子、复杂句子以及句子里令人困惑的难点，是把文字翻译做到更高层次的有效方法。

[1] Murmurously beyond their windows, yet so close they might be in the cloud of it, the beech accepts, leaf upon leaf, shelves and stairs of continuous dripping, the rain.

误译：窗外的山毛榉离得这么近，他们的房间大概也在它的树冠下面，它发出低沉和不停顿的响声，用一片片叶子把雨水接受下来，然后再让它们一层层一阶阶地连续流淌下来。

改译：他们的窗户上方在沙沙作响，不过窗户或许离枝叶茂盛的树冠很近，山毛榉把雨接住，叶子层层叠叠，持续不停的雨滴在层层下淌，在节节下淌。

评析：这句话的核心成分，也就是主句，是"the beech accepts the rain"（山毛榉把雨接住），主、谓、宾分明，只是中间插入了两个短语，误译的问题是没有按这样的句序去处理，而是颠倒语序，乱加词汇。改译基本是顺着原文往下翻译的。

[2] Town after town numbingly demonstrated to him that his life was a paltry thing, roughly duplicated by the millions in settings where houses and porches and trees mocking those in Mt. Judge fed the illusions of other little boys that their souls were central and important and invisibly cherished.

误译：看到了这些千篇一律的城镇他才意识到他的生活是多么微不足道，它们的众多街景差不多是同一个模子造出来的，跟贾基山的房屋、门廊和树木十分相似，而生活在贾基山的其他小男孩看来却有一个错觉，以为他们便是世界的中心，他们的生活是有声有色和令人神往的。

改译：小镇一个接一个悄无声息地在前面展现，让他明白他的生活是一种渺小的东西，被芸芸众生大同小异地复制出来，所处环境是和贾奇山的那些建筑差不多的房舍、门廊和树木，它们让小孩子们产生幻觉，以为他们的灵魂是中心，很重要，被无形地宠爱着。

评析：这段英语究竟是什么意思并不容易弄懂。它不仅体现了一个作家遣词造句的风格，也因为里面有几个从句和许多修饰成分而显繁复。误译中增加了许多表达语，但仍令人不知所云。关键是译者没有搞懂"numbingly demonstrated to him, roughly duplicated by the millions in settings, fed the illusions"到底指什么。这个英文句子虽然长，但是也只有第一行是主要成分，其余都是围绕这个核心深入阐释的。

[3] I have looked after the wild stock of the town, which gave a faithful herdsman good deal of trouble *by leaping fences*.

误译：我也曾守护过城区的野兽，使忠于职守的牧人要跳过篱笆，遇到过许多的困难。

改译：我曾看守过该镇的野兽群，它们常跳过围栏，让忠于职守的牧人吃尽了苦头。

评析："leaping fences"的主角是野兽群，而不是忠于职守的牧人。本译文及以下译文均采自美国著名作家大卫·梭罗的《瓦尔登湖》的译本（苏福忠，2006：272）。

[4] Though the view from my door was still more contracted, I did not feel crowded or confined in the least. There was pasture enough for my imagination.

误译：虽然我的门口望出去，风景范围要狭隘，我却一点不觉得它拥挤，更无被囚禁的感觉。尽够我的想像力在那里游牧的了。

改译：尽管从我的门边一眼望去，视野比较狭窄，但是我却没有感觉到拥挤或局促，一点也没有。牧场有的是，够我想像了。

评析：原译句法、逻辑不通，改译重新作了调整。

[5] The heroic books, even if printed in the character of our mother tongue, will always be in a language dead to degenerate times, and we must laboriously seek the meaning of each word and line, conjecturing a larger sense than common use permits out of what wisdom and valor and generosity we have.

误译：如果这些英雄的诗篇是用我们自己那种语言印刷成书的，这种语言在我们这种品德败坏的时代也已变成死文字了；所以我们必须辛辛苦苦地找出每一行诗每一行字的原意来，尽我们所有的智力、勇武与力量，来寻思他们的原意，要比通常应用时更深更广的原来的意义。

改译：这些写英雄的书籍，即使用我们的母语印刷出来，在世风日下的时代也会变成一种僵死的文字，我们必须孜孜不倦地把每个单词和每句话的意思弄清楚，用我们的智慧、幻想和气量推断出超乎一般用法的意义来。

评析：英文原句有点饶舌，误译为了传达原意，也跟着绕，结果叫人不知所云。在翻译时必须把主谓语弄清楚才行。

本节练习四

[1] He *was studying* Greek sculpture of the *primitive* and *classical periods*.

[2] *The D. D. T.* and *rat extermination squads* set to work.

[3] The Red Army soldiers marched from the *southeast* to the *northwest of China*...

across some of the highest *mountains* and the greatest *rivers of Asia*.

[4] The *X-ray* or *post-mortem examination* reveals many broken bones.

[5] In 1945 he *returned to* his Paris museum and teaching posts.

[6] What are the *perspectives of the national liberation movement* and *the relations between China and the Third World countries*?

[7] But his titanic determination, his powerful mind and *his fierce commitment to the mission of his class* and *the lofty principles* of *the Party* overrode all physical handicaps.

[8] If there were no gravity, you would *not* be able to *talk* or *shout* or *hear* anything *at all*.

[9] I take it *that Comrade Lee has gone for the tickets* and *we are to meet him at the theatre*.

[10] Your sentences should be direct and straightforward, not *too long* or *too complicated for others to grasp easily*.

本章推荐阅读书目

林纪熹. 英语形似句辨异[M]. 福州：福建人民出版社，1982.

林相周. 英语理解与翻译讲话[M]. 上海：上海译文出版社，1985.

钱歌川. 翻译的技巧[M]. 北京：商务印书馆，1982.

张道真. 实用英语语法[M]. 北京：外语教学与研究出版社，2002.

第三章　翻译的技巧篇

"技巧",按照《辞海》的释义,指"较高的技能"。《高级汉语大词典》指"巧妙的技能"。在《牛津高阶英语词典》(第六版)中,"technique"指"a particular way of doing sth, especially one in which you have to learn special skills"。所谓的翻译技巧,说到底就是对语言差异的"灵巧"处理(孙致礼,2003:81)。译文要获得理想的传播效果,就必须讲究表达的技巧和方法。翻译技巧,是一种熟练而巧妙的技能。它是译者熟练而巧妙地运用各种翻译手法,完美地表达思想内容的技能。普通心理学认为,技能是在个体身上固定下来的自动化的行动方式,是一些巩固了的概括化的系统,它以操作训练的方式为人所掌握,是后天获得的东西。它可以在长期反复的"操作训练"中为人所掌握。

总结归纳各种翻译教科书里的翻译技巧,其最基本的有如下几种:拆译、词性转译、精简、增补、倒置、反译、虚译和实译、词语褒贬翻译、被动式翻译、数字倍数翻译等。这些翻译技巧互相穿插,互为补充。同一个句子的翻译,可以用几种技巧加以解释或运用,即它可以是拆译、词类或句法转换、增补等。试以下面段落翻译为例,说明翻译的各种技巧是紧密结合的。

Her presence brought memories of such things as Bourbon roses, rubies, and tropical midnights; her moods recalled lotus eaters and the march in *Athalie*; her motions, the ebb and flow of the sea; her voice, the viola.

看见她的神情,就叫人想起布邦玫瑰、鲜红的宝石和热带的中夜;看见她的意态,就叫人想起食莲人和"亚他利"里的进行曲;她的步伐就是海潮的荡漾,她的声音就是中提琴的幽婉。——张谷若译文

评析:译文打破了原文形式的框架,重新组织句式,变动词性,增减词语。通过这些技巧,译文达到了神似,并使之具备了一种对偶的语言美。再比如:

On one of those sober and rather melancholy days in the latter part of autumn, when the shadows of morning and evening almost mingle together, and throw a gloom over the decline of the year, I passed several hours in rambling about Westminster Abbey. There was something congenial to the season in the mournful magnificence of the old pile; and, as I passed its threshold, it seemed like stepping back into the regions of antiquity, and losing myself among the shades of former ages.

时方晚秋,气象肃穆,略带忧郁,早晨的阴影和黄昏的阴影,几乎连接在一起,不可分别,岁云将暮,终日昏暗,我就在这么一天,到西敏寺去散步了几个钟头。古寺巍巍,森森然似有鬼气,和阴沉沉的季候正好调和;我跨进大门,觉得自己已经置身远古,相忘于古人的鬼影之中了。

评析:译者没有拘泥原文的语序、用语,而是充分发挥译语的语言优势,如句读短,用语简洁等,并综合运用增词、减词、词类转换等技巧,将原文的意义和神韵,通过铿锵的音调,肃穆森然的气氛,传达得淋漓尽致。

为了学习的方便,我们将相对独立地介绍这些技巧。真正在使用时应该是"运用之妙,存乎一心",化定法于万变之中。

第一节 拆 译

英语的句法连绵,一个主句可以与众多的修饰词组、短语、从句共同组成,讲究一气呵成,几乎不容读者喘息机会。汉语句法短促,从容不迫。英汉翻译中最重要的手段就是拆译,翻译即拆译,即在译文中将原文打破重组,或抽词拆译、或抽短语词组拆译,否则,英文里读起来流畅自然的句子,如照搬进中文,就会变成"上下三十六根牙齿嚼不烂"(叶圣陶语)的"翻译腔"。这是翻译之大忌。但要特别提醒的是,文学翻译中,涉及作者文体风格的行文常须保持原文特有的节奏、句法、用词等,如有的句法缠绵(如 Henry James),有的句法干脆利落(如 Earnest Hemingway),这时的拆译或许需特别加以考虑。

一、从译文比较看拆译

译文的语言形式必须符合译文的语言习惯。原文语言中最习见最自然的表现法,在译文中也必须用译文语言中最习见最自然的表现法来翻译。但麻烦的是译者一碰上这些英文句法时,就忍不住要直接移植过来,结果是语句生硬。这时就必须用译文语言中习见自然的表现法去代替原来的表现法。

[1] He crashed down on a *protesting* chair.
　　生硬译文:他猛然坐到一张吱吱地发出抗议声的椅子。
　　自然译文:他猛然坐到一把椅子上,椅子<u>被压得吱吱作响</u>。
评析:在英文中"protesting"可以直接修饰后面的词,汉语则行不通。此时可将这类词所含的内容从句中拉出来,单独加以表述,使中文句子通畅。

[2] *This season saw* an ominous dawning of the tenth of November.
　　生硬译文:这一季节看见11月10日的不祥的破晓。
　　自然译文:<u>在这个季节</u>,11月10日黎明时分的景象是个不祥之兆。
评析:这是英语非人称主语句使用了拟人动词,翻译时必须转换,否则译句不通。

[3] *Darkness* released him from his last restraints.
　　生硬译文:黑暗把他从最后的顾忌中解放出来。
　　自然译文:<u>在黑暗中</u>,他就再也没有什么顾忌了。

[4] *The bitter weather* had driven everyone indoors.
　　生硬译文：寒峭的天气已经把每个人都赶到室内。
　　自然译文：天寒地冻，人人都已躲在室内。

[5] People who value their privileges above their principle soon lose both.
　　生硬译文：把利益看得比原则高的人很快就会把两者都失掉。
　　自然译文一：置利益于原则之上，利益与原则皆失。
　　自然译文二：重利轻义，利义皆失。
评析：根据原文重新加以锻造，没有了原文的词句，但最充分地表现了原文的词义句义。

[6] The only *concession* he made to the climate was to wear a white dinner jacket.
　　原译：他对气候的唯一让步就是穿了一件白色的短餐衣。
　　改译：面对这样的天气，他只好穿一件白色短礼服赴宴。

[7] He accused her of talking childish nonsense *not very flattering to the intelligence of her audience*.
　　原译：他责备她讲了一些对听众的智慧颇有不恭敬之处的幼稚的废话。
　　改译：他责备她讲了一些幼稚的废话，把听众当傻瓜看待。

[8] This proposal of his, this plan of marrying and continuing at Hartfield—the more she contemplated it the more pleasing it became. His evils seemed to lessen, her own advantages to increase, their *mutual good* to outweigh every drawback.
　　译文一：他的这种建议，这种结婚与继续停在哈特飞尔德的计划——她越想越高兴。他的不幸似乎在减少，他自己的利益似乎在增加，他们共同的好处似乎超越了任何障碍。
　　译文二：他提出的既能结婚又能留在哈特菲尔德的主意，她越思量越觉得妙。对他既无害，对她也有益，两全其美，尽可为之。
评析：译文一啰啰嗦嗦，稀松平淡，远不及译文二。

[9] A few of the pictures are worth mentioning both for their technical excellence and interesting content.
　　译文一：其中有些照片既由于其技术高超又由于其内容有趣而值得一提。
　　译文二：有些照片技术高超，内容有趣，值得一提。
评析：很明显，每一对译例的第二句都要优于第一句，因为这些句子顺应了汉语的构句方式。这种构句方式大多体现在描述语篇中。

[10] This film is a dramatic treatment of a threatened stoppage in a factory.
　　直译：本片是对一家工厂的一场可能发生的罢工，进行戏剧性的处理。
　　改译：本片用戏剧性手法，体现一家工厂是如何面临罢工威胁的。
评析：不抽词拆句，嚼不动，看不懂。抽词拆句译成两个分句来表达两层意思，变换句型和词类，添几个词，层次分明。

[11] She was a tall silent woman with a long nose and grey troubled eyes.
　　译文一：她是一个沉默的高个子女人，有着长长的鼻子和忧郁的灰眼睛。
　　译文二：她个子挺高，沉默寡言，长长的鼻子，一双灰眼睛，流露出忧郁的神情。

[12] The idea grew with him as he grew into manhood.

直译：那个思想随着他长大成人而成熟了。

改译：他成年了，而他的想法也随之成熟了。

评析：改译句采取倒译法，把原句拆开，先译状语从句，再译主句，整个译文从容不迫。

[13] Illness indisposes a man for enjoyment.

译文一：人病得这种样子，还有心思娱乐吗？

译文二：人病了，不想娱乐了。

评析：这比死译"疾病使人不想娱乐"要强几倍。

[14] Age incapacitated him for war.

译文一：他年纪老迈，不能打仗了。

译文二：他年纪大了，不能参加战争了。

评析：这比死译"老年使他无能力参加战争"要强几倍。

[15] On October first, *I shall have Czechoslovakia where I want her*.

译文一：到10月1日，我将<u>要捷克斯洛伐克乖乖听我的话</u>。

译文二：到10月1日，<u>我叫捷克向东，她就不敢向西</u>。

评析：这不但忠于原文的内容，而且忠于原文的形式。

[16] A new dignity crept into his walk.

译文一：走路的姿态不知什么时候开始给人一种庄重的印象。

译文二：走起路来，不觉平添了几分尊严。

评析：这两句译文都很精彩。译者都在"new"和"crept"上下工夫，加以锤炼，第二句译文里用"平添"来表达"new"，用"不觉"来译"creep"，使得整个句子都译活了。对译词的锤炼最能体现译者中外文功底之厚薄。

[17] The men and women throughout the world who think that a living future is preferable to a dead world of rocks and deserts will have to rise and demand, in tones so loud that they cannot be ignored, that common sense, humanity, and the dictates of that moral law which Mr. Dulles believes that he respects, should guide our troubled era into that happiness which only its own folly is preventing.

译文一：希望有一个可以活下去的世界而不要一个到处是岩石和沙漠的死亡的世界的各国男男女女，必须起来用一种人们不能置之不理的洪亮声音大声疾呼，要求让理智、人道和杜勒斯先生所说他所尊重的道义原则，来引导这个多事之秋的时代进入只有时代本身的愚蠢在阻止人们到达的幸福境地。

译文二：充满生机的未来世界胜于遍布岩石和沙漠的荒野，凡持此观点的世人，都应该行动起来，用无比洪亮的声音唤醒众人：正是我们今天的愚蠢做法在阻碍着人类走向幸福，我们必须依靠理智、仁慈，以及杜勒斯先生所倡导的道义原则，来引导这个动乱的时代迈入幸福的殿堂。

评析：原文一句话长达71个单词，其中套着三个定语从句、三个宾语从句和一个状语从句。译文一显得十分生硬，仅主语就达40字之多，表达如此笨重！译文二将句式做了调整，清爽许多。

[18] Translating consists in reproducing in the receptor language the closest natural equivalent of the source-language message, first in terms of meaning and secondly in terms of style. (E. Nida, 1969/1982: 12)

译文一：所谓翻译，是指在译语中用最切近而又自然的对等语再现原语的信息，首先在语义上，其次是文体上。——孙致礼译文

译文二：翻译就是接受语言复制出与原语信息最接近的自然等值体——首先是就意义而言，其次是就其风格而言。——柯平译文

译文三：所谓翻译，是指从语义到语体在译语中用最切近而又最自然的对等语再现原语信息。——谭载喜译文

译文四：翻译是指从语义到文体在译语中用最切近而又最自然的对等语再现原文的信息。

评析：翻译研究专家笔下的译文竟也如此的不同，可见译无定法。

二、长句拆译

英语句子之所以需要拆译，是因为中文表述无法按照其英文句法展开。中文最忌讳的是长长的一句话中间不带一个标点符号，非拆不可。

[19] They represented a worthy beginning to the *reshaping* of the United Nations concept of *collective effort* in international and national economic development.

这个宣言和行动纲领表明了一个可贵的开端，那就是在国际和国家经济发展方面，联合国提出了一个同心协力的新概念。

评析：译者把"reshape"一词拆开来译：先译"shape"，作"提出"，便于跟主语"联合国"相搭配；再译前缀"re-"作"新"，修饰宾语"概念"。这充分表明译者那熔铸锤炼和匠心独运的工夫。其次，"collective effort"译成"同心协力"，从而避开了"集体努力"的框框。一个精益求精的译者必然要根据上下文去推敲，而不能死抱着词典的"努力"不放。

[20] *Their skill as horsemen and archers halted Persian and Macedonian invasion* but they remained a nomadic people until their disappearance during the Gothic onslaughts of the 3rd century AD.（*Macmillan Encyclopaedia*）

<u>他们（西徐亚人）善骑术、精弓箭，故能拒敌波斯人和马其顿人</u>。他们一直是游牧民族。公元3世纪遭哥特人屠杀后消亡。

评析：主语"Their skill as horsemen and archers"被做了高度的转化分解，分别译成两个动词句"他们善骑术、精弓箭"，原文的谓语短语经翻译，以"故能"和前面译句构成因果关系，再现原文之意。

[21] The thought that she would be separated from husband during his long and dangerous journey saddened Mrs Brown.

布朗太太一想到丈夫踏上那漫长而危险的旅途，而在此期间，她又不能跟他在一起，心里不禁难过。

评析：译文首先改变了"the thought"的词性，继而改变句型，把句子一拆为三，其中第二句是从原来一个状语"during his long and dangerous journey"变出的，并补充谓语"踏上"使之成句。通过改变词性和句型，这就使译文文理通畅自然，成流走之势。

[22] There is a *bewildering variety* of acoustics and vibration measurement equipment now available to the noise control engineer.

目前，可供给控制噪音工程师用的音响装置和振动测量设备，<u>种类繁多，令人眼花缭乱</u>。

评析：把"bewildering variety"抽出，译成两个小句，置于句末。如果直译成"各种各样迷惑人的"，不仅啰嗦，而且文字欠简洁。这就是抽词拆句法。

[23] Accident may put a *decisive blunderer* in the right, but *eternal defeat and miscarriage* must attend *the man of the best parts*, if cursed with indecision.

容易出错的人，若遇事果断，仍可取得意外的成功；哪怕是最有才干的人，若优柔寡断，也定遭屡屡失误。

评析：把"decisive, blunderer, eternal defeat and miscarriage, the man of the best parts"等一一抽出，拆开译成汉语分句。这句的英文本身是一句高难度句，较抽象，多使用名词。

[24] Their fortress, built on a hill, *commanded an extensive prospect* of the bright and beautiful lake and its surrounding forests.

从他们建立在一座小山头上的堡垒望去，可以远眺一片广阔的地域，明澄美丽的湖泊及环绕湖面的森林也尽收眼底。

评析：把一句原文抽词拆句译成三个不定人称句，层次分明。

[25] A notion has taken hold in the United States to the effect *that* the only people *who* should be encouraged to bring children into the world are those *who* can afford them.

在美国有一种根深蒂固的观点，说是只有那些抚养得起子女的人才应鼓励其生育。

评析：抽词拆句译成汉语无连接词复句，用副词"只有……才"承上启下。

[26] Rome, as we all know, was not built in a day *which was a step-by-step process involving many individuals.*

大家都知道，罗马不是一天建立起来的，这是一个逐步完成的过程，一砖一瓦少了谁也不行。

评析：这个句子出自约翰·盖伊的《英国列王记》，是个复句，译文按原文顺序从容断开，"一砖一瓦少了谁也不行"译得极为精彩。

[27] I could not venture to approach her, or to communicate with her in writing, for my sense of the peril in which her life was passed was only *to be equaled by* my fear of increasing it.

我不敢和母亲接近，也不敢和她通信，因为我一方面深感她的处境已经十分危险，一方面又深怕增加她的危险。

评析：中译用"一方面……一方面又"来体现"to be equaled by"的涵义，而且为了突出原句对比的强烈程度，还加了两个"深"字，即"深感"和"深怕"。这不但逼近原作，还保持汉语惯常表达的特色。

三、短句拆译

[28] on one *sunshiny* morning in June…

在6月里的一天早上，天气晴朗……

评析：译者运用"抽词拆句法"，把"sunshiny"一词抽出，独立成句，这样拆译比译成"在六月里的一个晴朗的早晨"显得更具姿态，更明畅老练（黄邦杰，2003）。

[29] I'm not the first man who has made mistakes.

自来出错的人多了,我又不是头一个!

评析:这是个复合句,句子短,结构简单,如果译成"我不是第一个犯错误的人",也未尝不可,但过于平淡和呆板,体现不出人物的性格和语气。因此,可把句子拆开译,改成并列句,这就活龙活现地把那种不肯认错的无赖态度勾画出来了。

[30] This was a delight he could not forgo. (*Vanity Fair*)

他认为这是无上乐趣,不肯割舍。

评析:这一句本来也可以译成单句,比如:这是他难以放弃的乐趣。但高明的译者把句子拆成了上面两句话。

[31] The air seemed almost *sticky* from the scent of *bursting buds*.

花蕾初绽,散发出一股芳香,这时空气似乎给人一种粘糊糊的感觉。

评析:这句译文十分高超。译作采取层层剥开的方法,把一句拆成三句:倒过来先译"bursting buds",然后引出"scent",最后归结到中心词"sticky"上。在翻译过程中,还运用了"抽词拆句法",让"bursting buds"和"scent"一词分别独立成句,充分发挥汉语句法简短的特色。尤其值得注意的是,末句用了"这时"来连接上两句,使整句脉络分明,主次有别(黄邦杰,2003)。

[32] He had left a note of welcome for me, *as sunny as his face*.

他留下一封短信,对我表示欢迎;那信写得热情洋溢,一如其人。

评析:这一句看着简单,安排起来颇不容易。关键在于"sunny"一词,很不好译,因为它既跟"note"搭配,又要照顾"his face",而"his face"本身,如直译为"脸"或"脸色",也必定索然无味。译者把原来的一句话,断成四句,不脱不黏,文理自然。译者在拆句上下过很大工夫,否则译笔不可能如此老到。"sunny"译成"热情洋溢",这就有可能同时跟"note"和"his face"相搭配,而"as his face"译成四字词组"一如其人",不仅不落俗套,又接应了"热情洋溢"。

[33] Why should it be made longer than is necessary?

为什么拖得太久呢?用不着嘛。

评析:这句如果译成"为什么要使它拖得比需要的更长呢?"就不成中国话了。

[34] I pass my hands *lovingly* about the smooth skin of a silver birch.

我抚摸着白桦光滑的树表,爱不释手。

评析:"lovingly"拆译成句。

[35] His announcement got a *mixed* reaction.

他的声明引起了反应,褒贬不一。

评析:"mixed"拆译成句。

[36] The town *boasts* a beautiful lake.

镇上有个美丽的湖,人人以此自豪。

评析:"boasts"拆译成句。

[37] He was *thunderingly* insistent that something should be done about it.

他大发雷霆,坚持必须对此事采取措施。

评析:副词被拆成一句话。

[38] His *informality* impressed me deeply.

他不拘小节,给我留下深刻印象。

评析:名词拆成动宾结构。

[39] His attitude did not incline me to help him.
我看了他这种态度,想帮他的心都冷了。

评析:这比死译"他的态度使我不想帮助他"要强几倍。

[40] These *alternations of mood* were the *despair and* joy of Ethan Frome.
她这样一会儿一种心绪,叫伊坦时而灰心,时而高兴。

评析:"alternations of mood"是这句话的难点,这个名词化短语从汉语角度上看非常生硬,如果不能化开,就可能译成"这些情绪上的交替变化"。译者吕叔湘把它译成"一会儿一种",后面的"and"译成"时而……时而……",这样整个句子都盘活了,堪称佳译。

[41] He went hot and cold *by turn*.
他一阵发热,一阵发冷。

评析:把"一阵"重复一遍,显得顺当。

[42] You are talking *delightful nonsense*.
你虽信口胡诌,倒也蛮有情趣。

[43] His irritation could not withstand the silent beauty of the night. ——Maugham
面对这宁静的良宵美景,他的烦恼不禁涣然冰释了。——叶子南译文

总结:可以看出,英语尚长句,省用标点符号,汉语则喜短句,多用标点符号,使表达从容不迫。明白了这一点,我们在翻译中就应设法应用拆译技巧,以破解翻译句法欧化的毛病。

本节练习

[1] It was a town of sighs and silence, with none of the studied advertisements of sorrow.

[2] But they had become nomads of the desert, living on the ground and under the sky, and they loved it.

[3] They scarcely made a pretense of hiding the bug in your hotel room.

[4] His (Hitler's) discourse, says Speidel, "became lost in fantastic digressions."

[5] The morning of June 27th was clear and sunny, with the fresh warmth of a full-summer day; the flowers were blossoming profusely and the grass was richly green.

[6] His addition completed the list.

[7] She made tea for us *in a most agreeable manner*.

[8] A man without tears is a man without heart.

[9] Nothing is impossible to a willing mind.

[10] Good to the last drop.

第二节 转 换

有人认为,英语是一种静态型的语言结构,动作意义常借用其同源名词或其他词类来表

达。一般说来,初级英语、中级英语和高级英语的重要区别就是名词化和介词化的程度多深多浅了。在高级英语表达中,更多地使用了名词化和介词化,主谓宾甚至从句的结构少见了。名词化和介词化现象越高,译成中文时越需要译者抓得住短语和整句的大意,而后化整为零,在充分理解的基础上把译文搞通、搞活,让译文出彩。(苏福忠,2006:70)汉语则更偏向动态,多用动词表达动作意义,因而动词使用频率较高。转换可以分为词类转换和句子成分转换。英语和汉语词汇最大差别之一是,英语讲究词性。英语中的词可以根据词义、句法作用和形式特征分为十大词类(parts of speech):其中和词类转译密切相关的有:名词、形容词、动词、副词、介词、冠词等。在翻译中,一种语言里属于某种词类的词并非一定要翻译成另一种语言的相应词类,而且也不可能这样做。一般地说,英汉语的词性转换也有一定的规律,比如,英语比较喜欢多用名词和介词,而汉语则是动词用得多一些。要摆脱词性的纠缠,就应明确地意识到:在翻译中,词性不予考虑,一切以译文能否自然流畅地传递意义为准。对翻译初学者来说,他们常容易受限制于原语的词类,而不敢大胆地转换词类。其中,对初学者构成最大影响的是名词化动词(verbalized noun),它是使译文生硬拗口、晦涩难懂的原因。现将几个关键的词性转译问题列举如下。

一、名词的转换

名词的转换又可分为"不转也可"和"非转不可"两类。

1. 不转也可

[1] My *admiration* for him grew more.

我对他的敬佩与日俱增。

我对他越来越敬佩。

评析:admiration 的词性如果照直翻译,未尝不可,这样也更省事。但如果把这个名词和后面动词 grew more 结合在一起,转化成动词,亦佳。

[2] The international food shortage *had a direct impact on* Kuwait and other barren desert countries.

直译:国际粮食的缺乏对科威特和其他不毛的沙漠国家产生了一种直接的影响。

改译一:由于世界普遍粮食缺乏,这就直接影响到科威特和其他不毛的沙漠国家。

改译二:全球性食品短缺现象直接影响了科威特等贫瘠的沙漠国家。

评析:直译按照原词性翻译显得僵硬,但还说得过去。改译一变换了许多词的词性,把原来的主语部分变成了原因状语成分,使整个句子灵活。改译二则只将 a direct impact on 动词化,显得更简洁。

2. 非转不可

[3] Indo-China is a *drain* on French resources.

印度支那战争不断地消耗法国的资源。

评析:drain 只能译成动词"消耗",否则不像话。

[4] It's mighty to make him work Saturdays, when all the boys is having holiday, but he hates work more than anything else, and I've got to do some of duty by him, or I'll be the *ruination* of the child.

要说星期六别的孩子都在过假日你让他干活儿很难倒还罢了,可他压根儿就恨透了干活儿,比什么都恨,我真的是看不过去,非尽些责任不可,要不我非把这孩子毁了不可。

评析：很难想象在马克·吐温俚语充斥的口语体小说《汤姆·索亚历险记》中会出现如此名词用法！他为什么不写成："or I'll ruin the child"？而这在中文里非译成动词不可！

[5] He admires the President's stated *decision* to fight for the job.

他对总统声明为保住其职位而<u>决心</u>奋斗表示钦佩。

评析：英语的谓语动词只有 admires 一个词，其它用的是过去分词(stated)、动词性名词(decision)、不定式(to fight)和介词(for)。汉语没有词形变化，但可以几个动词连用。在本句中，decision 转化成动词"决心"。

二、形容词的转换

[6] Perhaps she would prod at the straw in her *clumsy impatience*. ——Sredni Vashtar

也许她会<u>迫不及待</u>地、<u>笨手笨脚</u>地翻弄那个草铺。

评析："clumsy impatience"是移就格。"clumsy"和"impatience"分别修饰谓语"prod at"。

[7] Buckley was in a *clear* minority.

巴克利<u>显然</u>属于少数。

评析："clear"跟它所修饰的名词没有语义联系，它是全句的修饰语，且有评论性质。

[8] Doctors have said that they are not *sure* they can save his life.

医生们说他们<u>不敢肯定</u>能否救得了他的命。

三、介词的转换

[9] He is a jovial giant, *with* a huge appetite *for* food, drink and women.

他生性乐观，身材魁梧，<u>贪</u>吃<u>贪</u>杯又<u>贪</u>色。

[10] The man ran back down *into* the cellar.

那个男子跑了回来，<u>进了</u>地窖。

[11] "Coming!" Away she skimmed *over* the lawn, *up* the path, *up* the steps, *across* the veranda, and *into* the porch.

"来啦！"她转身蹦着跳着地跑了，<u>越过</u>草地，<u>跑上</u>小径，<u>跨上</u>台阶，<u>穿过</u>凉台，<u>进了</u>门廊。

[12] *At the news* they were quite surprised.

<u>听了这消息</u>他们感到十分惊奇。

四、副词的转换

[13] He is physically weak but mentally sound.

他<u>身体</u>虽弱，但<u>心理</u>健康。

评析："physically"和"mentally"都分别是限定副词，缩小、限定了表语的语义范围。英语通过词性手段限定了表语的范围，而汉语则是借助主题语限定评述语的范围。限定人、事或地域范围的主题语是范围主题语(申小龙，1996：311)，在上述译句中，主题语是"他"，而"身体"和"心理"分别在评述语里做范围主题语。

五、非人称主语句的转换

英语中有大量非人称主语句,使用抽象名词或事物做主语。这种句式常带有拟人化修辞色彩,语气委婉、含蓄、结构严谨,言简意赅,是典型的英语句式。(连淑能,2006)非人称主语句在翻译成汉语时,常必须在汉语中采用人称主语句。两者之间的句法转换势在必行,否则译句生硬,甚至不成句子。

[14] Then came the struggle and parting below. *Words refuse to tell it.* ——Vanity Fair
　　接着是楼下告别时的忙乱,当时的情形真是难以言语形容。——杨必译文

评析:"难以言语形容"原文是"Words refuse to tell it",是个典型换个说法最好的例子。中文忌用事物做主语,现在把"words"换成了人,问题就解决了。

[15] This almost caused Jemima to faint with terror. "Well, I never," said she, "what an audacious—" *Emotion prevented her from completing either sentence.* The carriage rolled away; the great gates were closed; the bell rang for the dancing lesson. *The world is before the two young ladies*; and so, farewell to Chiswick Mall. (*Vanity Fair*)
　　吉米玛吓得差点儿晕过去,说道:"嗳哟,我从来没有——好大的胆子——"她的感情起伏得太厉害,因此两句话都没有说完。马车走了,大铁门关上了;里面打起铃子准备上跳舞课。两个女孩子从此开始做人了。再见吧,契息克林荫道!——杨必译文

评析:"Emotion prevented her from completing either sentence"译成"她的感情起伏得太厉害,因此两句话都没有说完",非常精彩。"两个女孩子从此开始做人了"也同样把"the world"的主词换成了"人"。

[16] *His failure* made a mockery of the teacher's great efforts to help him.
　　由于他考试不及格,老师辅导他的一番心血白费了。

评析:原主语转化为汉语的原因状语,将"teacher"一词拉出来做主语。

本节练习

1. 英语名词转化为汉语动词

[1] An *acquaintance* with world history is helpful to the study of current affairs.

[2] The *discovery* of a new dish does more for the happiness of mankind than the discovery of a new star.

[3] The beauty of the scenery baffles *description*.

[4] There has been a tremendous *expansion* of nurseries and kindergartens in both town and villages.

[5] A *view* of the West Lake can be *obtained* from this house.

[6] He is a *lover* of Chinese painting.

[7] He is no *smoker*, but his father is a chain *smoker*.

[8] He is a lot better *actor* than you think he is.

2. 英语介词或介词短语转化为汉语动词

[9] I found him *at his book* when I came into the room.

[10] The road to development is long but we are firmly *on* it.

3. 英语形容词转化成汉语动词

[11] We are not *content with* our present achievements.

[12] They were *suspicious* and *resentful* of him.

[13] Hussein was a *puzzled* man.

4. 副词转化为动词

[14] Sorry I wasn't *in* when you rang me up.

5. 动词转化为名词

[15] The landing was *designed* to cut the peninsula in two.

[16] On that day they were *escorted* to the Great Wall of China.

[17] A well-dressed man, who *looked* and *talked* like an American, got into the car.

6. 形容词转化为名词

[18] They are going to build a school for *the blind and the deaf*.

[19] All *the wounded* were sent to the hospital right away.

[20] They showed a *sympathetic* understanding of our problem.

7. 名词转化为形容词

[21] I recognized the *absurdity* of dealing with them through intermediaries.

[22] He was still more surprised at the *singularity* of the stranger's appearance.

[23] We are deeply convinced of the *correctness* of those policies and firmly determined to pursue it.

[24] He is a man of cool *courage*.

8. 名词用作表语形容词

[25] The garden-party is a great *success*.

[26] The music is a *gas*.

[27] They say my story is a *yawn*.

9. 副词转化为形容词

[28] He was *deeply* impressed by what they did in the critical moment.

[29] "I suppose boys think *differently* from girls," he said.

10. 英语形容词转化为汉语副词

[30] At last, he whispered a *hurried* good-bye to his host and darted toward the door.

11. 名词转化为副词

[31] He had the *kindness* to show me the way.

[32] I had the *fortune* to meet him.

[33] We found *difficulty* in solving the housing problem.

12. 非人称主语转换成人称主语

[34] The *thought* of returning to his native land never deserted him amid his tribulation.

[35] A *look* of pleasure came to her face.

[36] The *application* of electronic computers makes for a tremendous rise in labour pro-

ductivity.

[37] Failure *did not deter* him from trying again.

[38] His *words* sent a quiver through my body.

第三节 精简与增补

精简与增补是英译汉极其重要的手段。英语句法结构重"形合",句子各个成分间都有适当的连接成分表达它们的相互关系,强调语法关系的一致、协调。汉语句法结构重"意合",句子各个成分间的关系多靠意会,比较少用连接成分,结构形式比较松弛,词句也就比较简洁。这是英语和汉语的重大差别。在英译汉时,译者须把握这种差别,省去汉语里可以不要的连接成分,使译文流畅自如,避免生硬累赘,将可有可无的字词尽量省去。正如莎士比亚名言:Brevity is the soul of wit(言以简洁为贵)。根据对翻译共性的研究分析发现(柯飞,2005),译文语言同原文语言相比,会呈现出简化(simplication)、显化(explicitation)、扩增、净化(sanitisation)和隐化(implicitness)等现象。翻译过程中会不同程度地发生对原文的模仿,从而使汉译本有从意合转形合的潜在显化趋势,并且形成介乎原文与译文之间的"语际语"。我们要力争行文地道,努力避免对原文的机械模仿,就要掌握好"隐化"(精简)和"显化"(增补)的辩证关系。照顾到汉语表达习惯而做隐化处理的翻译通常比不做隐化的仿译(imitation)更为地道。因此我们尤其要充分发挥汉语的简练优势。

一、精简

[1] He used poetry as a medium for writing in prose.
   仿译:他以诗歌作为写散文的媒介。
   隐化:他用诗歌来写散文。

[2] Eczema may be found *in all age groups* and *in both sexes*.
   仿译:所有年龄组和两种性别都可患湿疹。
   隐化:男女老少都可患湿疹。

[3] A doctor's duty is to make every effort to *save the dying and help the wounded*.
   仿译:医生的职责是尽一切力量挽救垂死者和帮助受伤者。
   隐化:医生的职责是尽心尽力地救死扶伤。

[4] If you take this medicine, your illness will surely be cured.
   仿译:你要是服用这个药,你的病肯定能治好。
   隐化:这药吃了准好。

[5] You needn't care about the affairs in the home.
   仿译:你不必担心家里的事。
   隐化:家里的事,不用你操心。

评析:英译汉时做一定的隐化处理,译文会更地道,也比较简洁。仿译则将外语的表达法引入汉语,对于汉语来说,已经在形式上显化了,即本可以隐化表达的意思外在地显示出来了。这一类情况在英译汉中表现得非常明显和频繁。

[6] It was one of the few gestures of sentiment he was ever to make.

仿译：那是他在感情方面所做出的很少的几次表示中的一个例子。

隐化：他很少表露感情，这是难得的一次。

评析：采用隐化策略，减少重复，避免长定语，则可译得更符合汉语的表达习惯。

[7] Vast lawns extend like sheets of vivid green, with here and there clumps of gigantic trees, heaping up with rich piles of foliage.

原译：草地宽阔，好像地上铺了鲜艳的绿绒似的毡毯，巨大数株，聚成一簇，绿叶浓密，一眼望去，草地上东一簇，西一簇，这类的大树可不少。——《中国翻译》(1993/5)译文

改译：宽阔的草坪宛如翠绿的地毯，成片的参天大树点缀其间，绿叶浓密，层层叠叠。——马红军译文

评析：原译共61字，按照原译者的看法是："汉语的神韵与气势好像正是来自这种短促有力、潇潇洒洒、疏连自如、形离而神聚的语句之中"，但和改译相比，显得节奏缓慢、拖沓，赘词颇多，译文甚至比原句长！改译句简洁明快，字数省去一半，只有35字。

[8] The *system* of strong public services and social solidarity has deep roots in French history.

原译：法国历史中有很强的公共服务和社会团结的<u>体制</u>。

改译：强调公共服务和社会团结一直是法国的历史传统。

评析：文中的"system"总是被译成"体系"、"系统"等，这样译显得别扭。叶子南(2003：143)认为，"system"一词完全可以在译文中省去，或用其他词取代。改译不仅意思准确，而且行文也更流畅。这里用"传统"取代"体系"应该是可以的。

[9] People were variously impressed, intrigued, outraged, frightened, and perplexed by my arguments.

我的观点使有的人印象深刻，有的深感兴趣，有的气愤之极，有的惊恐万状，有的困惑不解。

评析：本句中的"variously"被保留了反而无法翻译成像样的中文，如译成"人们不同地……"会使行文别扭，它的意思已经融合在句子中，不必单独出现在译文中。

[10] We passed two neighbors. Havel nodded to both *wishing them a good day*.

我们路过两个邻居，哈维尔向他们点头，以示问候。

评析：wishing them a good day 是一个习惯表达语，英文的细节没有必要说出来，说了反而不像中文。

[11] The Western system is characterized by the *existence* of competitive elections.

原译：西方制度是由竞选的<u>存在</u>为其特点的。

改译：西方制度的一个特点是<u>竞选</u>。

评析：在本句中的"existence"在中文里没有必要表达出来，译出"存在"更显生硬。

二、四字格精简法

恰当运用汉语里的四字词组，也大大有助于表达上的简洁和生动。

[12] All evils are to be consider'd with the good that is in them, and with what worse attends them.

译文一：所以，考虑到所有坏事的时候，应当想到坏事中还有好事，还应当想到，坏事中还可能有更坏的情况呢。——黄杲炘译文

译文二：当我们遇到坏事的时候，我们应当考虑到其中所包含的好事，同时也应当考虑到更坏的情况。——徐霞村译文

译文三：真是，我怎么不想想祸福相倚和祸不单行的道理呢？——郭建中译文

[13] Scientific exploration, the search for knowledge has given man the practical results of being able to shield himself *the calamities of nature and the calamities imposed by other man*.

科学的探索，知识的追求，使人类获得了避免天灾人祸的实力。

评析：原句末11个词，译成四字格"天灾人祸"，精炼贴切。

[14] They developed a simple hunting and fishing culture *suited to the conditions of the region*.

他们因地制宜地发展了简易的狩猎业和渔业。

评析：这句天然的英语表达出自《麦克米伦百科全书》，和汉语成语吻合得天衣无缝，纯属巧遇。

[15] He was mature in years and *tried in wars* but had *the old, inbred arrogance of his family*.

他正当壮年，久经沙场，但是却带有他的家族的那种年深月久，代代相传的傲慢习气。

[16] His speech was Irish throughout, *versatile*, *witty* and occasionally pointed.

他的演说自始至终带有爱尔兰人的风格：洋洋洒洒，妙趣横生，有时则很犀利深刻。

三、增补

增补的目的就是使译文显化、明晰化、明朗化：一是出于句法上的考虑，即将原文句法上的省略成分按汉语习惯补出；一是根据原文上下文的意思、逻辑关系，在译文中增添有助于译文读者理解的显化表达，或者说将原文隐含的信息显化于译文中，使意思更明确，逻辑更清楚。形象点说，译者应善于给原文"圆话"，但不是画蛇添足。

1. 增补词语使译文句法完整(重复)

[17] I fell madly in love with her, and *she with me*.

我狂热地爱上了她，她也狂热地爱上了我。

[18] They began to study and analyze *the situation of the enemy*.

他们开始研究敌情，分析敌情。

[19] He became an *oil baron*—all by himself.

他成为一个石油大王——一个白手起家的石油大王。

2. 增补解释性的辅助动词，使汉语符合搭配习惯

[20] In the evening, after the *banquets*, the *concerts* and the *table tennis exhibitions*, he would work on the drafting of the final communiqué.

晚上在参加宴会、出席音乐会、观看乒乓球表演之后,他还得起草最后公报。

评析: "after the *banquets*, the *concerts* and *the table tennis exhibitions*"如直接译成"在宴会、音乐会、乒乓球表演之后",则太生硬,这时加上动词,形成三个动宾词组,那就使意思明确,读起来也较通顺自然,符合汉语习惯。

3. 增补语气词,英语里的语气可以通过汉语的语气词再现

[21] Don't tell me you've missed the train!
恐怕你赶不上火车了吧?

[22] I declare, John, you've grown a foot.
说真的,约翰,你长高一尺啦。

4. 增补解释性的词(阐译),不补则译文晦涩费解

[23] And *the years flipped off* the calendar like dry leaves from a lawn.
岁月催人,日历一张张撕掉,好像落在草坪上的枯叶一样。

[24] There are friends and friends.
朋友有各种各样,有益友,有损友。

评析: 原文过于简洁,不增补则意义无法显现。

[25] I buried my head under the *miserable* sheet and rug and cried like a child.
译文一:我把头埋在悲惨的被单和毯子下面,像孩子样地哭了起来。
译文二:我把头埋在那仿佛感染了我的悲惨心情的被单和毯子里,像孩子样地哭了起来。
译文三:我非常难过,一头扎进被单和毯子里,像孩子一样哭了起来。
译文四:我把头埋在被单和毯子里,像孩子一样哭得好伤心。
译文五:我把头埋在被单和毯子里,孩子似的哭了起来,而那被单和毯子也仿佛感染了我的悲伤。

评析: "miserable"的修饰位置有点匪夷所思,英语里可以说"悲惨的被单和毯子",汉语里却不行,就别扭。译文一称得上是"忠实"的典型,它将"the miserable sheet and rug"直接换成"悲惨的被单和毯子",形式上一一对应,但不符合汉语搭配;译文二、三则试图在忠实原文的同时还照顾"汉语的表达习惯",译文二显得十分啰嗦,译文三"miserable"过于前提;译文四过于简单;译文五把这个形容词拆出来,放到后面阐译,使句子语义比较完整。

[26] She tried hard to perform well, but the costume was *not cooperating*.
译文一:她努力试图表演得好,但服装就是不合作。
译文二:她努力好好地滑,但是服装就是不听话。
译文三:她尽了最大努力,但运动衣上掉下来的带子总是影响她。——叶子南译文
译文四:她尽了最大努力,但运动衣上掉下来的带子妨碍了她的发挥。

评析: 原文是一位体育评论员现场介绍一位滑冰运动员比赛时说的。译文一照单词"cooperating"直译,显得生硬,译文三和四则增补了语境因素,使译文意思显豁,表达自然。以下数例摘自叶子南(2003)。

[27] Collin Powell was the *worst kept secret*.
译文一:克林·鲍威尔是保守得最差的秘密。
译文二:克林·鲍威尔要当国务卿这早已是人人皆知的了。

译文三:克林·鲍威尔将军要当国务卿已是公开的秘密了。

评析:译文一是直译,译文二采用了正说反译的技巧,但太过于直露,译文三则根据语境,对"worst"做了较好的处理。

[28] His eight-minute valedictory was everything that Gore wasn't during his 18-month campaign: graceful, authentic, inspiring.

译文一:他那8分钟的告别演说非常成功,可这些偏偏在18个月的竞选中没有:有风度、可信、鼓舞人心。

译文二:他那8分钟的告别演说展示给众人的恰恰是他18个月竞选中没有的:有风度、可信、鼓舞人心。

译文三:他那8分钟的告别演说有风度、可信、鼓舞人心,应有尽有,这些偏偏是那18个月的竞选中从来没有表现出来的。

译文四:他在8分钟的告别演说中表现得既有风度、又可信,十分鼓舞人心,可惜来得太晚了,在过去18个月的竞选中这些却偏偏毫无踪影。

评析:译文一、二基本按照原文顺序,译文二增补了"展示给众人的",译文三增补了"应有尽有",译文四则做了非人称主语的转化,并增补了"可惜来得太晚了",也是原文作者心中想说而没有说出的话,当然,如果为了含蓄,也可以不增补。

[29] I believe the eight dead journalists are *policy*.

我相信那八个新闻记者的死亡是蓄意谋杀。

评析:这句话就不能译成"我相信那八个死去的新闻记者是政策"。"policy"一词必须根据其原意有所补充添加,才能把话说清楚。

[30] The child pawed *inquisitively* at the *lively* images on the screen.

那小孩好奇地抓着电视屏幕,想知道里面怎么会有人活动。

评析:inquisitively 和 lively 都必须加词发挥,才能把意思表达清楚。

[31] Condit came out with his *political* smile.

康迪特走出去时,脸上带着政客惯有的笑容。

评析:这句如译成"政治的笑容"显得生硬,故作了补充。

[32] Announcer's Voice: At 11:15 this morning, the Prime Minister, speaking to the nation from No. 10 Downing Street announced that Great Britain is at war with Germany.

译文一:广播员的声音:今天上午11点15分,首相在唐宁街10号向全国发表了讲话,宣布英国与德国处于交战状态。

译文二:广播员的声音:今天上午11点15分,首相在唐宁街10号——英国首相府邸向全国发表了讲话,宣布英国与德国处于交战状态。

评析:译文一忠实地译出了原文的字面层意义。但对"唐宁街10号"这一隐含文化意象的地名不做些补充说明的话,相信绝大多数中国普通观众会茫然不知其所云。译者宜对上述译文作恰如其分的增补修润,通过增补"英国首相府邸",观众这才真正认识到了"唐宁街10号"的具体所指。

本节练习

一、精简

1. **精减代词**

   精减人称代词

   [1] As he approached the village he met a number of people but none of whom he knew, which somewhat surprised him.

   [2] As we lived near the road, we often had the traveler or stranger visit us to taste our gooseberry wine.

   [3] I sent you yesterday all the books you wanted, have you received them?

   [4] When anyone among the people breaks the law, he too should be punished.

   [5] While reading does not allow yourself to regress, but keep reading ahead in every sentence, even when you come across a new word.

   精减物主代词

   [6] She listened for a moment with her rounded eyes.

   [7] They came in their thousands.

   [8] He wore a ragged, dusty coat that reached only to his knees.

2. **精减连接词**

   精减并列连接词

   [9] The early autumn day was warm and charming.

   [10] He looked gloomy and troubled.

   [11] He is kind and he knows a lot.

   [12] She is just the person—so quiet and so bright.

   [13] The doors opened and the audience came crowding in.

   [14] He is not honest, so he is not fit to be a cashier.

   [15] There must be somebody in, for I heard a voice.

   精减从属连接词

   [16] The grandmother said she would tell them a story if they would keep quiet.

   [17] I should not have time to see him even if he were here.

   [18] As the temperature increases, the volume of water becomes greater.

3. **精减冠词**

   [19] More often we would go for a weekend to Camp David.

   [20] He would never have to sleep in a strange bed.

   [21] He pushed open the door gently and stole out of the room for fear that he should awake her.

4. **精减介词**

   [22] By autumn of 1984, I was in Moscow bound for China.

   [23] Life in the White House is active and intense.

   [24] Rumours had already spread along the streets and lanes.

[25] Smoking is not allowed in the store-house.

5. 为行文简洁所作的词语精减

[26] A few months after this I crossed the sea eastward again.

[27] He realized the subtlety of China's messages, the gap between her hot rhetoric and her cool action.

[28] Men will reap as they sow.

[29] Allen had a long discussion with Nassar. He got nowhere.

[30] It was in mid-August, and the repair section operated under the blazing sun.

[31] As you read, make a conscious effort to screen the nouns, pronouns and verbs from the other words.

[32] Where there is a will, there is a way.

二、增补

1. 补动词

[1] This is essential for the *victory* of the revolutionary cause.

[2] In spite of yesterday's *rainstorm* the crops lay lush and green in the early light.

2. 补名词

[3] Nassar, with *statesmanship* and infinite patience, persuaded his quarreling brothers to sign an agreement.

[4] The *grief* of the people took charge.

[5] The development of Chinese industry remains one of the *priorities* of the government.

[6] I was struck by their *cordiality* to each other.

[7] He allowed the *father* to be overruled by the *judge*, and declared his own son guilty.

[8] A new kind of aircraft—*small*, *cheap*, *pilotless*—is attracting increasing attention.

3. 补形容词或副词

[9] They *lingered* long over his letter.

[10] At the meeting he made a speech —*eloquent* and *energetic*.

[11] In this mood, I went to diplomatic circles, *earnest* but only *sketchily* informed.

4. 补概括性词语

[12] We have achieved rapid progress in industry, agriculture, commerce, education and culture.

[13] The social systems of China and the U.S are fundamentally different.

5. 补概念词

[14] The car stopped in front of *the Nile Hilton*.

[15] Chen is thirty-two and mother of *two*.

6. 补数量词

[16] *A stream* was winding its way through the valley into the river.

[17] I was extremely worried about her, but this was neither the place nor the time for *a lecture or an argument*.

[18] *A red sun* rose slowly from the calm sea.

[19] This too was *a complete* lie.

7. 补显示复数的修饰词语

[20] The lion is the King of *animals*.

[21] The very earth trembled as with the tramps of *horses* and murmur of angry *men*.

[22] Most were absorbed into the Russian empire through colonial expansion under *the Tsars*.

8. 补语气词

[23] Their host *carved*, *poured*, *cut bread*, *talked*, *laughed*, *proposed healths*.

[24] Don't take it *seriously*. I'm *just* making fun of you.

9. 补词使译文清晰

[25] In April, there was the "*ping*" heard around the world. In July *the ping "ponged"*.

[26] All one needed was one lucky break and *the doors* would open.

[27] The weather was warm and sultry and everyone *seemed to be on edge*.

[28] But they still came, *by car*, *by donkey and on foot*. Thousands came from other Arab countries.

第四节　实译与虚译

中国文化思维方式具有较强的具象性，而西方文化思维方式则具有较强的抽象性。汉文化"尚象"的文化传统形成了偏重具象的思维方式，西方文化"尚思"的文化传统形成了偏重抽象的思维方式（包惠南，2001）。这两种不同的思维方式必然直接反映在句子词汇的使用层面上。汉语重实，重形象，喜用具体的表现法，较少使用表示抽象概念的名词。在英语中抽象名词的使用频率明显高于汉语。因此，在英译汉时，除了注意抽象名词的词性转化外，还要考虑实译与虚译的关系。所谓实译，是指词义或词组义从抽象引向具体，从一般引向特殊，从概括引向局部，从"虚"引向"实"的过程。所谓虚译，是指词义或词组义从具体引向抽象，从特殊引向一般，从局部引向概括，从"实"引向"虚"的过程（连淑能，2006）。

一、实译取向

实译，是采用译语特有的表达形式来使译文充实化，常常体现为归译。

[1] Gwendolen: Ernest has a strong upright nature. He is the very soul of truth and honour. *Disloyalty would be as impossible to him as deception.*
……他绝对不会见异思迁，也不会做假骗人。——余光中译文

评析：抽象名词这么多，中文最难消化。末句如果译成"不忠对于他将如欺骗一样不可能"，那是非常糟糕的。这是王尔德 *The Importance of Being Earnest* 中的一句台词，必须听起来"响亮而稳当，入耳便化"（余光中，2001）

[2] Lady Bracknell: Sit down immediately. *Hesitation of any kind is a sign of men-*

tal decay in the young, of physical weakness in the old.
犹豫不决,无论是什么姿态,都显示青年人的智力衰退,老年人的体力虚弱。
——余光中译文

评析:本句的抽象名词也不少。尤其句首的一词,如果只译成二字词组"犹豫"或"迟疑",都会显得突兀不稳。

[3] *Wisdom* prepares for the worst; but *folly* leaves the worst for the day it comes.
——R. Cecil.
聪明人防患于未然,愚蠢者临渴掘井。——包惠南译文

[4] In line with latest trends in fashion, a few dress designers have been sacrificing *elegance* to *audacity*.
有些时装设计师为了赶时髦,舍弃了优雅别致的式样,而一味追求袒胸露体的奇装异服。——包惠南译文

评析:[3][4]两例中的抽象名词 wisdom 和 folly, elegance 和 audacity,对于习惯于抽象思维的英美读者来说,词义明确、措词简练;但对于习惯于具象思维的中国读者来说,必须将这些抽象名词所表达的抽象概念具体化,才符合汉语读者的思维习惯和汉语遣词造句的行文习惯。

[5] He wished to try his luck by inviting the beautiful, young lady to dance, but *met with a rebuff*.
他想试试运气,请那位年轻貌美的女士跳舞,结果碰了一鼻子灰。

评析:"met with a rebuff"指"遭到断然拒绝",上面的译文更为具象。

[6] Western table manners compel us to sip our soup *noiselessly* and eat our food *quietly with the least expression of enjoyment*.
所谓的西方礼节,是强迫我们鸦雀无声地喝汤,闷头吃饭。

评析:"noiselessly"译作"鸦雀无声"、"quietly with the least expression of enjoyment"译作"闷头",既形象又简洁。

[7] However, such measures *touch only the tip*, but not address the basis of the problem.
然而,这样的措施只不过是蜻蜓点水,并没有触及问题的根源。

评析:原文中的"touch only the tip"如果译作"只不过是碰了碰问题的尖端",读起来文理不通、让人费解,译作"只不过是蜻蜓点水"是表达此含义的精彩中文说法。

[8] *Action and foresight* will be needed as well as *learning and reputation*.
不但需要有博学德高的学者,而且需要有远见卓识的实干家。

评析:原文中"learning and reputation","action and foresight"都是抽象词语,在译文中宜转化成具体词语。

[9] In the meantime, charlatans are all too happy to exploit people's ignorance by selling them "miracle" diets or *products* that are *worthless* and may even be dangerous.
同时,庸医们都轻而易举地利用人们的无知,向人们推销"神奇的"饮食配方,以及一文不值甚至对人们有害的"灵丹妙药"。

评析:把"worthless"、"products"引申译成"一文不值"和"灵丹妙药",正是原文内容所

表达的意思。

[10] The company applauded the *clever deception*, for none could tell when Chopin stopped and Liszt began.

在座的人对这种移花接木的巧妙手法,无不啧啧称赞,因为谁也不知道在什么时候肖邦停了下来,由李斯特接着弹奏下去。

评析:"deception"确有"欺骗"之意,但在此具体场合译为"移花接木的巧妙手法"比译为"骗术"要好得多。

[11] Nixon was to play the China game with the skill and *cynicism* it required.

尼克松随后在处理中国问题上真是手腕巧妙,竭尽纵横捭阖之能事。

评析:"cynicism"引申译成"纵横捭阖",真实地再现了原文所指"运用政治和外交手段达到联合或分化瓦解之目的"。

[12] He became engaged to Isabel. This was no surprise to Mrs. Bradley since they *had been inseparable* for years and one knew that Isabel was in love with him.

他和伊莎贝尔订了婚。这件事,布莱德太太倒不诧异。因为两人耳鬓厮磨已有多年,而且人们都知道伊莎贝尔爱他。——周熙良译文

评析:"耳鬓厮磨"的形象性从内容转移到形式上。

[13] Home after seven years, Home. The word had meant *so much* to him.

家,阔别了七年的家。这个字对他多亲切呀。

[14] This is why Postgate was moved to say that the principle of faithfulness was set up as a merit of true translation "*by general consent, though not by universal practice.*"(*The Art of Translation*)

波斯哥特因此感叹道:提出忠实的原则,其优点在于能够指导准确的翻译,这"谁都同意,尽管并非人人都这么做"。

二、虚译取向

虚译,或谓意译。由于原文的修辞表达结构直译过来会造成误解或牵强,译文只好取其基本义而弃其喻体。

[15] I learned yesterday that their eldest son has been twice sent to prison. I wonder how many other *skeletons they've got in their cupboard*.

我昨天才听说他们家大儿子坐过两次牢。真不知道他们家还有多少见不得人的事情。

评析:原文成语"skeletons in the cupboard"的喻义为"想要掩盖的丑事、隐私"。此处无法直译,只能意译之。

[16] Foreign competition has *taken the wind out of the sails* of the U. S. automobile industry.

国外的竞争势力已经使美国的汽车工业陷入颓势。

[17] The plan for a new swimming pool had to *go by the board*.

建新游泳池的计划只能落空了。

评析:[16][17]中出现的两个英语常规隐喻词组对中文读者缺乏实践感受,因此均无法再现原文的表达结构。

[18] "I know I have the body of a weak and feeble woman," she said in 1588, "but I have the *heart and stomach* of a king, and a king of England too."

实译:"我知道我有一个软弱的无力的女人的身子,"她在1588年说,"但是我有一个国王的心和胃,而且还是英格兰国王的。"

虚译:"我知道我长就了一副柔弱女子的身躯,可我有一个一国之君的气度,而且还是英格兰的君王。"

评析:这是英国女王伊丽莎白一世说的一句很有名的话,实译译文貌似十分忠于原文,但对"body, heart and stomach"理解太死。这三个词语汉语的同类词一样,都有转义,如"志趣"、"心胸"和"胃口"等等。

[19] *See-sawing* between partly good and faintly ominous, the news for the next four weeks was never distinct.

在那以后的四个星期内,消息时而部分有所好转,时而又有点不妙。两种情况不断地交替出现,一直没有明朗化。

[20] There were times when emigration *bottleneck* was extremely rigid and nobody was allowed to leave the country out of his personal preference.

过去有过这种情况:移民限制极为严格,不允许任何人出于个人考虑而迁居他国。——包惠南译文

本节练习

1. 实译

[1] Gulangyu is a *must* for most visitors to Xiamen.

[2] At twenty-two, he had first learned *what* it is to be a Negro.

[3] The baby can't walk, he can't talk, he can't feed or bathe himself, and in that he has an *unmixed blessing*.

[4] Vietnam was his *entrée* to the new Administration, his third incarnation as a foreign policy consultant.

2. 虚译

[5] Arabs *rub shoulders* with Jews, and have been doing so from the earliest settlement of the territories.

[6] There is a mixture of the *tiger* and the *ape* in the character of the imperialists.

[7] Every life has its *roses* and *thorns*.

[8] He chose *the gun* instead of *the cap and gown*.

第五节 褒译与贬译

任何语言的词语都有褒贬之分。词语翻译的褒义与贬义是由语篇上下文所决定的,但

最终是落实在词语翻译上。原文中有些词语本身就表示褒贬意义,就应该把褒贬意义相应地表达出来;但也有些原文词语孤立起来看似乎是中性的,译成汉语时就要根据上下文恰如其分地把它们的褒义或贬义表达出来。

一、原文词语褒贬义明显,翻译时相应译出

[1] He was a man of high renown.
他是位有名望的人。(褒)

[2] His notoriety as a rake did not come until his death.
他作为流氓的恶名是他死后才传开的。(贬)

[3] The tasks carried out by them are praiseworthy.
他们进行的事业是值得赞扬的。(褒)

[4] Henry keeps boasting that he has talked to the President.
亨利总是吹嘘说他曾同总统谈过话。(贬)

[5] Girls *were all smiles* on hearing the good news.
初译:姑娘们听到这个好消息都满脸堆笑。(贬)
改译:听到这个好消息,姑娘们个个笑逐颜开。(褒)

评析:原文的"were all smiles"显然是个褒义用法,而初译里的四字格"满脸堆笑"有故意做作的意味,含有明显的贬义色彩,"眉开眼笑"也不合适。用一个褒义四字格"笑逐颜开"正好。可见,翻译中的四字格还必须注意到感情色彩。

二、根据上下文决定褒贬义

(1) 译成褒义词

[6] Then Mr. Tekoah proceeded, after citing many *colourful* incidents, to refer to my statement to *Al-Muharrer*.
在列举了许多大肆渲染(×耸人听闻)的事件之后,特科先生进而提到我对《解放者报》的谈话。

评析:翻译成"耸人听闻"实际上是一种离开了原词的词义、无视原词的色彩的意译。要译好这个词,首先应紧紧扣住它的词义。抓住它的特色,结合发言人的态度,同时还要考虑到在联合国这样的外交场合,发言人的话一般都是比较含蓄的;而"耸人听闻"则语气太重。体现"colourful"这个词的色彩,恐怕还得从"色"这一原义出发,那么,改为"大肆渲染"也许比较合适。

[7] In 1974, while driving along the San Diego Freeway from Clemente to Los Angeles, he was asked to reflect on his hopes and *ambitions*.
1974年,有人同他一起驱车从克利门蒂沿圣地亚哥公路去洛杉矶,途中请他谈了他的希望和抱负。

[8] The two politicians talked for no more than five minutes, at a significant moment in their *careers*.
两位政治家交谈了仅仅五分钟。这次谈话是在他们一生事业的重大时刻进行的。

(2) 译成贬义词

[9] In our Second Address on the war, five days after the advent of *those* men, we

told you *what they were*. (*The Civil War in France*)

在这伙人上台五天以后,我们在关于前次战争的第二篇宣言中已经向你们说明他们究竟是些什么货色了。

评析: 选择词义时,还要考虑到词在原文中所含有的政治色彩、褒贬义。此句中,those(那些)译成"这伙";what they were(他们本来是什么样子)译成"他们究竟是些什么货色"或"他们的本来面目"。

[10] But it would be ludicrous today to attempt recounting the merely preliminary atrocities committed by the bombarders of Paris and the fomenters of a slaveholders' rebellion *protected* by foreign invasion.

但是今天要试图一一列举出那些轰击巴黎,在外国侵略者的卵翼下发起奴隶主叛乱的人们的暴行(而这些暴行仅仅是开始),那就太可笑了。

[11] Many of the old Orleanist stagers *had merged into* the Bonapartist lot.

很多奥尔良的老角色也与波拿巴派同流合污了。

评析: 以上两句,protect(保护)译成"卵翼";had merged into(消没于)译成"同流合污"。这些都是有意译成贬义的。

[12] He was a man of integrity, but unfortunately he had a certain *reputation*. I believe the *reputation* was not deserved.

他是一个正直诚实的人,但不幸有某种坏名声。我相信他这个坏名声是不该有的。

评析: "reputation"意为"the opinion that people have about what sb./sth. is like, based on what has happened in the past",中文的对应词是"名誉"、"名声"。这常给人印象是个褒义词,英文中其实是个中性词,可以说成"to have a good/bad reputation",有好/坏名声。但英语里该词常不加修饰词,只好根据上下文而定。

[13] They arrested me as a "spy" and *sent* me *out* through Poland.

他们把我当作"间谍"而逮捕了我,并取道波兰把我驱逐出境。

[14] He had lied to me and made me the tool of his wicked *deeds*.

他欺骗了我,使我成了他罪恶勾当的工具。

[15] As a *demanding* boss, he expected total loyalty and dedication from his employees.

他是个苛刻的老板,要求手下的人对他忠心耿耿,鞠躬尽瘁。

本节练习

1. 原文词语本身带有褒贬意义,翻译时相应译出

[1] That fat *jap*!

[2] I will say the very thought of you makes me *sick* and that you treated me with miserable cruelty.

2. 根据上下文来决定褒义或贬义

[3] Next Edison turned his inventive genius to another *ambitious* project—the invention of a means of lighting streets and buildings by electricity instead of by gas; the in-

vention of an electric-light bulb.

[4] Our conference did in the end make detailed plans for the *invasion*. The date was to be 1 May, 1944.

[5] He is bright and *ambitious*.

[6] "For people of my generation," he said, "Nixon had a certain *reputation*. I needed to assure myself the *reputation* was not deserved."

[7] Mr. Brown *felt greatly flattered* when he received the invitation to deliver a lecture.

[8] Hans was too *obviously flattering* the gentleman by saying he was the most courageous man he had ever seen.

[9] I'll let everybody at Lowed know *what you are* and *what you have done*.

[10] Those who do not remember the past are condemned to *relive* it.

第六节　倒译与顺译

英语和汉语的表达结构均是由其民族思维和语言发展长期积累沉淀而成的,这两种语言由于使用者观察世界的角度不同,思维习惯不同,导致表达结构也常常截然不同。翻译时就必须意识到这种差别,并视具体情况保留或改变原文的顺序,也就是要进行词法、句法顺序的倒译或顺译。严复在《天演论》例言里曾经论述道:"词句之间,时有所颠倒附益,不斤斤于字比句次。"这就是针对倒译而言的。在英汉翻译中,倒译的使用频率明显高于顺译。

一、倒译

"倒译"这一技巧并不是独立存在的,它与之前和之后论及的诸种翻译技巧,尤其是"拆译"和"被动式的译法"是相辅相成,密切结合的。"拆译"中有"倒译","倒译"中见"拆译"。只要我们再回顾一下前面的翻译技巧,就可以充分地感受到这一点。倒译可分为词或词组倒译和句子倒译。词或词组倒译一般比较简单,而且相对固定,如,absent-minded(心不在焉);well-conducted(行为端正的);northeast(东北);southwest(西南)。在词组方面,英语一般会说,north, south, east, west,而翻译则习惯译成"东、南、西、北"。句子倒译则涉及到更复杂的情形(陈廷祐,1980),不同的译者会采用不同的倒译技巧,甚至不一定倒译。句子倒译主要体现在以下几个方面:

1. 复合句倒译

[1] They were sons of the men who had left their homes and taken to the mountains with their broad swords by their side. —R. G. Gammage

他们都是那些抛妻别子、身带大刀进入深山的好汉们的后代。

评析:如果不作部分颠倒,顺着句子顺序译下来:"他们是好汉们的后代,那些好汉们曾经抛妻别子、身带大刀进入深山",气势就差了很多。英语中的限定性定语从句一般紧接着被修饰词,而在译成汉语时,这个限定性定语从句的意思习惯放在被修饰词的前面,形成

"……"的结构。

　　[2] Reason was the sole guide that Mr. Johnson accepted in his quest.
　　　　约翰逊先生在探索时,说理是他接受下来的唯一指导原则。

评析:这一句作了彻底颠倒,"约翰逊先生"被放在前面,这样读者才不会误解为有两个人。

　　[3] Don't scamp your work because you are pressed for time.
　　　　不要因为时间紧迫就马马虎虎。

　　[4] You will fail unless you work harder.
　　　　倘若你不努力工作就会失败。

　　[5] Thermoplastic plastics become soft if they are heated.
　　　　热塑塑料一经加热,就会变软。

评析:一部分带有状语从句的复合句,翻译时需要作大调整。汉语习惯于以时间先后、原因、结果、条件的顺序来安排句子,即先发生的事情放在句前,后发生的事情放在句后,先讲原因后讲结果,先讲条件后讲结果。而英语则往往反其道而行之。

2. 被动句子的倒译

　　[6] Everything possible was done to conceal our movements from the enemy and to mislead him. —W. Churchill
　　　　我们采取了一切可能的措施,以便对敌人隐瞒我们的活动情况,并迷惑他们。

评析:这句话中的真正主人虽未点出,但是清楚的,是"我们"。作者用了被动式,若照原样译成中文,不符合中国读者的习惯,文字也不通顺。

　　[7] Accounts are given of huge mountains sinking, of former plains seen heaved aloft, of fires flashing out amid the ruin. —J. Jackson
　　　　译文一:大山沉陷,平原隆起,火焰喷射,周围是一片废墟,这些都有记载。
　　　　译文二:据记载,大山沉陷,平原隆起,火焰喷射,周围是一片废墟。

评析:译文一将次序全部颠倒。译文二也别出心裁,非常巧妙。这些译法都避免了被动语态。有关被动式的翻译,详见本章第八节。

3. 用否定性副词或条件副词开头的句子的倒译

　　[8] No possibility of alleviating adverse opinion of them should be overlooked.
　　　　我们不应忽视能够缓和他们反对我们的任何可能性。

　　[9] Nothing was gained by all the overcaution.
　　　　所有这些谨小慎微的措施,到头来是一无所得。

　　[10] Hardly had she arrived at the station when it began to rain.
　　　　她刚到车站就下雨了。

　　[11] In no way can we consider air as a good conductor.
　　　　我们绝不能认为普通的空气是良导体。

评析:副词如 no, never, hardly, scarcely, no longer, not until, only 等引导的英语句型,其目的在于强调。翻译时,常将主语提前,加一些适当的字眼来加强语气。

4. 带有介词短语的句子的倒译

　　[12] Don't sleep with the windows open.
　　　　睡觉时别开窗子。

评析：若照英文排列,译成"不要睡觉开着窗子",就不太符合中国人的表达习惯。

[13] These data will be of some value in our research work.

这些资料对于我们的研究工作有些价值。

评析：of some value 作表语用,但后面又跟上一个介词短语 in our research work,是修饰 value 的,因此将它放到中间。译文"有些价值"则放在了最后。

[14] A worker from Birmingham enlivened the audience with some admirable specimens of racy old English humor, which were most gratefully received. —R. G. Gammage

一位来自伯明翰的工人讲了一些相当典型的、饶有风趣的英国古老幽默话,使听众活跃起来,他的话受到他们衷心的欢迎。

评析：这一句话的主语是 worker,介词短语 from Birmingham 是作为定语修饰主语的,因此放在"工人"之前,成为"一位来自伯明翰的工人"。谓语是 enlivened,它和宾语 audience 还不能马上译出来,因为有一个 with 引导的介词短语及其有关部分要先说明一下,这就是:"讲了一些相当典型的、饶有风趣的英国古老幽默话",这才"使听众活跃起来"。最后再补上一句:"他的话受到他们衷心的欢迎"。

[15] Aristotle could have avoided the mistake of thinking that women have fewer teeth than men, by the simple device of asking Mrs. Aristotle to keep her mouth open while he counted.

原译:亚里士多德本来能够避免这个错误的认识,即女人的牙齿比男人要少些;他只要用这个简单的方法,就是请亚里士多德夫人张开嘴巴,让他来数就行了。

改译:亚里士多德错认为女人的牙齿比男人少。其实,他只要请自己的夫人张一张口让他数一数,本是可以避免这个错误的。——郭建中译文

评析：原译者只知道按原文语序来翻译,因此译文十分拗口。译文语序重组后,形成和原文次序相反的倒译,而意思得以完美传递。

[16] It is popular for the fine views from the summit of the mountain.

从山顶远眺,湖光山色,尽收眼底;这儿风景绝佳,遐迩闻名。

评析：原句被切分成三部分,或三个相对完整的翻译单位。from the summit of the mountain 这一介词短语,译成汉语无主句的一个分句;for the fine views 这一介词短语,译成一个主谓结构,构成一个分句。译者从最后一个介词短语译起,倒着译到第二个介词短语,最后才译原句主谓结构。这是典型的倒译句。它同时也是一个拆译句,属于短句拆译,更见功夫。

[17] One could account for what was observed equally well on the theory that the universe had existed forever or on the theory that it was set in motion at some finite time in such a manner as to look as though it had existed forever.

当时有两种理论摆在大家面前:一种理论认为,宇宙是一直存在的;另一种理论则认为,宇宙是在某一个有限的时刻启动的,但给人的印象却似乎是一直存在的。但是,不管按照哪种理论,我们都可以很好地解释所观察到的事实。

评析：这个长句译起来从容不迫。译者先把 the theory that the universe had existed...处理掉,前面加了一个主题句"当时有两种理论摆在大家面前",然后分别说明"一种理论认为,……另一种理论则认为,……"最后才译出原英文的主句结构。

[18] Scientists all over the world are now trying to harness this energy by a process similar to one that occurs on the surface of the sun. This is called continuous thermonuclear fusion and involves causing hydrogen atoms to rush together and release vast amounts of energy.

原译：世界各国的科学家，正在试图利用这种类似在太阳表面所发生的过程产生的能源。这一过程叫做连续热核聚变，它促使氢原子冲集在一起并释放出极大热能。

改译：在太阳表面，发生着一种连续性的热核聚变过程。这个过程使氢原子冲集在一起，并释放出大量的热能。目前，世界各国的科学家，正在试图利用这种能源。——郭建中译文

评析：原译按原文的词序，逻辑混乱。改译对原文进行了重写。先说明太阳表面有一种连续发生的热核聚变；然后叙述什么叫热核聚变及其作用；最后谈到各国科学家正试图利用这种热核聚变所产生的能源。逻辑清楚，合乎汉语行文习惯（郭建中，2004：114）。值得注意的是，本例的倒译已经跨越了单句的范围而横跨了两个句子，我们称之为句群层面的倒译。

二、顺译

英汉两种语言的句子结构千变万化，我们得根据具体情况灵活处理译句，不能生搬硬套固定模式。重要的是，首先要细心琢磨作者的意图，他想说的是什么；到了中文阶段，要按照汉语习惯重作安排，力求通顺流畅而又不失原作的思想和文风。正如前面所述，更换次序是英汉翻译的主要做法，但有时说话人或作者出于修辞或场合的需要，其句法顺序并不能随心所欲地予以颠倒，否则效果将大打折扣，这倒是我们应特别加以注意的地方。另外，如果译者技法娴熟，对全文胸有成竹，也可以在不更动原句序的情况下，见招拆招，顺水推舟。

[19] Always obey your parents—when they are present.

父母的话总是要听的——当然是他们在身边的时候。

评析：这是美国作家马克·吐温在一次关于学生该不该听从父母的管教的演讲时，所讲的第一句话。它妙就妙在将限定语（如相声里的解包袱）放在了后面，这其实是对前面忠告的一种否定，听者当能心领神会。

[20] It is a truth universally acknowledged that a single man in possession of a good fortune must be in want of a wife.

译文一：凡有产业的单身汉，总要娶位太太，这已经成了一条举世公认的真理。——王科一译文

译文二：有钱的单身汉总要娶位太太，这是一条举世公认的真理。——孙致礼译文

译文三：饶有家资的单身男子必定想要娶妻室，这是举世公认的真情实理。——张玲、张扬译文

译文四：举世公认，一个拥有一大笔钱财的单身男人，必定想要一个女人做太太。这已成为一条真理。——义海译文

译文五：世间有这样一条公认的真理——凡财产丰厚的单身男人势必想娶个太太。

评析：从句法上看，英语原文可视为"圆周句"（periodic sentence）。"读者开始以为作者

将郑重其事地宣告一个举世公认的真理,然而读到最后一个词却出乎意料地发现,所谓'举世公认'的真理,只不过是市侩的庸俗意识而已。作者独具匠心,以庄重高雅的形式把读者的期待引向高峰,而最后一个词所代表的庸俗内容,却又将读者的期待降到谷底,产生强烈的讽刺效果,耐人寻味,使人难忘"(马红军,2000:98)。翻译 Austen 这句名言时,我们应充分考虑原文的这些特征,即"先庄后谐"。但译文一至四都改变了句法结构,形成"先谐后庄"。只有译文五保留了原文"先庄后谐"的表达结构。

[21] Recent breakthroughs in physics, made possible in part by fantastic new technologies, suggest answers to some of these longstanding questions.

最近,物理学的研究之所以取得了一些突破,部分应归功于新技术的飞速发展;而这些物理学上的突破对于回答那些长期以来悬而未决的某些问题是有所启发的。

评析:英语原文的主句是 Recent breakthroughs in physics... suggest answers to some of these longstanding questions,而 made possible in part by fantastic new technologies 是过去分词短语作定语,修饰 breakthroughs。译文把这一从属结构译成主谓结构,形成一个独立的分句,可算是按照原文次序就地安置,再把原文的主句也译成一个独立的分句,两个分句并列,把英语的枝杈结构转换成了汉语由两层波浪构成的流水句结构(郭建中,2004:114)。

[22] Modern scientific discoveries lead to the conclusion that energy may be created from matter that in turn may be created from energy.

现代科学的发现得出这样的结论:物质可以产生能量,能量又可以产生物质。

评析:英文原文包含一个同位语从句,在这一同位语从句中又包含了一个定语从句,汉语译文成了三个并列的独立分句。译文包含了一个顺译:即原文的主句结构"现代科学的发现得出这样的结论";同位语从句和其中的定语从句内部又各用了一个倒译:"物质可以产生能量,能量又可以产生物质"。因此,倒译和顺译是相辅相成的。

本节练习

[1] I'm sure that it is a better book as a result of his keeping my nose to the grindstone.

[2] This, Hawking's first book for the nonspecialist, holds rewards of many kinds for the lay audience.

[3] As interesting as the book's wide-ranging contents is the glimpse it provides into the workings of its author's mind.

[4] In this book are lucid revelations on the frontiers of physics, astronomy, cosmology, and courage.

[5] Hawking is attempting, as he explicitly states, to understand the mind of God.

[6] We go about our daily lives understanding almost nothing of the world.

[7] We give little thought to the machinery that generates the sunlight that makes life possible, to the gravity that glues us to an Earth that would otherwise send us spinning off into space, or to the atoms of which we are made and on whose stability we fundamentally depend.

[8] In our society it is still customary for parents and teachers to answer most of these

questions with a shrug, or with an appeal to vaguely recalled religious precepts.

[9] But much of philosophy and science has been driven by such inquiries.

[10] And this makes all the more unexpected the conclusion of the effort, at least so far: a universe with no edge in space, no beginning or end in time, and nothing for a Creator to do.

第七节 反 译

反译是指译文以与原文相反的表达方式传递原文的意义。它属于引申和修辞范围。反译包括词语反译、语言差异决定的反译和运用技巧的反译。以下部分例句摘自连淑能(2006)。

一、词语中的反译

词是翻译的基本单位，因此，即使一个单独的词语，也能体现反译技巧。

anxiety	不安
a barren tract of land	不毛之地
be at a loss	不知所措
be fatally ill	不可救药
failure	不成功
keep... within bounds	不偏不倚
life sentence (imprisonment)	无期徒刑
prove worthy of our trust	不辜负众望
safe and sound	万无一失；安然无恙
soon enough	不久
supreme authority	至高无上
wet paint	油漆未干
with dignity	不卑不亢

二、语言差异决定的反译

1. 回答否定词问句的译法

在回答反义疑问句时，英语国家的人考虑的是自己的答复是肯定还是否定的，肯定用 yes，否定用 no。中国人考虑首先是问句的命题是否正确，命题正确用 yes，命题不正确用 no。正好与英语逻辑思维相反。学习和翻译英语时极容易搞混淆。

[1] Are you *not* prepared to do this work?

你不打算做这项工作吗？

Yes, I am. <u>不</u>，我打算做。

No, I'm not. <u>是的</u>，我不打算做。

[2] It's not going to rain, is it?　不会下雨,是不是?
　　　No.　是的,不会。
　　　Yes, It's going to rain.　不,会下雨的。
[3] Look here, some boats are coming this way, *don't you see* them?
　　　瞧,有几条船往这边来了,你看见吗?
[4] I like Beijing very much, *don't you*?
　　　我很喜欢北京,你呢?

2. 英语非人称结构影响

[5] The name *slipped* from my memory.
　　　我一时想不起这个名字。
[6] The meaning *eludes* me.
　　　我弄不懂这个意思。
[7] This was a view which seemed to *have escaped* the Prime Minister.
　　　首相似乎没有看到这一点。
[8] Make yourself at home.　别客气。

3. 否定句译成肯定句

[9] I *couldn't* feel better.
　　　我感觉好极了。
[10] *No* man *can* have *too* much knowledge and practice.
　　　知识和实践越多越好。
[11] These scientists *could not* believe the two Curies *more*.
　　　这些科学家完全相信居里夫妇。
[12] There are *no winners* in a divorce.
　　　原译:在离婚中没有胜者。
　　　改译:离婚的人都是两败俱伤。

三、运用技巧的反译

[13] He thought, not very vividly, of his father and mother.
　　　正译:他并不是很鲜明地想到了他的爸爸和妈妈。
　　　反译:他模模糊糊地想到了他的爸爸和妈妈。
[14] No one knows where the shoe pinches like the wearer.
　　　正译:没有一个人会像穿鞋者那样知道鞋子挤脚。
　　　反译:哪儿挤脚,穿鞋人最清楚。
[15] Even the pine logs which burned all day in the fireplace couldn't keep my little house warm and dry.
　　　正译:火炉里成天烧着松柴,还不能使我的小屋子温暖和干爽。
　　　反译:火炉里成天烧着松柴,可我的小屋还是又冷又潮。

评析: 反译才显得是地道的中国话。

[16] ... whether the German memorandum was *really his last word*.
　　　德国的备忘录是不是果真绝无商量余地……

评析：这是《第三帝国的兴亡》(*The Rise and Fall of the Third Reich*)中张伯伦问及希特勒的态度的一句话。把肯定词译成否定词"绝无商量余地"用的是反译法。

[17] Mattie's hand was underneath, and Ethan kept his clasp on it *a moment longer than was necessary*.

玛提的手在下，伊坦把它握住，<u>没有立刻就放</u>。——吕叔湘译文

评析：句中的 a moment longer than was necessary 如果直译非常生硬。译者采用"同义反译"方法。类似的例子还有：

[18] Now, Clara, *be firm with* the boy!

听我说，克拉拉，对这孩子<u>可不能心软</u>！

评析：如译成"对这孩子要坚定"则较生硬。或许也可直译成"对这孩子就得严格"，这样能和原文表达形式更吻合。

[19] Wait, he is *serious*.

当心，他<u>不是说着玩的</u>。

评析：这是用了反译法，不然"当心，他可是认真的"也是很顺的。

[20] If all three of you take part in it, there can be *no further questioning* of your courage.

如果你们三位都参加，那就<u>足以说明</u>你们是有勇气的。

评析：正面译不顺，不妨反面着笔，以求尽量发挥翻译技巧灵活多变的特点。翻译之所以成为艺术，就是它本身具有创造性。既然英汉语两个民族的思想逻辑和表达方式不一样，同一个概念，一个民族正面说，认为是合乎习惯的，而另一民族则认为反着说才顺嘴。翻译就应考虑到这种差别。

[21] This makes the task of the Negro a more *healthful* and reasonable one. (*Uncle Tom's Cabin*)

这使得黑人所干的活比较<u>不伤身体</u>，也比较合乎情理。

[22] In Homer, as in all great writers, matter and manner are inseparably blended... and if we put Homer straight into English words *neither* meaning *nor* manner *survives*. (*The Art of Translation*)

和所有伟大作家的著作一样，在荷马的著作中，内容和风格浑然一体，密不可分……如果把荷马的著作逐字译成英语，则<u>意义和风格皆失</u>。

[23] This football team was organized three years ago and it *had yet to win a single game*.

这足球队三年前组队，<u>至今未胜一场</u>。

[24] The criminal is still *at large*.

罪犯还<u>未捉拿归案</u>。

[25] The project is yet all *in the air*.

这计划<u>尚未落实</u>。

[26] The world will be *long* forgetting their evil.

世人<u>不会很快</u>就忘掉他们的罪行。

[27] This is *the first time* I have heard of him.

<u>以前我从未听说过他</u>。

[28] The beauty of the scenery *passes* all power of description.
风景之美，<u>非</u>任何言语<u>所能</u>形容。

四、英汉告示语中的正反译

英语和汉语的告示语常常从不同的视角表达，几乎已成定式。

[29] No Thoroughfare（没有通路）
禁止通行

[30] Authorized Cars Only（只有准许的车辆才可入内）
未经许可车辆不得入内

[31] Employees Only（员工专道）
顾客止步

[32] Passengers Only（只有旅客才可通行）
送客止步

[33] Please Tender Exact Fare（请付确切的车钱）
恕不找零

评析：这是无人售票公共汽车收款箱上的提示。

[34] Courtesy Seats
老、弱、病、残、孕专座（爱心专座）

[35] 20％ Off
八折优惠

[36] Nothing Can Come of Nothing. ——William Shakespeare
物有其本，事有其源。——莎士比亚

本节练习

1. 正—反翻译(动词)
  [1] I *fail to understand* your meaning.
  [2] He *kept his eyes off* Gesse's feet.
  [3] Your legs are *young enough to hold you*.
  [4] These are days when *nerves are worn thin*.
  [5] They had better keep *their promise*, because everything hinges on that right now.

2. 正—反翻译(副词)
  [6] He needed Jack *too much to* risk making him angry.
  [7] We tried *vainly* to measure the voltage.
  [8] All these questions have only been *partially answered*.
  [9] They resumed their seats *moodily*.
  [10] *Slowly* he pulled the letter out of the envelope, and unfolded it.
  [11] He can read *fairly easily*.

3. 正—反翻译(形容词)
  [12] *Free from anxiety*, the old are living a happy life in the home for the aged.

[13] Pure metals have *few useful* properties.

[14] It seems that this was simply an *innocent* preparation for maneuvers planned long ago.

[15] A desert is a *barren tract* of land.

4. 正—反翻译(介词)

[16] But in the midst of those plans he died, and was succeeded by his son.

[17] There is one great issue *in the balance* here today.

[18] But that's very extraordinary. It seems *against* nature.

[19] His answer is *beside the mark*.

5. 正—反翻译(连接词)

[20] Any use of the atomic bomb on Manchurian targets would be more for purpose of panic *than* of destruction.

[21] Don't come in *unless* I call you.

6. 正—反翻译(名词)

[22] They look after the interests of their own *to the exclusion* of those of all others.

[23] Herb may be dying somewhere, calling out for his mum and dad, and *only strangers round him*.

[24] Osborne was Sedley's godson, and had *been one of the family* anytime these 23 years.

[25] *Silence* reigned all over for a while.

[26] Her *abstraction* was not because of tea party.

7. 正—反翻译(词组、句)

[27] You should *seize the opportune moment* to put in a good word for me.

[28] The news of the assassination of President Lincoln *spread like wildfire*.

[29] The pioneers *made light of* difficulties and dangers.

[30] Miss Fairlie *kept to her room all day*.

[31] Haste *makes waste*.

[32] I want everybody to *have a fair deal*.

8. 反—正翻译(动词)

[33] He *was not sorry* to get off his cold.

[34] I *never hear such a story* but I laugh.

9. 反—正翻译(副词)

[35] He is *not seldom* ill.

[36] An opportunity is *not likely to repeat itself*.

[37] Many agreed that the Prime Minister had in effect resigned *dishonorably*.

10. 反—正翻译(形容词)

[38] He entered the city *unopposed* in the early hours of 15 April.

[39] They were not, however, left long *undisturbed*.

11. 反—正翻译(名词)

[40] They charged him *with dishonesty*.

[41] *Misunderstanding* leads to *mistranslation*.
[42] His spies were *not going to lose sight of* me.

第八节 被动式的翻译

被动式在英语,尤其在科技英语文体中中广泛使用。除了用"be+过去动词分词",还用其他形式表现。

一、英语被动式表达

1. 名词

名词后缀-ee 表示动作的承受者,是被动的。
trainee 受训者
employee 雇员
addressee 收件人

2. 形容词

以-able,-ible 结尾的形容词,以及由过去分词转换的形容词,大多数含被动意义。
visible stars 看得见的星星
navigable rivers 可通航的河流
exchangable 可更换的
the accused 被告
the wounded 负伤者

3. 介词短语

in question 正被谈论的
on show 上映
past recovery 无法康复
under discussion 在讨论中
under repair 正在修理中
beyond control 无法控制
near completion 即将竣工

4. 动词

① 在及物动词"need, want, require, deserve, stand"等后面,可接主动形式的动名词表达被动含义。

[1] This is one of those questions that don't need answering.
　　这是一个不需要回答的问题。("answering"="to be answered")

② 某些不及物动词,如 draw, sell, wash, cook 等的主动形式,可表示被动意义。

[2] These goods sell like hot cakes.
　　这些货物十分畅销。(sell=are sold)

③ 表示状态特征的连系动词，如"look, smell, sound, prove, appear"等的主动形式表示被动意义。

[3] The results proved to be correct.
  此结果证明是正确的。

④ 不定式的主动形式有时也表示被动意义。

[4] These small houses are to let at low rental.
  这些小屋将以低价出租。

[5] I'm the one to blame.
  该受责备的是我。

二、汉语的被动式表达

汉语虽然较多使用主动式，但被动式的表达法还是有一些的。例如：

被：被打，被杀
叫：叫人说得一文不值
给：给他打了
挨：挨打
遭：遭劫，遭灾
受：受骗，受压迫
由：由人宰割
让：让人摆弄
获：获救，获罪，获准
为……所……；被……所……；让……给……

在古汉语中，表示被动式的还有：
见：表示被动，相当于"被"。
不见保。（《孟子·梁惠王上》）
见犯乃死。（《汉书·李广苏建传》）
诚恐见欺。（《史记·廉颇蔺相如列传》）
悲独见病。（唐·柳宗元《柳河东集》）
又如：见笑于人；见重于当时；见执（被捉拿）；见罔（被诬陷枉屈）；见害（被害）；见款（承蒙款待）。
于：在被动句中，引出动作、行为的主动者，相当于"被"。
不拘于时。（唐·韩愈《师说》）
苦于多疾。（宋·苏轼《教战守》）
伤于缚者。（清·方苞《狱中杂记》）
择于自然。（清·薛福成《观巴黎油画记》）
劳心者治人，劳力者治于人。治于人者食人，治人者食于人，天下之通义也。（战国·孟轲《孟子》）
吃：表示被动，用法同"被"。如：吃惊受怕（受惊骇）；吃孽（遭殃）；吃板子（挨板子）；吃拳（被拳打）；吃笑（被耻笑）。

栾廷玉须不是三头六臂,直恁惧怕他,日间吃他打败,夜间又要提防。(明·施耐庵《古本水浒传》)

完全不用:飞鸟尽,良弓藏;狡兔死,走狗烹。(《史记·越王勾践世家》)

三、被动式的翻译法

1. 被动式译成被动式

[6] Robert *was dismissed* by the boss of the factory.
   罗伯特<u>被</u>工厂的老板<u>开除</u>了。

2. 被动式译成主动式

[7] The result of the invention of the steam engine was that human power *was replaced by mechanical power*.
   蒸汽机发明的结果是,<u>机械力代替了人力</u>。

[8] Seamless tubes without joins *are made* in various ways.
   可用不同方法<u>制造</u>没有接缝的无缝管。

[9] Friction can be reduced and the life of the machine prolonged by lubrication.
   润滑能减少摩擦,延长机器寿命。

[10] Modern scientific discoveries lead to the conclusion that energy *may be created from matter*, which in turn, may be *created from energy*.
   现代科学的发展得出这样的结论:<u>物质可以产生能</u>,<u>能又可以产生物质</u>。

[11] In the afternoon rush of the Grand Central Station *his eyes had been refreshed by the sight of Miss Lily Bart*.
   在中央火车站午后的旅客洪流中,他<u>一眼瞥见了丽莉·巴特小姐的身影,顿时觉得眼目清新,精神为之一振</u>。

评析:原句细致生动,传达一个男青年对一年轻女子的感觉。原文用了被动式"his eyes had been refreshed by the sight of Miss Lily Bart",但是译者把内在主语拉出来,对"refresh"和"sight"做了发挥,使译文十分传神。

四、被动式在语篇中的翻译

被动语态是英语语言表达客观化的手段之一,这在英语科技文体中表现得特别突出(冯树鉴,1995),使用的频率特别高。相比较,汉语则少用被动态,因为这个"被"字可以多种方式被化解掉。翻译中就要考虑到汉语这个特点。试以下列例子为证。

[12] As oil *is found* deep in the ground its presence *cannot be determined* by a study of the surface. Consequently, a geological survey of the underground rocks structure *must be carried out*. If *it is thought* that the rocks in certain area contain oil, a "drilling rig" *is assembled*. The most obvious part of a drilling rig *is called* a "derrick". It *is used* to lift sections of pipe, which *are allowed* into the hole *made by* the drill. As the hole *is being drilled*, a steel pipe *is pushed* down to prevent the sides from falling in. If oil *is struck* a cover *is firmly fixed* to the top of the pipe and the oil *is allowed* to escape through a series of valves.
   因为石油深埋在地下,靠研究地面,<u>不能确定石油的有无</u>。因此,对地下岩层结构

必须进行地质勘探。如果认为某地区的岩层含有石油,就在该处安装"钻机"。钻机中最显眼的部件叫做"井口铁架"。井架用来吊升分节油管,把油管放入由钻头打入的孔中。当孔钻成时,放入钢管防止孔壁坍塌。如发现石油,则在油管顶部加盖紧固,使石油通过一系列阀门流出。

评析: 这一段英文126个单词,含14个谓语动词,使用了13个被动语态。译文皆做了巧妙的转换,大都变成无主语句,避免使用"被"、"受"等字眼,更为自然。

[13] One of the most famous monuments in the world, the Statue of Liberty, *was presented* to the United States of America in the nineteenth century by the people of France. The great statue, which *was designed* by the sculptor August Bartholdi, took ten years to complete. The actual figure *was made of* copper *supported* by a metal framework which *had been especially constructed* by Eiffel. Before it *could be transported* to the United States, a site had to *be found* for it and a pedestal had to *be built*. The site *chosen* was an island at the entrance of New York Harbour. By 1884, a statue which was 151 feet tall, *had been erected* in Paris. The following year, it *was taken* to pieces and *sent* to America. By the end of October 1886, the statue *had been put* together again and it *was officially presented* to the American people by Bartholdi. Ever since then, the great monument has been a symbol of liberty for the millions of people who have passed through New York Harbour to make their homes in America.

世界上最著名的纪念碑之一,自由神像是法国人民19世纪时赠送给美利坚合众国的。这座由雕塑家奥古斯塔·巴托尔德设计的巨大铜像,用了十年功夫才造成。它的身体部分是用铜制作的,支持身体的金属支架是由埃弗尔专门制造的。在自由女神铜像运往美国之前,须先找寻一个安放的地点,并建造一个基座。所选地点在纽约港进口处的一个岛上。到1884年,这个151英尺高的雕像在巴黎建成。第二年,雕像被拆卸成件运往美国。1886年10月末,雕像又拼装起来,并由巴托尔德正式赠予美国人民。从那时起,这座巨大的纪念碑对于通过纽约港口来美国建立家园的亿万人们,一直是自由的象征。(连淑能,2006)

评析: 本段182个单词,含19个谓语动词、不定式和过去分词短语,被动语态就占了14个。译文中真正使用"被"字的只有1个,"是……(动词)……的"占3个,"由……的"占3个,其他则转为无主语动词。

本节练习

1. 转化成主动结构,保留原来主语

[1] The article had been translated into English, but with little elegance to speak of.

[2] The decision cannot be delayed, not even for a single day.

[3] The sense of inferiority that he acquired in his youth has never been totally eradicated.

2. 转化成主动结构,主语变成宾语

[4] China's presence is felt, more than ever, all over the world, assuming historic di-

mensions in the world political situation.

  [5] It must be dealt with at the appropriate time with appropriate means.

3. 习惯语结构

  [6] It was rumoured that the dinner had been planned to please Lawrence.

  [7] It is generally considered not advisable to act that way.

  [8] It was believed that a loose meeting like this could hardly come to any important decisions.

4. 译成被动语态

  [9] Hitler was also washed away by the storms of history.

  [10] Robert Finn was dismissed by the boss of the factory.

  [11] He got observed two days after his arrival.

  [12] The plan was especially supported by those who wished to have more exposure to the literary theory.

5. "为……所"被动结构

  [13] Mother is a sentimental woman. Her heart is good and easily moved by tears and frailty.

  [14] The right of asylum may not be involved by any person guilty of a crime against peace, a war crime or a crime against humanity.

  [15] He was forced by family circumstances to leave school at sixteen.

6. 其他被动译法

  [16] She was criticized in front of everyone.

  [17] Most letters from his wife are read to him by the nurse in the hospital.

  [18] Every country will be represented by its prime minister.

第九节　数字和倍数的翻译

数字和倍数是翻译中一个较为棘手的问题,因为汉语和英语在表达上方式不一样。一个数字之差,可能会让业主赔上百万,真正马虎不得。

一、数字的翻译

数字信息反映的是客观、具体、重要的事实,因此译者必须保证数字信息得到准确如实的传递。然而,英、汉两种语言在数字的表达上存在较大的差别。

首先,英汉数字的分段方式不同。英语以"个、十、百"每三位数为一个段位,即"个、十、百","T(thousand)、十T、百T",然后是"M(million)、十M、百M"等,每个段位最后的落脚点都在"百"上。汉语数字是以"个、十、百、千"每四位数为一个段位,即"个、十、百、千","万、十万、百万、千万",然后是"亿、十亿、百亿、千亿"等。

其次,英汉数字的命数法不同。英语每一段位由低到高依次用"thousand"(千)、"million"(百万)、"billion"(十亿)、"trillion(万亿)"等词表示。汉语每一段位由低到高依次用

"万"、"亿"、"万亿"等词表示。如下表所示：

```
英： 个    百十个   百十个   百十个   百十个      ——分段
     4，   321，    987，    654，    321
     t         b         m         th           ——命数
汉： 个    千百十个      千百十个      千百十个        ——分段
     4，   3219，        8765，        4321
     万亿         亿           万                      ——命数
```

不难看出,英汉数字在分段和命数上存在较大差异,英语不以汉语的"万"和"亿"来命数,而汉语也不以英语的"million"和"billion"来命数,这就造成了翻译的困难,请看下面的对比图：

4	3	2	1	9	8	7	6	5	4	3	2	1
trillion				billion			million			thousand		
万亿	千亿	百亿	十亿	亿	千万	百万	十万	万	千			

从上面的比较图中我们可以看出,汉语中的"万"、"十万"、"千万"、"亿"、"百亿"、"千亿"在英语中都找不到直接的单一对应词。

因此要进行相应的转换,如下：

1 万	10 千	ten thousand
10 万	100 千	one hundred thousand
1000 万	10 百万	ten million
1 亿	100 百万	one hundred million
100 亿	10 个十亿	ten billion
1000 亿	100 个十亿	one hundred billion

同时,应当注意英美数字的命数也有所不同,"billion"在美国指"十亿",在英国则指"一兆(一万亿)"；"trillion"在美国指"万亿",在英国则指"百万兆(百亿亿)"。

大数字的基本译法

nine thousand, seven hundred and forty-three　9,743

a hundred and seventy-four thousand, three hundred and one　174,301

eighteen million, six hundred and fifty-seven thousand, four hundred and twenty-one　18,657,421

seven hundred and fifty million　750,000,000

four billion（美式）或 four thousand million（英式）　四十亿

twenty billion　二百亿

three hundred billion　三千亿

four million million　四万亿

数字的英汉翻译虽然有一定的难度,但是只要针对难点,加强练习,就能较好地掌握。

二、倍数的翻译

英语中常用"times"来表达倍数,但"times"和汉语中的"倍"用法却有所不同。"times"

是用来表示"乘"的(used to indicate multiplication),"n times"就是"乘以 n"的意思。我们可以这样理解：英语倍数的表达与汉语有所不同,英语在表述或比较倍数时,无论使用什么句型都包括基础倍数在内,因此都不是净增或净减,而是都包括基数 100%在内。所以表示倍数增加的英语可以译为"A 是 B 的 n 倍",或译为"A 比 B 多(n-1)倍"。

英语中倍数的减少译成汉语时,通常换算成百分数或分数来表示。因为"减少了多少倍"不合汉语的逻辑,倍是表示增加,而前面是减少,显然造成前后矛盾。因此汉语中通常说"减为几分之一"或"减少到几分之一","减少了几分之几"或"减少了百分之几"。所以表示倍数较少的"n times"可以译为"A 是 B 的 1/n",或"A 比 B 少(n-1)/n"。

请看下列英语中常用的表示倍数增减的句式：

① A is n times **greater**(smaller, more, …) than B.

② A is n times as **great**(small, much, …) as B.

③ A is n times the **size**(length, amount, …) of B.

④ A is n times **upon/over** B.

⑤ increase/decrease n times/n-fold

⑥ increase/decrease **to** n times

⑦ increase/decrease **by** n times

⑧ increase/decrease **by a factor of** n

1. A is n times greater(smaller,more,…) than B…

A 比 B 大(n-1)倍或小(n-1)/n

也可译为：A 的大小是 B 的 n 倍或 1/n

[1] Asia is four times larger than Europe.

　　误译：亚洲比欧洲大 4 倍。

　　正译：亚洲比欧洲大 3 倍。

　　或：亚洲的面积是欧洲的 4 倍。

评析：亚洲面积为 4400 万平方公里,欧洲面积为 1016 万平方公里。由此可知,亚洲面积应该是欧洲面积的四倍,即亚洲比欧洲大 3 倍。

[2] The volume of the earth is 49 times larger than that of the moon.

　　地球比月球大 48 倍。

　　或：地球的大小是月球的 49 倍。

[3] Sound travels nearly 3 times slower in lead than in copper.

　　声音在铅中的传播速度几乎是在铜中的 1/3。

　　或：声音在铅中的传播速度几乎比在铜中慢 2/3。

评析：在铅中在的传播速度为 710 m/s,声音在铜中的传播速度为 2100 m/s,可见声音在铅中的传播速度是在铜中的 1/3,即比在铜中慢了 2/3。

[4] The plastic container is five times lighter than that glass one.

　　这个塑料容器的重量是那个玻璃容器的 1/5。

　　或：这个塑料容器比那个玻璃容器轻 4/5。

2. A is n times as great(small,much,…)as B.

A 的大小是 B 的 n 倍或 1/n

[5] The oxygen atom is nearly 16 times as heavy as the hydrogen atom.

氧原子的重量几乎是氢原子的16倍。

评析：经查，氧原子的原子量为15.9994,氢原子量为1。

[6] The hydrogen atom is nearly 16 times as light as the oxygen atom.

氢原子的重量几乎是氧原子的1/16。

[7] The mercury atom is about 5 times as heavy as calcium atom.

汞的原子重量大约为钙的5倍。

评析：经查，汞的原子量为200.59,钙的原子量为40.08。

3. A is n times the size（length，amount，…）of B.

A的大小是B的n倍

[8] This book is three times the length of that one.

这本书的篇幅是那本书的3倍。

[9] The newly broadened square is four times the size of the previous one.

新扩建的广场是未扩建时的4倍大。

4. A is n times upon/over B.

A比B增加了(n-1)倍

也可译为：A增加到B的n倍

[10] The industrial output in our factory this year is ten times over that of 1999.

误译：今年我们工厂的产量比1999年的增加10倍。

正译：今年我们工厂的产量比1999年的增加9倍。

或：今年我们工厂的产量是1999年的10倍。

[11] He is five times upon your age.

他的年龄是你的五倍。

5. increase/decrease n times/n-fold

增加到n倍或减少到1/n

也可译为：增加了(n-1)倍或减少了(n-1)/n

[12] The cotton output in the county has increased four times.

该县棉花产量增加了3倍。

[13] The sales of TV set have risen 3.5-fold.

电视机销售量增加了2倍半。

[14] The weight of the bicycle has decreased 3 times.

这种自行车的重量减少了2/3。（即减少到1/3）

[15] The length of the rope has been shortened 5-fold.

绳子的长度缩短了4/5。（即缩短到1/5）

[16] If there were a bridge here, the distance would be shortened 4 times.

如果这里有座桥,距离将缩短3/4。（即缩短到1/4）

6. increase/decrease to n times

增加到n倍或减少到1/n

也可译为：增加了(n-1)倍或减少了(n-1)/n

[17] The number of the students has increased to three times.

学生人数增加到3倍。

[18] The production of integrated circuits has been increased to three times as compared with last year.

集成电路的产量比去年增加了两倍。

或：集成电路的产量增至去年的三倍。

7. increase/decrease by n times

增加到 n 倍或减少到 1/n

也可译为：增加了(n−1)倍或减少了(n−1)/n

[19] The steel output has increased by two times.

钢产量已增加了一倍。

[20] The error probability of the equipment was reduced by 2.5 times through technical innovation.

通过技术革新，该设备的误差概率降低了 3/5。

评析：reduced by 2.5 times，汉语中不说"降低到二点五"，这时应换算成整数分母，1/2.5＝2/5，即降低到"五分之二"，或降低了"五分之三"。

[21] By using a new process the prime cost of the television set was reduced by 3.4 times.

采用新工艺使这种电视的主要成本降低了 71%。

评析：算成整数分母，1/3.4＝5/17，即"降低到 5/17"或"降低了 12/17"，但这样仍不符合汉语习惯。在不要求绝对精确的情况下，可进一步换算成百分数，即"降低到 29%"或"降低了 71%"。

8. increase/decrease by a factor of n

增加到 n 倍或减少到 1/n

也可译为：增加了(n−1)倍或减少了(n−1)/n

英语单词"factor"有"因子"、"因式"、"系数"这样一些词义。"increase /decrease by a factor of n"，就是增/减一个 n 的因子(或系数)。"因子"、"因式"、"系数"和原值就是"乘"的关系。因此，虽然数字 n 后面没有跟"times"，但仍然表示倍数。

[22] The speed exceeded the average speed by a factor of 2.5.

该速度超过平均速度的 1.5 倍。

[23] The price of farm tools has decreased by a factor of 4.

农具降到原价的 1/4。（即降低了 3/4）

[24] This equipment will reduce the error probability by a factor of 5.

这种设备使误差概率降低到原来的 1/5。（即降低了 4/5）

综上所述，我们可以稍加总结：以上八种表达基本表示同样的意思，前四种句型可以译为：以上四种句式可应译为："A 的大小(长度,数量,……)是 B 的 n 倍"，或"A 比 B 大(长,多,……)(n−1)倍"。后四种句型可以译为："增加到 n 倍或增加了(n−1)倍"，或是"减少到 1/n 或减少了(n−1)/n"。后四个句型中的"increase"可以用其他表示增加意义的动词来替代，如：rise, grow, go up, step up, multiply, be；"decrease"可以用其他表示减少意义的动词来替代，如：reduce, shorten, go down, decrease, fall, cut, decline, contract.

除上述八种常用句式外，英语中还有一些用来表示倍数的词汇和表达。

1. …half as many（long，large…）again as…；

或：…half again as many（long，large…）as…。

可译为：…是…的一倍半，比…多(长，大…)半倍；

[25] This machine turns half as fast as again as that one.

（＝This machine turns half as fast as that one.）

这台机器转速比那台快半倍。

或：这台机器转速是那台的一倍半。

[26] This wire is half as long again as that one.

这根电线的长度是那根电线的一倍半。

或：这根电线比那根长半倍。

2. …as many（long，large…）again as…，…again as many（long，large…）as…，

可译为：…是…的两倍，比…多(长，大…)一倍

[27] A is as long again as B.（＝A is again as long as B.）

A 的长度是 B 的 2 倍。

[28] This year we have produced as many tractors again as they.

（＝This year we have produced again as many tractors as they.）

今年我们生产的拖拉机是他们的两倍。

3. double，twice 可译为：是…的 2 倍；增加了 1 倍；

treble，triple 可译为：是…的 3 倍；增加了 2 倍；

quadruple 可译为：是…的 4 倍；增加了 3 倍

[29] He demanded double the usual fee.

他要了比平常多 1 倍的路费。

[30] The grains in the area have trebled this year.

今年这个地区的粮食增加了 2 倍。

[31] Output should triple by next year.

到明年产量应增至三倍。

[32] Our income has been quadrupled in the past four years.

在过去的 4 年中，我们的收入增至 4 倍。（即翻了两番）

[33] By 2020, China's GDP will quadruple that of 2000 to approximately USD 4 trillion.

到 2020 年实现国内生产总值比 2000 年翻两番，达到 40,000 亿美元左右。

上面所讲的都是表示变化的倍数，下面我们来看一下表示直接变化量的英语译法。值得注意的是：表示增减意义的词后若跟具体数值或百分数时，所表示的是净增减数，只需照译即可。

[34] The turnover of this company has gone up by 10.9%.

这家公司的营业额增加了 10.9%。

[35] The ex-factory price of industrial goods dropped by 2.9 percent.

工业品出厂价格下降了 2.9%。

[36] Net Earnings of $17.6 million represents a growth of 1,676%.

1760 万美元的净收益增加了 1676%。

[37] Brazil trade volume amounted to US＄29.7 billion, an increase of 46.4％.
巴西贸易额高达 297 亿美元,增长了 46.4％。

[38] The total volume of import and export reached US＄113.8 billion in the first quarter, up 15.9 percent on last year's same period.
一季度,进出口总额 1138 亿美元,同比增长 15.9％。

[39] The global chip sales have gained a year-on-year increase of 11.5％ in July 2005.
2005 年 7 月全球芯片销量同比增长 11.5％。

[40] The output of grain this year has increased by 23％ over last year.
今年的粮食产量比去年增长两成三。

评析:一成即 10％,60％即六成。所以"23％"可以说是 2 成 3。
其他常和数字与倍数搭配的动词有:
表示总计的:be, amount to, total, come to, reach, stand at, add up to;
表示暴涨:climb, jump, surge, soar, rocket, vault, shoot up;
表示暴跌:plummet, plunge, slash, tumble, take a tumble on;

三、数字修辞的夸张功能及翻译

在自然科学的世界里,数字的功能是计算、标记,是毫厘分明、严谨精确的实数,表达纯粹的数量意义。而在人文科学的领域里,数字往往并不表示确切的数量概念,而只是一个泛化的虚数。

许多中文诗句中的数字就已经不是表示精确的实数,而是表示一个泛化的虚数,用夸张的手法突出所谈论的主题,例如:
● 飞流直下三千尺,疑是银河落九天。
● 两岸青山相对出,孤帆一片日边来。
● 桃花潭水深千尺,不及汪伦送我情。
● 飞起玉龙三百万,搅得周天寒彻。
● 长安一片月,万户捣衣声。
● 后宫佳丽三千人,三千宠爱在一身。
● 千里之行,始于足下。
● 三日不见,当刮目相看。

同样,英文有些表达中的数字也失去了它们原有的计算、确切的数量概念,有些已经成为习惯用语,有了自己特定的含义,例如:
● a thousand and one ways 千方百计
● the eleventh hour 最后时刻,危急的时刻
● be dressed up to the nines 穿着非常考究;打扮得很华丽
● at sixes and sevens 乱七八糟
● strike twelve 达到最高目标
● in twos and threes 三三两两
● the fifth wheel 累赘
● a nine-day's wonder 轰动一时(极其短暂)

既然数字在很多情况下都不表示精确记数而作为一种夸张手段,我们在翻译的时候就要特别小心。如果译者不能领会作者的意图和语用含义,则难免如实译出,吃力不讨好。应仔细推敲原文的修辞特色,着重从文采上考虑,精心选择适当词语,译出其形象,译出其语势。

[41] Across the street on the side of a house was painted a giant woman with a *five-foot smile* and long blond hair, holding out a giant bottle.

误译:街对面的墙上有一幅画——一个披着金色长发女郎张开足有<u>五英尺长</u>的笑口,手里扬着一个大瓶子。

改译:街对面房子的墙上有一幅画——一位肩披金色长发的女郎,<u>笑容满面</u>,手里举着一个大瓶子。

评析:five-foot 中的数词 five 仅表示一个模糊概念,不表示实数,它起着夸张的修辞作用。译者稍不小心就会失手。

[42] Keep a thing *seven years* and you will find a use for it.

误译:东西存放<u>七年</u>,总会派上用场。

改译:东西<u>放着</u>,总会派上用场。

评析:句中 seven 不是表示实指意义的数目字,而只表示一个不确定的、含糊的数目,因此译文不必把这个数字非译出来不可。

[43] "He is *seventy-six years* of age," said Mr. Smallweed.

Mrs. Smallweed piped up: "*Seventy-six pounds! Seventy-six thousand bags of money! Seventy-six hundred thousand million of parcels of banknotes!*"

"他今年<u>七十六岁</u>",斯默尔维德先生说。

斯默尔维德太太尖叫起来"<u>七十六镑</u>! <u>七十六万袋钱</u>! <u>七十六万万包钞票</u>!"

评析:句中 seventy-six hundred thousand million of parcels of banknotes,如按实数直译,就是"七万六千亿包钞票",尽管形似精确,但却影响了语义的连贯和语势的递增,译者依据语境,摒弃了数字的实指意义,巧妙地译为"七十六万万包钞票",与前面的"七十六镑"和"七十六万袋钱",形成了语势递增的层递修辞格,读来顺口,语义贴切,形象地刻画了一位爱钱如命、见钱眼开的人物形象。(包惠南,2001)

[44] There were 60 million Americans at home working to turn out the *thousand and one* things required to wage war.

美国国内有六千万人在生产<u>成千上万</u>种军需品。

评析:英语数字"the thousand and one"如直译成汉语,没有夸张或比喻的含意,只能产生"1001"的确切数字概念,改译成"成千上万"则符合汉语表达习惯。

[45] His brother is known to be no better than himself in inclination… In the old phrase it is *six of one and half a dozen of the other*… ——R. Stevenson, *The Master of Ballantrae*

人家都知道他兄弟的品性并不比他好……用句老话来说,也就是<u>半斤八两</u>……

评析:英语的"six of one and half a dozen of the other"译为"半斤八两",符合汉语的表达习惯。

还有一些英语表达中的模糊数字是不必译出的,例如:

[46] *One* man's meat is *another* man's poison.

人各有所好。

[47] I'll love you *three score and ten*.

我会<u>一辈子</u>爱你的。

[48] *Ten to one* he has forgotten it.

<u>很可能</u>他已经忘了。

[49] His mark in math is *second to none* in the class.

他的数学分数在班上是<u>名列前茅的</u>。

[50] I always believe my *sixth* sense.

我总相信我的<u>直觉</u>。

[51] He talks about you *nine times out of ten* when we have a chat.

每次我们闲聊他<u>几乎都</u>谈及你。

[52] The parson officially pronounced that they became *one*.

牧师正式宣告他们<u>成婚</u>。

[53] I used to study in France in *the year one*.

我<u>早年</u>曾在法国学习。

本节练习

1. 精确数字翻译

[1] to be double that of last year

[2] to be more than double the 1965 figure

[3] to be a dozen times that of 1949

[4] to be five times that of last year

[5] three times as many as ...

[6] The diesel output of oil for farm use has more than doubled.

[7] During this period its territory increased ten-fold.

[8] The output of chemical fibre has been increased three times as against 2000.

[9] Between 1999—2000, production of cars was up 8-fold.

[10] These machines increased productivity three fold.

[11] The output of chemical fertilizer was more than 2.5 times greater.

[12] It is four times as big as Europe.

[13] Wheel A turns as fast again as wheel B.

[14] The production of integrated circuits has been increased to three times as compared with last year.

[15] The hydrogen atom is nearly 16 times as light as the oxygen atom.

[16] This sort of membrane is twice thinner than ordinary paper.

[17] Switching time of the new-type transistor is shortened 3 times.

[18] When the voltage is stepped up by ten times, the strength of the current is stepped down by ten times.

[19] The equipment reduced the error probability by a factor of 5.

[20] The principal advantage of the products is a two-fold reduction in weight.

2. 模糊数字翻译

[21] At noon, the sky was as dark as at the close of the day. Many of us grew impatient and wandered out of our tents to discuss the weather *in twos and threes*.

[22] Jurgis was a young giant, broad of back, full of vigor, *a workingman in a thousand*.

[23] It used to be a well-run business, but then disagreements arose between the partners, and now things are *at sixes and sevens*.

[24] "What is it? What hurts you?"

"My eyes. They're hurting like *sixty*."——J. London, *The Valley of the Moon*

[25] When the patient's condition was critical, the doctor stayed with her for days and had *only forty winds* in the daytime.

本章推荐阅读书目

黄邦杰. 译艺谭[M]. 北京：中国对外翻译出版公司, 2003.

连淑能. 英译汉教程[M]. 北京：高等教育出版社, 2006.

思果. 翻译研究[M]. 北京：中国对外翻译出版公司, 2002.

第四章　翻译的文采篇

翻译即写作,翻译就是再创作,这是不少翻译研究家们早已形成的共识。傅雷在提出"神似"的观点时,也曾说过:"理想的译文仿佛是原作者的中文写作"(傅雷,1984:559)。思果曾提出"翻译为重写"(2001:1)。他认为,不会写中文而要把外文译成中文,等于没有米还要煮饭。中文都写不通,翻译还能通吗?不能写作的人最好不要学翻译。这都说明了翻译和写作的密切关系和重要性。纵观古今中外翻译杰作,因精彩的译文写作而产生的佳作不胜枚举。中国古代佛经翻译家鸠摩罗什非常注重译文语言的精美,他曾认为,"天见人,人见天"在言过质,采用了僧睿的译文:"人天交接,两得相见。"清朝翻译家严复主张"信、达、雅",引用孔子的"言之无文,行之不远",他的译文被认为"足与周秦诸子相上下"。作为文学家、文论家、诗人的林纾译笔精湛,颇具马、班、韩、柳的神韵和传统文学的风采,正因为他具有深厚的古文素养,才使他具有无与伦比的写作才华,写就了中国翻译史上精彩的译文。正如古人云:"文心者,言为文之用心也。"作文的"用心",就是讲"文之枢纽",讲文章的"纲领"。林纾能以自己的"文心"洞悉西方文学作品的"文心",故能写出绝妙的文字来,连当代学者钱钟书都为之佩服,他"宁可读林纾的译文,不乐意读哈葛德的原文","理由很简单:林纾的中文文笔比哈葛德的英文文笔高明得多"(钱钟书,1984:719—720)。当代翻译家许渊冲提出翻译的"优势论"、"竞赛论",也是强调如何把译文写得更好,甚至可以超越原文。

当代学者辜正坤则从英、汉两种语言的特性提出了英译汉中注重译文文采的必要性和重要性。其基本原理(2003:432)是:汉语是描写性特强的语言;英语则是逻辑性特强的语言,因此,相对来说,汉语多华丽修饰语,而印欧语要少得多。也就是说,汉语言文字先天地就在艺术表达上更富于表现性,更具美感性。这就是所谓的"归化还原增色法"。它指的是译者根据原语作品和译语作品所处时代、区域、读者对象、翻译目的、审美需求等若干因素,灵活地采取使译入语更加生动、富于文采的译法。可简括如下:

英译汉——简→繁;归化还原增色法:可近似程度地将英语的本色罩上汉语的浓妆。
汉译英——繁→简;归化还原减色法:可近似程度地将汉语的华丽色彩淡化为英语的本色。

因此,在进行英译汉时,一个汉语水平较高的译者笔下的译文总是情不自禁地具有很多增色的地方。这种增色在很多场合是势所必然的。译文的语言优势来源于对原文深刻的洞察理解,结果于译文的深刻的精确表达。原文优美,译文也优美;原文简练,译文也应简练。

也就是说,要体现原文的风格。翻译写作活动的最终目的是准确、流畅地表达原文作者的思想,使读者发生兴趣,能够理解和接受。

其次,文采来自译者较高的艺术修养,即译者的文才、才华,它包括译者运用译文语言的能力,掌握各种表达方式、表现技巧的能力,是从翻译主题的总体表达能力来说的。狭义的文采,是指遣词造句、修辞达意的能力,是从译者驾驭语言文字这一单项能力来说的。须知,原文是有文采的作品,翻译应该还之以文采,而不是平淡、稀松。译文的语言经过修饰,能切当地、艺术地表达思想感情,富有美感,这就是文采。文采的主要特点是艺术表达力强,具有审美效应。文采是增强译文感染力的重要因素。正如孔子所言,"言之无文,行之不远"。

再者,和写作一样,翻译写作也要积累语言材料:语言材料主要指词汇。词汇丰富是语言丰富的一个重要标志,有了丰富的词汇,遣词造句才能得心应手,左右逢源;提笔行文,才会随意生姿,挥洒自如。"辞不足不可以为成文"(韩愈)。词汇不丰富,语言贫乏,就会"一词之立,旬月踟蹰"(严复)。积累语言材料的一个办法是向优秀作品学习语言。现代的、古代的、中国的、外国的经典作品,它们的语言规范化程度高,特别是优秀文学作品的语言,很值得我们学习借鉴。许多精美的成语、典故、警句、妙语,都能丰富我们的语言材料,增添我们写作、翻译的文采。因此要特别注意以下两点。

要善于锤炼语言:锤炼译文语言的基本要求是有分寸感。所谓分寸感,就是译者的语言灵敏度强,能够精细入微地辨别词义,恰如其分地运用语言。具体来说,要做到准确:准确是文采的前提,是掌握分寸感的具体表现。语言准确,首先用词要求准确。辨别词语还要求准确地区分词语的感情色彩,选用词语要褒贬恰当。其次,选择句式要准确。语言的句子形式多种多样,不同的句式有不同的表达效果。长句严密、精确、细致;短句简洁、明快、有力;整句形式整齐、声音和谐;散句形式多样,富于变化;陈述句语气平稳,疑问句语气强烈;祈使句用来表示要求和希望;感叹句用来抒发强烈的感情。

务必适度:修饰必须适度。强调修饰绝不是允许不分文体、不分场合,可以乱用、滥用修饰。文采并不意味着要文辞华丽,而要干净利落。锤炼语言要反复修改,求简洁之美。古今中外那些名篇佳作,差不多都是改出来的。"文不厌改",只有通过反复的修改,才能做到精益求精,臻于完美。

总而言之,译者必须具有良好的中文修养,才能发挥译文优势,写出富有文采的译句,而有了无数精彩的译句,才能形成精彩的译篇。下列小节中数种方法是提高译文质量的重要手段。

第一节　巧用中国古代诗文典籍词语、句法

中国古代文化博大精深,古文作为一种承载体,对继承传统文化起了巨大的作用,虽然如今已不再在现代社会中起交流和传递信息的工具,但在现代汉语语体中,它的词语和部分句法仍然十分活跃。鲁迅曾说过:"恰当借用一些文言词汇,演化改进一些古文句式白话文,发挥古文的优点,使语言更为洁简精炼,多姿多彩,既明白晓畅,又有一种典雅的气韵,同时也强化了语言表现功能。"(《我是怎样做起小说来》《鲁迅全集》)余光中先生也说:

动用文言,一则联想较富,意味较浓,一则语法较有弹性,也更简洁,乐得摆脱英文文法的许多"虚字"。……在白话文的译文里,正如在白话文的创作里一样,遇到紧张关头,需要非常句法、压缩字词、工整对仗等等,则用文言来加强、扭紧、调配,当更具功效。这种白以为常、文以应变的综合语法,我自己在诗和散文的创作里,行之已久,而在翻译时也随机运用,以求逼近原文之老练浑成。(2002:190)

此话确实鞭辟入理。适当运用,可使译文不同凡响,回味无穷。当然,这不是提倡今人用古文写作和翻译。再说,现代译者想必也没几个有这本事做到。能不能做到是修养问题,要不要做到是策略问题,无须大惊小怪。当然,使用文言文词语和句法必须看文体、场合,还要有个度的限制,即,必须是浅显畅晓,切不可用上那些艰深晦涩、诘屈聱牙的词句来故弄玄虚,食古不化。有道是,运用之妙,存乎一心。

一、古词语的引用

[1] She set what was conceded to be the finest table in White House history. Sometimes she wondered whether the President *really appreciated the food*. He wolfed it down with such incredible speed. (*The Glory and the Dream*)

她的食谱据说是白宫历史上最讲究的。不过胡佛吃饭时总是那么狼吞虎咽,他的夫人有时怀疑总统是否会<u>食而不知其味</u>。(王宗炎译文:《光荣与梦想》)

评析:译文划线部分语出《大学章句》,其文曰:"心不在焉,视而不见,听而不闻,食而不知其味。此谓修身在正其心。"该译文非常巧妙地套用了其中一句。它又没有太深的译语文化气息,用得恰到好处!

[2] *Wonderful waves rolling in*, *enormous clouds of foam*, made one marvel that anybody could have got ashore at the landing.

<u>惊涛拍岸,卷起大片大片白云样的泡沫</u>,这使人难以相信,竟会有人能从海上登上滩头。

评析:苏东坡的"惊涛拍岸,卷起千堆雪",意境与此相近,稍作改动,便得佳译,读过苏词者会有此联想。划线部分如译成"惊人的浪涛滚滚而来,还有大片白云般的浪花",似乎也没大错,但在修辞和韵味上就平淡许多。

[3] As it is, called to imperial office, as I have been, by the consent of Gods and men, I have been moved by your high character and patriotism to offer you in peace the principate for which our forefathers *fought*, and which I obtained in war.

我实际上是由于诸神和人民的拥戴才取得皇位的,现在我受到你的崇高品格和爱国精神的感动,打算以和平方式把皇帝的统治权交给你;要知道,我们的祖先都是<u>马上得天下</u>,而我也是通过战争才取得政权的。

评析:《史记·陆贾列传》中有这样的话:"居马上得之,宁可以马上治之乎?"马上得天下,也是后来人们常用的话,意思是以武力夺取天下。这里将 fought 译作"马上得天下",很合说话者的口气,而且也可与下句"通过战争才取得政权"不重复。(陈廷祐,1980)

[4] But today, re-reading the passages in his lectures, it is impossible not to see that he himself was the *unnamed* hero.

但是今天重读他讲演中的这些段落,不难看出,那没有说破的英雄就是他自己。

评析:这句话参照《三国演义》中评论曹操、刘备煮酒论英雄一节中的话:"说破英雄惊煞人",将"unnamed"译成"没有说破",颇能传神,意味浓郁。译成"未指明的"则平淡了。

[5] We are going to try to *run the same by* forging a cynical alliance with the very members of Congress who tried to destroy him a year ago.

我们打算<u>以其道还治其人</u>,与国会中一年前力求打倒他的议员结成联盟,不再讲什么道义。

评析:非常简单的"run the same by"(做相同的事)译成了"以其道还治其人"。宋·朱熹《中庸集注》第十三章:"故君子之治人也,即以其人之道,还治其人之身。"这里的转用,精彩绝伦,其内涵义远比英文深刻,这就是充分发挥译文语言优势!

[6] The bomb "is the greatest thing in history," Truman boasted. Nor was he sorry he had used it. Noting the "unwarranted attack on Pearl Harbor," the President explained to a journalist, "when you deal with a beast you have *to treat him as a beast.*" ——*America, Russia and the Cold War*

杜鲁门大言不惭地说,原子弹是"历史上最伟大的东西"。他并不因为使用了原子弹而感到内疚。总统对一位记者解释说:"请注意偷袭珍珠港这件事。对付一头野兽,唯一的办法是<u>以其道还治其身</u>"。——《美苏与冷战》

评析:译文也是套用改造了朱熹的"以其人之道,还治其人之身",这是根据上下文锻造出来的。

[7] Some cautions must be mentioned——for example *good tools are essential to do the job well.* ——*Oxford Advanced Learners' Dictionary*

有些警句必须提及,如:<u>工欲善其事,必先利其器</u>。——《牛津高阶英汉双解词典》

评析:good tools are essential to do the job well 用典雅的古文词句表达显得不同凡响。这样的译法有何不可?

[8] The first requisite of an English translation is that it shall be English, or that a translation should be able *to pass itself off* as an original and show all the freshness of original composition. ——*The Art of Translation*

用英文翻译,首先要做到译文地道;译文应<u>出落</u>得像原文,就像是创作出来的,清新生动。——《翻译的艺术》

评析:"出落"是中国古典文学作品中常用来比喻少女体态容貌变化、成长的词语,元·王实甫《西厢记》第四本第二折:"出落得精神,别样的风流"。这里用来翻译 pass itself off 可谓妙绝。

[9] She was more like her father than her younger sisters, for Carreen, who had been born Caroline Irene, *was delicate and dreamy*, and Suellen, christened Susan Elinor, prided herself on her elegance and ladylike deportment. ——*Gone with the Wind*

比起两个妹妹,她更有乃父之风,因为悄玲是生就一个<u>多愁多病身</u>,苏纶又是硬要学文雅,都跟她自己的脾气不能融洽。——《飘》(傅东华译文)

评析:"delicate and dreamy"译成"多愁多病身"恰好又是元·王实甫《西厢记》第一本第四折《雁儿落》里的词语。《红楼梦》中也用在主要人物的描写上。

[10] When I was as young as you are now, *towering in confidence* of twenty-one, little did I suspect that I should be at forty-nine, what I now am.

我在你这个年纪的时候,二十出头,小荷尖尖,意气风发,哪里会想到49岁今天的我呢?——毛荣贵译文

评析:"小荷尖尖"四字,把"towering"一词的"精、气、神"一并译出。"小荷尖尖"四字,借自宋代诗人杨万里《小池》:"泉眼无声惜细流,树阴照水爱晴柔。小荷才露尖尖角,早有蜻蜓立上头。"这使得译文具有了丰富的联想意味。

[11] Men who had never previously been accustomed to seeing themselves in print were flattered by the proud distinction; and, though they sometimes experienced a difficulty in detecting their own portraits, the overdone colouring of the artist was *not uncongenial to their tastes*. (History of the Chartist Movement)

以前从来不习惯于看见自己的名字在报上出现的人都受宠若惊;虽然有时他们很难辨认出本人的肖像,但是,艺术家的过分着色不能不说是深得其心。

评析:"was not uncongenial to their tastes"若译成"并非不合他们的口味"、"正是投其所好",都不如用"不能不说是深得吾心"更有风趣。

[12] I have been a stranger in a strange land. —*Exodus* 2:22

独在异乡为异客。

评析:英文与王维诗句"独在异乡为异客"(《九月九日忆山东兄弟》)如出一辙。此乃文心相通也。

[13] What millions died that Caesar might be great!

一将功成万骨枯。

评析:巧妙借用中国古诗句"一将功成万骨枯",异曲同工。道尽古今中外丰功伟绩背后的不堪。

[14] Where's Caesar gone now, *in command high and able*? (Jacopone, *De Contemptu Mundi*)

那雄才大略,君临一切的恺撒如今安在?

评析:"安在"二字,胜过"哪里"十倍!

[15] The *shadows are lengthening* for me. The twilight is here. My days of old have *vanished tone and tint*; they have gone glimmering through the dreams of things that were.

译文一:我的影子在延伸。黄昏来到了这里。我的往日已经消失了;它们只是在过去事情的梦中闪烁而去。

译文二:我已是日薄西山的人了。黄昏已然来临。往日早已烟消云散,只是在梦回往事时,它还闪闪烁烁。

评析:"日薄西山"最早见于《汉书·扬雄传上》:"临汨罗尔自陨兮,恐日薄于西山。"此词语多见于古文中,而以晋·李密《陈情表》中的表达最为有名:"但以刘日薄西山,气息奄奄,人命危浅,朝不虑夕,……是以区区不能废远。"译者不读书,何以写出这样的句子?

[16] But then a sudden *fit of anger seized* him.

译文一:突然,一阵愤怒攫住了他。

译文二:他忽然怒从心上起。——吕叔湘译文

评析：吕叔湘译文语出《五代史平话》："朱温未听得万事俱休,才听得后,怒从心上起,恶向胆边生。"《水浒传》中常见使用。

[17] In 1931, he *failed* to reach it in the submarine Nautilus. (*Macmillan Encyclopaedia*)

1931年他驾驶"鹦鹉螺号"潜艇前往斯匹次卑而根群岛,未果。

评析：晋陶潜《桃花源记》："南阳刘子骥,高尚士也,闻之,欣然规往。未果,寻病终。"宋欧阳修《与程文简公书》："某自病起,益疲,不能复旧,岂遂衰邪？碌碌处此,思去未果。"清纪昀《阅微草堂笔记·如是我闻一》："拟请刘石庵补书,而代葺此屋……因循未果,不识何日偿此愿也。"

二、古文笔法的运用

[18] Some fishing boats were becalmed just in front of us. Their shadows *slept*, or almost *slept*, upon the water, a gentle quivering alone showing that it was not complete *sleep*, or if *sleep*, that it was *sleep* with dreams. (*Mark Rutherford*)

译文一：眼前不远,渔舟三五,凝滞不前,樯影斜映水上,仿佛睡去,偶尔微见颤动,似又未尝熟睡,恍若惊梦。——高健译文

译文二：渔舟三五,横泊眼前,樯影倒映水面,仿佛睡去,偶尔微颤,似又未尝深眠,恍若惊梦。

评析：译文运用古文笔法,意境深远,胜过原文,直令人想起范仲淹的《岳阳楼记》中的"至若春和景明,波澜不惊,上下天光,一碧万顷；沙鸥翔集,锦鳞游泳,岸芷汀兰,郁郁青青；而或长烟一空,皓月千里,浮光跃金,静影沉璧；渔歌互答,此乐何极！"它又令人联想到唐人张祜在《题金陵渡》中的佳句胜景："潮落夜江斜月里,两三星火是瓜洲。"看来,作为一个优秀译者,中国古典文化知识修养必不可少。这类译文句子不是该不该用的问题,而是会不会用的问题。

[19] The land did not move, but moved. The sea was not still, yet was still. ——R. Bradbury, *The Vacation*

大地止而亦行,大海动而亦静。——晓兰译文

[20] Paradox flowed into paradox, stillness mixed with stillness, sound with sound. —R. Bradbury, *The Vacation*

万寂交而万籁和,若真若假,若是若非。——晓兰译文

[21] Great is the art of beginning, but greater is the art of ending. —Henry W. Longfellow

善始固然不易,善终尤为难得。

评析：若译成"善始固然伟大,善终更为伟大"则太直。

[22] Our birth is nothing but our death begun. —Edward Young, *Night Thoughts*, 1742: 6

我辈之生,无非死之发端,岂有他哉。

[23] He that is not handsome at twenty, nor strong at thirty, nor rich at forty, nor wise at fifty, will never be handsome, strong, rich, or wise. —George Herbert, *Jacula Prudentum*, 1651

人而二十不英俊,三十不健壮,四十不富有,五十不明智,则永无英俊、健壮、富有、明智之日矣。

评析:其行文意气与金圣叹所言:"人生三十而未娶,不应更娶;四十而未仕,不应更仕;五十不应为家;六十不应出游"遥相呼应。

[24] He is fool who can not be angry, but he is really a wise man who will not.
译文一:常言道:愚者不知怒,智者能制怒。
译文二:常言道:愚者不会怒,智者而不怒。

评析:原文很容易理解,但要用恰当的汉语表达出来颇为不易。

[25] Isabella is one of the most beautiful characters in the pages of history. She was well formed, of middle size, with great dignity and gracefulness of deportment and a mingled gravity and sweetness of demeanour. Her complexion was fair; her hair auburn, inclining to red; her eyes were clear blue, with a benign expression, and there was a singular modesty in her countenance, gracing as it did, a wonderful firmness of purpose and earnestness of spirit. —Washington Irving

伊莎贝拉是史篇中的绝代佳人之一。她修短合度,纤秾得体,举止端庄而不失优雅,仪态严肃而不乏温馨。肌肤白皙,秀发金褐,碧眸明彻,目光祥和。她既有温和而谦逊的外表,又具有坚强的意志与执著的精神。

评析:这一段译文用词典雅,有古文词句的运用以增强时代感;结构对称,增强端庄的效果,给人一种仪态万方的古典美人的意象,又造就一种可望而不可及的令人敬畏感。

[26] After that, he kept looking out his window for her, *mourning the decade they had let slip by while married to other people.*

打那以后,他总是透过窗户意欲寻觅她的身影,哀叹十年光阴瞬息过,却与旁人共枕席。

评析:"哀叹十年光阴瞬息过,却与旁人共枕席"就是不受原句形式束缚的佳译,它浸润着浓厚的古汉语行文神韵。

[27] On one of those sober and rather melancholy days in the latter part of autumn, when the shadows of morning and evening almost mingle together, and throw a gloom over the decline of the year, I passed several hours in rambling about Westminster Abbey. There was something congenial to the season in the mournful magnificence of the old pile; and, as I passed its threshold, it seemed like stepping back into the regions of antiquity, and losing myself among the shades of former ages.

译文一:时方晚秋,气象肃穆,略带忧悒,朝曦和暮色,几乎相接。一年将息,终日阴暗。此时的我,到西敏寺去独步半日。古寺巍巍,森森然似有贵气,和阴沉沉的季候正好相吻;踏入门槛,仿佛我已经置身于远古,相忘于旧时的冥府之中。

译文二:这是晚秋的清冷而又有点难受的日子,早晨的影子和黄昏的影子,几乎接在一起,一年即将过去,天色晦暗。我就在这一天,到西敏寺去散步了几个钟头,古老的高大建筑的悲哀的华丽,和这个季节似乎一致。我踏入大门,似乎回到了那古老的地域,在古代的黑暗里失去了我自己。

评析:这是 Washington Irving 所写的小品文"Westminster Abbey",原文非常典雅,译

文一也具有那种韵味。它让人想起郦道元《三峡》:"每至晴初霜旦,林寒涧肃,常有高猿长啸,属引凄异,空谷传响,哀转久绝。"译文二虽然传递了意思,但有何情趣可言?

[28] *Their skill as horsemen and archers halted Persian and Macedonian invasion* but they remained a nomadic people until their disappearance during the Gothic onslaughts of the 3rd century AD. (*Macmillan Enclopaedia*)

<u>他们(西徐亚人)善骑术、精弓箭,故能拒敌波斯人和马其顿人</u>。他们一直是游牧民族。公元三世纪遭哥特人屠杀后消亡。

评析: 主语"Their skill as horsemen and archers"被做了高度的转化分解,分别译成两个动词句"善骑术、精弓箭",有古文句法之韵,原文的谓语短语经翻译,以"故能"和前面译句构成因果关系,再现原文之意。"拒敌"一词见于《水浒传》(第四十一回):"宋江又题起拒敌官军一事。"

[29] One of our ancient prayers says,
"Common be your prayer; Common be your purpose; Common be your deliberation; Common be your desires; Unified be your hearts; Unified be your intentions; Perfect be union among you."

我国古代的一篇祷文说道:
"愿同祈祷,目标无二,意志合一,谋虑与共,冀求相通,一体同心,众志成城,固此联盟。"——(连淑能,2006)

评析: 从译文的修辞考虑,对于原文中多次重复但并无不同含义的词——如果这种重复不是一种修辞手段的话,译时可以选择汉语中的同义词来表达,避免重复而造成译文单调。上面是印度的一篇古祷文,用古汉语四字句来翻译。其中的"common"一词,如都以"共同"来译,则显得太单调,故用"无二"、"合一"、"与共"、"相通"等词来加以变换,充分发挥了译文的语言优势。

[30] He was condemned to be hanged in 1463 but was banished from Paris instead, and *nothing is known of him after that date*. (*Macmillan Encyclopaedia*)

1463年被判处绞刑,但代之以驱逐出巴黎,<u>从此不知其所终</u>。

[31] ... such as the UK, where both legislature and executive are *largely in the hands of the same individuals*. (*Macmillan Encyclopaedia*)

在英国,立法和行政大都<u>同操于一些人之手</u>。

[32] Sandringham House, a 19th—century Tudor-style building, remains a royal residence. *It was the birthplace of George VI, who also died there*. (*Macmillan Encyclopaedia*)

桑德灵厄姆宅邸是一座19世纪都铎风格的建筑,现仍是皇家行宫。<u>乔治六世曾生于斯卒于斯</u>。

[33] The controversial Adoration of the Lamb altarpiece was probably begun by his elder brother Hubert van Eyck and *completed by Jan after Hubert's death*.

其颇有争议的圣坛背壁装饰画《羔羊的崇拜》很可能是由他的兄长胡贝特·凡·爱克着手画起,<u>兄死后,弟继之</u>。

评析: 以上四例表明,套用文言文词语、句法明显较之用白话文要简练得多,译文质量明显提高。

三、钱钟书古文译法赏析

钱钟书提出了文学翻译的"化境"说,他认为"把作品从一国文字转变成另一国文字,既能不因语文习惯的差异而露出生硬牵强的痕迹,又能完全保存原作的风味,那就算得入于'化境'"。下面精彩译文录自钱钟书《管锥编》,译文真正达到"化境",宛如原创,而且把文言翻译运用到极致。郑延国赞之为"下笔妍雅,片言生辉"(1990)。余光中认为,钱钟书的文言翻译,能"去芜存菁,不黏不脱,非仅曲传原味,即译文本身亦可独立欣赏,足称妙手转化(adaptation),匠心重营(recreation)。"(2002:189)

[34] Making small thing appear great and great thing small. ——古希腊辩士语
小物说似大,大物说似小。

[35] Let such teach others who themselves excel, and censure freely who have written well. —Alexander Pope
能手方得诲人,工文庶许摘病。

[36] Men are good in one way, but bad in many. ——亚里士多德所引谚语
人之善者同出一辙,人之恶者殊途多方。

[37] But if the top of the hill be properest to produce melancholy thoughts, I suppose the bottom is the likeliest to produce merry ones. (*Tom Jones*)
脱在山颠宜生愁思,则在山足当发欢情。

[38] A friend in power is a friend lost. —Herry Adams
朋友得势位,则吾失朋友。

[39] Get a livelihood, and then practise virtue. (《理想国》)
先谋生而后修身。

评析: 译者笔酣墨饱,以与《管锥编》语体色彩相一致的笔调,精彩翻译。"properest to produce"译成"宜生","likeliest to produce"译成"当发",将"Get a livelihood"译成"谋生","practise virtue"译成"修身",尤其贴切。至于将"who themselves excel"译成"能手","who have written well"译成"工文",则更是这样别出心裁、曲尽其妙了。

[40] Not too slender nor too stout, but the mean between the two. ——古希腊诗称美人
不太纤,不太浓,得其中。

评析: "得其中"三字译得妙极。这不正是战国楚辞赋家宋玉"增之一分则太长,减之一分则太短;著粉则太白,施朱则太赤"的翻版吗?东汉文学家傅毅在《七激》中赞美人道:"红颜呈素,蛾眉不画,唇不施朱,发不加泽。"三国时期魏国的杰出诗人曹植在《洛神赋》中说:"秾纤得中,修短合度。"很明显,钱钟书的这句译文正是从这里化解而来的。拜伦在诗中赞美人也有这样的诗句:"One shade the more, one ray the less, had half impair'd the nameless grace"(发色增深一丝,容光减退一忽,风韵便半失)。

[41] What is smells, and what does not smell is nothing. —F. H. Bradley
物而有,必可嗅;嗅不得,了无物。

[42] Divide the living child in two, and give half to the one, and half to the other. (《圣经·旧约》)
剖儿为两,各得其半。

[43] I never could dance in fetters. ——19世纪一英国诗人语
击链而舞,非吾所能。

[44] Happy the people whose annals are tiresome. Happy the people whose annals are vacant. ——孟德斯鸠
国史沉闷,国民幸运。国史无录,国民有福。

[45] Take mine eyes, and thou wilt think she is a goddess. ——西方古语
尔假吾眸,即见其美。

[46] Here lies one whose name was writ in water. ——济慈自撰墓铭
下有长眠人,姓名书水上。

[47] So think thou wilt no second husband wed; but die thy thoughts when thy first lord is dead. (*Hamlet*)
不事二夫夸太早,丈夫完了心变了。

评析：译者突破了原文表层形式的束缚,直探原文字里行间的含义与情趣,并以具有中国特色的三言、四言、五言或七言句译出。这些译文既清新悦目,又摇曳生姿;既工整典雅,又爽爽有神。

[48] Next dreadful thing to battle lost a battle won. —Wellington
战败最惨,而战胜仅次之。

[49] You could not step into the same rivers, for other waters are ever flowing on to you; into the same rivers we step and do not step; we are and are not. ——古希腊哲人语
重涉已异旧水,亦丧故我;我是昔人而非昔人,水是此河而非此河。

[50] Just as we see the bee settling on all the flowers, and sipping the best from each, so also those who aspire to culture ought not to leave anything untasted, but should gather useful knowledge from every source. ——古希腊文学家语
独不见蜜蜂乎,无花不采,吮英咀华,博雅之士亦然,滋味遍尝,取精而用弘。

[51] Not of the letter, but of the spirit; for the letter killeth, but the spirit giveth life.
意在言外,得意忘言,不以词害意。

[52] Grace of style comes from arrangement.
词意位置得当,文章遂饶姿致。

[53] The passage is remarkably like a central tenet of Buddhism, a cult of which Hume could hardly have heard. ——O. Elton, *A Survey of English Literature*
[此节]酷似佛教主旨,然休谟未必闻有释氏也。

评析：这句话换了白话文来翻译,就不如钱译的文言这么简练浑成。

[54] Everything is the same, but you are not here, and I still am. In separation the one who goes away suffers less than the one who stays behind. ——Byron
此间百凡如故,我仍留而君已去耳。行行生别离,去者不如留者神伤之甚也。

评析：这是拜伦致其情妇(Teresa Guiccioli)书云。余光中(2002：189)评曰：这一句情话,语淡情深,若用白话文来译,无非"一切如常,只是你走了,而我仍在此。两人分手,远行的人总不如留下的人这么受苦。"文白对比,白话译文更觉其语淡情浅,不像文言译文这么意

远情浓,从《古诗十九首》一直到宋词,平白勾起了无限的联想、回声。

本节练习

[1] No greater misfortune can befall a country than to be governed by an old tyrant.

[2] The more one gardens, the more one learns; and the more one learns, the more one realizes how little one knows. —Victoria Sackville West

[3] Seeing falsely is worse than blindness and speaking falsely than silence.

[4] The good and the beautiful do not always go together. —Shakespeare

[5] The person who knows how will always have a job. But the person who knows why will be his boss.

[6] Give me a fish and I will eat today. Teach me to fish, and I will eat for a lifetime.

[7] No one else could *get within a mile of him*.

[8] This one chance missed, the game is as good as lost.

[9] If Egypt *ever* truly *emerges from* its backwardness, Heikal will *deserve much credit*.

本章推荐阅读书目

四书章句集注(大学、中庸、论语、孟子)

古文观止

唐诗三百首

宋词三百首

史记

中国四大名著(三国演义、水浒传、西游记、红楼梦)

第二节 巧用汉语四字格词语

　　四字格是中国语言艺术的结晶,它是中国古典文籍中重要的叙事表情形式。虽然古文作为一种文化传递载体已不具鲜活力,但四字格表达结构却得以在白话文中熠熠生辉。汉语拥有纷繁的"四字格"词组。它涵意深刻,构型短小,生命力旺盛,表现力强。四字格有两大类(冯树鉴,1995:304):一类是汉语成语,因袭定型,词序固定,不能随意拆散或组合;另一类是普通词语,结构松散,可以根据一定的语境灵活组合。本节所讲的"四字格"词组,是广义的概念,包括成语和非成语。从内容上讲,"四字格"词组言简意赅;从形式上讲,它整齐匀称;从语音上讲,它顺口悦耳。由普通词语形成的"四字格"比用五字词语和三字词语要精彩得多,如"奋笔疾书"、"满脸堆笑"、"洗劫一空"。"四字格"在译文中如果运用得当,不但使译文大为增色,而且能发挥"锦上添花"的作用。朗读起来抑扬顿挫,起落跌宕,可以享受语音上的和谐美感。这种通过增强音感给人留下深刻印象的效果，是普通的二字词组、三字词组或五字词组、六字词组所不能得到的。但要注意的是，原文语言正规、行文流畅，尤其是在使用对偶、排比和平行结构等情况下，我们可用四字格来传达原文的语言效果。在译文中运用四字格时，我们还必须充分考虑到感情色彩、语言特征、人物塑造等方面的问题。

一、使用"四字格"词组的语言优势

1. 有助于笔墨经济，以少胜多

"四字格"词组是经过反复锤炼、相沿习用而成型的。寥寥四字，言简意赅。在忠实于原文的内容和风格的前提下，恰当采用，译文就显得凝炼、贴切，具有高度的概括力。

[1] Over the past several weeks, she had grown increasingly *restless*.

过去几周，她越来越<u>六神无主</u>。

[2] Scientific exploration, the search for knowledge has given man the practical results of being able to shield himself *the calamities of nature and the calamities imposed by other man.*

科学的探索，知识的追求，使人类获得了避免<u>天灾人祸</u>的实力。

评析：原句末 11 个词，译成四字格"天灾人祸"，何其精炼贴切。

[3] *The nation at large was exhausted from the searing effects* of the Civil War and Reconstruction.

由于南北战争和"重建"造成的<u>百孔千疮</u>，<u>举国上下</u>被搞得<u>筋疲力尽</u>。

[4] With ten years of Sorbonne and the prospect of a Nobel, Pierre was *a rising star* in the galaxy of scientists.

皮埃尔·居里在索邦大学任教十年，并有希望获得诺贝尔奖金，因而在科学界名流中是<u>后起之秀</u>。

评析：a rising star 如译为"正在成长的名家"，不免啰嗦。

[5] The fact that a plane is up in the air and cannot stop if anything goes wrong, makes it perhaps *a matter of life or death* that its performance is absolutely dependable.

飞机在空中飞行时，如果部件发生故障，它是不能停下来的，因此，其性能必须绝对可靠，这是一个<u>生死攸关</u>的问题。

评析：在科技翻译中同样可以运用"四字格"。关键在于它能否忠实于原文。

[6] The list of chiral objects *could go on*, but examples of two kinds of sea-shells *tell the story.*

手性物<u>不胜枚举</u>，但以两类海贝为例，即可<u>盖其全貌</u>。

评析：两个"四字格"正确、贴切地表达了用其他字眼难以表达的原文含义。

2. 有助于译文通顺流畅，雅俗交融

由于英汉语表达习惯迥然不同，对号入座的死译，常违反汉语表达的"约定俗成"，使译文生硬别扭，难以达到确切和通顺。因此，根据上下文的内在联系和关联，由表及里，恰当运用"四字格"，就能收到良好的效果。

[7] Eisenhower later recalled, when MacArthur felt slighted he was capable of expressing himself in "an explosive denunciation of *politics*, *bad manners*, *bad*

judgment, broken promise, arrogance, unconstitutionality, insensitivity, and the way the world had gone to hell." (William Manchester, *The Glory and the Dream*)

艾森豪威尔后来回忆往事时说，只要麦克阿瑟感到有人对他不够尊重，就"发起脾气来，破口大骂人家好耍权术，不懂礼貌，乱出主意，出尔反尔，狂妄自大，违反宪法，神经迟钝，麻木不仁，如今世道真是见鬼，等等。"

评析：译文中连续使用八个四字格。

[8] Wartime Marseilles was such a *bubbling* stew of political *double-dealing*, financial *corruption*, racial and nationalist *crisscrossings*, *refugee* agonies and tragedies, and Mediterranean *finagling* dating back to Phoenician times, that compared to Gaither's *daily grind*, *melodramas* and *spy* yarns *paled*. (Herman Wouk, *War and Remembrance*)

战争年头的马赛本来就已成一锅<u>上下翻腾</u>的大杂烩：政治上<u>狗苟蝇营</u>，钱财上<u>巧取豪夺</u>，种族和国籍的<u>混淆纠缠</u>，<u>离乡背井</u>的难民们的苦难和悲剧，以及从腓尼基人时代以来就已盛行在地中海沿岸的<u>尔虞我诈</u>、<u>勾心斗角</u>，所以和盖瑟的<u>例行公事</u>相比起来，什么离奇曲折的剧情和阴险诡谲的故事都要<u>黯然失色</u>。

评析：译文中用了十一个四字格。这些四字格既忠于原文，也显得异常生动，更加有效地表达了原文的意义。试想，假如把这些四字格都改换成参差不齐的二字、三字、五字或六字词组，那么译文的表达效果就必然要逊色得多。

[9] *In the savage fighting, Germany itself* was laid waste, *the towns and countryside were devastated and ravished, the people decimated.* (William Manchester, *The Glory and the Dream*)

德国全境受到了<u>野蛮战争</u>的洗劫，<u>市廛萧条</u>，<u>田野荒芜</u>，<u>生灵涂炭</u>，<u>十室九空</u>。

[10] Drew Pearson, a thirty-four-year-old reporter, described them as "*ragged, weary, and apathetic*," with "*no hope on their faces.*" (William Manchester, *The Glory and the Dream*)

有一位34岁的记者，名叫德鲁·皮尔逊，他描写那些退伍军人，说是"<u>衣衫褴褛</u>，<u>筋疲力尽</u>，<u>神情木然</u>，<u>满脸愁容</u>。"

[11] One of Eisenhower's friends was Moseley, whom Eisenhower later described as "*a brilliant*" and "*dynamic*" officer "*always delving into new ideas.*" (William Manchester, *The Glory and the Dream*)

莫斯利是艾森豪威尔的朋友。艾森豪威尔后来说他是个"<u>才气横溢</u>"、"<u>生气勃勃</u>"、"<u>富于创见</u>"的人。

[12] He was *canny, openhanded, brisk, candid, and modest.* (William Manchester, *The Glory and the Dream*)

他为人聪明<u>大方</u>，<u>生气勃勃</u>，<u>忠厚耿直</u>，<u>谦虚谨慎</u>。

[13] Although *lonely in a new land*, Matzeliger was described by his fellow workers and students as *cheerful, of a friendly nature, honest, and modest.*

虽然马泽利格<u>单身一人</u>，又生活在<u>异乡客地</u>，但正如他的同事和学生所描述的那样，他为人<u>活泼开朗</u>，<u>温文尔雅</u>，<u>诚实谦虚</u>。

[14] Since modern Western culture is *highly diverse*, something that has *faded completely* from one segment of a society can still *flourish* in another.

鉴于现代西方文化<u>千差万别</u>,有些事物在某个社会的一部分地区已经完全<u>销声匿迹</u>,而在另一部分地区可能仍然<u>方兴未艾</u>。

[15] Albert's thoughts *whirled*, and he was *thrilled* and *excited*. For the first time, he sensed that there were things in nature could not been seen, could not be touched, could *hardly be imagined*.

阿尔伯特<u>思潮起伏</u>,<u>心情激动</u>。他第一次意识到自然界里还有看不见、摸不着、<u>几乎不可思议</u>的东西。

3. 有助于译文生动活泼,形象鲜明

"四字格"成语,很多是凭借一定的积极修辞手段而构造的,以实指虚,具体生动,形象鲜明。运用恰当,有助于再现原文的语感、情态和形象,增加译文的感染力。

[16] You may have read stories in which the hero gets into his spaceship and "*blasts off*" into the *outer reaches of space without a worry* about fuel.

你大概读过这样一些故事吧。它们描写一位英雄坐上飞船,"<u>风驰电掣</u>",直冲<u>九霄云外</u>,<u>毋须</u>为燃料<u>担心发愁</u>。

[17] Many men have recognized the similarity of plants to the behavior of animals, and have *dreamed wistfully*, but *forlornly*, upon some *method or source of rejuvenation* such as Ponce de Leon sought in the Fountain of Youth several centuries ago.

许多人认为,植物的习性与动物相似,于是<u>梦寐以求</u>地去探求什么"返老还童"的"灵丹妙药",就像数百年前彭斯·德·利昂在青春泉祈求仙水一样,结果只能是<u>竹篮打水</u>。

评析:将"have dreamed wistfully"译成"梦寐以求",将"forlornly"译成"竹篮打水",将"method or source of rejuvenation"译成"'返老还童'的'灵丹妙药'",深刻地体现了作者的否定态度,增强了感染力。

4. 提高译文语言的整齐匀称和韵律感

吕叔湘在《现代汉语双单音节问题初探》(《中国语文》,1963/1:14)中指出:"2+2的四音节是现代汉语里的一种重要的节奏倾向。"他还指出:"四音节的优势特别表现在现代汉语里存在大量四音节成语即'四字格'这一事实上。"绝大部分"四字格"词组中,四个字音节清晰,富于变化,连续运用时,形成对仗,琅琅上口,抑扬顿挫,起落跌宕,十分和谐,具有语音上的美感,给人深刻印象,从而提高译文语言的节奏感,平添不少文采。

[18] *The dust, the uproar and the growing dark* threw everything into chaos.

<u>烟尘滚滚</u>,<u>人声嘈杂</u>,<u>夜色愈深</u>,一切都陷入混乱之中。

[19] *The sea thundered on, over and past, and as it roared by it revealed a hideous sight.*

<u>狂澜霹雳</u>,<u>隆隆滚远</u>,<u>汹涌波涛</u>,<u>呼啸喧闹</u>了一阵后,一片惨状顿显眼前。

[20] The very earth trembled as with *the tramps of horses and murmur of angry men*.

连大地都震动了,仿佛<u>千夫怒吼</u>,<u>万马奔腾</u>。

[21] But there had been *too much publicity* about my case.
　　但我的事现在已经搞得满城风雨,人尽皆知了。

[22] Target *priorities* were established there.
　　目标的轻重缓急,孰先孰后,是在那里决定的。

[23] Whatever initial worries we had about the plane soon *vanished*.
　　不管开始我们对这架飞机有什么不放心,不久就烟消云散了。

[24] If this was a time of *triumph* for the many, it was a *painful* period for the few.
　　多数人兴高采烈之日,却是少数人伤心失意之时。

[25] Peter has always *enjoyed claiming* that it was he and not George, who was the first to reach the summit of the mountain.
　　彼得一直津津乐道的是,第一个到达山顶的实际上并不是乔治,而是他自己。

5. 切忌盲目追求词藻华丽而超出"信"的范围

任何事物一旦超出适当的"限度",就会走向自己的反面。"四字格"在译文中的运用也是如此。这里讲的"限度",是指"信",即忠实于原文,不仅内容忠实,而且连形式、风格也要尽可能地忠实。恰当地运用"四字格"是提高译文质量的手段之一。因此,使用"四字格"词组要注意:

① 避免使用陈腐生僻、艰深古奥的词语,如"鱼质龙文";
② 避免使用汉语文化成语典故,如"罄竹难书"、"刻舟求剑"、"朝秦暮楚";
③ 避免使用带有汉字特征的词语,如"目不识丁";
④ 避免使用含有中国地名的词语,如"黔驴技穷"、"洛阳纸贵"、"稳如泰山";
⑤ 避免使用含有中国人名的词语,如"名落孙山"、"江郎才尽"、"阮囊羞涩"等,以免译文添加不应有的译语文化信息。

而一般性、通俗性的词语,如"千方百计"、"软硬兼施"、"纤尘不染"等则尽可使用。总之,四字格(成语)的使用务必根据上下文根据其词语的褒贬色彩选择得当,切忌混淆。以下例句需要修改:

[26] This aircraft is *small*, *cheap*, *pilotless*.
　　原译:这种飞机小巧玲珑,价廉物美,无人驾驶。
　　改译:这种飞机体积不大,价格便宜,无人驾驶。

评析:原译者片面追求形式上的均匀,滥用不恰当的汉语习语"小巧玲珑"和"价廉物美",纯属画蛇添足,使译文出现一些在原文中所没有的含义。

[27] Thousands and thousands of pear trees died of san-scales several years ago and *one need not look for a lesson*.
　　几年前,数以万计的梨树死于梨园蚧的侵害,殷鉴不远。(连淑能,2006)

评析:"殷"指中国古代殷朝,具有浓厚的汉语民族特色,同时这个"四字格"也较生僻,不妨改为"这种教训,记忆犹新"。

[28] After the fall of Troy she *was reunited* with Menalaus. (*Macmillan Encyclopaedia*)
　　原译:特洛伊陷落之后她又与墨涅拉俄斯破镜重圆。
　　改译:特洛伊陷落之后她又与墨涅拉俄斯重新团聚。

[29] The Tories were later associated with the rebellious Jacobites and were excluded

from politics until the 1780s, where they re-emerged, led by William Pitt the Younger.（*Macmillan Encyclopaedia*）

原译：托利党人因与叛乱的詹姆斯党联系在一起而被排挤出英国政坛，直到 18 世纪 80 年代才在小皮特领导下东山再起。

改译：……小皮特领导下复出。

[30] The country was a member of the *short-lived* Federation of the West Indies from 1958 to 1961.（*Macmillan Encyclopaedia*）

原译：1958 年至 1961 年曾是昙花一现的西印度联邦成员国。

改译：1958 年至 1961 年曾是为期短暂的西印度联邦成员国。

评析：上述三例皆过度使用了四字格成语，"破镜重圆"和"东山再起"包含太浓厚的中国历史典故色彩，尤其是"破镜重圆"，海伦的被诱拐和中国成语故事中比喻的夫妻离散后又重新团聚根本是风马牛不相及，一个是城破而被带回，一个是夫妻以信物相约来日再见，可谓滥用成语之极！修正的办法是将它们淡化处理，以一般词语表达之。[30] 的"昙花一现"也过于夸张。

二、"四字格"词组的场合使用

1. 英语原文中的非成语译成汉语四字格，使译文生动有力

原文的单词译作成语

[31] A minute later the head of John was handed to the *frightened* Salome.

不大会儿，约翰的首级就交给了魂飞魄散的莎乐美。

[32] Love is a climate—a climate of *the heart*.

爱的情感是一种气氛——一种心心相印的气氛。

[33] We associate China with vitality, *enormous* vitality.

我们提到中国就想起朝气，这是蓬蓬勃勃的朝气。

[34] The *hopeful young* writers should *flock* to the traditional artistic center to pour out their new-found creative strength.

年轻有为的作家会对这个传统的艺术中心趋之若鹜，以便在这里倾泻他们新获得的创造力。

[35] Everyone's life should have *room* for such loves.

每个人的生活都应该为这种爱留下一席之地。

[36] His success in this field has pushed his forerunners' point into the *background*.

他在这方面的成就使其前辈们的论点黯然失色。

[37] Over the past several weeks, she had grown increasingly *restless*.

过去几周，她越来越六神无主。

[38] It is clear that he was one of the *outstanding* pilots in the whole program.

事实很清楚，在整个执行计划中他是出类拔萃的驾驶员之一。

[39] I was nervous before *crowds*.

我在大庭广众之前感到紧张。

[40] It was a privilege revocable at any time on *whim* of the authorities.

这种恩赐只要当权者心血来潮随时可以取消。

[41] Dulles greeted me with a *bemused* look.
杜勒斯欢迎我时,满脸是呆若木鸡的表情。

[42] It was Monday, February 21, 1972, and Richard Nixon was about to achieve an *authentic* "first"; a presidential visit to China.
这一天是1972年2月21日,星期一,理查德·尼克松就要实现一件货真价实的"创举"了:美国总统访问中国。

[43] The Weimar Republic was about to *expire*. (*The Rise and Fall of the Third Reich*)
魏玛共和国即将寿终正寝。——董乐山译文

[44] To many Americans, China is still a *faraway* place—*unknown*, *unseen*, and *fascinating*.
时至今日,仍然有许多美国人觉得中国远在天涯海角,鲜为人知,令人心驰神往。

原文的短语译作汉语四字格

[45] The problems of the human environment are, to some of us, *an old story*.
人类环境问题对我们之中某些人来说是老生常谈。

[46] Internationally speaking, it amounts to *the ultimate aspiration* of all human beings to usher in an era of understanding and fraternal co-operation.
从国际意义来说,这无异于引进全人类梦寐以求的互相谅解,兄弟般合作的新纪元。

[47] John, however, conscious of his high duty as a minister of Jehovalh's will, found it impossible *to remain silent* before so wicked a deed.
然而,约翰作为奉行耶和华旨意的使者,他明白自己的崇高职责,而对这种丑恶行径噤若寒蝉,那绝对办不到的。

[48] Emma, handsome, clever, and rich, with a happy disposition, seemed *to unite some of the best blessing of existence*.
爱玛漂亮、聪颖、富有、天性开朗,称得上得天独厚。

[49] But against *the vast expense* of the sky, the parachute looked *very small*.
但和广阔无垠的天空相比,降落伞看起来渺小若蚁。

[50] The German penetration of the Allied lines was a *damning commentary* on the supposed *invulnerability* of the Maginot Line.
马其诺防线据说是固若金汤这一点,已被德军突破盟军防线这件事驳得体无完肤了。

[51] It is he that *enjoys tremendous popularity in the world*.
就是他闻名遐迩。

[52] They scoffed at him and *walked away*.
他们奚落他一番后扬长而去。

[53] He is *slow and stupid in attending to affairs*, *mediocre and incompetent*.
他麻木不仁,庸碌无为。

[54] After hearing what you said, I was *not a little bewildered*.
听了你的话,我大惑不解。

[55] Yesterday he was *righteously indignant while speaking* at the meeting.
昨天他在会上慷慨陈词。
评析：这是董乐山译的《第三帝国的兴亡》里的一句话，译文的表达力显然强于原文。

[56] The latter part of the fifteenth century prepared *a train of future events*. —Quentin Durward
15世纪下半叶酝酿着后来的风云变化。
评析：如果译成："15世纪后半部分准备了一系列的未来事件"，似乎也可以算是准确的翻译。但是汉语表达方式丰富，我们还可以考虑选用"酝酿"、"揭开序幕"、"铺平道路"、"鸣锣开道"等词。上句译文也许更能传达这本历史小说的风格，这就是发挥了译语的优势。

[57] Behind him I see the long grey rollers of the Atlantic *at work*. —Durrel
在他的背后我看见大西洋上的灰色巨浪，汹涌起伏。

[58] What I like best are *the stern cliffs*, with *ranges of mountains soaring* behind them, *full of possibilities*, peaks to be scaled only by the most daring.
我最喜爱那悬崖峭壁，它的背后是高耸云端、神秘莫测的层峦叠嶂。

2. 原文中的成语处理

2.1 套用汉语成语

[59] They *wisely kept their own counsel* and did not express their opinion too loudly.
他们明哲保身，决不大声发表议论。

[60] "Maybe it won't come off. There's many a slip," Pamela said.
"也可能不会成功，说不定功亏一篑，"帕米拉说。

[61] Don't believe about him for he is only *a sugar coated*.
不要相信他，因他只是一个口蜜腹剑的人。

[62] Why do you love *to find fault with* someone? It seems that the only person who is always right is yourself.
你为什么总爱吹毛求疵，总是认为自己是对的。

[63] I *took* the news *with a grain of salt*.
我对这个消息半信半疑。

[64] Unless you've *got an ace up your sleeve*, we are dished.
除非你有锦囊妙计，否则，我们是输定了。

[65] He *went through fire and flood* to save his mother.
他赴汤蹈火去救他的母亲。

[66] You *have a lucky star above you*.
你真是福星高照。

[67] She is now *between the devil and the deep sea* on this matter.
她在这个问题上真是进退维谷。

[68] She is *reaping what he has sown*.
她这是咎由自取。

[69] That fellow is always *fair without but foul within*.
那个家伙总是口蜜腹剑。

[70] Well, there's no need for us *to beat around the bush*.

我们现在没有必要*旁敲侧击*。

2.2 同一个成语可有多种译法

[71] He *was on tenterhooks* of expectations during our conversation.

在我们谈话时,他因有所期待而*如坐针毡*。

[72] I found him *on tenterhooks* when he was waiting for his girlfriend.

我发现他在等女朋友时显得*局促不安*。

[73] His parents *were on tenterhooks* all the time until they got his letter.

他的父母在收到他的信前,一直是那样*心烦意乱*。

[74] The students were *on tenterhooks* before the examination began.

考试开始前,学生们的心里*七上八下*。

[75] The poor boy *was on tenterhooks* when his father was searching for a stick.

那个可怜的男孩见父亲到处找棍子,感到*六神无主*。

[76] The hen-pecked man was *on tenterhooks* when his wife scolded her way into the room.

当妻子骂骂咧咧闯到房间来时,这个得了"气管炎"的男人便有些*手足无措*。

[77] She *was on tenterhooks* when she heard of her mother's illness.

她得知母亲病了,*坐立不安*。

2.3 原文的中性成语有时译成带有褒贬含义的成语

[78] Unfortunately, John had excellent reason to find fault with the private life of his sovereign. Herod, the Tetrarch, was *a chip of the old block*.

不幸的是,约翰掌握了谴责国王私生活的充足理由。分封王希律跟他父亲乃是*一丘之貉*。

评析:"a chip of the old block"意为"跟父亲一模一样的儿子",在此译成贬义的"一丘之貉"。

[79] Yesterday he received a letter from his sister about whom there *had been no news whatsoever*. It was like *a bolt from the blue*.

昨天他收到他姐姐一封信,原来他姐姐一直杳无音信,这真是*喜出望外*。

评析:"a bolt from the blue"含有"晴天霹雳"之意,但在汉语中这一成语一般与坏事相连,故译成"喜出望外",有褒义。

[80] For the first time Nora saw her husband *for what he was*... *a selfish, pretentious* hypocrite with no regard for her position in the matter.

这是娜拉有生以来第一次认清了丈夫的真面目:原来他是一个*道貌岸然、自私自利*的伪君子,在这个问题上根本不把她的处境放在心上。

评析:"what he was"注意不要译成"庐山真面目"。

[81] Where he faced us again, he was *huge and handsome and conceited and cruel*.

再次面对我们时,他已变得*身材魁梧、相貌英俊、心高气傲、冷酷无情*。

[82] She remember how in Nascosta even the most beautiful fell quickly under the darkness of time, like flowers without care; how even the beautiful became *bent and toothless*, their dark clothes smelling, as the mamma's did, of smoke and manure.

她想起,在那斯科斯塔,最美丽的娇娃,因为不堪时艰,很快便姿容消退,就像无人护理的花朵一般;绝美佳人很快也就弯腰驼背,皓齿尽落,一身皂衣,就像老妈妈一样,散发着火烟和粪肥的臭味。

[83] He must make us feel that they are twins indeed, *one dying if the other dies, one flourishing if the other flourishes.*

他必须使我们觉得,他们实际上是一对孪生兄弟,一枯俱枯,一荣俱荣。

[84] In heaven an angel is *nobody* in particular. —G. Shaw

在天堂,天使们也是芸芸众生。

3. 四字格的修辞结构

比较而言,汉语语言更注重语言的表现艺术。在英语句子中,有时候并没有使用重复,但为了使汉语译文生动,使译文渐入"雅"境,有时候也可以采用下列重复手段。

3.1 运用词的重叠

无论是在古汉语中还是在现代汉语中,词的重叠都是一种常见的修辞手段。在英译汉中,我们可以适当采用词的重叠,尤其是四字重叠词组,即 AABB 结构,以使译文生动活泼。

[85] In order to solve this problem, they have been working *day and night* for two weeks.

为了解决这个问题,他们两周以来一直日日夜夜地忙碌着。

[86] The kid is always *in rags* as if he were an orphan.

那个孩子总是穿得破破烂烂,就像个孤儿似的。

[87] Long-stemmed models *ankled* through the lobby. (*Time*)

身材修长的模特儿们袅袅婷婷地走过大厅。

[88] You will always find his *tardiness* and *carelessness* in everything he does.

你会发现他做任何事情都是磨磨蹭蹭,马马虎虎的。

3.2 运用四字对偶词组

汉语中许多四字对偶词组中前后两对词组形成对偶,往往具有相同或类似的含义。英译汉时对此类词组的恰当使用,同样也可以达到生动活泼的效果。

[89] Whatever initial worries we had about the plane soon *vanished*.

不管开始时我们对这架飞机有多少担心,这种顾虑不久就烟消云散了。

[90] Don't *fancy* any longer. To you, he is absolutely a man of *loyalty*.

别再胡思乱想了,他对你绝对是一心一意的。

[91] If this was a time of *triumph* for the many, it was a *painful* period for the few.

多数人兴高采烈之日,却是少数人伤心失意之时。

3.3 运用两个四字词组

作为汉语一大特点的四字词组,意义比较精炼,读起来朗朗上口,有节奏感,如运用恰当,可使文字生动活泼,增强修辞效果。在符合忠实、通顺的标准前提下,在译文中可酌情运用两个同义或近义的四字词组。

[92] But there had been too much *publicity* about my case.

但我的事现在已经搞得满城风雨,人人皆知了。

[93] Facing a critical moment, you should make clear the *priorities* first.

在紧急关头,你首先必须弄清事情的轻重缓急,孰先孰后。

[94] He showed himself *calm* in an emergency situation.

在危急情况下,他从容不迫,镇定自若。

[95] The questions were evidently unexpressed to the slow-witted spokesman, who instantly found himself *tongue-tied*.

这些问题显然使得这位反应迟钝的发言人感到意外,他立即显得张口结舌,哑口无言。

[96] During the Second World War, China had been *overrun* by Japanese invaders.

二战期间,日本侵略者在中国横行霸道,无恶不作。

4. 四字格词组与普通词语的译文比较

汉语行文,特别是记述、描写类文字中,有一种明显的以词组(尤其是四字格词语)为句段构建句子的倾向。这种句段构成的句子比一般散句音韵感好,简劲有力。郭绍虞在《汉语语法修辞新探》中称这种句子为"词组堆迭句"。李运兴(1998)认为,在我们的翻译实践(尤其是记叙、描写文字体)中也完全可以,而且应该顺应汉语的这种构句特点,提高译文质量。试比较:

[97] A few of the pictures are worth mentioning both for their technical excellence and interesting content.

译文一:其中有些照片既由于其技术高超又由于其内容有趣而值得一提。

译文二:有些照片技术高超,内容有趣,值得一提。

评析:每一对译例的第二句都要优于第一句,因为这些句子顺应了汉语的构句方式。

[98] I repair to the enchanted-house, where there are lights, chattering, music, flowers, officers (I am sorry to say) and the oldest Miss Larkins, *a blaze of beauty*. (*David Copperfield*)

译文一:我来到那迷人的住宅,那里有灯光、谈话、音乐、鲜花、军官们(看见使我难过),还有最大的拉京士小姐,一个美的火焰。——董秋斯译文

译文二:我现在朝那家仙宫神宇走去,那儿灯光辉煌、人语嘈杂、乐音悠扬、花草缤纷、军官纷来(这是我看着极为痛心的),还有拉钦大小姐,简直仪态万方,艳若桃李。——张谷若译文

评析:把"a blaze of beauty"译为"一个美的火焰",让人费解,译为"仪态万方,艳若桃李",就鲜明多了。

[99] It was an old woman, tall and *shapely still*, though *withered by time*, on whom his eyes fell when he stopped and turned.

译文一:他站住,转过身来,定睛一看,是个年迈的妇女。她身材很高,仍然是一副好模样,虽然受了时间的折磨而有点憔悴。

译文二:他停下脚步,转过身来,定睛一看,原来是个上了年纪的妇女。她身材修长,虽然饱经风霜,显得有点憔悴,但风韵犹存。——李端严译文

评析:"风韵犹存"比"仍然是一副好模样"要更加生动。"饱经风霜"也比"受了时间的折磨"来得精炼。

[100] The mayor of Toledo said in 1932: "I have seen *thousands of* these *defeated, discouraged, hopeless* men and women, *cringing and fawning* as they come to ask for public aid. It is a *spectacle* of national degradation." (William Manches-

ter,*The Glory and the Dream*)

初译：托莱多市长在1932年说过："我见到数千万遭受了挫折的、失去了信心和希望的男人和女人又奉承地又乞怜地前来请求救济。这么一个情景给国家丢了脸。"

改译：托莱多市长在1932年说过："我见到成千上万的山穷水尽、灰心绝望的男男女女前来请求救济。他们低声下气，苦苦哀求。此情此景，真是丢尽了美国的脸。"

评析：初译对原文中的划线部分没有采用四字格进行翻译，从而使译文在形式上失去平衡，在读音上缺乏节奏，使整个表达效果受到了较大的影响。如果对原文中的划线部分改用四字格译法，就会得到言简意赅、节奏强烈、形式工整、形象生动的效果。

[101] His irritation *could not withstand* the silent beauty of the night.

原译：他的烦恼经不起这宁静的良宵美景的感染。

改译：面对这宁静的良宵美景，他的烦恼不禁烟消云散了。

三、"四字格"词组翻译赏析

[102] They refused to *call off the attack*.

他们不愿就此偃旗息鼓。

评析：这比直译"他们拒绝结束这场进攻"生色。

[103] They have against them the whole of the Aristocracy, nine-tenths of the gentry, the great body of the clergy, and all the pensioners, sinecurists and bloodsuckers that feed on *the vitals of the people*.

反对他们的是所有的贵族、十分之九的绅士、庞大的牧师队伍和一切养老金的领取者、无功受禄的冗员、以民脂民膏为生的吸血鬼。

评析："vitals"意为"生命中最重要的器官，命门，要害"。这里借用中国俗话"民脂民膏"，与原文意思是贴切的。

[104] But they were *overwhelmed* at last.

可是到后来寡不敌众，直败下来。

评析："overwhelmed"译成了"寡不敌众，直败下来"，也比原文精确。

[105] Nixon was pleased by the distinction, but not *overwhelmed*.

尼克松对这种破格的礼遇感到高兴，但并没有喜出望外。

评析："overwhelmed"结合上下文的又一种译法。

[106] Oh, Lord knows! I suppose the woman wants to live her own life; and the man wants to live his; and each tries to drag the other on to the wrong track. *One wants to go north and the other south*; and the result is that both have to go east, though they both hate the east wind.

天知道！大概女人想过女人的生活，男人想过男人的生活，彼此都想把对方拉到相反的方向去；南辕北辙，结果两人都被拉向东边，虽然双方都不愿意。

评析："one wants to go north and the other south"用来译"南辕北辙"，虽不中不远矣！

[107] Every time I come back from a business trip it makes *a new man of me*.

我每到外头跑一趟生意回来，这个地方就叫我耳目一新，精神一爽。

评析：原文中"a new man of me"如按字面译成"重新做人"，跟原文内容大相径庭。对原文略加引申为"耳目一新，精神一爽"，符合汉语修辞习惯。

[108] It is very much like communicating with an *accurate* robot who has a very small vocabulary and who *takes everything literally*.
它很像<u>一丝不苟</u>的机器人讲话那样，机器人只会很少的词汇，<u>事事刻板</u>。
评析："accurate"本义为"准确、精密"，这里译为"一丝不苟"，以符合拟人化的需要。

[109] It was just *growing dark*, as she shut the garden gate.
关上园门时，已是<u>暮色苍茫</u>了。
评析：这比用什么"天快黑了"要好百倍。

[110] As I must therefore conclude that you are not serious in your rejection of me, I shall choose to attribute it to your wish of increasing my love *by suspense*, according to the usual practice of elegant females.（*Pride and Prejudice*）
因此我不得不认为：你这一次并不是当真拒绝我，而是仿效一般高贵女性的通例，<u>欲擒故纵</u>，想要更加博得我的喜爱。——王科一译文
评析：以"欲擒故纵"译"by suspense"，不但意思准确，而且符合人物口吻，确是生动。

[111] They have only a few anti-aircraft guns, but their *aim is mostly true*.
他们的高射炮虽然为数不多，但他们<u>弹无虚发</u>，命中率极高。
评析：运用汉语成语"弹无虚发"起到言简意赅的作用。

[112] This is the policy upon which we will act, *come what will*.
这就是我们奉行的政策，<u>成败利钝</u>，<u>在所不计</u>。
评析：比直接译成"无论发生什么情况"要高明许多。

[113] While the West *goes about its business*, Russia *gains nothing* by going off into a corner to sulk.
西方依然<u>我行我素</u>，而俄罗斯<u>一无所获</u>，只好缩在旮旯里生气。
评析：这个句子非常形象："to go about one's business"的意思是"该干什么还干什么"；"go off into a corner to sulk"，直译是"走开到一个角落里生气"；"gain nothing"，什么也没有得到。

[114] The opposition leader's speech *stole the headlines* from the government.
反对党领袖的演讲在报纸上<u>大出风头</u>，使政府相形见绌。
评析：直译是：反对党领袖的演讲从政府手里偷走了报纸的通栏大标题。

[115] The girl is *treated very much as if she were a daughter of the family*.
这家人把这个女孩<u>视同己出</u>。
评析：这比译成"这女孩被对待非常像这家的亲生女儿一样"要言简意赅。

[116] Their relationship is a *mixture of affection and exasperation*.
他们的<u>恩怨难分</u>。
评析：不要受原文拘束，而要用译文的说法来表达。

[117] A month ago, he was *a man of men*. Today he seemed truly *touched* by divine spirit, which *spiritualized and elevated him*.
一个月前，他是一个<u>凡夫俗子</u>。今天，他似乎真正得到了圣灵的<u>造化</u>，<u>超凡入圣</u>了。

评析:"凡夫俗子"、"超凡入圣",非常精到;touched 译成"造化",恰如其分。

[118] I spent three or four hours on two short chapters—savoring each paragraphs, *lingering* over a sentence, a phrase or even a single word, *building a detailed mental picture* of the scene. No longer was I in Sydney, Australia, on a sticky heat-wave night. *Relishing* every word, I joined foreign correspondent Sheean on a mission to China.

短短两章,我就读了三四个小时之久——对每个段落,我仔细品玩,一唱三叹;对每个句子,每个段落,甚至是每个词,我都<u>流连徘徊,依依不舍</u>;书中胜境在我脑海里,<u>历历入画,一览无余</u>。这时,我已不在澳洲的悉尼,置身于<u>热浪滚滚、汗流粘袂的夜晚</u>了。<u>津津有味</u>地品评每一词句,我已和外国记者谢安一起,专程访问中国。

评析:以上译文恰如其分地使用了四字格表达,尤其使用了汉语叠词,音韵极佳。

[119] The rocks presented a high impenetrable wall, over which the torrent came tumbling in a sheet of feathery foam, and fell into a broad, deep basin, black from the shadows of the surrounding forest.

山岩壁立,不可逾越。岩顶上一道瀑布,飞流直下,水花四溅,雾气弥漫,山泉轰然落入一个宽广的深潭,周围树林的影子,使得潭水一片黝黑。

评析:此译文充分发挥中文句法写景优势,让读者见到了山涧水流的一幅动势图,译者的形象思维丰富,熟谙中文写景技法。

[120] Gradually the river grows wider, the banks recede, the waters flow more quietly, and in the end, without any visible break, they become merged in the sea, and painlessly lose their individual being.

其后,河面逐渐展宽,两岸相距愈远,水流趋缓,最后则流入大海,与海水融为一体,海天一色,平心静气地结束其单独存在的那一段历程。

评析:毛荣贵先生评论道:原句中的"without any visible break"和"painlessly"均为翻译难点,译者居高临下,不受制于字词转换,而立足于一种意境的造设与渲染。"海天一色"拔高了原词的意境,而"平心静气地"则强化了拟人意境。译文用几个长短相近的句式的舒缓排列,烘托了大江下游烟波浩渺、天水合一之景。

[121] Tapestry weaving *has been practised since antiquity* but it only flourished in Europe from the 14th century.

壁毯纺织<u>古已有之</u>,但 14 世纪才在欧洲兴旺发达起来。

[122] ... improved technology and the use of plastic body forms *have resulted in greater degrees of realism.*

技术的改良及塑料模型的使用,使标本<u>几可乱真</u>。

[123] The Argonauts *were protected* by the *superior* singing of Orpheus.

阿尔戈船英雄们则靠奥尔甫<u>技高一筹</u>的歌唱才<u>平安无事</u>。

[124] All dialects *are linked historically* and *all developed from a common ancestor*, Proto-Slavonic.

所有这些方言从历史上说皆<u>一脉相承</u>,<u>源出一宗</u>,即原始斯拉夫语。

评析:以上五例基本能表现出成语在译文中的运用,它确能收到言简意赅的功效。

译文欣赏

War and Remembrance
Herman Wouk
(An Excerpt)

Here in Cairo people are still *rattled* by the *closeness* of Rommel, but *encouraged* by your planes, tanks, and trucks *pouring to* our Eighth Army via the Cape of Good Hope, and *on direct convoy* past Malta. Talky has it straight from Churchill—Winnie flashed through here twice this month, *raising a cloud of bloody nonsensical* trouble—that all this is *a drop in the bucket* compared the Niagara of equipment that you're *flooding* to the Russians. When or how your countrymen produce all this, I don't know. Your country *baffles* me: a luxurious *unharmed* lotus land in which *great* hordes of *handsome dynamic* people either wallow in deep *gloom*, or *play like overexcited* children, or fall to *work* like all the devils in hell, while the press *steadily* drones detestation of the government and *despair* of the system. I don't understand how America works, any more than Frances Trollope or Dickens did, but it's an *ongoing* miracle of sorts.

In London things are *as bad*. The repair of the blitz devastation goes *sluggishly*. People *drag themselves* through the *rubble* in *sticky* weather on *dwindling rations*.

But bad as the surrender of Tobruk *hit* London, it was *nothing to* what went on here in Egypt. We missed the worst of it, but we hear it was like the fall of France. Rommel *came roaring along* the coast, all fueled up and rearmed with *masses of stuff* he captured at Tobruk. By the time he halted at El Alamein, two hours by car from Alexandria, *government bureaus*, *military headquarters*, and *rich big shots* were all fleeing eastward to Palestine and Syria in every available train and *vehicle*. *Less-favored* folk *were clogging the roads on foot*. *In the cities* there were *strict curfews*, *empty hotels*, *abandoned streets* and *offices buildings*, *looters*, *trigger-happy patrols*, and *all the rest*. Little of this *got past* the tough censorship.

Things are less *scary* now. Some of the *skedaddlers* are *sheepishly drifting back*, but the more prudent ones are staying where they are. Obviously Rommel is *retooling* and *gassing up for another try*.

战争与回忆
霍尔曼·沃克著
(节选)

在开罗这儿,人们因为隆美尔<u>近在咫尺</u>而仍有风声鹤唳之感,但是你们经由好望角以及护航舰队取道马耳他海面<u>直路行驶</u>,支援我们第八军的<u>源源而来</u>的飞机、坦克和卡车,却使此间<u>人心大振</u>。韬基直接从丘吉尔口中知道——温尼在本月内两次匆匆路过这儿,以致使<u>谣诼纷起</u>——比起你们像尼亚加拉大瀑布一样倾斜给俄国人的装备来,所有这一切只不过是<u>九牛一毛</u>。你的同胞们是在什么时候、用什么方法生产出这许多东西来的,我可不知道。

你们的国家真叫我觉得不可思议：仙境般无忧无虑的国度、容光焕发、精力充沛、熙熙攘攘的人群，他们不是沉溺在忧郁悲观的深渊中，就是像欣喜雀跃的儿童一般游戏作乐，要不然就像入地狱的鬼魂一般辛苦工作，而你们的报纸则是无休无止地指责政府，宣称你们的制度无可救药。我丝毫不比特罗洛普和狄更斯他们二位更加懂得美国是怎么回事，而只知道它正在日新月异地显露一桩桩奇迹。

伦敦情况不佳。闪电战的毁坏，修复进展迟缓。天气湿热，配给日减，人们在断垣残壁间艰难度日。

托布鲁克的易手虽使伦敦蒙受重创，但和这儿埃及相比，却是不可同日而语。我们没有碰上最严重的时日，但是听说那一阵子简直就和法国沦陷的时候一样。隆美尔利用他在托布鲁克缴获的大批辎重，加足了燃油，重新装备了武器弹药，沿着海岸浩浩荡荡，长驱直入。他在阿拉曼暂时停留的时候，离开亚历山大只有两个小时的汽车路程，此间的政府机关、军事总部、豪富钜子都纷纷向东逃往巴勒斯坦和叙利亚，所有的火车和大小车辆都用上了。徒步出去的无财无势的人们充塞道途。各处城市都严格实行宵禁，饭店旅舍都已人去楼空，大街小巷行人绝迹，办公大楼门可罗雀，歹徒趁火打劫，巡逻队动辄开枪杀人，完全是一片兵荒马乱景象。这种情形是难以通得过严厉的检查制度而得见诸报端的。

现在的情形已不那么惊慌失措。有一些仓皇出走的人已经提心吊胆地陆续回来，一些比较谨慎的人仍在外地逗留。隆美尔显然在重整旗鼓，加足汽油，还要卷土重来。

评析：译文大量使用了四字格，这实在是中文的行文特色。如果不用四字格，势必行文拖沓啰唆，意味不足。

本节练习

[1] General Thomas *gave up the sword for the plough* in 1987.
[2] There are *one thousand and one* people watching the games in the stadium yesterday.
[3] His chances of getting into Harvard are *one out of hundred*.
[4] I am *at a loss* what I ought to say on that occasion.
[5] But once I made the decision, I went at it *with all flags flying*.
[6] I *took* the news *with a grain of salt*.
[7] Unless you've *got an ace up your sleeve*, we are dished.
[8] She is now *between the devil and deep sea* on this matter.
[9] He is *reaping what he has sown*.
[10] She is an easy-going woman. She always *throws her cares to the winds*.
[11] That fellow is always *fair without but foul within*.
[12] He looks like *up to the air*.
[13] She found the keys she had lost last month and was overjoyed.
[14] Just as the postwar period witnessed the *disintegration* of old empires, the epoch we are entering now will see the end of neo-colonialism.
[15] Parents love their children and the love is *perfect*.
[16] Britain has no such natural protection from a *flood* of Hollywood products.
[17] Thus, the question of the United Nations peace-keeping efforts in Cyprus begins to

assume the dimensions of a *dilemma* for the Organization—indeed, several *dilemmas*.

[18] The Council could have been spared a long *harangue*.

[19] He discharged the responsibilities of the presidency with the ease and adroitness of one long *familiar with* the working of the United Nations.

[20] She *sailed* into the room.

[21] He was *a tall, thin, elegant man with the air of thorough-bred grace*.

[22] They *met just once* at the dinner table.

[23] The palace is surrounded by *a marvelous group of old trees*.

[24] But he *was building* on ruins.

[25] His popularity would *soar*.

[26] He is an expert in *floating things*.

[27] But there was *little* Eden *could do*.

[28] But Dictator Attlee, he can *get away* with *blue murder*.

[29] We have only *begun to see some* of the effects.

[30] This was a theme that *kept on recurring*.

[31] She has grown increasingly *restless*.

[32] They tried *in vain* to make him tell.

[33] They were *elegant of dress*, *free with money*, *vague as to their antecedents*.

[34] They left the shop *without a word*.

[35] She *sneers* at all opinions but her own.

[36] The weather is wonderful, and very *exhilarating*.

[37] I haven't been doing anything *sensational*; just working.

[38] He was *very constant* during all our difficulties.

[39] I was very lucky. It was *touch and go*.

[40] The strange news *completely dumbfounded* us.

第三节　巧用汉语习惯语

一、译文比较

在英汉翻译中除了适当运用四字格词语外，善于使用汉语其他习惯语（熟语），包括二字词组、三字词组、五字词组或六字词组，也是发挥译文优势的有效手段。它们也能使译文文字表现得更生动活泼。

[1] Beggars *can't* be choosers.

原译：饥不择食。

改译：要饭的<u>不能嫌馊</u>。

评析：这是《牛津高阶英汉双解词典》前言里专门提出来讨论欣赏的译句。评论者认为，改译准确表达出can't所承载的无奈，所以妙译并非一定要用成语才能表达其意。

[2] She smiled falsely at his jokes.

原译：她以虚假的微笑回答他的笑话。

改译：她听了他的笑话假装笑了。

评析：原译生硬，改译自然，不见斧凿痕迹。

[3] In the vestibule below was a letter box into which no letter would go, and an electric button from which *no mortal finger could coax a ring*. —O. Henry

译文一：楼下通道里有一个信箱，但是永远不会有信投进去；还有一个电钮，非得神仙下凡才能把铃按响。

译文二：……还有一个电钮，只有鬼才按得响。

评析：这是欧·亨利在《麦琪的礼物》(*The Gift of the Magi*)中描写电铃时说的。否定词"no mortal hand"（不是凡人的手）译成肯定的"神仙下凡"，用的是正译法。但用"只有鬼才按得响"更深刻地表现其涵义，第二种译文显然比第一种译文生动。

[4] Bettors lose inevitably.

打赌的无可逃避地输钱。（×）

赌钱的免不了输钱。

逢赌必输。

[5] It occurred to him that one cigarette would *comfort* him.

原译：这时，他想到，一支香烟也许能给他带来点安慰。

改译：这时，他想到，吸支香烟也许能解解愁。

[6] Every day sees the boy cleverer.

原译：每天看到这个男孩渐渐聪明了。

改译：这个男孩日益聪明了。

[7] In a wagon, you can be *one place today and another the next day*.

原译：坐着马车，你今天可以在一个地方，明天又可以在另外一个地方。

改译：坐着马车，你可以今天看山，明日玩水。

评析：原句要表达的是，自己忙忙碌碌，而对方却悠闲自在。原译不能算错，但过于死板，原文那种羡慕的涵义没有表现出来。还是改译"今天看山，明日玩水"能够曲尽其妙。

[8] It was remarked that the clock began to strike, and I began to cry, *simultaneously*.

据说，钟开始敲，我也开始哭，两者同时。——董秋斯译文

据说那一会儿，当当的钟声，和呱呱的啼声，恰好同时并作。——张谷若译文

据说，钟声当当一响，不早不晚，我就呱呱坠地了。——许渊冲译文

评析：许渊冲认为，董译对等，只能使人知之；张译用了"当当"、"呱呱"，发挥了汉语叠字的优势，可以使人好之；许译用了"不早不晚"发挥了汉语四字词组的优势，可以使人乐之，是最好的表达方式。

[9] The dress set off to perfection the seventeen-inch waist, the smallest in three counties, and tightly fitting basque *showed breasts well matured for her sixteen years*.

她的腰围不过十七英寸,穿着那窄窄的春衫,显得十分合身。里面紧紧绷着一件小马甲,使得她胸部特别隆起。她的年纪虽只十六岁,乳房却已十分成熟了。——傅东华译文

她的腰围只有十七英寸,三个县里就数她腰身最细,那身衣服把她腰肢衬托得更见纤细。虽说年方十六岁,乳房却长得非常成熟。熨帖的紧身上衣把她乳房裹得格外显眼。——陈廷良译文

她的腰围不过十七英寸,是附近三个县里最细小的了,而这身衣裳更把腰肢衬托得恰到好处,再加上里面那件绷得紧紧的小马甲,她的虽然只有十六岁但已成熟了的乳房便跃然显露了。——戴侃、李野光译文

她的十七英寸的腰围,在附近三个县里算是最细小的了,这身衣服把她的细腰束得尽善尽美,年方十六岁的她,乳房已经十分丰满,那紧而贴身的小马甲,更使其跃然显现。——毛荣贵译文

评析:傅译紧扣了原文的"matured"一词即足,但以"成熟"两字形容"乳房"显得拘谨。陈译在紧扣的同时,译笔略作发挥,但基本上停留于述实层次,"裹得"两字欠自然。戴李译用了"跃然显露"四字,译笔活泼,演绎了原文表述的潜在美,但句式略显欧化,"乳房"前的定语过长。毛译则综合了以上之长做了精彩处理。

二、译文评析

[10] He's everything I've *dreamed of*.
    他是我最中意的人。

评析:如果按字面译成"他处处都符合我理想",虽然也通顺,但精神、味道都不如原译。

[11] And *dressing Empire in seductive colours* and *calling it* Commonwealth cannot alter the facts.
    给帝国乔装打扮,涂脂抹粉,美其名曰联邦,也不能改变现实。

评析:这是一篇题为《忘恩负义的非洲》(*Ingratitude of Africa*)中的一句话。"乔装打扮,涂脂抹粉"用的是"拆词法","美其名曰"是加词法,并且比"*calling it*"更加深了该句的讽刺意味。

[12] But to *stand idly by and see* the enemy win a victory seems *the worst of all courses*.
    但是袖手旁观坐视敌人取得胜利,似乎是最下策(×一切方针中最糟的)。

[13] The enemy was *extremely disturbed*.
    敌人慌了手脚(×被弄得慌张极了)。

评析:以上两句译文与括号内的普通译文相比,功力立显。

[14] This large body of men had met on the previous night, *despite the elements which were opposed to them*, a heavy rain falling the whole of the night and drenching them to the skin.
    这一大群人头天晚上还是聚集到了一起,可惜天公不作美,整夜下着倾盆大雨,大家被淋得浑身湿透。

评析:若将"天公不作美"改为"天气跟他们作对",就差劲多了。

[15] Kissinger felt the massive bombing would *strengthen the President's hand* in

China. (*Kissinger*)

基辛格觉得这场大规模的轰炸会使总统在中国的<u>腰杆子硬</u>一些。

[16] "Hyde Park you said, didn't you? I'll be there to *cheer* you."

"It's *a promise*," he said. (*Betrayed Spring*)

"你说海德公园,是不是?我准来给你<u>打气</u>。"

"那就<u>一言为定</u>,"他说。

[17] The Flower Girl: ... Will you pay for them?

The Daughter: Do nothing of the sort, mother. *The idea*!

卖花女:……你肯给钱吗?

女儿:一点不要给她,母亲。<u>她想得倒好</u>!

评析:按许渊冲的看法,[15]中"腰杆子硬"是改了原文。[16]中"打气"、"一言为定"、[17]中"想得倒好"都是比原文表达力更强的语言形式。这是发挥译文优势的结果。

[18] The reverberations of fighting between the forces of India and Pakistan are reaching us *in increasing volume*.

印度和巴基斯坦两国部队的<u>杀伐声一阵紧似一阵</u>传到我们这里来。

评析:"volume"在这儿作"音量"解。但如把 in increasing volume 译作"声音越来越响"或"音量不断增大",都不像句话。这个状语本身就不容易译得通顺,要想把这一词组的色彩表现出来就更难了。在译文里,"杀伐声一阵紧似一阵"的译法,真亏译者想得出来!不仅意思贴切,更妙的是把这一词组的特色充分表现无遗。这使人想起《三国》、《水浒》这一类运用民间语言的小说,写到两军对阵,其间喊杀声、战鼓声,就是用这种富有生命力的文字来形容的。译者信手拈来,恰到好处(黄邦杰,2003)。

[19] ... that we here highly resolve..., that this nation under God, shall have a new birth of freedom, and that government *of the people*, *by the people*, *for the people*, shall not perish from the earth.

所以我们应在这里表示最大的决心……;这个国家在上帝保佑下,一定要获得自由的新生;而这个政府也要<u>民有、民治、民享</u>,才不会从地球上消失。

评析:上句引自美国第十六任总统林肯在葛底斯堡国家公墓发表的著名演说的最后一句,其中 of the people, by the people, for the people, 是那样简练有力、铿锵可诵,一向脍炙人口。中译以"民有、民治、民享"相匹配,不论从形式、精神和朗诵方面,都大致逼似。

[20] Sandringham is a village in E England, in Norfolk. The Sandringham estate was bought by Queen Victoria for the Prince of Wales (late Edward VII) in 1861. Sandringham House, a 19th-century Tudor-style building, remains a royal residence. *It was the birthplace of George VI, who also died there*.

桑德灵厄姆是英格兰东部诺福克郡一村镇。1861年维多利亚为威尔士王子(后之爱德华七世)买下该处房地产。桑德灵厄姆宅邸是一座19世纪都铎风格的建筑,现仍是皇家行宫。乔治六世曾<u>生于斯卒于斯</u>。

评析:这种锤炼使表达更简洁别致。

[21] John *prefers* film to stage plays.

约翰觉得电影比戏剧<u>更合他的口味</u>。——黄邦杰译文

评析:这"更合他的口味"就是把"prefer"一词,甚至把整个句子都译活了。这比译成

"比起戏剧来,约翰还是喜欢电影"要胜一筹。

[22] His *best* jokes *fell flat*.

他那些<u>最能逗人乐</u>的笑话都<u>不灵了</u>。——黄邦杰译文

评析：把 best 译成"最能逗人乐"是根据词的搭配。

[23] He once again imparted to us his *great* knowledge, experience and wisdom.

我们又一次领受了他的<u>广博</u>的知识、丰富的经验和无穷的智慧。

评析："great"一词的意思是"很多"。考虑汉语的习惯说法,故译。

[24] Too clearly, it is a topic we shall *do no justice to* in this place. —T. Carlyle: *On Heroes and Hero-worship*

很显然,像这样一个题目,我们是不可能在这里<u>讲得透彻</u>的。

评析："do justice to"意为"公平对待"、"适当处理",但在句子里还要结合上下文,对这个词组加以锤炼。"讲得透彻"是译者根据上下文研炼得来的。同一个词组,在另一个句子里,又得根据上下文来重新塑造新译。

[25] Many volumes, rather than pages, would be required to *do justice to* the statesmen, soldiers, philosophers, poets, historians, and other famous men of the Sung Dynasty.

要论述宋朝那些政治家、军人、哲学家、诗人、史学家和其他知名人士,用少量篇幅是不够的,恐怕要用若干卷次才能说个分明。

评析："do justice to"是个不好译的词,译文非常地道。

[26] When he might well have *acted with boldness*, he found himself filled with doubts, scruples and equivocations, *in addition to* the *ordinary fears* of a *lover*.

等到他不妨放胆去追求的时候,他却迟疑不定,顾虑重重。至于<u>一般坠入情网的人</u>那种种常有的提心吊胆的心理,<u>那就更是难免的了</u>。

评析：这是一个在炼词方面比较集中而又比较突出的例子。译者将一些词语加以重铸,把"when"译成"等到……的时候",把"act with boldness"深化为"放胆去追求",把"a lover"译成"一般坠入情网的人",把"ordinary fears"译成"种种常有的提心吊胆的心理",把"in addition to"译成"那就更是难免的了"。这些词和词组经过加工锤炼之后,焕然一新,这就是翻译炼词的魅力。

[27] It was all very well to say "Drink me," but the wise little Alice was not going to do that *in a hurry*. (*Alice's Adventures in Wonderland*)

说"喝我"还不好吗?但是那个聪明的小阿丽思决不会这样地<u>冒失</u>。

评析："冒失"用来译"in a hurry"是神来之笔(思果,2004)。

[28] However, this bottle was not marked "poison," so Alice *ventured* to taste it, and finding it very nice, she *very soon* finished it off.

然而这一回瓶子上并没有"毒药"的字样在上,所以阿丽思就<u>大着胆</u>尝它一尝,那味儿倒很好吃,所以<u>一会儿工夫</u>就稀里呼噜地喝完了。

评析："ventured"译为"大着胆","very soon"译为"一会儿工夫",都很巧妙。译文"稀里呼噜"原文里没有,添得很好。

[29] In the hearings which followed, Kissinger *gave a lesson in the art of pleasing*

that would *have done honour to* Lord Chesterfield *at his most amiable*.

在随后的意见听取会上,基辛格使人领教了一套讨好人的艺术,其手段之高明,就连处于最吃香时期的切斯特菲尔德勋爵也要甘拜下风。

评析:"讨好人"、"吃香"、"甘拜下风"都是多么自然地道的文字啊!

[30] It is *typical* of him to slander others.

他这个人就是喜欢诽谤别人。

评析:一个极普通的"就是",把一个人活灵活现地刻画出来。这比说"诽谤别人是他的典型作风"要地道,才是中国话。

[31] They are *formal* with each other.

他们彼此很客气。

评析:如果译成"他们彼此十分正式",那是用中文写的外国话。

[32] ...and not all his large estate in Derbyshire could then save him from having a most *forbidding, disagreeable* countenance...（*Pride and Prejudice*）

……他既然摆起那么一副讨人嫌惹人厌的面貌,那么,不管他在德比郡有多大的财产,也挽救不了他……

评析:这句中的两个形容词"forbidding"和"disagreeable"译为"讨人嫌惹人厌",非常得体。该书中"I would not be so fastidious as you (Darcy) are"译文为"我可不愿意像你那样挑肥拣瘦",这里的"fastidious"译为"挑肥拣瘦",恰如其分地描绘了达西对舞伴的苛求挑剔。

[33] With Franco, I started from a point of hostility, discovered how profoundly he had misrepresented and reached the stage of "*grudging admiration*".

对于佛朗哥,我最初是怀有敌意,后来却发现人们对他有很大的误解,终至有了"三分仰慕之情"(×勉强的钦佩)。

[34] For the work performed, each man received a *starvation pittance* of two pence per day.

从事这项工作,每人每天所得只是两个便士的难以糊口的(×饥饿的微薄)工资。

[35] And if we are no longer *paramount*, neither are we pawns of destiny.

尽管我们不再是凌驾一切的主宰,也绝不是任命运摆布的小卒。

评析:把"paramount"译成"凌驾一切",同时为了呼应后面的内容加上"主宰",既不损害原意又使译文搭配合意,读起来也顺口。

[36] At night, cities *belong to them*.

在夜间,这些城市都是他们的天下。

评析:这比直译"在夜间,这些城市属于他们",内涵义得到深化,更合乎中文习惯。再比如,"maybe the 21st century will belong to them"当然可以译成"二十一世纪可能属于它的",但译成"也许二十一世纪将是他们的天下",不是更显精彩吗?

[37] I had the story, *bit by bit*, from various people...

这个故事我是东一点西一点从许多人那儿得来的……

评析:"bit by bit"可译为"一点一滴",但现译加了"东"和"西",很生动。

[38] "You had better return to your partner and enjoy her smiles, *for* you are wasting your time with me."(*Pride and Prejudice*)

"你还是回到你的舞伴身边去欣赏她的笑脸吧,犯不着把时间浪费在我身上。"

评析：介词"for"译为"犯不着",想得到吗？

[39] Earlier in the day we had a tussle over the words "mug" and "water". Miss Sullivan had tried to impress it upon me that "mug" is mug and that "water" is water, but I persisted in confounding the two. *In despair* she had dropped the subject for the time, *only to renew it at the first opportunity*.

那一天我们已经为"mug"和"water"这两个词纠缠过一番了。沙利文小姐想让我知道"mug"就是"mug"(茶缸子),"water"就是"water"(水),可是我老把这两个词搞混。她没有办法,只好暂时放下这个话题,等有机会再说。

评析：原文"in despair"是绝望的意思。但此处讲的只是教师对"我"感到失望而已,照字典上的意义译就太重了,故只译为"没有办法"。后面的"only to renew it at the first opportunity"译成"等有机会再说"也译得非常灵巧。

[40] "My husband and I were liberal people—giving *the benefit of the doubt* to everyone, bending over backwards to be fair," she recalled.

"我和我的丈夫都很宽厚,总觉得大家都是好人,总是尽量做得公正,"她说。

评析："the benefit of the doubt"本是法律术语,意为"在证据不足情况下先假定无罪"。在此处则指对周围的人行为均作善意解释和理解。译文根据上下文及口语的语体特点译成"觉得大家都是好人",准确而得体。

[41] Gonna fight with me? Tell 'em I'm *ready for it*. I'm always *ready for it*.

想和我打架？告诉他们我奉陪,我随时奉陪。

评析：把"ready for it"译成"奉陪"也比"准备好了"自然得多。

[42] a pisingwhile

撒泡尿工夫

评析：这是莎士比亚戏剧《维洛那二绅士》四幕一场二十一行里的词语,和汉语里的天然表达可谓一字不差。

[43] you three inch fool

三寸丁(柯平,《英汉与汉英翻译教程》)

评析：这是莎士比亚戏剧《驯悍妇》四幕一场二十七行里的词语,那不正是《水浒》里的"三寸丁谷树皮"吗？

[44] I don't think I need your *protection*.

你大可不必为我操心啦。

评析：译文非常灵活,"大可"表达出了句子的语气。protection(保护)变通为"操心",颇见功夫。

[45] "Any one who knew how to please Aunt Julia has a right to her money," Miss Bart rejoined *philosophically*.

"谁要是会讨朱利亚姑妈的欢心,谁就有权得到她的钱！"巴特小姐逆来顺受地说。

评析：这句的难点在"philosophically"的翻译,它一般被译为"善于迁就"、"世故地"、"富有哲学意味地"等西化词儿。译者译出"逆来顺受"是为了原文中说话的内容,因话里面有"讨……欢心"和"得到她的钱"这类行为上的应承和物质上的好处；"逆来顺受"在这里也涵盖了巴特小姐一种想得到好处的心态(苏福忠,2006)。"逆来顺受"在这里用"豁达地"来表示也不错,"He accepted their conclusion philosophically"可译成"他豁达地同意了他们的结论"。又如"She took the bad news philosophically"可译成"她镇定地面对这个坏消息"。

[46] Perhaps *I am in the way*, then?

这么说，我碍你事了？

三、吕叔湘《伊坦•弗洛美》佳译赏析

文学翻译最能展现译者运用文采的能力。当译者的水平高于原作者时，译者就有可能随心所欲地对原作进行"美化"或修改；而当译者的水平低于原作者时，译者往往会碰到一些他无法解决的困难，留下的译作就会是漏洞百出的"伪译文"（王宁，2006）。最理想的翻译应当是：译者与原作者的水平相当或大致相当。只有这样，译者写出的译文才能达到原文的水平，甚至高于原文的水平。美国著名女作家伊迪丝•华顿的中篇小说《伊坦•弗洛美》（*Ethan Frome*）小说原文细腻而典雅，用词明快简练，描写到位（苏福忠，2006），吕叔湘先生的译文就充分显示了译者在把握原文的意境内涵、发挥中文遣词造句上的译写水平非常高超，译作的艺术表达丝毫不逊于原作。

[1] People *struggled on* for *years* with troubles.

许多人有毛病，可以带病延年一年年混下去。

评析：英文句子里"struggled on"和"years"都翻得非常好。

[2] Sickness and trouble: that's what Ethan's had *his plate full with*, ever since the very first *helping*.

病和祸害，这是伊坦的家常便饭，从他能吃饭时候算起。

评析："plate full with"译为"家常便饭"，"helping"译为"吃饭"，天衣无缝。

[3] But the bay was *as good as Frome's word*, and we pushed on to the Junction through *the white, wild scene*.

但是那老栗马不辜负弗洛美的话，我们在漫天风雪中终于到达车站。

评析："as good as Frome's word"译成"不辜负弗洛美的话"，非常自然；"the white, wild scene"译成"漫天风雪"，不死板，又极有意境。

[4] Mattie's hand was underneath, and Ethan kept his clasp on it *a moment longer than was necessary*.

玛提的手在下，伊坦把它握住，没有立刻就放。

评析：句中的"a moment longer than was necessary"如果直译非常生硬。译者采用"同义反译"方法。

[5] The builder refused genially, *as he did everything else*.

建筑师的拒绝是很婉转的，这人无往而不婉转。

评析：译句改变了原句的主谓宾关系，为后面的句子作铺垫，"这人无往而不婉转"的译法比原句高明。

[6] She's a pauper that's hung onto us after her father'd done his best to ruin us.

她是个小叫花子，她的父亲拐了我们的钱，这会儿她又赖在我们身上。

评析：利用英语语法中的先后时态，把句子处理得干净利落。

[7] Now and then he turned his eyes from the girl's face to that of the partner, which, in the exhilaration of the dance, *had taken on a look of impudent ownership*.

他时而转移他的目光从女子的脸上到她的舞伴的脸上,那张脸在跳舞狂热中*俨然有"佳人属我"的神情*。

评析: "had taken on a look of impudent ownership"译成"俨然有'佳人属我'的神情",非常超逸。"ownership"的发挥很有特色,不同凡响。

[8] Now, in the warm, lamp-lit room *with all its ancient implications of conformity and order*, she seemed infinitely farther away from him and more unapproachable.

这会儿在温暖的有灯亮的屋子里头,*自古以来的伦常和规矩好像都摆在这儿*,她变得远远而不可接近。

评析: "with all its ancient implications of conformity and order"译成"自古以来的伦常和规矩好像都摆在这儿",译得很实在,让一般译者感到望尘莫及。原文若直译还真无从下手。

[9] She stood silent, her hands lying cold and *relaxed* in his.

她站在那儿不作声,她的手放在他那手里,冰冷的,*一丝力气也没有*。

评析: "relaxed"在句子里当形容词,大多数译者都会顺手译成"放松的",这里译作"一丝力气也没有",很好地反映了女主人公的身心状态,极传神。

[10] She remained motionless, as if she had not heard him. *Then* she snatched her hands from his, threw her arms about his neck, and pressed a sudden drenched cheek against his face.

她一动不动,好像没有听见他的话,*过了一会儿*,她挣脱了双手,一把抱住他的脖子,把她的湿透了的脸蛋儿偎在他的脸上。

评析: 原文是两个句子,但是译者为了强调一对情人难舍难分的情景,把"then"译作"过了一会儿",让主人公的动作有了停顿感,使得下面三个动作"挣脱了双手"、"一把抱住他的脖子"和"偎在他的脸上"有层次地加强,产生力度。"threw her arms"是复数形式,译者用"一把"来处理。

[11] The words were like fragments *torn from his heart*. *With them came the hated vision* of the house he was going back to—of the stairs he would have to go up every night, of the woman who would wait for him there.

她这些话像是*从他自己心里掏出来的*。*跟着这些话来的是那个想起来就恨的景象*——他今晚上要回去的屋子,天天晚上要爬上去的楼梯,在那儿等着他的那个女人。

评析: "torn from his heart"翻译成了"从他自己心里掏出来的",非常有神韵。"with them came the hated vision"翻译成了"跟着这些话来的是那个想起来就恨的景象",简练、传神。

[12] Her somber violence constrained him, she seemed the *embodied instrument of fate*.

她的阴沉的威力制服了他;她好像是*命运的化身*。

评析: "the embodied instrument of fate"如果翻译成"命运具体化的器械"会非常生硬,这里译成"命运的化身"非常自然。

[13] The sky, *swollen* with the clouds that announce a thaw, *hung as low* as before a summer storm.

天上涨满了预告融雪的云,<u>直压到人头顶上</u>,像夏天里暴风雨之前一样。

评析:"swollen"译作"涨满","hung as low"被发挥成"直压到人头顶上"。

[14] They spoke *in smothered whispers*, as though the night were *listening*.

他们说话的声音<u>低到不能再低</u>,好像怕黑夜也在<u>偷听</u>。

评析:"in smothered whispers"中的"smothered"是个难词,这里译成"低到不能再低","listening"补充成"偷听"。

[15] Ethan, a moment earlier, had felt himself *on the brink of eloquence*; but the mention of Zeena had paralysed him.

伊坦早一刻觉得自己的<u>话多得很</u>,但是一提细娜的名字,好像再也张不开嘴了。

评析:"on the brink of"是"处在……的边沿",但直译不自然。

[16] The cat, who had been a puzzled *observer* of these unusual movement, jumped up into Zeen's chair.

那个猫儿一直莫名其妙地在旁边<u>看着</u>这些和平常不同的行动,这个时候一跳跳上细娜的椅子。

评析:"observer"是"观察者",但万万不可用在这里。翻译时做了词性调整。

[17] "It was a pretty bad smash-up?" I questioned Harmon, looking after Frome's *retreating* figure...

"他受的伤很不轻吧?"我问哈蒙,一边望着弗洛美的渐行渐远的后影……

评析:这里的现在分词"retreating"译为"渐行渐远",把现在分词所包含的动作正在进行的意思译活了。

[18] Her mind was a store-house of innocuous anecdote and *any question about her acquaintances brought forth a volume of detail*; but on the subject of Ethan Frome I found her unexpectedly reticent.

郝尔太太的肚子里装满了无恶意的奇闻轶事;<u>只要是她认识的人,随便问起哪一个,她都能原原本本地给你说半天</u>,可是关于伊坦·弗洛美,完全出于我意料之外,她非常缄默。

评析:这句中的"any question about her acquaintances brought forth a volume of detail"译得多么灵活,译文完全不受原文结构的影响,将"any question about her acquaintances"译为"只要是她认识的人,随便问起哪一个";把"brought forth a volume of detail"译为"她都能原原本本地给你说半天",真是把原文短短一句中字里行间的意思表达无遗。特别是把"a volume"译为"原原本本","of detail"译为"半天",这样译再切合原意也没有了,而且译文又地道通顺。

[19] Zeena herself, from an *oppressive reality*, had faded into an *unsubstantial shade*.

连细娜这人也由<u>咄咄逼人</u>的实体褪成一个<u>虚无缥缈</u>的影子。

评析:这"虚无缥缈"和"咄咄逼人"译得实在绝!译者具备雄厚的功力,译出来得心应手。

四、杨必《名利场》佳译赏析

英国小说家萨克雷的《名利场》(*Vanity Fair*)是一部冷嘲热讽皆成文章的佳作。杨必的译文是英译汉的一个很好的译本,其中的佳译值得欣赏学习。

[1] Those virtues which characterise the young English *gentlewoman*, those accomplishments which become her birth and station, *will not be found wanting* in the amiable Miss Sedley, *whose industry and obedience* have endeared her to her instructors, and *whose delightful sweetness* of temper has charmed her aged and her youthful companions.

英国<u>大家闺秀</u>所特有的品德,在她家世和地位上所应有的才学,温良的赛特笠小姐<u>已经具备</u>。<u>她学习勤勉,性情和顺</u>,博得师长们的赞扬,而且<u>她为人温柔可亲</u>,因此校内无论长幼,一致喜爱她。

评析:"gentlewoman"译成"大家闺秀"多么妥帖!"will not be found wanting"译成"已经具备"是反译,也可圈可点,译者已经摆脱了原文,另用中文来表达。"whose industry and obedience"另起一句,尤其巧妙。下面"whose delightful sweetness"又切断了,另外提出,妙不可言。

[2] In fact, the Lexicographer's name was always on the lips of this *majestic* woman, and a visit he had paid to her was the cause of *her reputation and her fortune*.

这位<u>威风凛凛</u>的女人嘴边老是挂着词汇学家的名字,原来他曾经来拜访过她一次,从此使她<u>名利双收</u>。

评析:"威风凛凛"、"名利双收"是极可称赏的译文。

[3] During their interview Pitt Crawley made a great stroke, and one which showed that, had his diplomatic career not been blighted by early neglect, he might have *risen to a high rank* in his profession. When the Countess Dowager of Southdown *fell foul of* the Corsican upstart, as the fashion was in those days...

他们在一起说话的时候,毕脱·克劳莱耍了一下子聪明不过的手段,由此可见若是他早年有人提携,事业上没受挫折的话,做起外交来一定能<u>出头露角</u>。莎吴塞唐老太太随着当时的口气,痛骂那<u>一朝得志的科西嘉小人</u>,……

评析:原文"risen to a high rank"译文用"出头露角"成语,可称"铢两悉称,天衣无缝"。随后的"痛骂那一朝得志的科西嘉小人"译"fell foul of the Corsican upstart"也很精彩。

[4] ...who is a *good* Christian, a *good* parent, child, wife or husband.

……<u>虔</u>诚的教徒,<u>慈爱</u>的父母,<u>孝顺</u>的儿女,<u>贤良</u>的妻子,<u>体贴</u>的丈夫。

评析:根据"词无定译"的原则和译一词应视所搭配的另一词而转化的精神,把"good"这个极通俗的字眼译得五彩缤纷,搭配得恰如其分。

[5] ...on the day Amelia went away, she was in such a passion of tears, that they were obliged to send for Dr Floss...

……爱米丽亚离校那天她哭得死去活来,校里的人只好请了弗络丝医生来……

评析:原来"哭得死去活来"原文是"such a passion of tears",真是巧妙。译者遇到难译的词语只有找中文适当的字词重写。

[6] ...yet Pitt *spoke to her heart* when he lauded both her idols; and by that single speech *made immense progress in her favour*.

可是毕脱对她两个偶像的一顿夸奖,正<u>碰在她心坎上</u>。这一席话,就帮他<u>得了老太太的欢心</u>。

评析:"碰在她心坎上"和"得了老太太的欢心"译文非常地道。反观一下,这两个中文怎么翻译成英文?

[7] James Crawley, when his aunt had last beheld him, was a gawky lad, at that *uncomfortable age* when the voice varies between *an unearthly treble and a preternatural bass...*

詹姆斯的姑妈最后一次看见他的时候,他还是一个笨手笨脚的大孩子。男孩子长到这么<u>尴尬的年龄</u>,说起话来不是<u>尖得像鬼叫</u>,就是<u>哑得怪声怪气</u>……

评析:"尴尬"用来译"uncomfortable"妙极。"unearthly treble"(非人间的童音最高声)译为"尖得像鬼叫","preternatural bass"(异常的低音)译为"哑得怪声怪气"是神来之笔。

[8] "I think you were speaking of *dogs killing rats*," Pitt remarked mildly, handling his cousin the decanter to "buzz."

毕脱把壶递给他,让他喝个干净,一面温和的回答道:"好像是<u>狗拿耗子</u>?"

评析:英文表达和中文表达有同曲同工之妙。

[9] Lady Bareacres and the chiefs of the English society, stupid and irreproachable females, *writhed* with anguish at the *success of the little upstart* Becky, whose poisoned jokes quivered and rankled in their chaste breasts. But she had all the men on her side. She *fought* the woman *with indomitable courage*, and they could not talk scandal in any tongue but their own.

英国上层社会里的尖儿,像贝亚爱格思夫人之流,全是德行兼备的蠢婆子,看着蓓基<u>小人得志</u>,难得<u>坐立不安</u>。蓓基取笑她们的话说得非常刻薄,好像一支毒箭戳进了她们纯洁的胸膛,直痛到心窝里。所有的男人全帮着蓓基。对于那些女的,她拿出<u>不屈不挠</u>的精神跟她们<u>周旋</u>,反正她们只会说本国的语言,不能用法文来诋毁她。

评析:"小人得志"用来译"success of the little upstart"真是可圈可点。其他译文如"坐立不安"、"刻薄"、"不屈不挠"、"周旋"等非常地道。

[10] His blood boiled with honest British exultation, as he saw *the name of Osborne ennobled* in the person of his son, and thought that he might be the progenitor of *a glorious line* of baronets.

这老头是老实的英国人本色,一想到儿子<u>光耀门楣</u>,成了贵人,以后<u>一脉相承</u>,世代都是光荣的从男爵,自己便是老祖宗,不禁得意得浑身暖融融的。

评析:译文把原文句首"his blood boiled"放到最后去,表示结果,这是通盘考虑的功夫。

[11] Of what else *have* young ladies *to think*, but husband? ——*Vanity Fair*

小姐们的心思转来转去不就想着丈夫吗?

评析:谓语动词"have to think of"译为"心思转来转去不就想着",生动得很,添加"转来转去"这些词很有必要。

五、姚克《推销员之死》佳译赏析

美国阿瑟·密勒最著名的剧本《推销员之死》(*Death of a Salesman*)由姚克译成中文,是"极罕见的佳译"(思果,2004)。姚克的翻译能做到完全摆脱原文的桎梏,充分运用舞台语言特点来把握译文,其台词和提示词的译文都非常精彩。其翻译艺术亦同样适用于电影翻译。

[1] A melody is heard, played upon a *flute*. It is *small and fine*, telling of *grass and trees and the horizon*. The curtain rises.

横笛吹来幽雅的曲子,诉说着芳草,佳树和天涯。幕启。

评析:这是《推销员之死》话剧的开场白,是对场景的描写。译文意境优美隽永,其中"横"、"芳"、"佳"都是按照剧情加上去的。而"small and fine"译成"幽雅"、"horizon"译成"天涯",妙绝!仅此一句,译者精妙中文功底展现得淋漓尽致,仿佛原创。"佳树"一词尤佳。佳树,嘉树,良木也。《新唐书·王义方传》:"为御史时,买第,后数日,爱廷中树,复召主人曰:'此佳树,得无欠偿乎?'又予之钱。"唐温庭筠《酬友人》诗:"闲云无定貌,佳树有余荫。"宋苏舜卿《蓝田悟真作》诗:"满岩佳树尤朴檄,赫赤如霞间浓绿。"宋尹洙《水调歌头》:"危亭好景,佳树修竹绕回塘。"

[2] The flute plays on. He hears but *is not aware of it*.

笛声洋洋盈耳,还在吹奏着,可是他好像没听见。

评析:"好像没听见",非常自然,不过思果认为改译成"听而不觉"更好。

[3] (*resigned*) Well, you'll just have to take a rest, Willy, you can't continue this way.

(没话可说):那么,你只有休息一阵了,惟利,这样挨下去不是个办法。

评析:"没话可说"用来译"resigned"是大手笔,译成"叹口气"已经不错了(思果语)。"这样挨下去不是个办法"也很地道。

[4] (*with wonder*) I was driving along, you understand? And I was fine. I *was even observing* the scenery.

(暗暗称奇地):我一路开着车,你明白?我精神非常好。还贪看风景呢。

评析:"暗暗称奇地"原文里没有"暗暗"。译者有时觉得不加意思不明白或不连贯,这很重要。中文不就是这个意思吗?"贪看"也译得妙!译者看着外文,常常写不出自己的中国话。

[5] They don't need me in New York. I'm the New England man. I'm *vital* in New England.

我到纽约去,对他们没用处。我是跑新英格兰的。在新英格兰我可吃得开。

评析:整个句子处理得非常灵活。"I'm the New England man"成了"我是跑新英格兰的","vital"结合上下文译成了"吃得开",怎么也想不到!姚克的译文,真是雅到极致,俗得彻底。

[6] Linda You've got too much on the ball to worry about.

Willy *You're my foundation and my support*, Linda.

林达:像你这样精明能干的人,我还担什么心哪?

惟利:要是没有你,我在哪儿扎根儿?我靠谁撑腰?

评析:"扎根儿"全用来译"You're my foundation and my support",真是才人之笔,改写得天衣无缝(思果语),该句运用了拆译、词性转换等技巧。

[7] (*with enthusiasm*) Listen, why don't you come out West with me?

(提起兴致)你听着,你为什么不跟我一块儿到西部去呢?

评析:一般人可能译成"热情地、积极地",远不如"提起兴致"从容。

[8] Willy's form is dimly seen below the darkened kitchen. . . . Music insinuates itself as the leaves appear.

惟利的影子早已隐约可见。……树叶显现时,音乐依稀可闻。

评析:"隐约"、"依稀"都是极抒情的词。

[9] Terrific. Terrific job, boys. *Good work*, Biff.

绝!绝活儿,孩子们。功夫到家了,比夫。

评析:"功夫到家"原来译的是"Good work!"整句话都很精彩。

[10] Well, I borrowed it from the locker room.(He laughs *confidentially*)

得了,我是从储藏室"借"来的。(他会心地笑着。)

评析:"会心地"译的是"confidentially"。按译文用"借"来代替"偷",彼此自家人心照不宣,"会心"用得很巧妙。

[11] *You're supposed* to pass.

照规矩,你该传球才是。

评析:"You're supposed to"译成"照规矩"非常别致。

[12] (laughs *appreciatively*) You better go down and tell them what to do, Biff.

(欣赏地笑着)你不如下去,给他们出主意吧,比夫。

评析:思果认为译成"欣赏地"虽准确,但略嫌不很明白,建议改译"领略他的用意地"。

[13] Bernard is *not well liked*, is he?

勃纳德的人缘不太好,是不是?

评析:译成"不太讨人喜欢"已很不错,但用"人缘不太好"译 not well liked 更是妙极。

[14] Willy You go ahead. I'm not tired at the moment.

Happy (to Willy) *Take it easy*, huh? (*He exits*)

惟利:你先睡吧,这会儿我还不累。

海庇:(向惟利)别劳神了,呃?(下。)

评析:"Take it easy"译成"别劳神了"是根据上下文重写的。"下"上省去了"He",可见汉语惜墨如金的功能。

[15] (*hesitantly*) All right. You got cards?

(举棋不定地)得。你有纸牌吗?

评析:姚克对剧本中的提示词翻译真见功夫。"hesitantly"译成"举棋不定地"。其他佳译还有:with infinite patience(尽量忍耐着);lost(出神);with a deep sentiment(一往情深);enthralled(喜出望外);indignantly(愤愤不平);angrily(恼羞成怒、盛怒地、愤然、忿然);with youthful energy(洋溢着年轻的精力);The smile goes(笑容忽敛);with great feeling(情见乎辞);exploding at her(向她咆哮如雷);gallantly(彬彬有礼地);giving great weight to each word(字字千钧);getting angry(捺不住火);trying to stop them(慌忙阻止他);wildly enthused(欣喜若狂);furiously(怒不可遏)。

[16] I got nothin' to give him, Charley, I'm *clean*, I'm *clean*.

我没有什么给他,查理,我是两袖清风,两袖清风。

评析:"clean"原来可以如此译法。

[17] He is a *stolid* man, in his sixties, with a mustache and an *authoritative* air. He is utterly certain of his destiny, and there is an aura of far places about him.

他是个木讷的老人,年纪六十多岁。上唇一撮小胡子,俨然有一呼百诺的气概,他对自己的命运有绝对把握,他的周围有一种远方绝域的雾团。

评析:用"木讷"译"stolid"非常适合,用"一呼百诺"译"authoritative"也非常贴切。但"他的周围有一种远方绝域的雾团"显然不知所云,原文的表达也确实比较抽象,这就是翻译中的疑难杂症,高手如姚克也无可奈何,圣手如思果似乎也避而不谈。本处的译文应该是"他有种可望而不可及的气派"。

[18] (turning to him) *You ought to be ashamed of yourself*!

(转身向他)别死不要脸了!

评析:真亏译者能想得到这样的改写!照原文译出来不是中国人说的话。翻译的人容易给原文牵着鼻子走。这是对原文的改写。

[19] Willy That's just the way I'm bringing them up, Ben—*rugged, well liked, all-around*.

Ben Yeah?(to Biff)Hit that, boy—*hard as you can*.(He pounds his stomach)

惟利:我就是这样把他们教养长大的,本——要吃得起苦,人缘好,文的武的什么都拿得起。

本:是吗?(向比夫):打我一拳,孩子,下死劲儿打。(他捶打自己的肚子)

评析:"rugged, well liked, all-around"译得非常地道;"下死劲儿打"原来译的"hard as you can",也改得好。

[20] Why, Biff can fell any one of these trees *in not time*!

啊,这些树,随便哪一棵,比夫不消一眨眼的功夫,就能把它砍倒。

评析:"不消一眨眼的功夫"译的是"in not time",一般人都只会译成"立即、迅速"。

[21] Willy, the jails are full of *fearless characters*.

惟利,天不怕地不怕的好汉,监狱里满都是。

评析:"fearless characters"译成"天不怕地不怕的好汉",你想得到吗?

[22] (*sarcastically*) Glad to hear it, Willy. Come in later, we'll shoot a little casino. I'll *take some of your Portland money*.(He *laughs* at Willy and exits)

(缺德地):我听了都开心,惟利。待会儿进去,咱俩打几手卡西诺牌;你朴特兰的佣钱,好让我也沾点儿油水。(他在冷嘲热讽的笑声中下场)

评析:"Sarcastically"译"缺德地",换了说法。一般人肯定译成"讥讽地",思果认为这不是中国人的说法。"Laugh"根据上下文补充为"冷嘲热讽的笑声中",妙极。

[23] Business is *bad*, it's *murderous*. But not for me, of course.

市面不景气,简直是谋财害命。

评析:"bad"译成"不景气","murderous"译成"谋财害命"再好不过了。上面讲的是"business"(译成"市面"),当然和银钱有关,所以才用"谋财"。

[24] I'll *be late* for my train.

我要赶不上火车了。

评析:简单明了,非常口语化。

[25] I know, dear, I know. But he likes to have a letter. Just to know that *there's still a possibility for better things.*

我知道,好孩子,我知道。可是他盼着你来信。他只想知道:<u>瓦片儿也有翻身的日子</u>。

评析:"瓦片儿也有翻身的日子"是对原文巧妙改写。铢两悉称,天衣无缝,是高手的翻译(思果语)。

[26] No. You can't just come to see me, because I love him. (*With a threat, but only a threat, of tears*) He's the dearest man in the world to me, and I won't have anyone making him *feel unwanted and low and blue*.

不可能。你不能单只来看我,因为我爱他。(<u>泪汪汪地,但没哭出来</u>。)在我心目中他是世界上最亲爱的人,我不许任何人对他态度不好,<u>使他觉得消沉,忧郁,受人家厌弃</u>。

评析:括弧里的"泪汪汪地,但没哭出来"译的是"with a threat, but only a threat, of tears",原文的意思是要哭没哭出来,只流了泪,这样译完全译了出来而文字更简洁生动。后面的话"feel unwanted and low and blue"译成"使他觉得消沉,忧郁,受人家厌弃",译得自然好懂。

[27] Never had an ounce of respect for you.

一丁点儿没放你在眼里。

评析:非常妥贴!

[28] People are worse off than Willy Loman. *Believe me*, I've seen them!

比惟利·罗门更倒霉的人多着呢。<u>不冤你</u>,我亲眼看见过!

评析:"不冤你"原来译的是"Believe me"。如果译成"相信我"成什么话?当然也可以用"不骗你"、"说实话"都可以。

[29] But he's human being, and a terrible thing is happening to him. So *attention must be paid*.

可是他是一个人,而且眼前他正在大难临头的关口。一定要<u>小心照顾他</u>。

评析:"小心照顾他"原文只是"attention"这个字,又是一个不容易译的。

[30] Those *ungrateful* bastards!

这帮子没良心的狗杂种!

评析:"ungrateful"译成"没良心的",妙极!

[31] Last month…(*With great difficulty*) Oh, boys, it's so hard to say a thing like this! He's just a big stupid man to you, but I tell you *there's more good in him than in many other people*.

上个月……(<u>嗫嚅地</u>)呃,孩子们,这样的事简直说不出口!你们觉得他不过是个大傻瓜,可是我告诉你们:<u>要论心肠好,比不上他的人多着呢</u>。

评析:括弧内"嗫嚅地"用来译"With great difficulty",真亏他想得出来,这是"才人之笔"(思果语,2004:190)。"there's more good in him than in many other people"也不容易译,所以反过来说,也就是换个角度来说。这些都表现出译者活译的聪明智慧,也可以教会人怎样活译。

[32] (kissing her) All right, pal, all right. It's all settled now. I've been remiss. I know that, mom. But now I'll stay, and I swear to you, I'll apply myself. (Kneeling in front of her, *in a fever of* self-reproach) It's just-you see, Mom, I

don't fit in business. Not that I won't try. I'll try, and *I'll make good*.

(亲亲林妲):得了,好妈妈,得了。现在什么都解决了。我一直没尽我的责任。我是知道的,妈。可是现在我不走了,我对你起誓,我一定争气。(跪在她面前,痛心疾首地责备自己)只为——你明白,妈,我做生意不合适,并不是我不肯努力。我愿意努力,我要争口气。

评析:"痛心疾首"译的是"in a fever of"(高度兴奋),甚好。"I'll make good"译成"我要争口气",很到位。

六、傅东华《飘》佳译赏析

[1] Their family had more money, more horses, more slaves than anyone else in the County, but the boys *had less grammar* than most of their poor Cracker neighbours.

他们家里的钱比人家多,马比人家多,奴隶人家多,都要算全区第一,所缺少的只是他哥儿俩肚里的墨水,少得也是首屈一指的。

评析:"grammar"译成"墨水"好极,"语法"在中文里没有引申义,而"墨水"有。

[2] She was hot-tempered and *easily* plagued by the frequent scrapes of her four sons.

她的脾气本来很暴躁,再经不得这四位少爷常常出岔子,所以动不动就大发雷霆。

评析:这句中的副词"easily"译为"动不动"非常生动传神;其次,这里的谓语动词被动语态"plagued"和后接的状语短语"by the frequent scrapes"也译得很顺。

[3] "You know there isn't going to be any war," said Scarlett, *bored*.

"哪来的什么战争!"思嘉不耐烦地说。

评析:"不耐烦"译"bored",好极。思果赞曰:"傅先生不愧为大译家,就凭这一句,他就在众人之上了"(2004:13)。

[4] "I do, and a sillier old lady *I never met in all my life*."

"这个我知道,一个傻老太婆,我一辈子也没见过第二个。"

评析:用"一辈子也没见过第二个"来译"I never met in all my life"非常好。

[5] The patient hounds lay down again in the soft red dust and looked *longingly* at the chimney swallows circling in the gathering dusk.

那一群猎犬也就在那软红土上坐了下来,馋涎欲滴地望着一群在暮色苍茫中盘旋的燕子。

评析:"longingly"译成"馋涎欲滴",而不是"渴望地"。

[6] Well, it wouldn't be right to make Jeems *face what we don't want to face*. We'll have to take him.

"不过,己所不欲,勿施于人,咱们自家儿受不了的事,也不该叫阿金去受。咱们还是带她同走罢。"

评析:"己所不欲,勿施于人"添进去很适宜。这可见傅先生的中文好。

[7] She was as *forthright* and simple as the winds that blew over Tara and the yellow river that wound about it, and to the end of her days she would never be able to understand a complexity.

她是一条肚肠通到底的,头脑非常简单,简单到象陶乐场上吹过的风,陶乐场边环流的水,因而直到她的末日,她也不会懂得一件机构复杂的东西。

评析:"一条肚肠通到底"是"forthright"的具体化。

练习题

[1] What we were offered was a *big fat zero*.

[2] Carter is *shooting at oil* now, but who will be next?

[3] *That notion is being nurtured* by people.

[4] You may go further and fare worse.

[5] She should learn and *indulge his habits*.

[6] Public opinion was *aroused* and the Republican spokesman held a press conference to *explain away the matter*.

[7] On Taiwan there was *little grace* and *less give*.

[8] My husband knew that I would not be *satisfied* to be merely an *official hostess*.

[9] Edward, later Duke of Windsor, rather *steals* the book.

[10] Ellsberg recalled that Kissinger was "*very, very critical*" of Nixon.

[11] Don't *sir me so much*.

[12] He sought *the distraction of distance*.

[13] No one had promised any man that life is *easy* here.

[14] I wasn't *born yesterday*.

[15] His visit *marked* the 30th anniversary of the university.

[16] You don't know *how much she means to me*.

[17] This truth *goes everywhere*.

[18] He *has known praise and hatred*, and *has gone from cheers to jeers*.

[19] Don't be taken in by *what he says*; it isn't true.

[20] The picture *flattered* her.

[21] I used to be a *politician*. But since I came back from Peking I have been a statesman.

[22] Feeling was inflamed by dispatches from London emphasizing the lack of *aggressive* spirit in the British troops.

[23] *To be something and somebody* was Harriman's fondest wish for Averell.

[24] She was a *force to be reckoned with*. She was *somebody*.

[25] "If we die," he once had said, "we want people to *accept it*."

[26] The country *not agreeing with* her, she returned to England.

[27] The President wants a Chinese face or two to add to *the fraternity*.

[28] John was *a fool for danger*.

[29] Foreign Minister Ismail Fahmy accused the Israelis *of bad faith*.

[30] Is it a *poor man* like me, that has to be *going the roads and singing in fairs*, to have the name on him that he took a reward?

[31] I suppose he will be *awfully proud*, and *I shall be treated most contemptuously*.

Still I must *bear my hard lot* as well as I can.

[32] She felt that she *must not yield*, she must go on leading her straightened, humdrum life. This was her punishment for having made a mistake. *She had made her bed, and she must lie on it.*——Theodore Dreiser

[33] They will be *ice-sating in hell* the day when I vote the aid for them.

[34] You'd better *pull up your socks* next term.

[35] She's the sort of woman who *likes to be very much in evidence*.

[36] In spite of *the Herculian efforts* made by the enemy, the plot ended in a fiasco.

[37] Where all think alike, no one *thinks very much*.

[38] At 22, he had first learned *what it is* to be a Negro.

[39] Hitler was *the fate* of the German people.

[40] It was *a veritable pandemonium*.

第四节 巧译英语意美、音美、形美

　　翻译不但要译意,还要译音、译形,争取意美、音美、形美(许渊冲,1984:52)。但要翻译得如此十全十美又谈何容易?因为在翻译过程中,我们很难在音位、字位、语法、词汇各层次做到和原文完全对等(equivalent),最多只能做到一个平面上的对等。这个理论对于翻译双关语、修辞表达等是有指导意义的。双关语之所以难翻,是因为要求译文在语义和修辞效果上和原有双关语平行对等是办不到的。译者只能两者取其一,或者翻译意义或者从修辞结构(音位、字形等)入手,尽量译出双关,而放弃意义。在这种理论指导下,甚至可以干脆追求其中的声音效果,而把原文的意义完全抛到一边。因为在原文中,语义是为形式服务的,而在译文中,既然原来的意义不能再为形式对等服务,那么译者完全可以把语义加以改变,以适应形式的对等。我们从电影《音乐之声》(*The Sound of Music*)中的歌曲"哆咪咪"发现四种译文的趣味对比:

[1] Doe, a deer, a female deer, Ray, a drop of golden sun.
　　译文一:Doe 是鹿,是一头母鹿,Ray 是金色阳光。
　　译文二:"哆"是一只小母鹿 /"来",一束金色阳光。
　　译文三:哆,我的朋友多 /来,大家来唱歌。
　　译文四:朵,美丽的花朵。/来呀,大家都快来!
Me, a name I call myself, Far, a long long way to run.
　　译文一:Me 是我,是我自己,Far 是奔向远方。
　　译文二:"咪"是称呼我自己 /"发"前面道路远又长。
　　译文三:"咪",呀大家笑眯眯 /发呀,发出光和热。
　　译文四:密,你们来猜秘密。/发,猜中我把奖发。
Sew, a needle pulling thread, La, a note to follow sew.
　　译文一:Sew 是穿针引线,La 跟在 Sew 后面走。

译文二:"索"是穿针又引线 /"拉"是音符跟着"索"。
译文三:"索"能拴住门和窗 /拉呀 大家来拉车。
译文四:索,大家用心思索。/拉,快点猜莫拖拉。
Tea, a drink with jam and bread. That will bring us back to doe.
译文一:Tea 是喝茶加点心。那就重又回到 Doe。
译文二:"梯"是饮料茶点 /然后我们来唱"哆"。
译文三:"西"太阳已归西 /然后我们来唱"哆"。
译文四:体,怎样练好身体,做茁壮成长的花朵。

评析:押韵是原文的主要特征,目的是增强趣味性。译文一和译文二基本都是死译原文的字、词,不能传递原文的妙处。译文三和译文四虽然有异,但思路是一致的,他们大胆抛弃原文的后半部,而根据关键词改造表达结构。这才是真正忠实于原文的功能和目的,较完美地体现了许渊冲所说的"意美、音美、形美"。(译文一、四摘自祝吉芳,2004;译文二、三摘自黄少政,http://www.culstudies.com)

[2] At last, a *candid candidate*!
终于找到了一个<u>厚道的候选人</u>!

评析:英文斜体部分的词形、音相近,如果译成:"到底找到了一个老实的候选人!"那就只传达了原文的意思而没有表达原文的音美。如果改成:"忠厚的"或"脸皮不太厚的候选人",那么,"厚"字和"候"字声音相同,多少传达了一点原文的音美和讽刺的意美。

[3] Able was I ere I saw Elba!
译文一:我在看到厄尔巴之前曾是强有力的。——钱歌川译文
译文二:不到俄岛我不倒。——许渊冲译文
译文三:落败孤岛孤败落。——马红军译文

评析:据说这是1814年各国联军攻陷巴黎后,拿破仑皇帝被放逐于地中海的厄尔巴(Elba)荒岛时人们对他的戏讽。该句的妙处在于它的形貌特征,因为无论从左看到右,还是反向看,英文字母的排列顺序都完全相同,是一个典型的回文句(palindrome)。这种形美,很不容易甚至是不可能翻译的。钱歌川只是译出了原文的意思,但原文的"妙味"则无法传递。许渊冲根据汉语"不见棺材不落泪",把这句译成:"不到俄岛我不倒。""岛"和"倒"同韵,"到"和"倒"、"我"和"俄"音似、形似,加上"不"字重复,可以说是用音美来译形美了。但更佳的译文当为译文三。译文和原文碰巧都是七个字。译文没有出现"厄尔巴"三字,而以"孤岛"代替,事实上厄尔巴岛也是孤岛,这个"孤"字更能体现出拿破仑的处境。而且,这个"孤"还和后面的"孤"相呼应,过去的皇帝称自己为"孤"。句首的"落败"二字表示拿破仑兵败滑铁卢后被囚于该岛之意,而句末的"败落"也是表示拿破仑的穷途末路。此译文的妙处是,顺念倒念意思完全相同,字也完全一样,是一个地道的汉语回文句,且具有一定的寓意。我们不能不佩服译者的精巧构思。

[4] It was a splendid population—for all the *slow, sleepy, sluggish-brained sloths stayed* at home.
译文一:这是一批卓越能干的人民——因为所有这些<u>行动迟缓、瞌睡稀稀、呆如树獭</u>的人都留在家乡了。——余立三译文
译文二:那是一批卓越的人——因为那些<u>慢慢吞吞、昏昏沉沉、反应迟钝、形如树獭</u>的人留在了家乡。——杨莉藜译文

译文三：这是一批卓越能干的人民——因为那些<u>行动迟缓、头脑迟钝、睡眼惺忪、呆如树獭</u>的人留在了家乡。——章和升译文

译文四：（出来的）这帮人个个出类拔萃——因为凡是<u>呆板、呆滞、呆头呆脑的呆子都呆</u>在了家里。——马红军译文

评析：在这个句子里，作者用了五个头韵词（Alliteration）与前面的"splendid"呼应，词义色彩则正好相反，造成了强烈的诙谐和幽默的效果。一般说来，谐音押韵，如头韵、尾韵等的修辞效果是"不可译"的，因为翻译时不得不照顾词义，而破坏了韵律与声调，虽然汉语有双声和叠韵，但把这句中的"slow, sleepy, sluggish-brained sloths stayed"五个词的头韵翻译出来，几乎是不可能的。前三个译文虽然有不少可取之处，但作为一句名言，在音、形、意、神方面还有很大差距，总觉得有令人不满意的地方，马红军则比较精彩地传递了这点。译者用五个"呆"字，翻译出了五个押"s"字母的头韵词，真可谓巧夺天工，拍案称妙。

[5] If we don't *hang together*, we shall most assuredly *hang separately*. —Franklin

译文一：咱们要不<u>摞到一块儿</u>，保准会<u>吊到一块儿</u>。

译文二：我们不<u>紧紧抱在一起</u>，准保会<u>吊在一起</u>。

译文三：如果我们不能<u>紧密地团结在一起</u>，那就必然<u>分散地走上绞刑台</u>。

译文四：我们不<u>紧紧团结一致</u>，必然<u>一个个被人绞死</u>。

译文五：我们必须<u>共同上战场</u>，否则就得<u>分别上刑场</u>。

译文六：我们必须<u>共赴沙场</u>，否则就得<u>分赴法场</u>。

译文七：如果我们不<u>抱成一团</u>，就会被<u>吊成一串</u>。

评析：这是富兰克林在《独立宣言》上签名时说的话，英文句子妙用两个"hang"。我们把译文和原文作一比较就会感到，原文掷地有声，意味深长，使人过目不忘，玩笑的口吻中透着严肃，具有名言警句的特征。译文一至四过于口语化，上下句联系不够自然、紧凑，在力度上与原文也有很大的差距。译文五至七则注意到用中文双关语重构，效果才能真正体现。译文五用两个"场"体现出原句的两个"hang"，其修辞效果和原文比较接近，但不够上口。译文七用"抱成一团"对应"hang together"，而"抱成一团"在中文里有团结在一起的含义，用"吊成一串"对应"hang separately"，同时"一团"和"一串"谐音。译文六与译文七一庄一谐，不分高下，皆是精致译文。

[6] I am never at a loss *for a word*; Pitt is never at a loss *for the word*.

译文一：我总是能凑合找个词儿说说，可是皮特什么时候都能找到恰如其分的词儿。

译文二：我总能找到<u>一个词</u>，而皮特总能找到<u>那个绝妙好词</u>。

译文三：我总能找到<u>一个觉得妙的词</u>，而皮特总能找到<u>那个绝妙的词</u>。

译文四：我总能找到一个意思相当的词，而皮特总能找到那个意思恰当的词。

译文五：我总是<u>滔滔不绝</u>，而皮特则是<u>字字珠玑</u>。——马红军译文

译文六：我和皮特都能出口成章，但我用的词大都<u>不可言妙</u>，而他用的总是<u>妙不可言</u>。

评析："a word"和"the word"系原句的精华所在，体现出英语的简约之美，不着一个修饰词，但意味深长。译文各个费尽九牛二虎之力。译文一略嫌啰嗦；译文二比较简洁明快，也最合原意，但略显平白；译文三用"觉得妙"对"绝妙"，但与原文前半句含义出入较大；译文四不如原文简明有力；译文五最为精炼，前后对比鲜明，但还是不如原文简约；译文六含文字

游戏,"不可言妙"对"妙不可言"。

[7] He tried to *shake* off his fear, and actually *shook* his head.

译文一:他想驱除内心的恐惧,但实际上只摇了摇头,仿佛表示驱除不了。

译文二:他拼命想摆脱内心的恐惧,结果只无奈地摆了摆头。

评析:从原文理解上说并不难,但从翻译的角度看,却相当难译,因为作者在这里使用了文字游戏——"a play of words",用了两个"shake"。前一个是"虚"的,因与"off"结合,把原义"摇晃"引申成"get rid of"(去掉);第二个是"实"的,用的是原词义。这里存在一个形式与内容的统一问题。译文二巧妙地在"摆脱内心的恐惧"和"摆了摆头"上达到了形式与内容的统一。

[8] A little more than *kin*, and less than *kind*.

译文一:超乎寻常的亲族,漠不相干的路人。——朱生豪译文

译文二:亲上加亲,越亲越不相亲。——卞之琳译文

译文三:比亲戚亲一点,说亲人却说不上。——曹未风译文

译文四:比侄子是亲些,可是还算不得儿子。——梁实秋译文

译文五:说不亲亲上亲,说亲又不亲。——张今译文

评析:比较起来,卞之琳译得最好,其他三家都着力不够,略逊一筹,译文五是对卞译的进一步改进。

[9] I love my love with an *E*, because she's *enticing*; I hate her with an *E*, because she's *engaged*; I took her to the sign of the *exquisite*, and treated her with an *elopement*; her name's *Emily*, and she lives in the *east*. (Dickens: *David Copperfield*)

译文一:我爱我的爱人为了一个 E,因为她是 Enticing(迷人的);我恨我的爱人为了一个 E,因为她是 Engaged(订了婚了)。我用我的爱人象征 Exquisite(美妙),我劝我的爱人从事 Elopement(私奔),她的名字是 Emily(爱弥丽),她的住处在 East(东方)。(董秋斯译文,1980)

译文二:我爱我的爱,因为她长得实在招人爱。我恨我的爱,因为她不回报我的爱。我带着她到挂着浮荡子招牌的一家,和她谈情说爱。我请她看一出潜逃私奔,为的是我和她能长久你亲我爱。她的名字叫爱弥丽,她的家住在爱仁里。(张谷若译文,上海译文出版社,1980)(转引自连淑能,2006)

译文三:我爱我的爱人,因为她很迷人;我恨我的爱人,因已许配他人;她在我心中是美人,我带她私奔,以避开外人;她名叫虞美人,是东方丽人。

译文四:我爱我的那个"丽",可爱迷人有魅力;我恨我的那个"丽",和他人结伉俪;她文雅大方又美丽,和我出逃去游历;她芳名就叫爱米丽,家住东方人俏丽。——马红军译文

译文五:吾爱吾爱,因伊可爱;吾恨吾爱,因伊另有可爱;吾视吾爱,神圣之爱;吾爱名爱米丽,吾东方之爱。

译文六:我爱我的心上人,因为她是那样地叫人入迷(Enticing)。我恨我的心上人,因为她已订婚将作他人妻(Engaged)。我的心上人花容月貌无可比拟(Exquisite),我劝她离家出走跟我在一起(Elopement)。她的名字叫爱米莉(Emily),她的家就在东城里(East)。我为我的心上人呀,一切都因为这个 E!

评析：原文是狄更斯小说《大卫·科波菲尔》第 22 章中的一首英文打油诗,全部运用嵌入句,即每一小句最后一个单词都是以同一字母"E"开头。译文一翻译出了原诗的命题意义,却没有处理好原文里的文字游戏,中英文混杂,是个半成品,让不懂英文的人费解。译文二读起来一气呵成,朗朗上口;译者把原文中重复出现的成分——字母"E",统一归化成汉语的双元音"ai"(爱),非常巧妙地同时传达出原文的指称意义和言内意义。遗憾的是,译文内容与原诗稍有偏离,如"不回报我的爱"、"挂着浮荡子招牌"、"住在爱仁里"都是原文所没有的。译文三就形式上看,基本做到了所有的诗行都以同一个"人"字结尾,从而再现了原文的艺术形象。但"虞美人"用得不恰当,"东方丽人"也给人误解。译文四也译得不错,只是"丽"字重复率太高(5 次)。译文五形式和内容上基本传递了原文,但在风格上用汉语的文言体显然与原文明快自然的笔调不符。译文六不仅在形式上完全再现了原诗的特征,而且在内容上也较贴切。里面的英文基本可以脱离译文,可惜晚节不保,问题出在最后一个"E"上面。这叫不懂英文的人如何明白?可否改译成"情意绵绵始终如一"?

［10］ Out of *sight*, out of *mind*.

　　译文一：眼不见,心不烦。

　　译文二：眼不见,心不念。

评析：从两个译文的谐音效果来看,译文二似乎更佳。

［11］ Without the sound of *drums*, *Cuba* would not exist.

　　没有鼓声,就没有古巴。

评析：鼓乐数百年前由非洲奴隶传到古巴,成为古巴音乐的支柱。一些古巴音乐家认为古巴应以鼓乐为国乐。上述这句话是一位音乐家说的。原文没有文字机关,但译文却在"鼓"和"古"上造出了谐音,可以肯定地说,这个译文胜过原文。

［12］ A fool and his words are soon parted; a man of genius and his money.

　　蠢才轻其言,天才轻其钱。

评析：原文后半部有省略。其意为：傻瓜记不住说过的话,天才存不住手里的钱。译文将"fool"译成"蠢才",正好和"天才"对仗。"言"与"钱"也押韵。这些修辞都是原文所没有的,可以说艺术性更高。

［13］ Better *late* than the *late*.

　　译文一：迟到总比丧命好。

　　译文二：迟了总比死了好。

　　译文三：宁愿晚点,勿要玩命。

　　译文四：宁迟一时,不辞一世。

　　译文五：慢行回家,快行回老家。

　　译文六：晚了总比完了好。

评析：这是美国高速公路上的一则安全警示语,叫人不要超速行驶。趣味就在这则公示语连用了两个 late。Late 一词含"迟到"和"已故"的双义。原文用词精准、含蓄幽默。译文一、二和三过于直白,中文忌讳这么写;译文四有音韵对仗,但不易上口;译文五传达出了形韵("回家"对"回老家")。译文六的音韵好,且含蓄,最佳。无独有偶,在深圳深南大道有这么一幅大型交通告示牌"飞速一时,毁人一世",堪称旗鼓相当。

［14］ Change is part of life and the making of character, hon. When things happen that you do not like, you have two choices：You get *bitter* or *better*.

变化是生活的一部分,而且也塑造了人的意志品德,亲爱的。当你不喜欢的事情发生了,你有两种选择:要么痛苦不堪;要么痛快达观。

评析:英语头韵(alliteration)得以在译文中完美体现。

[15] Romeo: What has thou found?

　　　Mercutio: No *hare*, sir.

　　　罗:你发现了什么?

　　　墨:倒不是野鸡,先生。

评析:这是莎士比亚《罗密欧与朱丽叶》第二幕第四场中 Mercutio 讽刺老乳母为娼妓时的对话。"hare"一词二义,既指野兔,亦指娼妓,但在中文里"野兔"并无"娼妓"这样的双关,与"娼妓"双关的是"野鸡"。因此梁实秋先生大胆地把"野兔"变"野鸡",形成完美的谐音。机巧之妙,堪称一绝。

[16] "Did you say '*pig*' or '*fig*'?" said the cat.

　　　"I said '*pig*'," replied Alice.

　　　"你刚才是说'猪'还是'鼠'?"那只猫问道。

　　　"我说的是'猪',"爱丽丝说。

评析:这是英语儿童读物《爱丽丝漫游仙境》中爱丽丝与猫的对话。句中"fig"的出现因与"pig"同韵,才使"猫"听不明白,如果将"fig"译成"无花果",只是照搬了原文的词语,不能体现原文的韵味,因此,译文大胆地将 fig(无花果)转译成"鼠",这里,"鼠"是为了配合"猪"的音韵的。举一反三,我们同样也可以用"虎"、"兔"或其他任何谐音字来替换。

[17] "Mine is a long and a *sad tale*!" said the Mouse, turning to Alice, and sighing.

　　　"It is a *long tail*, certainly," said Alice, looking down with wonder at the Mouse's tail, "but why do you call it *sad*?"

　　　那老鼠对爱丽丝叹了口气道:"唉,说来话长!真叫我委屈!"

　　　"尾曲?!"爱丽丝听了,瞧着老鼠那光滑的尾巴说:"你这尾巴明明又长又直,为什么说它曲呢?!"——马红军译文

评析:这真是绝妙译文:"委屈"和"尾曲"同音异形,修辞手法及幽默风趣基本相当。

[18] "I beg your pardon," said Alice very humbly, "you had got to the fifth bend, I think?"

　　　"I had *not*!" cried the Mouse, sharply and very angrily.

　　　"A *knot*!" said Alice, always ready to make herself useful, and looking anxiously about her. "Oh, do let me help to undo it!"

　　　"请原谅,"爱丽丝很恭顺地说:"我想你是讲到第五个弯了,不是吗?"

　　　那老鼠很凶很怒地道:"我没有到!"

　　　爱丽丝道:"你没有刀吗?让我给你找一把吧!"——赵元任译文

评析:译文用"到"和"刀"巧妙地再现了原文的幽默。

[19] dooooooooooooog ——James Joyce, *Ulysses*

　　　狗狗狗……天 ——萧乾译文

　　　猪猪猪…… ——金隄译文

评析:出现在《尤利西斯》(*Ulysses*)这本奇书里的这个词,是乔伊斯的妙用,是以"dog"为"god"的前后倒置,萧乾的译法是按语意译为"狗狗狗……天",而金隄译成"猪猪猪……",

这是用了汉语中"猪"与"主"同音。原文以变字形成趣,金译文改以谐音成趣,已尽力体现了原文化用字词的妙处,异曲同工。

[20] What flower does everybody have? —*Tulips*. (Tulips＝two lips)

人人都有的花是什么花？——泪花。

评析：可以看出,译文"泪花"已经不同于原文里的答案"郁金香"。译文的前半部是直译原文的,关键在后半部起了变化。它根据译文前半部重造,忠实于原文的修辞意图。由此类推,我们还可以"心花"、"脑花"和"老花"。

[21] The professor tapped on his desk and shouted："Young men, *Order*!"—The entire class yelled："Beer!"

译文一：教授敲击桌子喊道："年轻人,请安静!"——学生："啤酒!"[注：英语的"order"含歧义：请安静；点菜,要饮料]

译文二：教授敲击桌子喊道："你们这些年轻人吆喝（要喝）什么?"——学生："啤酒!"

译文三：教授敲击桌子喊道："小伙子们,你们叫什么叫?"
　　　　学生："叫啤酒!"

评析：译文一完全无法传递原文的妙处,只能做些解释,读者也许能懂,但译文本身是不成功的。译文二则机智地找到汉语谐音词来再现原文的机关,方能妙趣横生。译文三的"叫"也体现了这个字的多义性。

[22] You reckon your *Dodge* would help you up to all these *dodges* again?

译文一：你以为坐上你的道奇车就可以再次逃之夭夭?

译文二：你以为坐上你的道奇跑车就可以再次跑掉么?——马红军译文

评析：这是一个警官对他抓到的作案者说的一句话。句中"Dodge"是美国"道奇"牌小汽车,它与普通词"dodge"（逃跑）语义相关。原文透出该警官对作案者的讥讽,译文一无法体现这层含义,译文二则巧妙地加了"跑"字,这就使前后两个"跑"字发生了联系,原句的形韵和幽默味道多少有所体现。

[23] The *output* of the United Nations has not been commensurate with the *input*.

译文一：联合国的贡献与其花费已经不相称了。——《英汉翻译概要》

译文二：联合国的作用已难抵其费用。——马红军译文

评析：译文一未尝不可,意思也对,但译文的分量与趣味明显不如原文。英文中的"input"和"output"由于"形状"相近而形成明显的反差。译文一未能译出原文的形韵。译文二则简洁有力,非常成功。

[24] The *ballot* is stronger than the *bullet*.

译文一：选举权比子弹更具威力。

译文二：选票比大炮更具威力。

译文三：选票胜于枪炮。

译文四：选单胜过子弹。

评析：这是一句林肯的名言。林肯所以用"bullet"和"ballot"相比,是由于两者既音似且形似,译文一里"选举权"和"子弹"之间缺乏音韵及字形上的对称关系,因此译文不理想。译文二、三较好地传达了原文的音韵特征,但译文四在音韵和字形上和原文更加贴近。

[25] "Why is the river rich?"

"Because it has two *banks*."
"为什么说河水富有？"
译文一："因为它总向前(钱)流。"
译文二："因为它年年有余(鱼)呀。"
译文三："因为有(油)水呀。"

评析：原文"bank"是双关语，一指河岸，二指银行。中文当然不可能有这样的对等词。译文的谐音双关，和原文的一词多义表面上格格不入，但在修辞效果上是一致的。

[26] The life that is too *short* for the happy is too *long* for the miserable.
译文一：对幸福的人来说短暂的生活对受苦的人来说则是漫长的。
译文二：幸福的人嫌命短，受苦的人嫌命长。
译文三：幸福者苦命短，苦命者苦命长。

评析：译文一阅读吃力费解，译文二和译文三则从对仗、音韵等美学层次来还原汉语表达的本来面目。

[27] Paris n'a pas été bati dans un *four*.
建设巴黎非叹息(旦夕)之功。

评析：这是一句经过改造的法语成语，原形式是"Paris n'a pas été bati dans un jour"，作者借"four"(灶)与"jour"(日)的音似与形似。译文非常精致。虽是法汉翻译，但其理值得借鉴。

[28] *Coca Cola* 可口可乐

评析："Coca"乃南美产的药用植物，"Cola"则为非洲产的硬壳果树木。这两个字双声叠韵，念起来顺口。中译也双声(可、口)叠韵(可、乐)。

[29] *Pepsi Cola* 百事可乐

评析："pep"是活力之意，中译音义俱佳。

[30] *club* 俱乐部
[31] *Utopia* 乌托邦

第五节　巧译电影片名

电影翻译有区别于其他翻译的特殊性，即其译文要做到能见之于文，形之于声，达之于观众。片名就是电影的商标和广告，电影片名的翻译不是文体的翻译，而是广告翻译。电影片名虽然只有只言片语，但却是影片的点睛之笔，要让观众过目不忘，历久弥新，这就对电影片名的翻译提出了更高的要求。基本上我们必须遵循三大原则：信息传递原则、美学欣赏原则和文化重构原则(郑玉琪，2006：66)。好的片名不一定非要直译，也并不是必须意译，译名和原名能形神兼备又贴切传神固然好，但当形神难以兼得时，或英文片名不能传递足够信息时，不妨另辟蹊径，重铸佳译。

许多英文电影的片名大多比较朴实无华、简单直白，他们喜欢把影片的主人公或影片中心背景和地名作为片名。直译当然省事，但这样的中文译名不符合中文观众的审美情趣和文理。按照中文名称的特点，一般讲究对故事情节高度概括，最常见的是把外国电影的内涵与我国国情和文化传统紧密结合起来，用词典雅隽永，再加上使用了汉语四字格表达方式，给观众一种成语般朗朗上口的感觉，由此造就精彩译名。一些译制影片正是这样体现出译者的神思妙想，寓意深刻。因此，外国电影的名称虽然会局限翻译思路，但一旦发挥中文优势，就能为翻译提供广阔的发挥空间。许多译名比原名还要准确传神。这是中文之美，非原片名所能及。

但所谓过犹不及，有些译名似乎在这条路上走得太远，比如把《瑞贝卡》(Rebecca)翻成《蝴蝶梦》，意境虽美，但对于不懂庄子的观众来说，有点莫名其妙；且片中也看不见一只蝴蝶，何来梦有？而要求观众进电影院前都了解老庄，则不可能。再比如，电影 Lolita 在台湾译为《一树梨花压海棠》。这个译名出自宋代词人张先和苏轼的一则文坛趣话，张先在 80 岁时娶了 18 岁的女子为妾，好友苏轼做一首贺诗调侃："十八新娘八十郎，苍苍白发对红妆；鸳鸯被里成双夜，一树梨花压海棠。"这最后一句寓意老夫配少妻、白发对红颜，有一种情色的艳丽和含蓄。小说描绘的是老鳏夫亨伯特爱上自己年仅 13 岁的继女洛丽塔的畸恋故事，小说译本的副题就叫"鳏夫忏悔录"。因此"一树梨花压海棠"被用来比喻这个惊世骇俗的畸恋故事。有些评论家认为这个译名"令人叹为观止"、"喜出望外"（郑玉琪，2006：68），但事实上一般读者可能无法了解到这么深沉的含义。根据海明威名作 The Sun Also Rises（《太阳照样升起》）改编的同名电影译为《妾似骄阳又照君》也过于矫揉造作。因此，译名既要避免稀松平淡，又要避免晦涩艰深。

[1] *Waterloo Bridge*《魂断蓝桥》

评析：这是公认的佳译。原名若直译为《滑铁卢桥》，人们会以为这部电影和拿破仑的最后一仗有关，1817 年英国在泰晤士河上出资建造了滑铁卢桥，以此来纪念威灵顿公爵指挥英国军队打败拿破仑而取得滑铁卢战役的胜利。其实它是描述战争使情侣生离死别的故事。影片描绘了第一次世界大战期间，年轻漂亮的女演员玛拉在滑铁卢桥上结识了青年军官罗依，并成了恋人。而后，玛拉获悉罗依战死疆场，痛不欲生，为了生存沦落为妓。当罗依奇迹般地出现时，她无法面对现实，为了爱情和名誉，她再次来到与罗依初恋的地方，丧生在车轮滚滚的滑铁卢大桥上。而《魂断蓝桥》巧妙地引申到我国的传统戏曲《蓝桥会》。那是关于唐代文人裴航在陕西蓝田蓝溪蓝桥与仙女云英邂逅成亲、羽化登仙的故事。而"蓝桥相会"的传说与 *Waterloo Bridge* 故事情节有着许多异曲同工之处。所以译者把原名"滑铁卢桥"译成了"魂断蓝桥"。部分中国观众也许不了解"蓝桥会"的典故，但是从"蓝"的现代意象出发，也能领悟到这是一部关于爱情的电影。电影翻译中文化意象重构的意义在于它能及时有效地达到使译文与观众沟通，使观众心领神会。魂断于蓝桥，爱情就在"断"中永恒，而"蓝"又为这一出悲剧添加了一面凄美的色彩。

[2] *Gone With the Wind*《飘》；《乱世佳人》

评析：这是外国片中文译名中的经典之作，充分体现了中文的博大精深和丰富内涵。简单的一个字"飘"把原文"随风而逝"的意思表达得完整贴切。"乱世佳人"也恰如其分地传递出影片那战乱纷飞、颠覆传统的时代，主人公对命运的难以把握和无止无尽斗争的痛苦和无奈。当然，"飘"的译名源自傅东华中文译本。

[3] *Red Shoes*《红菱艳》

评析：英国电影 *Red Shoes* 播映时被译成"红舞鞋"，已经无可厚非。此片主要讲述了英国一名芭蕾舞女演员面对爱情与事业而不能作出正确抉择，最终走向断崖的凄婉的故事。

尽管"红舞鞋"正确无误地译出了英文的原意,也紧扣剧情,但直译得平铺直叙,没有更深的寓意。观众如果光看片名,确实难以激起任何联想的波澜。20世纪80年代后期,*Red Shoes*这部英国影片片名被译成了《红菱艳》,细细品味《红菱艳》这一译文,译者把那双纤巧的红舞鞋比作了中国观众妇孺皆知的红菱。它寓意红菱虽生长于浊水污泥,却娇艳迷人,特别是那两只弯弯的红菱角,犹如中国古代女子的三寸金莲,三寸金莲虽然小巧,但凝聚了多少女子的血泪,有的甚至为之付出了生命的代价。因此"红菱艳"这一片名隐含穿着如红菱般舞鞋的舞女艳丽却薄命。《红楼梦》(第五回)中有"千红一窟(哭),万艳同杯(悲)"一说。译者把这一极具中国文化特色的文化意象"红菱"注入其翻译中,从而成功地重构了一幅为广大中国观众所熟悉、能会意、肯接受的崭新的文化意象。文化意象重构(reconstruction of culture image)这一巧夺天工的翻译手法在电影翻译中随处可见。

　　[4] *Bathing Beauty*《出水芙蓉》

　　评析:若译成"浴水美人"则太白。这部经典音乐喜剧片在国内只有一个家喻户晓的名字《出水芙蓉》。这是最符合中国人思维习惯和中文韵味的译名,非此则何?

　　[5] *Hamlet*《王子复仇记》

　　评析:英文喜欢用片中人物的名字取名,如《哈姆雷特》,但对于不熟悉英国文学的观众来说,《王子复仇记》更能点题。它最早是由清末翻译家林纾根据剧本所译。中文片名加以袭用。

　　[6] *Sound of Music*《音乐之声》

　　评析:这个译名基本就是直译原名,但显得简明而优雅。香港的译名是《仙乐飘飘处处闻》,道出了影片中有美妙歌曲这一主要卖点,但嫌太长,且为了追求美的意境而过分修饰。它引自唐代大诗人白居易的《长恨歌》中的诗句:"骊宫高处入青云,仙乐风飘处处闻。"台湾译名《真善美》虽然有为主题点睛之用,但似乎太过宽泛,不着边际,哪部电影不在说"真善美"呢?

　　[7] *Thelma and Louis*《末路狂花》

　　评析:美国人总喜欢用地名或人名来做电影的名字,《末路狂花》的原片名就是用了片中两个女主角的名字:Thelma and Louis。但很难想像,中国观众会对一个名叫《赛尔玛和路易丝》的影片产生什么浓厚的兴趣。《末路狂花》点出了两个被迫走上绝路的女人最后的疯狂,译名的精气神全出。

　　[8] *Shining*《闪灵》

　　评析:Shining意为"正在闪闪发亮的意思"。《闪灵》一名不仅音近,更有神似,凸显出了库布里克苦心营造出的诡异恐怖、色彩明亮而调子低沉的骇人场面。男主人公性格突变,儿子有了超感应能力,都从一个"闪"字中渗透出来,而"灵"本身已囊括了片中所有奇幻诡异的细节。该片名经典到已成恐怖代言词。音义境皆备,马上有了恐怖片凉飕飕的腥风血气。

　　[9] *Speed*《生死时速》

　　评析:直译成《速度》过于简单,而故事里那辆永远停不下来的车,必须以高速驾驶才能避免炸弹爆炸的巧妙设计,只有在"生死时速"这四个字里才能表达完全。紧张、刺激,一目了然,让人难以抵抗其中的诱惑。这是英文标题难以和中文译名媲美的地方。可以说,精致中文的美学意境,远非外(英)文可以比肩。

　　[10] *Amadeus*《上帝的宠儿》

　　评析:这是英若成的译名,Amadeus意为"神宠爱者",取自莫扎特Wolfgang Amadeus

Mozart 的中名。由同名话剧改编的电影也是表现宫廷乐师长对莫扎特天才的嫉妒,痛恨上帝没有宠爱他自己,而设计害死莫扎特。

[11] *The Piano*《钢琴别恋》

评析:这是一部澳大利亚影片,国内的译名居然是《钢琴课》,把这样一部优秀的爱情电影翻译成了好像是一部科教片。香港的译名叫"钢琴师和她的情人",有那么一点味道,但是有一点媚俗。台湾的译名是"钢琴别恋",像个电影名,较可取。

[12] *The Italian Job*《偷天换日》

评析:该片直译为《意大利工作》,白得不能再白,这样的译名"除了大大缩小观众面外,别无他益"(郑玉琪,2006:66)。译者根据剧情巧妙地将其译为《偷天换日》,点出了影片的玄机,大大提升了其趣味性。

[13] *Catch Me If You Can*《有本事来抓我》

评析:本片据说在中国内地遭遇了令人大跌眼镜的票房惨败,原因之一就是片名译成《我知道你是谁》,这不但读起来拗口,而且作为一部主要讲述 FBI 捉拿通缉犯的悬念迭出的侦探片的片名,却显得语气平淡,气势薄弱,根本无法先声夺人。直译《有本事来抓我》或许更胜一筹。这部电影在港台地区和海外的其他译名还有《逍遥法外》、《智抓双雄》、《神鬼交锋》等。

[14] *Pretty Woman*《风月俏佳人》

评析:这部 1990 年上映的美国影片,在香港地区译为《麻雀变凤凰》,俗不可耐。大陆译成《漂亮女人》,略显直白。相比之下,台湾地区的译名《风月俏佳人》则文词隽永,令人赏心悦目。

[15] *Forrest Gump*《阿甘正传》

评析:这部 1995 年荣获奥斯卡 6 项大奖的经典影片被传神地译为《阿甘正传》,而不是音译为《福雷斯特·甘普》,是一个中西文化合璧的范例。译名借用鲁迅的《阿 Q 正传》点出这部电影是人物传记题材,"甘"又照顾了原片名,点出主人公的姓氏。"阿甘"这个中国式的亲切称呼极易上口,深入人心。

[16] *Spiderman*《蜘蛛侠》

评析:2002 年上映的 *Spiderman*,在台湾翻译为《蜘蛛人》,这就远没有大陆的《蜘蛛侠》来得传神。这个"侠"字为西洋电影增添了一分中国的侠士义气。这是把外国电影的丰富内涵与我国的文化精髓相结合的精彩译名。

[17] *Platoon*《野战排》

评析:"野战"两字加得好。

[18] *Boogie Night*《不羁夜》

评析:这简直是意译与音译的完美结合,叹为观止。

[19] *The Cold Mountain*《乱世情天》

评析:这部 2003 年奥斯卡热门影片被直译为《冷山》,在中国也未能引起预期的轰动效应。这其实是一部动人的反映美国南北内战时期的爱情片,描述的是受尽战火洗礼的男主人公漫长艰难的回家历程,他的家乡位于名为"冷山"的偏僻小镇,那里有他的爱人在等待着他。把这个没有什么名气的地点作为汉语片名虽然忠实于原文,但却无法吸引观众的关注。香港译为《乱世情天》就提纲挈领,既点出了战争的大背景,又蕴含了爱情这一主题。而同样是反应战地爱情的美国大片 *Pearl Harbor* 虽然直译为《珍珠港》却是一炮打响,这是因为中国观众对"珍珠港事件"早就耳熟能详。

[20] *Blood and Sand*《碧血黄沙》

评析：假如直译为《血与沙》，虽字面忠实，但无情无义。译者根据影片内容，增译了两个颜色词，译作《碧血黄沙》，"碧血"一词源于《庄子·外物》："苌弘死于蜀，茂其血，三年而化为碧。"现用以指为正义事业而流洒的鲜血。碧血丹心，黄沙万里，由此译名，定能让观众神驰广宇，遐思联翩。（包惠南，2001）

[21] *Tristan and Isolde*《王者之心》

这部史诗大片 2007 年引进中国时，该片的美方编剧迪恩表示，对中国发行方肆意改动原先的片名感到不满，他认为《崔斯坦与伊索德》这个名字更加直接，并称要起诉。对此，负责译制的八一电影制片厂译制片主任回应，外国影片的译名一定要符合国人的口味。他表示，在国内上映的国外的译名非常重要，在某种程度上能迅速拉近与国内观众的距离，勾起观众进电影院的欲望。原片名直译就是《崔斯坦与伊索德》，考虑这个名字过于普通，因此根据影片剧情和中国观众的需要，侧重于宏伟的史诗巨片角度，确定了《王者之心》这个名字。它很符合中国观众的口味——简短、上口、印象深刻，可以称得上是经典译名。至于国外有人指责影片的译名问题，说明他们对中国的观众、中国的文化还不熟悉。双方在译名问题上的分歧竟然导致原本定下影片编剧、导演及主演来华进行宣传的计划落空。可谓电影译名的典型案例。从翻译的角度上说，《王者之心》的改译名是正确的。

精彩电影译名欣赏，体验汉语表达韵味之妙：

All Quiet on the Western Front	西线无战事
Always	天长地久
Bridges of Madison County, the	廊桥遗梦
Cleopatra	埃及艳后
Dances with Wolves	与狼共舞
Enemy at the Gates	兵临城下
Entrapment	偷天陷阱/将计就计
Erotic Passion	如痴如醉
Fugitive, the	亡命天涯
Ghost	人鬼情未了
Great Waltz, the	翠堤春晓
Head Over Heels	神魂颠倒
How Green Was My Valley	青山翠谷
It Happened One Night	一夜风流
Jack	家有杰克
Lara Croft Tomb Raider	古墓丽影
Legends of the Fall	秋日传奇
Mirror Has Two Faces, the	双面镜
My Fair Lady	窈窕淑女
Net, the	网络惊魂

Nine Months	九月之痒／九月怀胎
Nun's Story, the	修女传
Once Upon a Time in America	美国往事
Random Harvest	鸳梦重温
Ring, the	午夜凶铃
Robin Hood: Prince of Thieves	侠盗罗宾汉
Rock, the	石破天惊
Scent of a Woman	闻香识女人
Showgirls	艳舞女郎
Silence of the Lambs, the	沉默的羔羊
Sister Act	修女也疯狂
Star Wars	星球大战
Stealing Beauty	偷香
Suspicion	深闺疑云
Terms of Endearment, the	母女情深
They All Laughed	哄堂大笑
Unforgiven	不可饶恕／杀无赦
Valley of Decision, the	空谷芳草
Walk in the Clouds, the	云中漫步
Wild at Heart	我心狂野

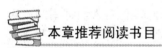

本章推荐阅读书目

梁实秋小品文
林语堂文集
余光中文集

第五章 翻译的文化篇

文化和语言的关系至关密切。语言是文化的载体,在传递文化的过程中,不同民族的文化都在他们的语言表达形式上留下强烈的印迹,因此也造成翻译的困难。

第一节 文化差异与表达差异

不同民族的文化差异直接体现在思维、表达差异上。在英语和汉语中,人们都用"心"来作为七情六欲的中心,人们常说"用心去爱",英语也说"give your heart to sb."(爱上某人)。但是在西非一些语言里,人们"用肝去爱"(love with the liver),而在中美洲的一些土著语言里,人们"用胃去爱"(love with the stomach) (Nida, 1993:2)。在英语中,人们说"white as snow",但在其他语言里,人们说"白如霜"、"白如白鹭毛"或"白如蘑菇"等等。其比喻手法一样,虽然具象不同。动物形象在不同的语言里常常会有不同的文化含义。汉语中带有"狗"字的成语往往带有贬义,但 dog 在英语中是中性偏褒的。汉语里还有多条涉及老虎的成语,因为在中国传统文化中,老虎被认为是"百兽之王",而在英语文化中却是狮子。这就造成英汉语中含义相仿,形象不同的表达方式。例如:

虎口拔牙 beard the lion(拔狮子的胡子)
狐假虎威 ass in the lion's skin(披着狮子皮的驴)
拦路虎 a lion in the way(拦路狮)
摸老虎屁股 twist the lion's tail(拨弄狮子尾巴)
虎落平阳被犬欺 Hares may pull dead lions by the beard(兔子也敢摸死狮子的胡子)

保留原文的表达形式,有利于原汁原味地传递原文的文化思想。但是,死抠原文字眼的形式对应,常会使译文不能正确传达原文意思。原文读者懂得,要理解一个成语的意义,不能看其字面,而应看其喻义,其文化涵义。但译文读者往往只能看到其字面,而无法理解其喻义,甚至会根据其字面,套用自己译语文化的喻义。有些动物在英语和汉语中代表的含义总是有细微的区别,如:

英语	汉语
pig：贪心、丑陋	猪：懒、笨
wolf：贪心	狼：凶狠
bear：脾气坏、没有规矩	熊：动作慢、笨拙
peacock：傲慢	孔雀：美丽
bee：忙碌	蜜蜂：勤劳

因此，在这种情况下，译者就要充分考虑到两种不同语言文字所表达的内涵，注意原文形式的迻译。奈达曾提出改变形式的五个标准：

1. 直译原文会使意义发生错误。

如在闪语(Semitic)里，"heap coals of fire on his head"的字面意义是"堆火团于他头上"，常常被人严重曲解为某种折磨人致死的刑法。其实它的意思是"使人羞愧交加"。

2. 借用语会构成语义空白，因而可能使读者填入错误意义。

3. 形式对应会引起严重的意义不明。

4. 形式对应会产生不为原作者有意安排的歧义表达法。

5. 形式对应会引起译文语法错误、语体不合。

总结起来只是一条：当形式对应容易使译文产生误解时，就应该改变形式。但奈达还提出一条重要的原则：有些重要的宗教标志，其含义虽然往往隐晦难懂，但为了保持《圣经》信息的完整统一，却不可随意变换。例如，"上帝的羔羊"、"十字架"等表达法必须予以保留，同时可加注说明。在西南太平洋岛群上的美拉尼西亚人认为猪是宠物，羊则榜上无名或为卑弃之物，乃用"上帝的小猪"(Little Pig of God)来取代"上帝的羔羊"(Lamb of God)。爱斯基摩人则译成"上帝的海豹"(Seal of God)，这在奈达看来是无法接受的。无独有偶，霍克斯在翻译《红楼梦》时，就忽略了译文正确传达中国文化中某些重要特征。霍克斯虽然深知"红"在中华文化中象征"吉祥"、"喜庆"、"富贵"乃至"爱情"等喜事，但他认为，"红"(red)在西方人心目中会和暴力流血产生联想，因此，他把它归化成西方人喜欢的"绿"，结果，"怡红公子"译成"Happy Green Boy"，而把"怡红院"译成"House of Green Delights"(快绿院)。就连书名《红楼梦》也按其另一个中文名字译成 The Story of the Stone (《石头记》)。虽然极尽巧妙之能事，但如果按照奈达的阐述，这是不能允许的。同样，我们也不能把"Lord forbid"译成"阿弥陀佛"，把"God of Heaven"译成"观音菩萨"，这是不同宗教文化的差别。"Talk of the evil and he will appear"也不适宜译成"说曹操，曹操就到"。

从严谨的角度上讲，在任何语境下都不应该这么译。但我们在许多译文中为何还能看到译语文化因素的介入呢？这种介入是不可避免的还是可以克服呢？这是翻译研究的一个重大问题。

第二节 直译、归译与译语文化因素的介入

翻译的过程，是源语文化进入译语文化的过程。但是，有时候译语文化常因为不同译者的主导性关系，会自觉或不自觉地反向侵入译文，增加译文的译语文化信息。这种情况的出

现,是和译者的直译、归译翻译思想紧密相连的。不同译者在处理译语文化介入上存在着侧重直译或侧重归译的现象。

为避免论述空洞抽象,我们将对英国文学名著 Robinson Crusoe 诸译本进行分析比较研究。Robinson Crusoe 的最早中文译本见于 1902 年沈祖芬的《绝岛漂流记》,又有从龛的《绝岛英雄》(1905)。可惜二译本今皆不见传。本节赖于分析的五个译本(按出版年代顺序)分别是:《鲁滨孙漂流记》(林纾、曾宗巩译,1905 年版,商务印书馆)[简称林译]、《鲁滨孙漂流记》(徐霞村译,1934 年初版,1959 年重新修订,人民文学出版社)[简称徐译]、《鲁滨孙漂流记》(郭建中译,1996 年 5 月版,译林出版社)[简称郭译]、《鲁滨孙漂流记》(义海译,1997 年 7 月版,海峡文艺出版社)[简称义译]、《鲁滨孙历险记》(黄杲炘译,1998 年 7 月版,上海译文出版社)[简称黄译]。本节依据的英文版本是 Robinson Crusoe(1991,牛津大学出版社)。从林纾、徐霞村译本到郭建中译本和黄杲炘译本,其间历时 93 年,基本涵盖了中国近现代以来翻译活动的历程,颇具典型性。《鲁滨孙漂流记》译本也经历了从文言文译本到白话文译本的演变。在译语文化介入问题上,既呈现出因时代不同形成的差异,也有因同时期不同译者而形成的差异。且看这些历代译者和同时代译者是如何阐译同一原作的。

在展开论述之前,我们有必要先探讨一下 Robinson Crusoe 的各种中文译名。自林纾将书名译成《鲁滨孙漂流记》后,随后的徐霞村译本、郭建中都沿用此名,已是约定俗成。义海译成《鲁滨孙漂流记》,大同小异。黄杲炘则提出不同译法,他认为,把鲁滨孙的名字同"飘流"挂钩未必妥当,而且易于造成误会。因为在笛福的笔下,鲁滨孙一生之中从来都不曾"飘流"过!(黄杲炘,1998)因此他将书名译成《鲁滨孙历险记》。现又有范纯海的《鲁滨孙漂流记》(2001),则把"飘"改成了"漂"。我们在论述时,暂且保持各译本的译名。

一、林纾译《鲁滨孙漂流记》的译语文化因素的介入

首先,作为古文家的林纾在译本的整体把握上就始终以传统的中国文化思想观念来审视原作。他在《鲁滨孙漂流记》的序言中就以儒家的"中庸之道"来观照小说中鲁滨孙父亲所描述的"守家守业、不冒险"的所谓当时英国中产阶级思想。按儒家的"中庸之道",其涵义远非如此。因为儒家的"中庸之道"不仅要求做到"不偏不颇","中立不倚",还要求防止极端,维护正道。一切绝对保持平衡(沈善洪,1998)。虽然,"中庸"一词现已广义化了,但作为译文文字,其特殊文化涵义还是无法彻底消除的。遗憾的是,随后的五部重译本无一例外地袭用。林纾还把鲁滨孙的行为喻为"兼义、轩、巢、燧诸氏之所为"。林纾在该译本序言中精辟地说道:"译书非著书比也,著作之家,可以抒吾所见,乘虚逐微,靡所不可;若译书,则述其已成之事迹,焉能参以己见?"尽管如此,我们还是在其译本中看到不少充满浓郁中国传统文化色彩的译辞。其中最典型者就是林纾在译本中多处使用"仁"这个含义较广泛的儒家道德概念。仁,本指人与人之间的亲善关系,也包括恭、宽、信、敏、惠等内容。可是,我们在林译本中连续读到"此岂仁者之所为"、"非仁也"、"谓之仁人"(1905:25)、"仁爱"(1905:78,106,194)"至仁至义"(1905:115)。林译中涉及儒家思想道德观念的表达语还有"勇而赴义,廉而知耻"(1905:148)、"忠心"(1905:156)"仗义讨之"(1905:174)、"竭忠相待"、"其人忠而且公"(1905:202)等。一些极具中国传统文化的表达词语也令读者有如阅读中国经典或说部的感觉,如"宠辱无惊"、"明哲保身"(1905:3)、"不期竟得贤主"(1905:25)、"为充军边远之人"(1905:49)。林纾把原文"my army"译成"羽林之军"(第 172 页),无形中徒增"羽林"二字。查《辞海》,"羽林"指:西汉武帝时选陇西、天水、安定、北地、上郡、西河等六郡良家子

宿卫建章宫,称建章营骑。后改名羽林骑,取其"如羽之疾,如林之多"的意思,属光禄勋,为皇帝护卫,东汉以后,历代禁卫军常有羽林之名。试想,让一个熟读中国诗书的读者看了会产生何种感想?难怪林语堂叹曰,林纾"把西洋的长篇小说变成《七侠五义》、《阅微草堂笔记》等的化身"(林语堂,引自罗新璋,1984:420)。更有意思的是,林译用了"舢舨"一词来翻译原文中的 boat,舢舨原为中国港湾和江河里的船只,根据《新牛津英语词典》,sampan(舢舨)词源正是来自汉语,大约在17世纪初叶才进入英语。

由此我们看到,林译从译文的表达方式(传统古文风韵)到表达的内容,都带有强烈中国传统文化色彩。其原因有二:一是林纾是个精通国学的古文家、小说家和诗人,他的这个优势因而在译文中发挥得淋漓尽致,为他人所不及;二是当时的翻译理论思想尚不成熟,且林纾本人不通外文,反而使他不那么受原文的束缚。顺便提及,林纾案例和翻译李白诗歌的美国诗人和翻译家庞德何其相似乃尔,可为翻译史上的特例。

二、《鲁滨孙漂流记》重译本的译语文化因素的介入

在林纾译《鲁滨孙漂流记》之后出现的重译本,在译语文化因素的介入上也表现出各自的特色,我们可以通过这些译本的汉语成语典故的运用,看出他们的差异。

[1] But it was enough to affect me then, *who was but a young sailor, and had never known any thing of the matter.* (1991:8)

徐译:我这时只是一个初出茅庐的水手,对于海上的事完全没有知识。(1959:6)

郭译:对我这个初次航海的年轻人来说,……因为我对航海的事一无所知。(1996:7)

义译:我不过是个第一次出海的水手,对海上的事情一无所知。(1997:9)

黄译:对于当时我这样一个毫无航海知识的年轻生手,这景象已足以叫我胆战心惊了。(1998:8)

评析:"初出茅庐"和"三顾茅庐"同样为中国读者所熟知。它是《三国演义》里的故事。它比喻初次出来做事,缺乏经验,还很幼稚。徐译在此添加的译入语文化成分显然是原文作者不可能想像到的,这也是过于追求归化的一种表现。林译文为"实为余放舟时所不经见者"(第6页)。

[2] I believe it was the first gun that had been fir'd there *since the creation of the world;* ...(1991:53)

徐译:我相信,自从开天辟地以来,在这岛上,这是第一次有人开枪。(1959:46)

郭译:我相信,自上帝创造这世界以来,第一次有人在这个岛上开枪。(1996:44)

义译:我相信,这一枪是这里开天辟地以来的第一枪。(1997:46)

黄译:我相信,自从上帝创造了世界以来,这还是那里响起了第一枪;(1998:55)

评析:"开天辟地"是中国古代神话传说,盘古氏开天辟地,开始有人类历史。比喻前所未有,是有史以来第一次。它和"上帝创造世界"是不同民族、不同宗教信仰产生的神话传说。徐译和义译采用归化译法,"开天辟地"所表现出的汉民族神话色彩非常浓烈。而郭译和黄译则保留了原表达涵义,避开了这种译语文化联想。类似这样的文化成语还有"前车之鉴(徐译,第3页;郭译,第5页)"、"强弩之末(徐译,第124页;郭译,第114页)"。从互文性(intertextuality)的角度上看,它令人联想到它的译语先前语篇,即该引语特有的传统中国文化典故。郭译和黄译避开了这一点,从而摆脱归化带来的冗余译语文化信息。

因此,统观其全书,作为第二部《鲁滨孙漂流记》重译本,徐译的归化处理也较明显。实际上这种译语文化对译文的侵袭常常是根深蒂固的,即使90年代出版的郭译、义译、黄译,也不能免。兹举二例:

[3] It is not easy for me to express how it mov'd me to see what extasy and *filial affection* had work'd in this poor savage, at the sight of his father, and of his being deliver'd from death; nor indeed can I describe half the extravagancies of his affection after this;...(1991:238)

徐译:一见他父亲已经绝处逢生,竟是这样大喜大狂,孝心流露,我内心的感动,简直无法表达。(1959:213)

郭译:见他父亲已绝处逢生,流露出如此无限的孝心,简直欣喜若狂,(1996:195)

义译:这个可怜的野人见自己的父亲被从死路上救了下来,真是欣喜若狂,用各种方式表达他对父亲的爱心。(1997:189)

黄译:见到他死里逃生的父亲,欣喜到这种地步,那份孝心竟如此强烈,(1998:244)

[4] I observ'd the poor *affectionate* creature every two minutes, or perhaps less, all the while he was here, turn'd his head about, to see if his father was in the same place,...(1991:240)

徐译:我冷眼旁观,只见这孝心真挚的家伙一边干着活儿,一边频频回过头来,看看他父亲是不是还坐在原来的地方。(1959:214)

郭译:我发现,星期五真是个心地诚挚的孝子。(1996:195)

义译:我发现,这个可怜的人真是太爱他的父亲了。(1997:191)

黄译:我看着这可怜的孝子,看他虽在这儿干着活,……(1998:246)

评析: 上述两段译文的一个关键字"孝"几乎所有译家都不能幸免地使用到了。"孝"所涵盖的也是汉文化独特的儒家伦理概念(例,不孝有三,无后为大《孟子·离娄章句上》),其涵盖义大于filial一词,但连国内几本权威英汉词典也做"孝"解,查"filial"一词,词源来自拉丁语,英语释义为"of, relating to, or due from a son or daughter"(《新牛津英语词典》)。我们怎么能以"孝子"称呼"星期五"这个尚未教化的、吃人的原始人呢?即使在当代中国文化里,"孝子"也是个意义很重的词。上述"孝子"之处是否可以译成"好儿子"?倒是在林纾译本(特指《鲁》)中,我们还没有发现他使用"孝"这个字。一个鲜明的例子是在新译本出现"孝心"的地方林译本处理成"父子之情"。不知是有意或无意为之?综观上述译例,义译规避得较好,但他在该译本其他地方,"孝道"(第9页)一词依旧赫然在目。可见译语传统文化烙印之深。由此看来,使用归化或异化不单单是译者策略的取向问题,还关系到源语与译语文化是否形成冲突的问题。

三、同一时期重译本异化与归化着重点的差异

从历时的角度上看,文学名著的重译的总体方向是从倾向归化向异化发展,但我们也应该看到,即使是同一时期的重译本,由于不同译者的翻译理念、翻译方法、学术修养和文学审美情趣存在着差异,每个译本也会有所侧重。拿翻译出版时间相差仅二、三年的郭译、义译和黄译相比,在涉及文化词语的处理上,我们发现郭译仍偏向于采用归化法,即趋向于使用译语特有表达方式。针对《鲁滨孙漂流记》的重译问题,郭建中教授在该译本的序中便提到

应"使语言更现代化,更通俗易懂"。他认为,译者采取何种翻译策略取决于三大因素:作者的意图、原作的性质(《鲁》虽是古典文学名著,但它原本是一部通俗小说),以及译文读者。因此郭译有意识地在归化上有所侧重。下面几个译例可管窥出其翻译用意:

[5] All this while the storm encreas'd, and the sea, which I had never been upon before, went very high, *tho' nothing like what I have seen many times since*; no, nor like what I saw a few days after... (1991:8)

徐译:虽然还没有像我后来几次以及过了几天所见到的那样凶,……(1959:5)

郭译:但比起我后来多次见到过的咆哮的大海,那真是小巫见大巫了;……(1996:7)

义译:这还不如我后来所经历的以及我以后几天所见到的那样凶猛;……(1997:9)

黄译:甚至同我稍后几天看到的相比,都还算不上什么。(1998:8)

[6] ... he rose immediately, for he swam *like a cork*, ... (1999:23)

徐译:可是他立刻浮出了水面,因为他游起泳来,像一个软木塞。(1959:19)

郭译:他在水里像鱼,游得极快。(1996:20)

义译:他水性很好,很快便像个鱼浮子似的冒出水面,游了起来,……(1997:22)

黄译:他水性极好,马上像个木塞似的浮上了水面,……(1998:24)

评析:在本例中,如此简短的译文居然形成有趣的比较。诸译家的译法各不相同。徐译是最彻底的异化(直译),保留了原表达语的修辞特征;黄译次之。郭译则归化得"如鱼得水"。几种译文各呈优势。另外,郭译还使用了"司空见惯(1996:26)"、"祸福相倚和祸不单行(1996:51)"等归化性极强的表达语。这种具体手法上的归化正是翻译思想观念上归化意识的反映。采用归化语言的优势在于译文语言地道、精炼。但过分归化亦有弊端。它丧失了原文鲜活的异样表达形式,不利于译语文化对外来文化的吸收。以"司空见惯"一词而言,译语文化对译文的侵袭偏重。因此,如何最大限度地采用异化翻译法又使译文读起来有归化的效果应是文学作品新译或重译的追求目标。

四、结论

从以上对《鲁滨孙漂流记》诸译本的分析看出,随着时代的发展,在对原文文本文化的诠释上走的是从归化译语到回归源语表达的演化过程。林译作为早期的翻译代表作,归化的色彩最为明显,从徐译起至黄译,在尽量避免译语文化介入上前进了一大步。在当代的几部《鲁滨孙漂流记》重译本中,郭译也表现出较多的归化特色。黄译和义译在异化方面做得更深入一些,但这并不意味着他们的译作就不沾染上一点译语文化气息。作为原作者的代言人,译者的母语文化意识会不可避免地掺和进去。另外,也会出现这种情况,有的译者此处采用归化法,彼处则用异化法,而另一个译者与之正相反,似乎令人捉摸不定,其实这里面有他们的指导思想及当时翻译状态下的创作思维所制约。意识到这些问题,有利于今后的重译者更自觉地开展这项工作。

概而言之,翻译活动的本质决定了它就是一种归化的行为,所谓"洋为中用",因为从一开始它就以译语取代源语。其次,当异化的表达语为译语文化接受、同化后,人们也就"见异不异,异久而归",成为本土文化的一部分。这样,掺和了异质文化的本土文化的异质容忍度就会越来越大。因此说,异化是手段,归化是目的。就翻译策略本身而言,随着时代的发展,

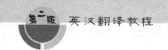

不同文化的日趋接触、弥合,今后的重译本在文化观念上会更自觉地取向异化翻译。而异化译文将随着译语读者的取舍而溶入到译语文化中去,最终成为译语文化的一部分。这就是归化与异化相互作用的结果。

第三节 英汉亲属词称谓的文化差异性及汉译处理

英语亲属称谓是一个貌似容易,其实很棘手的翻译问题。主要原因在于中西文化中称谓体系的不对应,而英语部分亲属词的模糊性使得翻译更为困难。

一

从对比的角度看,英汉语称谓体系出现种种不对应的现象,是不同语言、不同历史文化的必然结果。具有五千年传统文化的中国人注重家族宗法观念、尊卑长幼之分,形成一套较为完整、具体的称谓体系。相比之下,英、美民族的家族称谓体系就简单、笼统得多。这体现在"汉语亲属称谓为每条(血缘)纽带上的各个亲属分别设称呼语,英语亲属称谓则以同一个称呼语把一些亲属分为一类。前者为描述类型,后者为分类类型"(张蓓,1993:57—62)。英汉两种不对应的亲属称谓体系本身并无孰优孰劣的问题,因为它们在各自文化圈内交流时都不会造成障碍,对英美民族的人士来说,兄或弟都是"brother",即"man or boy having the same parents as another person"(《牛津高阶英汉双解词典》,1997),姐或妹就是"sister",即"daughter of the same parents as oneself or another person"(同上),无所谓长幼、先后之分。专门针对外国人学习英语而编写的《朗曼当代英语词典》(1978:1299)就明确指出:"There is no special word to show whether one brother or sister is older than another(没有特别一个词显示兄弟或姐妹长幼关系)"。而在中国传统文化里,同胞兄弟尚且要讲究"兄友弟恭","长兄如父"。在古汉语中,兄弟更细分为"伯、仲、叔、季",现代中国人已把这四种称谓简化为"伯、叔"二种。正如《普通语言学》书中所述,"古汉语与现代汉语在这方面的亲属称谓体系是不同的,古汉语用四分法,而现代汉语则用二分法。这种称谓体系之所以不同,是由于有贯时的演化事实插入其中,在口语中'伯伯'取代了'伯父',而'叔叔'则取代了'仲父'、'叔父'和'季父'三个旧称谓。"(杨茂勋,1993:129)

英语亲属称谓一些较为典型的模糊词语当为:"uncle"(伯父、叔父、舅父、姑父、姨父),"aunt"(伯母、婶娘、舅妈、姑妈、姨妈),"brother-in-law"(姐夫、妹夫、内兄、内弟、大伯、小叔),"sister-in-law"(兄嫂、弟媳、姑、姨)。在法语里尚有"cousin"和"cousine"的阳性和阴性之分,而英语中一个"cousin"就包括了堂(表)兄弟和堂(表)姐妹,真正的一词多义。从翻译操作的层面上看,我们将之称为"多义模糊词"。按照伍铁平的观点,这些亲属词的模糊性属于认识上的即人们头脑中的模糊性(epistemological fuzziness),而不是来自客观世界本身界限的不分明(伍铁平,1999:141)。上述这种种亲属词引起的麻烦甚至还影响到对非亲属成员使用亲属称谓的翻译处理,如"Uncle Sam,Uncle Tom"之类的称呼。有人认为,上述两个含有特殊意义的绰号不能算"从亲属称谓",即泛化的亲属称谓(张蓓,1993:57—62)。但它毕竟使用了亲属称谓词。事实上,美国文学名著 *Uncle Tom's Cabin* 书名的译法就一直存有争论,早期译者译成《汤姆叔叔的小屋》(唐均,1986),且已成定译。后来的译者改译成《汤姆大伯的小屋》(黄继忠,1982),即使是正确的,由于先入为主的影响,反倒让人感到怪怪的。一名之立,关系到全书的来龙去脉。《汤姆大伯的小屋》一书的译者为此在译著的前言还专门作了一番考证,并为之正名:

> 《汤姆叔叔的小屋》的译名也已流传较广,但英语中"uncle"一词,可指叔父、伯父、舅父、姑父、姨父中任何一位,从原作内容看来,称汤姆为"uncle"的人主要是他第一个主人谢尔贝的儿子乔治,而汤姆较谢尔贝大八岁,所以乔治应叫他"大伯"才对;况且汤姆在庄园上的黑奴中是比较年长而受人尊敬的人,因此大多数黑孩子都应称他"大伯",故改成今译名(黄继忠,1982:15)。

在文学翻译中,亲属词的模糊性导致的麻烦很大。法国著名作家巴尔扎克有两部名著: *La Cousine Bette* 和 *Le Cousin Pons*,有的译者将其译为《从妹贝德》和《从兄邦斯》("从"与"堂"同义),傅雷先生经过相当复杂的"换算"考证,将它们分别译为《贝姨》和《邦斯舅舅》。德莱赛的名著 *Sister Carrie*,书名中的 Sister 究竟是指"姐姐"还是"妹妹",仅从书名上就无法判断。根据考据,这个故事中嘉莉的原型就是德莱赛自己的一个妹妹,命运坎坷,结局悲惨,给年轻的德莱赛留下了深刻的印象。由此可知书名中的 Sister 实际上是指作者的妹妹,故书名定译为《嘉莉妹妹》(包惠南,2001)。在狄更斯小说 *David Copperfield* 一书中有一个 Aunt Betsey Trotwood,根据高克毅考证,"四本中文译本中,三个译者认为是 David 父亲的姨母,因此译作'姨婆',另一位译作'祖姑母'"(高克毅,1998:220)。孰是孰非?可见英语亲属词的汉译确实是个大问题。

中文译者由于受到母语文化的影响和制约,明知英文没有分得这么细,但在翻译时常常免不了非要辨个明白不可,要求译文一步到位,免得读者猜疑,其所依据的是翻译的语用原则,译者在称谓翻译上遵从译文表达习惯是必要的。现在的问题是,即使译者有心这样做,面对无法提供充足信息的上下文,译者会常常觉得力不从心。文学翻译中如此,非文学翻译中出现的亲属词概莫能外。

二

现以《麦克米伦百科全书》(*The Macmillan Encyclopaedia*,1997)中涉及亲属词的条目释文为例,说明英语亲属词的汉译困难。由于百科全书的条目释文受辞书编写体例要求和篇幅限制,表达常常难以充分,人物关系难免交代不清,即使遍查相关的条目,乃至相关工具书,也常不尽人意。因此,称谓翻译问题在百科全书翻译中特别突出。实例如下:

[1] According to legend, when the Trojan prince Paris abducted Helen, *her husband's brother*, Agamemnon, led a Greek force to recover her, captured Troy by the stratagem of the wooden horse after ten years' fighting, and destroyed it (Troy).

译文:根据传说,特洛伊王子帕里斯诱拐了海伦,海伦丈夫的兄弟阿伽门农率领希腊军队想把她夺回。战争持续了十年,最后希腊人用木马计攻克特洛伊城,并将其摧毁(特洛伊)。

评析:上文划线部分译成"海伦丈夫的兄弟"在读者看来实在是隔靴搔痒,其实译者的苦衷在于即使根据该条目上下文,仍然无法判定这"brother"指"兄"还是指"弟"。翻查本辞书的相关条目,仍不可得。我们试查了《英汉百科知识辞典》(1991),发现该辞书相关条目的称谓互相矛盾,极其混乱。其中一个条目称阿伽门农为弟(1991:13),两个条目称阿伽门农为兄(1991:635,1004),一个条目仍称阿伽门农为"兄弟"(1991:1005)。《简明不列颠百科全书》认定阿伽门农是哥哥(1991:7—717,6—80)。《英汉大词典》中的 Menelaus 词目(1991:1117)也认定阿伽门农是哥哥。但《剑桥百科全书》条目仍模糊地译成"兄弟"(1991:768)。众译者和研究者折腾了好半天,皆因"brother"一词模糊不清所致。

如果说神话故事纯属子虚乌有,不足为训的话,让我们再来看看《麦克米伦百科全书》中一些真实人物条目的称谓问题。

[2] In rivalry with his *brother-in-law*, Aristotle Onassis, he pioneered the construction of supertankers during the 1950s (Niarchos, S).

译文:20 世纪 50 年代与其连襟翁纳西斯激烈竞争,他首创建造了超级油轮(尼亚科斯)。

评析:仅凭该条目上下文,译者简直束手无策。此处的"brother-in-law",根据《牛津高阶英汉双解词典》的释义计有:1. brother of one's husband or wife(大伯子;小叔子;内兄;内弟);2. husband of one's sister(姐夫;妹夫);3. husband of the sister of one's wife or husband(妻子或丈夫的姐姐或妹妹的丈夫)。根据英文版《简明不列颠百科全书》(1988)"翁纳西斯"(1988,8:949)条目,翁纳西斯"1946 年和船王利瓦偌斯(Stavros Livanos)的女儿(Athina Livanos)结婚"。又,尼亚科斯的岳父(father-in-law)也是船王利瓦偌斯(8:674)。如此,两人都是利瓦偌斯的女婿,属连襟关系。《剑桥百科全书》(1996)的"尼亚科斯"(1996:836)条目指称"他在与其堂兄弟翁纳西斯的竞争中最先建造出超级油轮";《英汉百科知识辞典》(1991)的"尼亚科斯"条目(1991:700)中则干脆说"为与其兄弟翁纳西斯竞争,……",不知其依据是什么?以下是"brother-in-law"又一例。

[3] He was overshadowed by his *brother-in-law* Sir Robert Walpole and resigned (Townshend, Charles, 2nd Viscount)

译文:因其连襟罗伯特·沃波尔爵士权势盖过他而辞职(汤森)。

评析:《剑桥百科全书》"汤森"(1996:1204)条目称"与其表兄罗伯特·沃波尔……",不知依据的原文是什么?汤森生卒年为 1674—1738,沃波尔生卒年为 1676—1745,前者长于后者。《剑桥世界名人百科全书》的"汤森"(1998:943)条目的释文是:"汤森……成为其姻兄沃波尔为首的辉格党执政内阁的显要人物。"若参照此辞书,他们则是连襟。遍查手头各种资料,实在难于确认。再看下例:

[4] Ralph Wood I (1715—72) trained under John Astbury. His *cousin* Aaron Wood (1717—785) was employed by many Staffordshire potters as a modeller (Wood).

译文:拉尔夫·伍德(第一)(1715—1772)拜阿斯特伯里为师。堂弟艾伦·伍德(1717—1785)……(伍德)。

评析:从该条目释文中我们猜想,"Ralph"和他的"cousin Aaron"皆同姓 Wood,年龄相差 2 岁,当为堂兄弟无疑。在这条目里,称谓词背景比较完整,这算是《麦克米伦百科全书》条目撰写人所能提供的令译者较容易翻译的词条。

三

正如[1]所示,英语亲属词中缺乏排行称谓。而如果出现一家四兄弟,那么他们在英文上下文中是如何称呼的呢?且看下面一个完整的条目释文。

[5] **Siemens, Ernst Werner von** (1816—1892) German electrical engineer, who opened a telegraph factory in 1847 and, a year later, laid a government telegraph line from Berlin to Frankfurt. Together with *his brother* Karl Siemens (1829—1906), he established telegraph factories in a number of European cities. *A third brother* Sir William Siemens (Karl Wilhelm S; 1823—1883) moved to England in 1844. He invented the open-hearth steel process in 1861, based on the principle of heat regeneration previously patented by *a fourth brother* Friedrich Siemens (1826—1904).

直译：西门子 Siemens, Ernst Werner von (1816—1892) 德国电气工程师。1847年开设电报机制造厂。一年后，架设了从柏林至法兰克福的供政府使用的电报线路。他和兄弟卡尔·西门子(1829—1906)在许多欧洲国家建立电报机工厂。第三个兄弟威廉·西门子爵士(卡尔·威廉·西门子；1823—1883)于1844年移居到英格兰。他于1861年发明平炉炼钢法，所依据的是第四个兄弟弗里德利希(1826—1904)原先获得专利的热再生原理。

改译部分：……他和三弟卡尔·西门子(1829—1906)在许多欧洲国家建立电报机工厂。大弟威廉·西门子爵士(卡尔·威廉·西门子；1823—1883)于1844年移居到英格兰。他于1861年发明平炉炼钢法，所依据的是二弟弗里德利希(1826—1904)原先获得专利的热再生原理(西门子)。

评析：很明显，西门子家族四兄弟在英语原文中的称呼是按他们在原文出现先后排列的，如果照直翻译成中文，如本文的初译，即使他们的名字后面都附有生卒年月，仍会造成混乱，阅读不便。改译文毅然重新做了调整，按照他们兄弟的出生年月加以称谓，这样，四兄弟的长幼关系一目了然，符合中文读者的称呼习惯。

事实证明，只要百科全书条目撰写人多费一两个词，就能把很难办的事情澄清，避免语焉不详。但原英文条目撰写人由于受到英语亲属称谓习惯的影响，导致中国读者和译者阅读及翻译困难。可见，辞典编撰人要是能具有一点多文化意识(multicultural sense)，就能轻而易举地解决许多不成问题的问题。在这部百科全书有这么一例：原文称谓词非常到位，翻译时省了很多气力：

[6] ... was probably begun by his *elder brother* Hubert van Eyck and completed by Jan after Hubert's death (van Eyck, Jan).

译文：很可能是由他的兄长胡贝特·凡·爱克着手画起。兄死后，弟继之(凡·爱克)。

总而言之，英汉亲属称谓词的翻译不是一项轻而易举的事。译者要做大量考证工作，查阅许多资料。可见，译者的耐心细致至关重要。

第四节　翻译的意识形态影响

翻译除了受到译语表达形式、译语传统文化的影响外，还受到当前意识形态的制约，这种意识形态指译者所处社会的政治形势、思想道德观念、习俗和规范。严复当年翻译《天演论》，为了使那些封建士大夫能乐意接受西方的理论思想，采用"合乎中国古文传统的体式"（王佐良语）来写就译文。斯诺的 *Red Star Over China* 直译应为《红星照耀中国》，但由于抗战时期所处的环境，为了能在白区顺利发行出版，译者将其改写成了《西行漫记》这一游记的译名，淡化了原书名的政治色彩。强烈的本民族意识形态色彩还会导致译者偏向、袒护或淡化自己的民族、政府的问题乃至罪行。著名的例子就是，一名十四岁的犹太少女记录自己二战期间躲避德国纳粹、遭受纳粹折磨经历的日记本小说《安妮·弗兰克的日记》战后出现了三个不同的译本：荷兰语版本、德语版本和英语版本，但德语版本因为面向德国读者的缘故，抹去和弱化了一切有辱于德国人的篇章和段落，这显然也是由于意识形态的原因而造成的(Lefevere，1992)。

不同时期的译者对于"性"描写的处理也有所不同。古希腊剧作家阿里斯托芬的《吕西斯特拉特》这部喜剧中，女主人公请由裸体美女扮演的"和平"，把斯巴达的和平使者带来，说了这么一句话，直译过来就是"要是他不肯把手伸给你，就拉着他的阳具吧。"不同时期的英语译者是这样翻译的：希基(William James Hickie)的1902年译文是："要是有人不肯把手伸给你，就钩住他的鼻子走吧"。韦伊(A. S. Way)1934年的译本用"腿"取代"阳具"。菲特斯(Dudley Fitts)1954年的译文是："女士们，拖着他们的手吧；要是他们不愿意，那么随便拖什么也行"。帕克(Douglass Parker)1964年的译文用"把手"(handle)代替"阳具"。迪金森(Patrick Dickinson)1970年的译文是："要是他们不肯把手伸给你，就温文地拖他们的救生索(lifeline)吧。"(Lefevere，1992：177) 中文译成"命根子"是不错的选择。在一些外国电影译制片和外国文学作品中，译者、出品人和出版社也常对其中的一些涉及性及色情的片段加以技术处理，就连中国古典小说《金瓶梅》的再版发行，其中的猥亵色情描写也作了文字处理，删去四千三百字之多。但社会意识形态对作品及翻译作品的影响也随着时代的发展而变化。英国作家 D. H. Lawrence 的作品 *Lady Chatterley's Lover* 在20世纪20年代在英国国内被列为"淫书"而遭禁，但在欧洲大陆却得以发行。随着时代的推移，这部被认为"伤风败俗"的书早已被摆到英国的大小书店，并不止一次被改编成电影。目前该书已有至少两种中文译本。由此可见，意识形态对翻译，乃至图书出版影响至大至深。

 本章推荐阅读书目

辜正坤. 中西诗比较鉴赏与翻译理论[M]. 北京：清华大学出版社，2003.
谭载喜. 奈达论翻译[Z]. 北京：中国对外翻译出版公司，1999.
余光中. 余光中谈翻译[M]. 北京：中国对外翻译出版公司，2002.

第六章　翻译的语篇

语篇是指相对完整和独立的一个语言片段。内容相对完整的文章或著作节选均可称为语篇(李运兴,1998:69)。翻译的具体操作是在两个层次上进行的。一是词句层,也就是像作文一样的遣词造句过程。译者在这一层次上所思考的主要是词义的定夺及句式的安排。但译者只在句以下的层次上进行思考是不够的。因为有时会把原文的一句拆成两句,有时又会把原文的两句合成一句,有时一个词、一个结构的意义并非在本句的范围内就能解决,必须放在更大的语言单位中去分析思考。这就需要译者在句以上的语篇层次上进行操作,不仅要考虑一个句子,还要顾及几个句子、整个段落,以至整篇文章。这道理也正和作文一样,光遣词造句是不够的,还必须善于连句成篇,句与句之间的结构衔接、意义连贯也是保证译文质量的重要环节。因此,我们不仅要体味译者在选词造句上的精妙,也要纵观语篇层次上意义的连贯和流畅,作为自己翻译实践的借鉴。语篇的类型多种多样,从本科英汉翻译学习出发,我们选取以下几种语篇类型加以论述。必须注意,虽然每种语篇类型在措辞和文体上都有各自特点,但只要掌握了牢固的英汉语知识和基本翻译技巧,基本可以应付自如。

第一节　报刊语篇的翻译

报刊语篇属于新闻文体。从广义上讲,报刊语篇涉及政治、经济、军事、外交、科技、宗教、法律、家庭等各个方面。它强调的是内容的"纪实性"(factualness),即文章包含了多少"事实"(fact)或"信息"(information)。因此,报刊语篇可以分为三个层次。第一个层次为硬新闻(pure hard news),指的是新闻电讯报道,这类新闻纪实性最强,讲究客观事实的报道。第三个层次为软新闻(pure soft news),纪实性最弱,娱乐性最强,如社会新闻、杂文小品等。中间层次的各式文章被泛称为特写(feature articles),如专题报道、采访、人物介绍、每周专文、各类评述或杂议等(魏志成,2004)。报刊文章的特点是题材新颖,时效性强,通过派生、附加、合成、拼缀及缩略等产生的新词多。从语法上看,报刊语篇具有以下特征(孙致礼,2003):一是广泛使用直接引语和间接引语,以增添真实性和生动性;二是倾向于多用简单

句,并辅以定语、状语、同位语、插入语等补加成分,为读者提供更多的背景知识;三是以提供事实或消息为目的,避免使用带有个人感情或倾向性的语言。从翻译的角度上看,由于报刊语篇,尤其是新闻报道的翻译非常讲求时效性,这就不允许译者像翻译文学作品那样做到精雕细刻,译文出现的问题主要是翻译时间仓促,句法比较欧化、新词查找困难等。但即使这样,译文的准确和严谨仍是报刊语篇的基本要求。译者务必对当前的国内外时事有深刻的了解,关注事态的发展,这样才能胜任这项翻译工作。

例文[1]

The Most Important Speech of the Century

David Nyhan

We learned how far up he's come on New Year's Day when every Chinese newspaper heralded a 6000-word speech in which Deng signaled the end of thousands of years of Chinese xenophobia.

It may eventually come to be regarded the most important speech of the century. For in it, the Maximum Leader of the nation that comprises one-fourth of mankind served notice that China is joining the rest of the world (save Albania) in the 20th century.

"No country can develop by closing its door," said Deng. "We suffered from this, and our forefathers suffered from this." Reversing thousands of years of official hostility to the world outside the Great Wall, Deng said simply: "Isolation landed China in poverty, backwardness and ignorance."

This startling admission contradicts thousands of years of Chinese policy, going back beyond the Ming Dynasty to the Chin Dynasty, when the wall was erected to keep barbarians on horseback out in the wilds where they belonged.

Deng's message: Do not renounce Marxism, but adopt capitalist ideas where they make sense—"it cannot harm us." Economic reform, spearheaded by younger leaders, is the single most important bulwark for the nation's security, for only with economic strength can bombs, missiles and planes be purchased.

If China is trying to catch up to the rest of the world in the 20th century, maybe the 21st century will belong to them. They have people, brains and they can be impressively disciplined. And their industrial potential is awesome.

It may come to be commonly accepted in the next century that the most significant speech ever given by a fellow with a cowboy hat came not from Ronald Reagan but from an 80-year-old Chinese man. —*Boston Globe*

本世纪最重要的讲话

戴维·奈恩

在元旦这天,当中国每家报纸都发表了邓小平的一篇六千字的讲话时,我们了解到他迈出了多大的步子。这篇讲话标志着中国几千年恐外历史的终结。

这篇讲话最终有可能被认为是本世纪最重要的讲话。因为在这篇讲话中,占人类总数四分之一的国家的最高领导人宣布,中国在 20 世纪正在加入世界其他国家(除了阿尔巴尼亚)的行列。

邓说:"任何国家要发达起来,闭关自守都不可能。我们吃过这个苦头,我们的老祖宗也吃过这个苦头。"邓改变了几千年来官方敌视长城以外的世界的态度,他明确地说:"闭关自守把中国搞得贫穷落后,愚昧无知。"

承认这一点是令人吃惊的,这同中国几千年来执行的政策大不一样。这种政策可以追溯到明代以前直到秦代,当时修筑了长城,为的是阻挡居住在荒原上的骑马的野蛮人。

邓的意思是:不放弃马克思主义,但是只要资本主义的观念有道理,就采纳,因为"开放伤害不了我们"。由较年轻的领导人带头进行的经济改革是国家安全最重要的保障,因为只有经济实力雄厚,才能购买炸弹、导弹和飞机。

如果中国在 20 世纪设法赶上世界上其他国家,21 世纪可能属于它的。他们有人力,有人才,他们的纪律性很强。他们的工业潜力也是令人敬畏的。

下一世纪,人们可能会普遍同意,发表最重要讲话的戴牛仔帽的人不是罗纳德·里根,而是一位 80 岁的中国人。(《波士顿环球》)

评析:这是一篇报刊评论型的文章,所表现的主题是邓小平改革开放给中国带来的翻天覆地变化。作者是外国专栏作家,所传递的观点是客观、肯定和友好的。文章开篇以中国各家报纸刊登的演讲为引子,采用边叙边议的方式,对邓小平的一些重要言论加以评述,最后以耐人寻味的论断结束全文。全文共分七段。第一段实际上是一个包含了两个修饰性从句的长句,将原文简而化之,其主干句是"We learned how far he's come on New Year's Day",该段落难点在于如何把整个长句切分开,重新加以组合。对"Deng"的称谓在翻译中表达也是个问题。第二段又两个句子构成。其中第二句也是一个长句,包括两个从句。该段落的难点为从句,尤其是第二个从句的翻译。"save"对学生来说也是一个易出错的词。第三段中的"Isolation landed China in poverty, backwardness and ignorance". 是个典型的英语句型。第四段的句子包含一个分词短语和两个不同层次的从句。在"going back beyond the Ming Dynasty to the Chin Dynasty"中的"Chin"是一个极易混淆的词。第五段中,"renounce、purchase"看似容易,对学生都是难以处理好的词。第六段共有三句,由一个条件句引导,辅之以两个句子陈述理由。最后一段作为一个长句,也许是本文中最难的一句,包含一个从句,其中,"ever given by a fellow with a cowboy hat"是修饰"speech"的过去分词短语,其主要结构是"It may come to be... accepted... that the ... speech ... came not from Ronald Reagan but from an 80-year-old Chinese man"。要翻译好这最后一段,我们还要了解一些背景知识,即邓小平 1979 年访美时,曾应邀在得克萨斯州休斯敦观看马术表演,并获赠一顶牛仔帽。在美国人眼里,"牛仔"体现着一种勇敢、强悍和坚忍不拔的精神。这一历史性镜头通过电视的传播令人难忘。文章作者巧妙地联想到这一往事,信笔成趣。

本篇曾作为第一篇翻译作业让历届英语专业三年级学生试做,发现无论是哪一届学生,他们基本都会犯一系列相同的错译。现从以下三个方面加以分析。

1. 对翻译的认识问题

这里假设的一个前提是译者在理解上稍无大碍,但由于对翻译的性质、功能、要求等认识存在偏差,翻译被视为可任意改编、自由发挥的工作。于是,在文章的整体把握上就会出现如下问题:

任意改变称谓、语气:原文中"Deng"是英语行文中的习惯称谓,出自一个西方报刊作家的笔下,可直译成"邓"或"邓小平",但历届都有学生将其译成"小平同志"、"邓小平同志",有的人甚至于一口一个"小平同志",其口气俨然国内报纸的社论文章,以为不这样称呼就是不敬。岂不知,原文通篇并无"comrade"一词。

任意添加、发挥或删减:如在第一段中译者就无端写出了"随着新年钟声的敲响,中国各家各户报纸带着邓小平同志的一篇6000字的演讲飞进了千家万户"。其思路估计是说到新年必联想到新年钟声。肆意添加且不说,译文本身也是病句。更有无中生有,张冠李戴者,如"中华人民共和国主席邓小平"。第二段也被译得陈词滥调,如将"China is joining the rest of the world (save Albania) in the 20th century"译成"中国人民将在20世纪走出国门,面向世界"等。第五段中,"for only with economic strength can bombs, missiles and planes be purchased"看似简单,也是历届学生译错率最高的,误译如下:"只有经济实力雄厚,才能购买原子弹、导弹和飞机"(常识问题)、"只有把经济搞上去,外国的大炮、导弹和飞机才不敢来"、"……才能有效地增强国防力量"、"才会有强大的军事力量"、"……才能购买炸弹、导弹和飞机等防御设施"(画蛇添足)、"……才能购买高科技武器"。学生要么只粗略翻译大意,要么干脆捕风捉影,添油加醋。最后一段也被删减成"本世纪最举足轻重的演说并不是来自美国的里根,而是一位80岁的中国老人"。原文中的"ever given by a fellow with a cowboy hat"这样一个风趣而形象的表达语也荡然无存。当然,上述错译也不能完全归因于对翻译的认识问题,语法理解和词的理解也可能造成这些问题。

2. 语法理解问题

对于英语专业三年级学生而言,英汉民族思维习惯的差异、英汉语两种语言的结构差异造成他们在理解和表达上困难重重。从语言角度上看,主要原因在于英语的语法结构太复杂,修饰性短语太多且穿插于主句结构之间,造成视觉混乱,理不清其中的语法关系。例如第二段中"the Maximum Leader of the nation that comprises one-fourth of mankind served notice that China is joining the rest of the world (save Albania) in the 20th century",其主结构是"the Maximum Leader…served notice that China is joining the rest of the world"极容易受修饰语"that comprises one-fourth of mankind"干扰。原文最后一段是学生最易译错的部分,一方面,学生对当时的时代背景不甚了解,另一方面(也是主要方面),这个长句以"It may come to be commonly accepted"开头,后接一个长长的名词性从句结构,从句里的主语speech又受一个过去分词短语"ever given by a fellow with a cowboy hat"修饰,从句中的谓语动词结构是"came not from…but from…"。学生面对这个包含较多修饰短语的长句显然有点手忙脚乱,力不从心,出现如下误译:"本世纪最重要的演讲不是戴着牛仔帽的里根,而是中国的一位80岁的老人"或"演讲不是来自里根,而是出自一位80岁的戴着牛仔帽的中国老人"(评:"戴着牛仔帽的"的修饰对象偏差)、"下个世纪人们将会认为在20世纪领导人所作的讲话中,最重要的不是罗纳德·里根,而是一位80岁的中国老人"(评:基本正确,但"ever given by a fellow with a cowboy hat"没有翻译出来)。

3. 词的理解问题

词是语篇翻译中的基本单位,对词语理解不深,或一知半解,或因为粗心大意,必然造成误译,影响整个句子、段落乃至整个语篇。例如,"save"在文章中应为介词,表示"除了",而一些译文作动词解,断章取义地翻译成"拯救";"the Maximum Leader"应为"最高领导人",而不知有多少人将其译成"马克思主义领导人",盖"Maximum"为"Marxism"之误也!再说,"Marxism"能直接用来修饰"Leader"吗?第四段中的"Chin Dynasty","秦朝也",但将其译成"清朝"(Ching Dynasty)的大有人在。第五段中的"renounce"意为"放弃、抛弃",而有人译成"宣扬"("pronounce"之误)。"bomb"翻译成"炸弹"也就够了,有的偏要译成"炮弹"、"原子弹",原子弹可购买哉?"plane"不译"飞机",而要译成"军机"、"轰炸机"!"purchase"的误译五花八门,分别译成"拥有"、"制造"、"生产"、"追赶"(chase 之误)、"换来"、"引进",就是不译"购买"。最后一段中的"fellow"为口语词,有"男人、男孩、小伙子"之意,泛指"人",但一些学生将其与后面的"Ronald Regan"放在一起翻译,就有了"棒小伙子里根"、"年轻的美国总统里根"等译文,殊不知里根恰是个老年总统!坏就坏在对"fellow"一词的理解上。第七段中的"cowboy hat"竟也令不少人大费周折,各种译文纷纷出笼,分别有"草帽"、"帆布帽"、"鸭舌帽"等各种款式的帽子,乃至译成"牛仔裤"。这些问题大部分只要认真查阅词典,都可以解决,为什么会一而再出现在翻译作业中呢?这是语言水平问题,更是不求甚解、译风散漫的表现。当然,也有一些精彩的佳译。原文第一段中,"We learned how far up he's come on New Year's Day"在参考译文中为"……我们了解到他走了多远",似乎较生硬,有学生将其译成"我们了解到他迈出了多大的一步",这样的表达更透彻。原文第六段中"maybe the 21st century will belong to them"在参考译文中为"21 世纪可能属于它的"显得平直,有学生译成"也许 21 世纪将是他们的天下",则把其中的涵义表达得更充分。

在本文中还有一个重要的问题值得关注。那就是邓小平的几句讲话的翻译问题。由于这几句话是直接引语,说明它们是直接从中文翻译过去的,这就要求译者在资料允许的情况下查找出原文的确切说法。

由此可见,报刊题材翻译的基础还是基本技能,在此基础上再来谈发挥报刊题材翻译的特点不迟。

本节练习

第一篇(时政)

After a Hard Year, Signs of Rebounding Spirits at the UN

The past year has been a spirit-bruising period for the United Nations, disparaged by the Bush administration as irrelevant, excluded from the political transition in Iraq and institutionally rocked by the fatal bombing in August of its Baghdad headquarters.

"The morale was deeply affected by the various attacks on the relevance of the institution, and Aug. 19—we call it 'our 9/11'—was an enormous emotional setback with the loss of so many friends and colleagues," said Shashi Tharoor, undersecretary general for communications and public information.

Twenty-two people died in that blast, including the mission chief, Sergio Vieira de Mello. Soon afterward, Secretary General Kofi Annan withdrew all international United nations staff members from Iraq.

Now, the organization finds itself again at the center of things, and the dejection around the East River headquarters building is lifting. "There's definitely a bounce back in the step," said Mark Malloch Brown, administrator of the United Nations Development Program.

Since the start of the year, the United Nations has been wooed by its onetime detractors in the Bush administration to re-enter Iraq and chart the country's political future, scored a breakthrough in the decades-long struggle to reunite the feuding Turkish and Greek Cypriots, and acted with unaccustomed swiftness to authorize deployment of a multinational force to Haiti.

Mr. Tharoor traced the recovery from a low point last November—when the American-brokered agreement to transfer power in Iraq made no mention of any role for the United Nations—to the meetings here on Jan. 19—when L. Paul Bremer III, the American administrator of Iraq, and members of the American-appointed Iraqi Governing Council asked the United Nations to chart the political future in Baghdad.

"For the leading protagonists of that agreement to come to New York in January and say, 'We need you' certainly represented a significant change," Mr. Tharoor said.

The confrontational experience of the past year has bred wariness into the United Nations as it steps back into the Iraqi crisis.

Kishore Mahbubani, the ambassador from Singapore, often referred to as a possible successor to Mr. Annan, said that being excluded from Iraq was only one of "the two nightmares that Iraq offers."

"The other," he said, "is to be completely included."

"As it gets more and more into Iraq, the responsibility will become more and more the UN's, and we will have to be very careful to avoid a situation where, let's say, the election process in Iraq falls apart, and everyone will go around saying, 'There goes the UN, failing again.'"

What the new willingness of the United States to work with the United Nations means for the future is a subject of debate.

"I find no evidence that there is a fundamental shift in Washington's attitude towards the UN," said Michael W. Doyle, a professor of law and international affairs at Columbia who was a special adviser to Mr. Annan from 2001 to 2003. "It is still multilateralism a la carte. When it serves the US purpose, it will seek the UN's views. When it doesn't, it won't."

Mr. Malloch Brown said assessments of the status of the United States—United Nations relationship always tended to the extremes.

"It is never as bad as some think and never as good and euphoric as others would believe," he said. "That said, the bad karma has tended to prevail over the good karma more in this administration than the last."(*The New York Times*)

翻译提示：这是一篇有关联合国的文章，译者如果平时关心时事，那么一些背景知识将会对翻译有帮助作用。

第二篇（新闻）

Asian buyers help fuel Sotheby's art boom

Sotheby's had its best year in 2005 for at least 15 years as the art market boomed, fuelled in part by new Asian and Russian buyers.

Sotheby's yesterday said it sold $2.75bn in art last year, generating revenue of $513.5m and an 85 per cent rise in net income to $63m. Sales this year show prices continuing to rise across the board.

"Worldwide sales to date [this year] have been exceptional," the group said. Sotheby's and Christie's together sold a record $451m of artworks at last month's main London sales.

The strength of the market, especially in contemporary art, has led to questions about whether growth can be sustained. The previous art market boom 15 years ago ended abruptly. The prices of some works are still recovering.

Robin Woodhead, Sotheby's chief executive for Europe and Asia, said what is different now from the previous boom, which was driven by the Impressionists, is that the market is busy across practically all sectors.

"There are very high prices in old masters, in photography [and] renewed interest in decorative arts. There is a great depth of buying and a lot of property coming to the market for sale."

Mr Woodhead said growth in traditional areas such as Impressionist and modern art remained strong but the big increases were in contemporary art and nonwestern art, especially Asian and Russian.

He said Sotheby's would hold its first contemporary Asian art sale this month in response to demand, and it had seen a 10-fold increase in Russian art sales in the past five years.

"With the growth in the Chinese, Asian and Russian economies, there has been great interest in those countries in acquiring their historical and cultural works of art, to repatriate them," he said. More recently, wealthy Chinese and Russian families had started buying western works as well. Asians bought 11 per cent of the contemporary works sold at the Sotheby's London auction last month.

翻译提示：报刊类文章,注意其中数字和倍数的翻译。

第三篇(新闻)

Public's DNA to be exhibited alongside Mandela's

South Africans and international tourists are being invited to test their DNA to determine their ancestry and have the results exhibited alongside Nelson Mandela's.

The tests are being offered by the new Origins Center museum in Johannesburg to illustrate one of its themes, that "all human beings are related genetically and can trace their roots to a common ancestor who lived in Africa."

The DNA samples will be tested by the National Health Institute and the results will be given after two weeks. One can choose whether to remain anonymous or have one's ancestry exhibited in the museum.

Mandela's DNA results, taken from a sample a couple of years ago, show that he is descended from the earliest inhabitants of Africa, the San people. Their mitochondrial DNA (mitDNA) contains the earliest genetic print of all human beings, called L1. He also is descended from a group of Africans from the Great Lakes region in East Africa.

South Africa's African groups mainly originated from the Great Lakes area and moved down along the east coast to settle in South Africa.

The Origins Center is situated on the campus of the University of Witwatersrand and beginning next Tuesday will open to the public six days a week.

It is the brainchild of Mbeki who had the idea when he went walking in the Ukahlamba Drakensberg Mountains five years ago and found that he knew more about rock art than most of his guides. He wanted South Africa's impressive rock art collection and research exhibited to benefit the public at large.

The museum will also contain a significant repository of stone age tools and rock art, evidence of inhabitants of southern Africa from 2.6 million years ago.

Only later did people leave Africa to journey to the rest of the world, according to Francis Gerard, the creative director of the Origins Center. "People only go to the Americas about 18,000 years ago," he said.

翻译提示：报刊类文章，注意人名和地名的翻译。应尽量查找英汉人名地名词典，而不能根据读音自拟。

第四篇（报刊评论）

Guests Welcome
Peter Mayle

Tourists are guilty, so we are frequently told, of a number of crimes: upsetting the ecological balance of Mount Everest, parking wads of chewing gum under the benches of museums and art galleries, wearing unsuitable T shirts in Notre Dame, debauching the local peasantry and generally lowering the tone of everywhere they choose to set their benighted feet. Rarely has a group of people been so widely reviled, and I am one of them. So are you. I've been a tourist in Provence for about 15 years now, often on the receiving end of criticism or mild abuse from people who accuse me of having "ruined" the region by writing about it. Curiously, these complaints, which are sometimes offensive and invariably very shrill, do not come from the Provençaux themselves, who seem to regard me as a fairly benevolent oddity, but from my fellow tourists.

From their vantage points in London or Brussels or Boston, they deplore what they say has happened to Provence. They know, from investigations carried out during their brief annual vacations, that Provence has changed. The markets are more crowded, the prices have gone up, the restaurants are full, the sunniest cafe tables are taken, bakers run out of bread, waiters run out of patience, there is nowhere to park and nobody—but nobody—can be founded to fix a leaking poll.

Mass tourism in Provence started more than 2,600 years ago with the arrival of Greeks from Phocea, who founded Marseille. They were a civilizing influence and provided jobs for the locals, and could therefore be described as acceptable tourists. So were the Romans, who built the monuments and viaducts and amphitheaters that we still enjoy. Then came a bad patch, with the arrival of Visigoths, Ostrogoths and Franks. They amused themselves by terrifying the inhabitants and ravaging the countryside. Here, perhaps, is where it had its start: the reputation of tourists as slobs.

After many years of on-the-spot observation, I would like to put in a good word for this much-maligned species. The overwhelming majority of these visitors are amiable and considerate people who want nothing more than quiet enjoyment. They have come to Provence for sunshine and spectacular scenery, for the food and the wine, for a pleasant-break from real life. Of course there are crowds, particularly in July and August, but these tend to be confined to the towns and postcard villages. For those who want solitude, beautiful and empty countryside is only a short drive away.

Personally, I have never found the tourist season intolerable; indeed, there is reason to be grateful for some of its effects. If it weren't for the money that tourism brings, many of the chateaux and gardens open to the public would become derelict; monuments would be left to crumble; many restaurants could never survive on local custom alone; it wouldn't be worth putting on concerts or village fetes. Rural life would be the poorer.

Obviously, this is not true everywhere. Some parts of the world have been so thoroughly overexploited that they have lost whatever charm they once possessed. This is usually the result of local greed; but the tourist, not the rapacious developer, gets most of the blame.

翻译提示：旅游是否该为当地资源受侵袭而负责？旅游者是无辜还是有过？作者用了大量篇幅加以分析判定。

第二节 文学语篇的翻译

纽马克把翻译题材分成两类：真实性题材(fact)和虚构性题材(fiction)。真实性题材属于非文学翻译，虚构性题材属于文学翻译。非文学翻译基本上只是和词的本义打交道（如"树"、"椅子"），而虚构性题材涉及到想象事物，所表达的是寓言故事，是对现实进行评述而不是描述，本义只是作为例子，其中心在表达词的内涵意义：联想（玫瑰）、象征（剑）、隐喻、声韵修辞（头韵法和拟声）、押韵等。表达词本义的语言（窗户、小路）一般只需照字面译，这和文学题材，即想像文学，是相反的。文学翻译运用形象思维，创造出具有审美价值的艺术形象和典型。文学是以语言作为塑造形象的表达工具，因此文学是语言艺术。比起非文学翻译者，文学翻译家有更多的文化因素、语言现象要重新处理。文学翻译就是运用另一种语言将原有艺术形象和典型加以再创造，使之同样栩栩如生，宛如原创。一部东西方翻译史几乎就是一部文学翻译史。长期以来，翻译研究的主体就是文学翻译研究。因此有关文学翻译的要求和标准可谓多矣。钱钟书旗帜鲜明地说过："文学翻译的最高理想可以说是'化'。把作品从一国文字转变成另一国文字，既能不因语文习惯的差异而露出生硬牵强的痕迹，又能完全保存原作的风味，那就算得入于'化境'。"这是文学翻译的最高层次。以下我们对散

文和小说的翻译加以评述,感受文学翻译之美。

一、散文的翻译

以某一话题作为写作内容的散文(prose)可以分为正式散文体和非正式散文体。正式散文体在英语中称为"exposition",汉语又称其为"说明文"、"议论文"、"政论文"、"论述文",说理透彻,逻辑性强、结构严谨、用词讲究、风格凝重。非正式散文体侧重于一些轻松的话题,或写景或抒情。英语的"narration"(叙述文)和"description"(描述文)大体可以划归为非正式散文体,其特点是结构相对散漫,语言风格自由多样、生动幽默、轻松自然(魏志成,2004)。翻译之前,应该先广泛阅读各种中文散文,体会散文的写作风格和笔法,方能译出其中的妙味。

例文[2](写景)

A Londoner's Holiday
William Hale White

One Sunday we determined upon a holiday. It was a bold adventure for us, but we had made up our minds. There was an excursion train to Hastings, and accordingly Ellen, Marie, and myself were at London Bridge Station early in the morning. It was a lovely summer's day in mid-July. The journey down was uncomfortable enough in consequence of the heat and dust, but we heeded neither one nor the other in the hope of seeing the sea. We reached Hastings at about eleven o'clock, and strolled westwards towards Bexhill. Our pleasure was exquisite. Who can tell, save the imprisoned Londoner, the joy of walking on the clean sea-sand! What a delight that was, to say nothing of the beauty of the scenery! To be free of the litter and filth of a London suburb, of its broken hedges, its brickbats, its torn advertisements, its worn and trampled grass in fields half given over to the speculative builder; in place of this, to tread the immaculate shore over which breathed a wind not charged with soot; to replace the dull, shrouding obscurity of the smoke by a distance so distinct that the masts of the ships whose hulls were buried below the horizon were visible—all this was perfect bliss. It was not very poetic bliss, perhaps; but nevertheless it is the fact that the cleanness of the sea and the sea air was attractive to us as any of the sea attributes. We had a wonderful time. Only in the country is it possible to note the change of morning into mid-day, of mid-day into afternoon, and of afternoon into evening; and it is only in the country, therefore, a day seems stretched out into its proper length. We had brought all our food with us, and sat upon the shore in the shadow of a piece of the cliff. A row of heavy white clouds lay along the horizon almost unchangeable and immovable, with their summit-lines and the part of the mass just below them steeped in sunlight. The level of opaline water differed only from a floor by a scarcely perceptible heaving motion, which broke into the faintest of ripples at our feet. So still was the great ocean, so quietly did everything lie in it, that the wavelets which licked the beach were as pure and bright as if they were a part of the mid-ocean depths. About a mile from us, at one o'clock, a long row of porpoises appeared, showing themselves in graceful curves for half-an-hour or so, till they went out farther to sea off Fairlight. Some fishing-boats were becalmed just in front us. Their shadows slept, or almost slept, upon the water, a gentle quivering alone showing that it was not complete deep, or if sleep, that it was sleep with dreams. The intensity of the sunlight sharpened the outlines of every little piece of rock, and of the pebbles, in a manner which seemed supernatural to us Londoners. In London we get the heat of the sun, but not his light, and the separation of individual parts into such vivid isolation was so surprising that even Marie notices it, and said it "all seemed as if she was looking through a glass". It was perfect—perfect in its beauty—and perfect because, from the sun in the heavens down to the fly with burnished wings on the hot rock, there was nothing out of harmony. Everything breathed one spirit. Marie played near us; Ellen and I sat still, doing nothing. We wanted nothing, we had nothing to achieve; there was no curiosities to be seen, there was no particular place to be reached, no "plan of operations", and London was forgotten for the time. It lay behind us in the northwest, and the cliff was at the back of us shutting out all thought of it. No reminiscences and no anticipation disturbed us; the present was sufficient, and occupied us totally.

假日记游

威廉·海尔·怀特

某礼拜日我们决定出游。这事在我们颇是一番壮举,但是我们决心不变。那天适有游览车通往哈斯丁斯,于是埃伦、玛丽和我自己一清早即去了伦敦桥车站。那是7月中旬的一个可爱的夏日。由于天气炎热,尘土飞扬,一路上并不舒服,但是我们对此也并不在意,一心只盼看到大海。我们抵达哈斯丁斯时为11点左右,于是漫步向西,前去白克希尔。此行之乐,可谓妙极。散步于清浅的沙滩之上——此中的快乐,除了久伏不出伦敦蛰居者外,又有谁知!景色之佳姑且不说,仅仅能到海边已是多么欣快!伦敦郊外的垃圾污秽、断篱残砖、破烂招贴、乃至半由投机建筑商侵占践踏的大片草地,至此都一概抛在脑后;而代之以光洁无瑕的岸滩,步履其上,清风习习,不杂一丝烟气;这里再不是烟尘笼罩,晦暝凄其,而是天明气清,一望无际,沉埋在远处地平线下的船只,桅樯矗立,历历可见——看到这一切真是很大的幸福。也许这还够不上诗意般的幸福;然而这里的海天之清,至少也和海上的种种同样诱人的一点,则也是个事实,因而可说不虚此行。一天之间,自朝至午,自午至暮,其间的递嬗变化,唯有乡居才最能觉察,因此一天的时间在这里才显示出它的真正长度。我们携带着食物,坐卧在滩头悬崖的阴影之下,一团凝重的白色阵云低垂在水天之际,迄不稍动,云的顶端和下面的一部分都沉浸在阳光之中。坦荡乳白的水面,如若不是处于几乎难辨的喘动,简直如席地一般,在我们的脚下碎作丝丝涟漪。大海是那么沉着,海中的一切又是那么寂静无哗,拂激着海滩的细浪微波显得更加纯净澈滟,宛如出自远洋深底一般。午后一时许,离我们约一哩处,一长队海豚浮水面,翻舞嬉戏,颇为好看,半小时后才远过费尔莱特,向深海游去。眼前不远,渔舟三五,凝滞不前,樯影斜映水上,仿佛睡去,偶尔微见颤动,似又未尝熟睡,恍若惊梦。天上晴光炽烈,灼灼之下,砾岩卵石,纹理悉见,这在我们伦敦人看来,几非尘世所有。伦敦的太阳只授予人热而不授予人光,光热分离,竟到了如此程度,就连玛丽都察觉到了,所以她说,那里一切仿佛尽是"镜中窥物"。而这里一切无不完美,这完美不仅见于景物的佳妍,还来自许多东西,上自天端的丽日,下至岩上金蝇的微羽毛,无一不觉得和谐。

万类噫气,其魂则一。玛丽嬉游在一旁;埃伦与我则默坐其地,一事不做。此时我们与物无求,于愿无期;无珍奇瑰丽的事物可观,无特殊的佳胜之境要去,无"行动计划"须待执行,而伦敦乃得暂时去怀。它坐落在我们的西北,背后有悬崖阻隔,足使我们对之屏虑。往事未来,两不相扰;眼前之景,于我已足,其余则无暇蒽蒽过虑了。——高健译文

译评:本语篇为描述和叙述性散文。一般来说,描述及叙述文比较讲究语言美,特别是涉及绘景、状物、写人时,以达到给人们美感享受的目的(魏志成,2004)。为此,翻译时应该在语言运用上下工夫,最基本的要求是顺应原文,译文的清婉或华丽都应该以原文风格为基准。文章虽是游记,但能从中说开去,谈及天地,处处体现一种渴望远离尘世浮华、追求自然、自由、清新的生活。译者译到得意处,就挥洒出"眼前不远,渔舟三五,凝滞不前,樯影斜映水上,仿佛睡去,偶尔微见颤动,似又未尝熟睡,恍若惊梦"的精彩佳句,令人不能不想起范仲淹《岳阳楼》的诗句,这是阅读英语原文所无法感受到的。当然,也有译论者认为,该译文"文白杂用"现象过于突出,过多短句,过多的动宾倒装结构,过多的"四字结构",过多的古旧语汇(如古代汉语的叹词"噫")、生僻或废弃的语汇("蒽"字)等,在一定程度上使译文丧失了原文的清新美(魏志成,2004)。其实不然,如果我们打开梁实秋的闲适小品文一读,就会发现其字里行间散发出来的就是这么一股浓浓的典雅别致的气息。

例文[3](写景)

It was a typical summer evening in June, the atmosphere being in such delicate equilibrium and so transmissive that inanimate objects seemed endowed with two or three senses, if not five. There was no distinction between the near and the far, and an auditor felt close to everything within the horizon. The soundlessness impressed her as a positive entity rather as the mere negation of noise. It was broken by the strumming of strings.

译文一:

那是一个典型的六月黄昏。大气的平衡如此精微,传导力如此敏锐,就连冥顽的无生物也有了知觉——如果不是五种知觉的话,也有两三种。远和近已失去了差异,地平线以内的声音都仿佛近在咫尺。这一片寂静在她耳朵里并非是消极的默无声息,而仿佛是一种积极的实际存在。而这寂静却被拨弄琴弦的声音打破了。

译文二:

这是六月里特有的夏日黄昏。暮色格外柔和静美且极富感染力,连那些冥顽之物都仿佛平添了几分灵性,有了各种知觉。远近一切,难分彼此;天际间任何一丝声息,听来都恍如近在耳畔。她觉得这静寂并非单纯的悄无声息,而是一种实实在在的感觉。不想这静寂却被瑟瑟的琴声打破了。——马红军译文

评析:原文中一些词语非常抽象,如"equilibrium"(平衡、均衡),"transmissive"(能传送),"two or three senses, if not five"(如果不是五种知觉的话,也有两三种),"within the horizon"(地平线以内),"positive entity"(实际的存在)。也亏英语能写出这样的文字。译文一译得非常艰难,疲于应付,而译文二则将一段晦涩的文字译得诗情画意,彻底超脱原文文字的拘绊。

例文[4](游记)

Torcello, which used to be lonely as a cloud, has recently become an outing from Venice. Many more visitors than it can comfortably hold pour into it, off the regular steamers, off chartered motor-boats, and off yachts; all day they amble up the towpath, looking for what? The cathedral is decorated with early mosaics-scenes from hell, much restored, and a great sad, austere Madonna; Byzantine art is an acquired taste and probably not one in ten of the visitors has acquired it. They wander into the church and look round aimlessly. They come out on to the village green and photograph each other in a stone armchair, said to be the throne of Attila. They relentlessly tear at the wild roses which one has seen in bud and longed to see in bloom and which for a day have scented the whole island. As soon as they are picked the roses fade and are thrown into the canal. The Americans visit the inn to eat or drink something. The English declare that they can't afford to do this. They take food which they have brought with them into the vineyard and I am sorry to say leave the devil of a mess behind them. Every Thursday Germans come up the towpath, marching as to war, with a Leader. There is a standing order for fifty luncheons at the inn; while they eat the Leader lectures them through a megaphone. After luncheon they march into the cathedral and undergo another lecture. They, at least, know what they are seeing. Then they march back to their boat. They are tidy; they leave no litter. (Nancy Mitford, *The Water Beetle*)

　　托车罗往日寂寞如孤云,近来却成了威尼斯外围的游览点。来客多了,这个小地方就拥挤不堪。搭班船的,坐包船的,驾游艇的,一批批涌到,从早到晚,通过那条纤路,漫步进村观光。想看什么呢? 大教堂内装饰,有早期镶嵌画;表现地狱诸景的多经修复,此外还有容色黯然凛然的圣母巨像。拜占庭艺术是要有特殊修养才能欣赏的,而有特殊修养的游客十中无一。这些人逛到教堂,东张西望,茫茫然不知看什么好。踏上村中草地,看到一张石椅,听说是匈奴王阿提拉的宝座,就要照相:一个个登上大位,你给我照,我给你照。这些人惯于辣手摧花,见了野玫瑰决不放过。可怜含苞欲放的野玫瑰,岛上飘香才一昼,爱花者正盼其盛开,却给这些人摘下来,转瞬凋萎,给扔进运河。美国人光顾小酒店,吃吃喝喝。英国人声称花不起,自带食物进葡萄园野餐;真对不起,我不能不说他们把人家的地方搞得乱七八糟。德国人呢,每逢星期四就像出征一样,由队长率领,列队循纤路走来,到小酒店吃其照例预订的五十份午餐,边吃边听队长用喇叭给他们上大课。午餐后列队到大教堂,在里头还得恭听一课。他们至少知道看的什么。完了列队回船。他们倒是整洁得很,从来不留半点垃圾。——翁显良译文

　　评析：这篇东西写的是古已有之、于今尤甚、想看风景而又煞风景的游客。首句引"Wordsworth",原诗如译成五言,第一行"I wander lonely as a cloud"不妨化为"浪迹天地间,寂寞如孤云"。中国读者可以从"寂寞如孤云"联想到李白的"孤云独去闲",因而印象更深,艺术感更强。第三句的"sad, austere",译作"黯然凛然",用以形容 Madonna,也许比较恰当。第四句的"aimlessly"译成"茫茫然不知看什么好",神情差不离。第十二句的"lectures",就是我们常说的"上大课"。再说章法句法。只要用汉语整段构思,原文许多句子的结构形式势必打破。英译汉应该因汉语之宜,或分或合,或伸或缩,灵活处理,充分发挥我们在运用本族语方面固有的优势;这样才有可能做到译文与原文二者艺术效果大致相同,这样才是艺术上忠实于原作。读者能从末句的"倒是"二字看出作者的讪笑。真正得原著之味,才能因汉语之宜,用汉语之长;译文确能因汉语之宜,用汉语之长,才可以使读者得原著之

味。原著的艺术性越高,越要发挥汉语的优势。寻求汉语的最佳表达方式。汉译的技巧,无非是摆脱原文表层结构的束缚而自由运用汉语再创作的技巧。

例文[5](游记)

A Watering Place

Hayden

Saturday Night, 30 Sept. 1826

The Warwickshire Avon falls into the Severn here, and on the sides of both, for many miles back, there are the finest meadows that ever were seen. In looking over them, and beholding the endless flocks and herds, one wonders what can become of all the meat! By riding on about eight or nine miles farther however, this wonder is a little diminished; for here we come to one of the devouring WENS: namely, CHELTENHAM, which is what they call a "watering place", that is to say, a place to which East India plunderers, West India floggers, English taxgorgers, together with gluttons, drunkards, and debauchees of all descriptions, female as well as male, resort, at the suggestion of silently laughing quacks, in the hope of getting rid of the bodily consequences of their manifold sins and iniquities. When I enter a place like this, I always feel disposed to squeeze up my nose with my fingers. It is nonsense, to be sure; but I conceit that every two-legged creature, that I see coming near me, is about to cover me with the poisonous proceeds of its impurities. To places like this come all that is knavish and all that is foolish and all that is base; gamesters, pick-pockets, and harlots; young wife-hunters in search of rich and ugly and old women, and young husband-hunters in search of rich and wrinkled or half-rotten men, the former resolutely bent, be the means what they may, to give the latter heirs to their lands and tenements. These things are notorious; and, Sir William Scott, in his speech of 1802, in favour of the non-residence of the Clergy, expressly said, that they and their families ought to appear at watering places, and that this was amongst the means of making them respected by their flocks! Memorandum: he was a member for Oxford when he said this!

温泉胜地

海顿

1826年9月30日,星期六晚

华立克夏的爱望河在此流入色纹河,两河沿岸若干哩水草丰美,前所未见。草地上牛羊成群,沿途不断。看着这景色,这牛羊,心想这些好肉可作多少用途,不禁感到神奇。但是再向前骑八九哩,这神奇之感就破灭了;原来我们已到达一个毒瘤似的害人地方,名叫却尔特能,所谓温泉胜地是也。这地方充满了东印度的劫掠者,西印度的奴隶主,英国的税吏,吃客,酒鬼,淫棍,各色各样,男女俱全。他们听了一些窃窃暗笑的江湖郎中的鬼话,以为在做了多少丑事之后,一身孽障,可以到此一洗而净!我每次进入这等地方,总想用手指捏住自己鼻子。当然这话没有道理,但我一看见这儿任何一个两腿畜生向我走来,实在觉得他们肮脏不堪,像是一有机会就要将他们毒疮传染给我似的!来这地方的都是最恶劣、最愚蠢、最下流的人:赌鬼、小偷、娼妓,一心想娶有钱的丑老婆子的年轻男子,一心想嫁有钱的满脸皱纹、半身入土的老头子的年轻女子。这些少夫幼妻为了便于继承产业,不惜一切手段,坚决要为这些老妇衰翁生男育女!

这等丑事,尽人皆知。然而威廉•司各特爵士在1802年演讲,明白主张牧师不必定居教区,而应携眷到温泉游览,据说这样反而能得到他们教区子民的尊敬云云。查此人作此语时,官任代表牛津城的国会议员! ——王佐良译文

评析:这是一篇游记,夹叙夹议,"既有随笔小品的情致,又有政论文的锋利"(王佐良:《英国诗文选译集》)。文章措辞严谨、句式凝重、繁复,王佐良的译文用词洗练,不时运用文言文的典雅句式,同样传达了原文的文体风格。"the finest meadows that ever were seen"译作"水草丰美,前所未见",摆脱原文结构羁绊,灵活而得体。第二句拆译成两句。先将"endless flocks and herds"译为单独一句,再译原句中其余部分。在"for here we come to one of the devouring WENS: namely, CHELTENHAM, which is what they call a "watering place", that is to say, a place to which East India plunderers, West India floggers, English taxgorgers, together with gluttons, drunkards, and debauchees of all descriptions, female as well as male, resort, at the suggestion of silently laughing quacks, in the hope of getting rid of the bodily consequences of their manifold sins and iniquities"中,"a place"后所跟定语从句(to which...)中谓语动词为"resort, resort to"为"常去某地"之义。译者在处理此句时采用了拆译法。"at the suggestion of"和"in the hope of"两个介词短语被拆译成一个句子,译得十分自然、畅达。"少夫幼妻"和"老妇衰翁"译得精确而洗练。原文结尾颇为奇特,直译为:"备忘录:他讲这话时,任牛津城议员"。译文用故作公文腔调的措辞,译出了讥讽、针砭的内涵(李运兴,1998)。

例文[6](幽默小品)

Slow Boat from China
William Brown

The most convenient and leisurely means to Hong Kong is the "poor man's cruise," which I've taken at least 30 times. While buses are cheaper, you're stuck in a seat all day watching videos of gory Hong Kong gangster movies or Karaoke tapes, and you get in at night—just in time to spend $100 U.S. on a Hong Kong hotel room. (If you go to Hong Kong, by the way——stay in the Kowloon YMCA! Great prices, great rooms, awesome view, and located next door to the Peninsula Hotel, of James Bond fame). With the boat, you're free to roam about, or relax in your cabin, and the morning arrival helps offset the cost of one day's accommodation.

Buy tickets a week in advance at Heping Port(和平码头,Heping Matou) ticketing office (a ten minute walk from downtown harbor). Ship schedules change, but at the time of this writing (12:43 p.m.), the MV Jimei departs Xiamen once a week, and returns from Hong Kong once a week.

Note that depart times and prices are always subject to change—especially if you're in a hurry and have connections in H.K.

First class, which runs about 500RMB, gives you a cabin with a window and a private bath. You also get a cabin mate who inevitably is a chain smoker.

Second class saves you 60 RMB. It's also two to a room, but there's no window or bath, though you do have a sink to soak your head in when the tobacco smoke gets to you. Bear in mind that your roommate, like you, is cost conscious (that's why you're both in 2nd class), so he smokes a cheaper, more noxious grade of Chinese tobacco—like Petunia Cigarettes, or Great Ceiling.

Third class saves you another 60 RMB and lands you in a room with 18 to 20 people in bunkbeds. Smoking is not allowed while lying in bed, so everyone sits up in bed and smokes. The token foreigner is always assigned the upper berth in the corner where the smoke collects, but if you complain they'll just say you are blowing smoke. Third class mattresses are a 1/4″ thick piece of foam laid on top of plywood; authentic "room and board."

Fourth class, the lowest you can go in this classless society, gets you an assigned chair to sit in all night. I've tried it, and recommend throwing decorum out the port hole and lying on the floor. You'll sleep like a bug in a rug (or at least with the bugs in the rug).

Dinner and breakfast are available for a fee, and two shops sell snacks, alcohol, and cigarettes to resupply your chain smoking cabinmate.

Jesting aside, we highly recommend the boat, if for no other reason than that you can bring tons of luggage (like cheese!) and not pay a lot of overweight.

The 18 hour ride is a pleasant interlude in our all too busy life — except during typhoons. If you are prone to seasickness, just ask the front desk for seasickness pills. If you can't say "seasick pills" in Chinese, just throw up on the desk. But if you're shy, just ask for Yun Chuan Yao: 晕船药.

(Note: The MV Jimei has been remodeled and now has only 3 classes: 1st, 2nd, and Deluxe. Alas, the perils of progress).

来自中国的[悠悠]慢船
[悠悠慢船赴香江]
潘威廉

去香港,最方便也是最休闲的方式是搭乘号称"穷人航班"的廉价客轮,这船班我乘了至少30次。虽说坐大巴会更便宜,但你得一整天憋[窝、枯坐]在座位上看血腥的[打打杀杀的、血肉横飞的]香港警匪片[古惑仔影片],要不然就是卡拉OK歌带,动弹不得。而且到港时已经入夜,只好住进一晚100美元的酒店房间。(顺便提一下,到香港你可以住在九龙基督教青年会招待所,此处价钱实惠,房间奇大,景色优美。而且就在半岛酒店隔壁。半岛酒店曾因詹姆斯·邦德的入住而大扬其名。)要是坐船的话,你就可以在船上自由自在地逛荡,或者呆在船舱里休息。船到港的时间在早上,正好省掉你一夜的住宿费。

请提前一星期到和平码头售票处(离闹市区码头徒步仅十分钟的路程)买票。船班时时在变,不过在写这篇文章的时候(下午12:43),"集美"号内燃机船仍是一周一次往返于香港厦门。

请注意,发船时间和票价总是在变——当你急着赶路,且在香港要转乘车船飞机时更要特别注意。

头等舱,大约 500 元,那是一间带有窗户和私人卫生间船舱。另外加上一位舱友,此人必是烟鬼无疑[烟不离嘴的主儿、老烟枪]。

二等舱让你省掉 60 元,那也是一间双人房,只是没有窗户和卫生间。不过有一个洗手盆,这样当烟雾向你袭来时,你可以把头浸在水中。请你记住,你的室友和你一样都爱省钱[精打细算、很在意花销、用钱方面斤斤计较、怕花钱的人、节俭之人,也是个抠鬼、是个铁算盘](这是你们同在二等舱的原因[要不然你们怎么会同居一室呢?]),所以他抽的国产烟更便宜,毒性也更大——比如牵牛花牌或大云幕牌之类。

三等舱比二等舱又便宜[能为你再省]60 元,是 18 人到 20 人一间的上下铺床房间[但你就只有和 18 人至 20 人分享上下铺了]。由于禁止躺在床上吸烟,所以大家都坐着吸。那难得一见的[特征明显的、那聊作点缀的、徒有其表而实则囊中羞涩的]老外总被安插在船舱角落的上铺,那里正是烟雾缭绕的地方。但是如果你抱怨[发牢骚],他们反倒说你在无(雾)中生有[吞云吐雾]。三等舱的床垫是三合板上放一块 1/4 英寸厚的泡沫,真是名副其实"膳宿"齐备[一间房,一张床]。

四等舱,这是你在这个无阶级社会里所能去的最低阶层了。这里只提供一张椅子,让你坐着过夜[一人一张板凳,一夜坐到天亮]。我尝过这种滋味,因此建议你把斯文通通抛到舷窗外,直挺挺地躺倒在地板上,那样你会睡得舒舒服服,好比毯子躲着虫子(起码是与毯子里的臭虫同被共眠)。

正餐和早餐得自个儿掏腰包买,有两间小店卖快餐、酒,还有香烟,正好源源不断地接济给你的烟鬼舱友[以补充我们的烟枪室友的给养]。

玩笑归玩笑[言归正传、撇下笑话不说],我们还是力荐乘船,不为别的,就为了你可以携带上吨的行李(比如奶酪),超重也不必付太多钱。

这 18 小时的航行是我们忙碌不堪的生活中一段愉快的插曲—只要不碰上台风。如果你会晕船,就到服务台去要点晕船药。要是你不会用中文说"晕船药",干脆给它呕吐在前台上。如果你不好意思,还是学着说"Yun Chuan Yao"(晕船药)好了。

(注:"集美"号客轮经过装修,现只分成三等:一等舱、二等舱和豪华舱。哎呀,进步太快也是危险啊[这一改进可有危险失去客源哟])。

评析:在英语中有这么一句话:"There are translations and translations". 意为"译文有多种多样,有好的译文,有坏的译文"。抛开坏的译文不说,同一篇原文,好的译文肯定不止一种。原文一个句子或词组,译者一般只采用他认为最佳的一种表达语,其他的只好忍痛割爱,殊为可惜。事实上,原文一些表达词语在翻译中可发挥的余地很大。不同的译者有各种奇思妙想,神来之译笔。本译文采用一种新颖的编排法,把学生译文中精彩的表达萃集在一起,以体现翻译表达的奇特和趣味。本文是一篇幽默小品文。译文应力求体现作者的幽默、诙谐和夸张的风格,表达要活灵活现。原文也有一些容易被学生译错的词语:"connections"常被译成"有亲戚"或"有急事要联系";"token"也极不好译,其意为"只做象征性的、做装点的",有学生将其译成"徒有其表而实则囊中羞涩的"虽然不太符合词意,倒也是入木三分地刻画出一个在中国人眼里理应阔绰的"老外"居然也睡到下等舱;"bug in a rug"的尾韵效果也应该在译文中体现出来。"blowing smoke, room and board"都是颇费斟酌的词语。

例文[7](幽默小品)

Suppose you ignore the telephone when it rings, and suppose that, for once, somebody has an important message for you. I can assure you that if a message is really important it will reach you sooner or later. Think of the proverb: "Ill news travels apace." I must say good news seems to travel just as fast. And think of the saying: "The truth will out." It will. But suppose you answer the telephone when it rings. If, when you take off the receiver, you say "Hullo!" just think how absurd that is. Why, you might be saying "Hullo!" to a total stranger, a thing you would certainly think twice about before doing in public, if you were English.

But perhaps, when you take off the receiver, you give your number or your name. But you don't even know whom you are giving it to! Perhaps you have been indiscreet enough to have your name and number printed in the telephone directory, a book with a large circulation, a successful book so often reprinted as to make any author envious, a book more in evidence than Shakespeare or the Bible, and found in all sorts of private and public places. By your self-advertisement you have enabled stranger, bore, intruder, or criminal to engage you in conversation at a moment's notice in what ought to be the privacy of your own home.

假定电话铃响你置之不理，又假定刚好这次那人有重要的消息要告诉你。我可以向你保证，如果那消息时真正重要的话，它迟早总会传达给你听得。想到那句谚语，"恶事传千里"，我一定要说好的消息好像也同样地传达得很快的呀。再想想那句常言，"真相总会水落石出的"，确是如此。但是假定你听到电话铃响，你就去接。当你拿起听筒，如果你说"哈啰！"的话，试想这是多么荒谬呀。哼，你也许正在对一个完全不相识的陌生人在说着"哈啰！"如果你是英国国民的话，这确实是一件在人面前你要三思而后行的事。

但是当你拿起电话听筒的时候，也许你会把你的号码或是姓名告诉对方的。你甚至还不知道你在告诉的人是谁呢！也许你太轻率把你的姓名号码，随便就印在电话簿上去了，那是一本销数极多的书，任何作家都要羡慕的一本再三重版的成功的书，一本比莎士比亚或是圣经更要引人注目的书，在各种各样的公私场所都可见到的。由于你的自我宣传，你使得任何陌生人、令人讨厌的家伙、闯入者，或是罪犯之流，都能够侵入你在自己家里的私生活，随时来和你交谈。

评析：这是英国作家 William Plomer（1903—   ）的一篇随笔"On Not Answering the Telephone"中的一节。文笔中讽刺与幽默并用，再加上日常说的谚语，把接听电话这样简单的事写得极为生动有趣，这是典型的英国随笔风格。翻译时也应有那种调侃夸张的笔调。

例文[8]（论说）

Now, if you are to punish a man retributively, you must injure him. If you are to reform him, you must improve him. And men are not improved by injuries. To propose to punish and reform people by the same operation is exactly as if you were to take a man suffering from pneumonia, and attempt to combine punitive and curative treatment. Arguing that a man with pneumonia is a danger to the community, and that he need not catch it if he takes proper care of his health, you resolve that he shall have a severe lesson, both to punish him for his negligence and pulmonary weakness and to deter others from following his example. You therefore strip him naked, and in that condition stand him all night in the snow. But as you admit the duty of restoring him to health if possible, and discharging him with sound lungs, you engage a doctor to superintend the punishment and administer cough lozenges, made as unpleasant to the taste as possible so as not to pamper the culprit. A Board of Commissioners ordering such treatment would prove thereby that either they were imbeciles or else they were hotly in earnest about punishing the patient and not in the least in earnest about curing him. (*The Crime of Imprisonment*)

然而，志在惩罚，责令抵罪，非使人受苦不可。志在改造，则非教人向善不可。人是不会因遭罪受苦而回心向善的。企图一举而收惩罚与改造之效，无异对肺炎患者试行治罪兼治病的疗法。因为此人染上肺炎，危害社会，若是保养得宜，本来可以避免；所以必须狠狠教训一番，一则罚其失慎与肺弱，二则以儆效尤。根据这种理由，于是剥光他的衣服，要他赤身裸体，立雪通宵。可是，既然承认有责任尽可能使他复原，肺部健全而后释放，就要请医生监罚，同时给予咳糖含服；而这些咳糖又要极其难吃，以免姑息罪人。倘若有一委员会下令采取这种疗法，那就足以证明他们不是白痴，便是只有逞暴严惩之心而毫无治病救人之意。

评析：作者的观点很明确：企图一举而收惩罚与改造之效，那是荒唐的，因为人是不会因遭罪受苦而回心向善的。吃透原作，抛开原作，才能写出观点与原作基本相符的译文，才是真正忠实于原作。按照原文的精神，用笔宜悍。

例文[9]（论说）

Of Studies
Francis Bacon

STUDIES serve for delight, for ornament, and for ability. Their chief use for delight is in privateness and retiring; for ornament, is in discourse; and for ability, is in the judgment, and disposition of business. For expert men can execute, and perhaps judge of particulars, one by one; but the general counsels, and the plots and marshalling of affairs, come best from those that are learned. To spend too much time in studies is sloth; to use them too much for ornament is affectation; to make judgment wholly by their rules is the humor of a scholar. They perfect nature, and are perfected by experience: for natural abilities are like natural plants, that need pruning by study; and studies themselves do give forth directions too much at large, except they be bounded in by experience. Crafty men condemn studies, simple men admire them, and wise men use them; for they teach not their own use; but that is a wisdom without them, and above them, won by observation. Read not to contradict and confute; nor to believe and take for granted; nor to find talk and discourse; but to weigh and consider. Some books are to be tasted, others to be swallowed, and some few to be chewed and digested; that is, some books are to be read only in parts; others to be read, but not curiously; and some few to be read wholly, and with diligence and attention. Some books also may be read by deputy, and extracts made of them by others; but that would be only in the less important arguments, and the meaner sort of books, else distilled books are like common distilled waters, flashy things.

Reading maketh a full man; conference a ready man; and writing an exact man. And therefore, if a man write little, he had need have a great memory; if he confer little, he had need have a present wit; and if he read little, he had need have much cunning, to seem to know that he doth not. Histories make men wise; poets witty; the mathematics subtle; natural philosophy deep; moral grave; logic and rhetoric able to contend. *Abeunt studia in mores*. Nay, there is no stand or impediment in the wit, but may be wrought out by fit studies; like as diseases of the body, may have appropriate exercises. Bowling is good for the stone and reins; shooting for the lungs and breast; gentle walking for the stomach; riding for the head; and the like. So if a man's wit be wandering, let him study the mathematics; for in demonstrations, if his wit be called away never so little, he must begin again. If his wit be not apt to distinguish or find differences, let him study the Schoolmen; for they are *cymini sectores*. If he be not apt to beat over matters, and to call up one thing to prove and illustrate another, let him study the lawyers' cases. So every defect of the mind may have a special receipt.

译文一：

论 学 问

读书为学的用途是娱乐、装饰和增长才识。在娱乐上学问的主要的用处是幽居养静；在装饰上学问的用处是辞令；在长才上学问的用处是对于事务的判断和处理。因为富于经验的人善于实行，也许能够对个别的事情一件一件地加以判断；但是最好的有关大体的议论和对事务的计划与布置，乃是从有学问的人来的。在学问上费时过多是偷懒；把学问过于用作装饰是虚假；完全依学问上的规则而断事是书生的怪癖。学问锻炼天性，而其本身又受经验的锻炼；盖人的天赋有如野生的花草，他们需要学问的修剪；而学问的本身，若不受经验的限制，则其所指示的未免过于笼统。多诈的人渺视学问，愚鲁的人羡慕学问，聪明的人运用学问；因为学问的本身并不教人如何用它们；这种运用之道乃是学问以外，学问以上的一种智能，是由观察体会才能得到的。不要为了辩驳而读书，也不要为了信仰与盲从；也不要为了言谈与议论；要以能权衡轻重、审察事理为目的。

有些书可供一尝，有些书可以吞下，有不多的几部书则应当咀嚼消化；这就是说，有些书只要读读他们的一部分就够了，有些书可以全读，但是不必过于细心地读；还有不多的几部书则应当全读，勤读，而且用心地读。有些书也可以请代表去读，并且由别人替我作出摘要来；但是这种办法只适于次要的议论和次要的书籍；否则录要的书就和蒸馏的水一样，都是无味的东西。阅读使人充实，会谈使人敏捷，写作与笔记使人精确。因此，如果一个人写得很少，那么他就必须有很好的记性；如果他很少与人会谈，那么他就必须有很敏捷的机智；并且假如他读书读得很少的话，那么他就必须要有很大的狡黠之才，才可以强不知以为知。史鉴使人明智；诗歌使人巧慧；数学使人精细；博物使人深沉；伦理之学使人庄重；逻辑与修辞使人善辩。"学问变化气质。"不特如此，精神上的缺陷没有一种是不能由相当的学问来补救的；就如同肉体上各种的病患都有适当的运动来治疗似的。踢球有益于结石和肾脏；射箭有益于胸肺；缓步有益于胃；骑马有益于头脑；诸如此类。同此，如果一个人心志不专，他顶好研究数学；因为在数学的证理之中，如果他的精神稍有不专，他就非从头再做不可。如果他的精神不善于辨别异同，那么他最好研究经院学派的著作，因为这一派的学者是条分缕析的人；如果他不善于推此知彼，旁征博引，他顶好研究律师们的案卷。如此看来，精神上各种的缺陷都可以有一种专门的补救之方了。——水天同译文

译文二：

论 读 书

读书可以作为娱乐，作为装饰，作为能力的培养。娱乐的作用通常见于离群独处时；装饰的作用体现在高谈阔论中；至于才能，则表现在裁处事务上。行家里手虽能事无巨细——予以处理或判明是非，但运筹全局、合理谋划则少不了茂士英才。读书费时过多，无异于懒惰；装饰之用过滥，显得矫揉造作；办事只知照本宣科，实为书呆子气。读书弥补天性的缺陷，经验又弥补读书的不足：人的天性犹如自然的花木，需要学习予以整枝培育；读书自身无边无际，需要经验予以制约。取巧者蔑视学问，无知者羡慕学问，明智者运用学习；因为学问本身并没有教人如何运用；运用的智慧不在书中，而在书外，全凭观察所得。读书时不要与作者作对，不要诘难他；但也不要轻信，以为书上什么都对；更不要寻章摘句，用来炫耀；而应该着意掂量，仔细斟酌。有的书可供品尝，有的书只能吞食，少数的应该细细咀嚼，一一消化；那是说，有的书只需读其中一部分；有的书用不着读得太认真；但少数好书则需要认真细致地通读。有的书还可以请人代读，取其摘要就行；但这只限于不甚重要的论述和次等书籍；否则，经过摘录的书犹如经过蒸馏的水，变得淡而无味了。读书使人充实；交谈使人机敏；摘录使人精确。因此，一个人读书时如果很少摘录，则需有超群的记忆；如果他很少与人交谈，则应有随机应变之才；如果他很少读书，则需要取巧有术，让人觉得他并非孤陋寡闻。历史使人聪明，诗歌使人机智；数学使人精密；哲理使人深刻；道德使人正经；逻辑与修辞使人能言善辩：总之，读书能陶冶人的性情。读书当，决不会使人心智受损，只会益智增才。——何新译文

译文三：

说 学

学之为用有三：充娱乐、供装饰、长才干也。

充娱乐主要见之于退居独处之时，供装饰于谈吐之顷，而长才干则于事务之判断处理。

练达之人于具体事实类能逐一行之识之；至若贯通之识见，遇事多谋善理之长才，则又渊贯之士之所独擅。

以过多之时日耽溺于学便是怠惰；以其所学悉供装饰便成虚矫；断事但以书中之规律绳之，便又是文人学士难改之积习。

学以补天生之不足，然学问又必受经验之补益；天生之才干犹之天生之植物，其成长或赖学问之剪裁；然学问所能提供之指导恒过宽，不能不更受经验之约束，方不致漫无指归。

学问之事，巧黠者卑夷之，愚昧者惊叹之，惟有识之士能利用之；其所习者初非学问自身之用途；此种智慧恒不待于学问或高于学问，得诸观察者也。

读书之目的非为辩驳与争议也；非为尽信书言，视为当然也；非为交谈吐属而读，藉资谈助也；读书之目的在审度与寻绎。

书有供人尝之者，有供人吞食者，亦有不多之书为供人咀嚼与消化者；易言之，书有仅须部分读之者，有仅须涉猎然无须细玩之者，少数书亦有须全读者，而其读则必勤必细，必全神贯注。书甚至可由人代读，读后令做撮要，然此必限于书中之非重要内容，且亦必非重要之书；诚以过滤之书亦犹过滤之水，甚乏味也。

读书使人充实,谈话使人敏捷,动笔使人精确。

是故、疏于握管者,其记忆须强;交谈不足者,其才智须捷;腹中乏书之人,其狡黠也亦须大,有不知而实似知之之能。

史益人智;诗令人慧;数学教人缜密;自然哲学进人于深邃;伦理学启人之庄严;而逻辑修辞诸学则在授人以辩术,Aheunt studia in mores(学入人性格也)。

实则心智之各类窒碍固无不可藉适当之学习以匡正之,犹之躯体之疾病之可籍运动而祛除。诸如滚球健肾,射箭健肺,散步健胃,骑乘健脑等均属之。

是故人之心智有不专者,宜令其习数学,盖于证题之际,苟心智稍有游移,势不能不废而重演;其有不善指陈细节剖析入微者,宜令以经院学者为师,以此类学者均为细入毫芒之大家;其有不能审察明辨以此证彼者,则令习律师之办案。故曰心智之疾病固各有其良方也。——高健译文

译文四:

谈 读 书

读书足以怡情,足以傅彩,足以长才。其怡情也,最见于独处幽居之时;其傅彩也,最见于高谈阔论之中;其长才也,最见于处世判事之际。练达之士虽能分别处理细事或一一判别枝节,然纵观统筹、全局策划,则舍好学深思者莫属。读书费时过多易惰,文采藻饰太盛则骄,全凭条文断事乃学究故态。读书补天然之不足,经验又补读书之不足。盖天生才干犹如自然花草,读书然后知如何修剪移接;而书中所示,如不以经验范之,则又大而无当。有一技之长者鄙读书,无知者羡读书,唯明智之士用读书,然书并不以用处告人,用书之智不在书中,而在书外,全凭观察得之。读书是不可存心诘难作者,不可尽信书上所言,亦不可只为寻章摘句,而应推敲细思。书有可浅尝者,有可吞食者,少数则须咀嚼消化。换言之,有只须读其部分者,有只须大体涉猎者,少数则须全读。读时须全神贯注,孜孜不倦。书亦可请人代读,取其所做摘要,但只限题材较次或价值不高者,否则书经提炼犹如水经蒸馏,淡而无味矣。读书使人充实,讨论使人机智,笔记使人准确。因此不常作笔记者须记忆特强,不常讨论者须天生聪颖,不常读书者须欺世有术,始能无知而显有知。

读史使人明智,读诗使人灵秀,数学使人周密,科学使人深刻,伦理学使人庄重,逻辑修辞之学使人善辩:凡有所学,皆成性格。人之才智但有滞碍,无不可读适当之书使之顺畅,一如身体百病,皆可借相宜之运动除之。滚球利睾肾,射箭利胸肺,慢步利肠胃,骑术利头脑,诸如此类。如智力不集中,可令读数学,盖演题须全神贯注,稍有分散即须重演;如不能辨异,可令读经院哲学,盖是辈皆吹毛求疵之人;如不善求同,不善以一物阐证另一物,可令读律师之案卷。如此头脑中凡有缺陷,皆有特药可医。——王佐良译文

评析: Francis Bacon是与莎士比亚同时代的人,都处在现代英语的最初阶段,语言中还有不少古英语的痕迹,与现代英语有较大的差异。全文措辞表达协调优美,充满警句隽语;富于比喻和准确精当的排比,有格言体风格;结构细密严谨,层次井然,紧凑坚致;句子短小质朴,长短比较一致,用词简古,要言不繁;句间很少使用连词和转折副词,每个句子均表达一定的思想,可单独成句。在风格上似乎与我国唐宋八大家中的欧阳修和韩愈的作品有相似之处。翻译家王佐良运用了大量的文言句式以体现作品语言上的古雅风格,但译者用的又不是那种艰深古奥、诘屈聱牙的古文,而是浅近的文言,既体现了原作的语言风格,又浅显易懂。文章开头第一句话:"Studies serve for delight, for ornament, and for ability". 这句

话就言简意赅,很不好译。因为其中的"delight, ornament"和"ability"都是名词。译者将这几个词分别译为"怡情"、"傅彩"、"长才",贴切地传达了原意,干净利落。"ornament"一词的本意是"装饰"、"美化",引申为"添风致"、"增光彩"。这里则是"谈吐不俗"、"显露文采"的意思。译为"傅彩",文字简到了不能再简的程度,而意思则全出来了。"傅彩"便是添加文采。第二段的头一句:"Reading maketh a full man; conference a ready man; and writing an exact man". 这里的"full man, ready man"和"exact man"也很不好译。译者连同"maketh"译成"使人充实","使人机智",十分恰当。又如"They perfect nature, and are perfected by experience"前后两个分句,用了同一个动词,上下之间,不仅意思联系很紧,而且读起来有呼应,有声韵美。译文为:"读书补天然之不足,经验又补读书之不足。"两个分句的句式一样,用一个"又"字相连,由于重复"补……之不足",读起来也很动听。译文中使用了汉语四字结构,使译文更加简洁,如"独处幽居"、"高谈阔论"、"纵观统筹、全局策划"、"大而无当"、"寻章摘句"等。有时甚至将一个词也译成四字结构,如将"attention"译成"全神贯注","diligence"译成"孜孜不倦"。全文读起来,错落有致,节奏明快,符合汉语排比句的句式。译者的汉语根底坚实,运用自如,这才成就了一篇绝译。其他几篇译文相比之下,更显得王佐良译文的可贵之处,那就是王佐良译文最恰当地把握了译文的文言文体风格。王译的不足之处在标题处理,译得过于直白,明显和译文文体不合,倒是高健的"说学"较好,或者可译"为学",和清人彭端淑的"为学"正好遥相呼应,还可联想到韩愈的"进学解",及至荀子的"劝学篇"。

例文[10](演说)

Address at the Dedication of
the Gettysburg National Cemetery

Fourscore and seven years ago our fathers brought forth on this continent, a new nation, conceived in Liberty, and dedicated to the proposition that all men are created equal.

Now we are engaged in a great civil war, testing whether that nation or any nation so conceived and so dedicated, can long endure. We are met on a great battle field of that war. We have come to dedicate a portion of that field as a final resting place for those who here gave their lives that that nation might live. It is altogether fitting and proper that we should do this.

But, in a larger sense, we cannot dedicate—we cannot consecrate—we cannot hallow—this ground. The brave men, living and dead, who struggled here, have consecrated it, far above our poor power to add or detract. The world will little note, nor long remember what we say here, but it can never forget what they did here. It is for us the living, rather, to be dedicated here to the unfinished work which they who fought here have thus far so nobly advanced. It is rather for us to be here dedicated to the great task remaining before us—that from these honored dead we take increased devotion to that cause for which they gave the last full measure of devotion—that we here highly resolve that these dead shall not have died in vain—that this nation, under God, shall have a new birth of freedom—and that government of the people, by the people, for the people, shall not perish from the earth.

译文一：

美国总统林肯葛底斯堡演讲词

八十七年以前,我们的先辈们在这个大陆上创立了一个新国家,它孕育于自由之中,奉行一切人生来平等的原则。

现在我们正从事一场伟大的内战,以考验这个国家,或者说以考验任何一个孕育于自由而奉行上述原则的国家是否能够长久存在下去。

我们在这场战争中的一个伟大战场上集合。烈士们为使这个国家能够生存下去而献出了自己的生命,我们在此集会是为了把这个战场的一部分奉献给他们作为最后安息之所。我们这样做是完全应该而且非常恰当的。

但是,从更广泛的意义上来说,这块土地我们不能够奉献,我们不能够圣化,我们不能够神化。曾经在这里战斗过的勇士们,活着的和去世的,已经把这块土地神圣化了,这远不是我们微薄的力量所能增减的。全世界将很少注意到,也不会长期地记起我们今天在这里所说的话,但全世界永远不会忘记勇士们在这里做过的事。毋宁说,倒是我们这些还活着的人,应该在这里把自己奉献于勇士们已经如此崇高地向前推进但尚未完成的事业。倒是我们应该在这里把自己奉献于仍然留在我们面前的伟大任务,以便使我们从这些光荣的死者身上汲取更多的奉献精神,来完成他们已经完全彻底为之献身的事业;以便使我们在这里下定最大的决心,不让这些死者们白白牺牲;以便使国家在上帝福佑下得到自由的新生,并且使这个民有、民治、民享的政府永世长存。(张培基等:《英汉翻译教程》,1980)

译文二:

葛底斯堡演讲词

八十七年前,我们的先辈们在这个大陆上建立了一个以自由为理想、以人人平等为宗旨的新国家。

现在我们正进行一场大内战,考验这个国家或任何一个主张自由平等的国家,能否长久存在。

我们在这场战争中的一个大战场上集会,来把战场的一角献给为国家生存而牺牲的烈士,作为他们永久安息之地,这是我们义不容辞、理所当然该做的事。

但是,从更深刻的意义来说,我们不能使这一角战场成为圣地,我们不能使它流芳百世,我们不能使它永垂青史。因为在这里战斗过的勇士们,活着的和死去的,已经使这一角战场神圣化了,我们微薄的力量远远不能使它增光,或者使之减色。世人不太会注意、也不会长久记住我们在这里说的话,但是永远不会忘记他们在这里做的事。因此,我们活着的人更应该献身于他们为之战斗并且使之前进的未竟事业。我们更应该献身于是我们面前的伟大任务,更应该不断向这些光荣牺牲的烈士学习,学习他们为事业鞠躬尽瘁、死而后已的献身精神,更应该在这里下定决心,一定不让这些烈士的鲜血白流;这个国家在上帝的保佑下,一定要得到自由和新生,这个民有、民治、民享的政府一定不能从地球上消失。(许渊冲:《翻译通讯》)

译文三:

林肯在葛底斯堡的演说

八十七年前,我们的父辈在这块大陆上创建了一个新的国家。这个新的国家在自由中孕育,信奉人人生而平等的主张。

现在我们正在从事伟大的国内战争,来考验这个国家,或任何在自由中孕育,信奉人人生而平等的主张的国家,能否长久存在下去。

我们今天相聚在这场战争的一个伟大的战场上。我们相聚在这里是为了把这伟大战场的一部分奉献给那些为了我们国家的生存而献出了生命的烈士们作为最后的安息地。我们这样做完全是合情合理的。

但在更广泛的意义上来说,我们不能奉献这块土地,我们不能使这块土地神圣,我们不能使这块土地光耀。那些勇敢的人们,那些曾经在这里战斗过的,活着和死去的人们,已经使这块土地神圣了,远非我们所能增加或减少。世界不大会注意,也不会永久记住我们今天在这里所说的话,但世界决不能忘记他们在这里所做过的事情。我们这些活着的人,倒是应该在这里献身于他们长久以来如此高尚地推进的,尚未完成的工作。我们倒是应该在这里献身于留在我们面前的伟大任务:那就是继承这些光荣的先烈,对他们在这里作出最后全部贡献的事业,作出我们进一步的贡献;那就是我们在这里狠下决心,决不让这些先烈的死成为白白的牺牲;那就是我们的国家一定要在上帝底下获得新的自由;那就是决不让人民的政府,人民选举的政府,为了人民的政府从地球上消亡。——解伯昌译文

评析:这篇演说词简朴而脍炙人口。全文段落结构清晰,层次分明,一气呵成。作为演说词,它长句比较多,但结构紧凑、严密、有力。句法特征为多掉尾句、强调句及排比句。全文既充满哀婉动人情绪,又凸显奔放的爱国激情,具有强烈的鼓动性和宏大的气势。译文要尽力把原文典雅端庄和措辞、洗练有力的风格传达出来。以往的译文,包括译文一和二,都把"of the people, by the people, for the people"译成"民有、民治、民享"简洁有力又符合汉语习惯,成为定译。但也有人认为,如果原作是一篇书面文章,这种译法无懈可击,堪称上乘。但原作是一篇用口头表达的演说词。原作中"of the people, by the people, for the people"这几个重叠词,念起来琅琅上口,听起来铿锵有力,而且简单明白易懂。而"民有、民治、民享"则完全是书面语言。若用口头表达出来,让成千上万与会者听起来,就不易听懂,或虽然听懂了也印象不深,效果不免大为逊色。因此,译文三注重了作为口头表达的演说词的特点,并做了有别于前两种译文的翻译处理,颇为新鲜。

二、小说的翻译

小说的翻译是文学翻译的重头戏。这不仅因为其篇幅相对较长,还表现在它涵盖了散文、诗歌和戏剧的要素和成分,它以全景式的画面展现人生百态,风土民情。小说翻译也最能体现译者的语言功力、文学艺术修养和翻译技能。这主要体现在译文如何重现原作的风格。张今(1987)指出,文学译品的风格实际上是一种综合风格。上乘译品的境界应该是,译作能体现作者的风格,而译者的风格若隐若现。在翻译艺术中,不同作者的多种多样的风格化为译者风格的多样性。译者要善于表现不同作家的多种多样的风格,又有自己独特的翻译风格。在译文中,作者的风格是通过译者的翻译风格体现出来的。而作为某一译者的译作,它必然会带有该译者的遣词造句的行文风格。英国翻译理论家西奥多·塞弗瑞指出(1968):"文章的任何段落,无不在一定程度上显现作者的风格。作者如此,译者亦然。"译者在如何忠实完美再现原著风格上,应具有文学翻译中的辩证思维观念(郭建中,1983)。这种辩证思维观念就是,小说翻译中忠实地传递原文文字的部分表达结构,往往不能取得生动传神的效果,倒是脱离原文表层结构,根据原文深层内涵重新组织译文,更能圆满地反映原著的风格。以下我们通过对美国作家辛格(Isaac Bashevis Singer)短篇小说 *Gimpel The*

Fool(《傻瓜吉姆佩尔》)的三种译本所做的比较分析,感悟文学翻译中的辩证思维观念。

例文[11](短篇小说)

Gimpel the Fool
Issac Bashevis Singer
(An excerpt)

  I AM GIMPEL the fool. I don't think myself a fool. On the contrary. But that's what folks call me. They gave me the name while I was still in school. I had seven names in all: imbecile, donkey, flax-head, dope, glump, ninny, and fool. The last name stuck. What did my foolishness consist of? I was easy to take in. They say, "Gimpel, you know the rabbi's wife has been brought to childbed?" So I skipped school. Well, it turned out to be a lie. How was I supposed to know? She hadn't a big belly. But I never looked at her belly. Was that really so foolish? The gang laughed and heehawed, stomped and danced and chanted a good-night prayer. And instead of the raisins they give when a woman's lying in, they stuffed my hand full of goat turds. I was no weakling. If I slapped someone he'd see all the way to Cracow. But I'm really not a slugger by nature. I think to myself: Let it pass. So they take advantage of me.

  I was coming home from school and heard a dog barking. I'm not afraid of dogs, but of course I never want to start up with them. One of them may be mad, and if he bites there's not a Tartar in the world who can help you. So I made tracks. Then I looked around and saw the whole market-place wild with laughter. It was no dog at all but Wolf-Leib the Thief. How was I supposed to know it was he? It sounded like a howling bitch.

  When the pranksters and leg-pullers found that I was easy to fool, every one of them tried his luck with me. "Gimpel, the Czar is coming to Frampol; Gimpel, the moon fell down in Turbeen; Gimpel, little Hodel Furpiece found a treasure behind the bathhouse." And I like a golem believed everyone. In the first place, everything is possible, as it is written in the Wisdom of the Fathers. I've forgotten just now. Second, I had to believe when the whole town came down on me! If I ever dared to say, "Ah, you're kidding!" there was trouble. People got angry. "What do you mean! You want to call everyone a liar?" What was I to do? I believed them, and I hope at least that did them some good.

  I was an orphan. My grandfather who brought me up was already bent toward the grave. So they turned me over to a baker, and what a time they gave there! Every woman or girl who came to bake a batch of noodles had no fool me at least once. "Gimpel, there's a fair in heaven; Gimpel, the rabbi gave birth to a calf in the seventh month; Gimpel, a cow flew over the roof and land brass eggs." A student from the yesiva came once to buy a roll, and he said, "You, Gimpel, while you stand here scraping with your baker's shovel the Messiah has come. The dead have arisen." "What do you mean?" I said, "I heard no one blowing the ram's horn!" He said, "Are you deaf?" And all began to cry, "We heard it, we heard!" Then in came Rietze the Candle-dipper and called out in her hoarse voice, "Gimpel, your father and mother have stood up from the grave. They're looking for you."

  To tell the truth, I knew very well that nothing of the sort had happened, but all the same as folks were talking, I threw on my wool vest and went out. Maybe something had happened. What did I stand to lose by looking? Well, what a cat music went up! And then I took a vow to believe nothing more. But that was no go either. They confused me so that I didn't know the big end from the small.

I went to the rabbi to get some advice. He said, "It is written, better to be a fool all your days than for one hour to be evil. You are not a fool. They are the fools. For he who causes his neighbor to feel shame loses Paradise himself." ...

I wanted to go off to another town. but then everyone got busy matchmaking, and they were after me so they nearly tore my coat tails off. They talked at me and talked until I got water on the ear. She was no chaste maiden, but they told me she was virgin pure. She had a limp, and they said it was deliberate, from coyness. She had a bastard, and they told me the child was her little brother. I cried, "You're wasting your time. I'll never marry that whore." But they said indignantly, "What a way to talk! Aren't you ashamed of yourself? We can take you to the rabbi and have you fined for giving her a bad name." I saw then that I wouldn't escape them so easily and I thought: They're set on making me their butt. But when you're married the husband's the master, and if that's all right with her it's agreeable to me too. Besides, you can't pass through life unscathed, nor expect to.

I went to her clay house, which was built on the sand, and the whole gang, hollering and chorusing, came after me. They acted like bear-baiters. When we came to the well they stopped all the same. They were afraid to start anything with Elka. Her mouth would open as if it were on a hinge, and she had a fierce tongue. I entered the house. Lines were strung from wall to wall and clothes were drying. Barefoot she stood by the tub, doing the wash. She was dressed in a worn hand-me-down gown of plush. She had her hair put up in braids and pinned across her head. It took my breath away, almost, the reek of it all.

Evidently she knew who I was. She took a look at me and said, "Look who's here! He's come, the drip. Grab a seat."

I told her all; I denied nothing. "Tell me the truth," I said, "are you really a virgin, and is that mischievous Yechiel actually your little brother? Don't be deceitful with me, for I'm an orphan." "I'm an orphan myself," she answered, "and whoever tries to twist you up, may the end of his nose take a twist. But don't let them think they can take advantage of me. I want a dowry of fifty guilders, and let them take up a collection besides. Otherwise they can kiss my you-know-what." She was very plainspoken. I said, "It's the bride and not the groom who gives a dowry." Then she said, "Don't bargain with me. Either a flat yes or a flat no. Go back where you came from."

译文一：

傻瓜吉姆佩尔

艾萨克·巴什维斯·辛格

（节选）

我是傻瓜吉姆佩尔。我不认为自己是傻瓜。恰恰相反。可是人家叫我傻瓜。我在学校里的时候,他们就给我起了这个绰号。我一共有七个绰号:低能儿、蠢驴、亚麻头、呆子、苦人儿、笨蛋和傻瓜。最后一个绰号就固定了。我究竟傻些什么呢?我容易受骗。他们说:"吉姆佩尔,你知道拉比的老婆养孩子了吗?"于是我就逃了一次学。唉,原来是说谎。我怎么会知道呢?她肚子也没有大。可是我从来没有注意过她的肚子。我真的是那么傻吗?这帮人又是笑,又是叫,又是顿脚又是跳舞,唱起晚安的祈祷文来。一个女人分娩的时候,他们不给我葡萄干,而在我手里塞满了羊粪。我不是弱者。要是我打人一拳,就会把他打到克拉科夫去。不过我生性的确不爱揍人。我暗自想:算了吧。于是他们就捉弄我。

  我从学校回家,听到一只狗在叫,我不怕狗,当然我从来不想去惊动它们。也许其中有一只疯狗,如果它咬了你,那么世上无论哪个鞑靼人都帮不了你的忙。所以,我溜之大吉。接着我回头四顾,看见整个市场的人都在哈哈大笑。根本没有狗,而是小偷沃尔夫-莱布。我怎么知道这就是他呢?他的声音像一只嚎叫的母狗。

  当那些恶作剧和捉弄人的人发觉我易于受骗的时候,他们每个人都想在我身上试试他的运气。"吉姆佩尔,沙皇快要到弗拉姆波尔来了;吉姆佩尔,月亮掉到托尔平去了;吉姆佩尔,小霍台夫·弗比斯在澡堂后面找到了一个宝藏。"我像一个机器人一样相信每一个人。第一,凡事都有可能,正如《先人的智慧》里所写的一样,可我已经忘记书上是怎么说的。第二,全镇的人都对我这样,使我不得不相信!如果敢说一句,"嘿,你们在骗我!"那就麻烦了。人们全都会勃然大怒。"你这是什么意思?你要把大家都看作是说谎的?"我怎么办呢?我相信他们说的话,我希望至少这样对他们有点好处。

  我是一个孤儿。抚养我长大的祖父眼看快要入土了。因此他们把我交给了一个面包师傅,我在那儿过的是什么日子啊!每一个来烤一炉烙饼的女人或姑娘都至少要耍弄我一次。"吉姆佩尔,天上有一个市集;吉姆佩尔,拉比在第七个月养了一只小牛;吉姆佩尔,一只母牛飞上屋顶,下了许多铜蛋。"一个犹太教学堂的学生有一次来买面包,他说:"吉姆佩尔,当你用你那面包师傅的铲子在刮锅的时候,救世主来了。死人已经站起来了。""你在说什么?"我说,"我可没有听见谁在吹羊角!"他说,"你是聋子吗?"于是大家都叫起来,"我们听到的,我们听到的!"接着蜡烛工人里兹进来,用她嘶哑的嗓门喊道:"吉姆佩尔,你的父母已经从坟墓里站起来了。他们在找你。"

  说真的,我十分明白,这类事一件都没有发生;但是,在人们谈论的时候,我仍然匆匆穿上羊毛背心出去。也许发生了什么事情。我去看看会有什么损失呢?唔,大伙儿都笑坏了!于是我发誓不再相信什么了,但是这也不行。他们把我搞糊涂了,因此我连粗细大小都分不清了。

  我到拉比那儿去请教。他说:"圣书上写着,做一生傻瓜也比作恶一小时强。你不是傻瓜。他们是傻瓜。因为使他的邻人感到羞辱的人,自己要失去天堂。"……

  我要离开这儿到另外一个城市去。可是这时候,大家都忙于给我做媒,跟在我后面,几乎把我外套的下摆都要撕下来了。他们钉住我谈呀说的,把口水都溅到我的耳朵上。女方不是一个贞洁的姑娘,可是他们告诉我她是一个纯洁的处女。她走路有点一瘸一拐,他们说这是因为她怕羞,故意这样的。她有一个私生子,他们告诉我,这孩子是她的小弟弟。我叫道:"你们是在浪费时间,我永远不会娶那个婊子。"但是他们义愤填膺地说:"你这算是什么谈话态度!难道你自己不害羞吗?我们可以把你带到拉比那里去,你败坏她的名声,你得罚款。"于是我看出来,我已经不能轻易摆脱他们。我想他们决心要把当作他们的笑柄。不过结了婚,丈夫就是主人,如果这样对她说来是很好的话,那么在我也是愉快的。再说,你不可能毫无损伤地过一生,这种事想也不必想。

我上她那间在沙地上的泥房子走去;那一帮人又是叫,又是唱,都跟在我后面。他们的举动像耍狗熊的一样。到了井边,他们一齐停下来了,他们怕跟埃尔卡打交道。她的嘴像装在铰链上一样,能说会道,词锋犀利。我走进屋子,一条条绳子从这面墙拉到那面墙,绳子上晾着衣服。她赤脚站在木盆旁边,在洗衣服。她穿着一件破破烂烂的旧长毛绒长袍。她的头发编成辫子,交叉别在头顶上。她头发上的臭气几乎熏得我气也喘不过来。

显然她知道我是谁,她朝我看了一下,说:"瞧,谁来啦!他来啦,这个讨厌鬼。坐吧。"

我把一切都告诉她了,什么也没有否认。"把真情实话告诉我吧,"我说,"你真的是一个处女,那个调皮的耶契尔的确是你的小兄弟吗?不要骗我,因为我是个孤儿。"

"我自己也是个孤儿,"她回答,"谁要是想捉弄你,谁的鼻子尖就会弄歪。他们别想占我的便宜。我要一笔五十盾的嫁妆,另外还要他们给我募一笔款子。否则,让他们来吻我的那个玩意儿。"她倒是非常坦率的。我说:"出嫁妆的是新娘,不是新郎。"于是她说:"别跟我讨价还价。干脆说'行',或者'不行'——否则你哪里来就回哪里去。"——万紫译文

译文二:

傻瓜吉姆佩尔

艾萨克·巴什维斯·辛格

(节选)

我是傻瓜吉姆佩尔。我想我并不傻。恰恰相反。但是人们却这么叫我。我还在上学的时候,他们就开始给我起了这个绰号。我一共有七个绰号:低能儿、蠢驴、亚麻头、呆子、木头、笨蛋和傻瓜。这最后一个绰号一直叫到今天。那么我在哪些地方傻呢?我容易受骗。人家说:"吉姆佩尔,拉比[1]的妻子生孩子了?你知道吗?"于是我逃了学。嗨,原来是说谎。我怎么会知道呢?她肚子没有大呀。何况我从来没有瞧过她的肚子呀。这样就真的很傻吗?可是那帮人大笑大叫,又是踩脚,又是跳舞,又是唱晚安的祈祷文。女人生孩子,本应请吃葡萄干,可是他们却把羊粪塞到我手里。我并不软弱无能。要是我扇谁一巴掌,准会把他扇到克拉科夫去。不过我确实生性不爱打人。我心想:算了吧。所以人们总是捉弄我。

我放学回家,听到狗叫。我并不怕狗,但是我当然也不愿意惹它们。没准儿有一条是疯狗哩,要是被疯狗咬上一口,那世界上就连鞑靼人也帮不了你的忙。于是我拔腿就跑。我向周围一看,整个市场上的人大笑不止。原来根本不是什么狗叫,而是小偷沃尔夫—莱布在学狗叫哩。我怎么会知道是他呢?那声音听起来明明像是一只母狗在叫嘛。

那些好事之徒和促狭鬼们发现我容易受骗,于是个个都想在我身上试试运气。"吉姆佩尔,沙皇要来弗拉姆波尔了;吉姆佩尔,月亮掉下来落到图尔平了;吉姆佩尔,小霍代尔·富尔皮斯在澡堂后面发现财宝了。"我像机器人一样相信每一个人。首先,什么事情都是可能发生的,像《先智书》上写的那样,可是我忘记是怎么说的了。其次,全镇的人都这样对待我,我不能不相信!如果我胆敢说句,"哈,你们在骗人!"那就惹麻烦了。人们会勃然大怒。"你这是什么意思!你要把我们都说成是骗子吗?"我该怎么办呢?我只好相信他们,至少我希望这样做对他们也有点好处。

我是个孤儿。把我抚养大的祖父已是快入土的人了。于是大伙儿就把我交给一个面包师傅,我在那里过的是什么日子啊!每个来烤面条[2]的女人或姑娘至少都要捉弄我一次。"吉姆佩尔,天上有个集市;吉姆佩尔,拉比怀孕七个月,生了一头小牛;吉姆佩尔,一头母牛

飞上了屋顶,下了好些铜蛋。"有一次,犹太教学堂一个学生来买面包卷,他说:"你呀,吉姆佩尔,就在你站在这里用面包铲子铲来铲去的功夫,弥赛亚[3]降临了。死人都复活了。""你这是什么意思?"我问道,"我没听见有人吹羊角号[4]呀!"他说:"你聋了吗?"于是大家起哄说:"我们听到了,我们听到了!"接着蜡烛工莉兹进来了,她用沙哑的声音喊道:"吉姆佩尔,你的父母都从坟墓里出来了。他们正在找你呢。"

说真的,我十分清楚不会有这种事,但在人们谈论时,我还是匆匆穿上羊毛背心出去了。没准儿真的发生了什么事哩。我去看看会有什么坏处呢?嗬,你听大伙儿那个尖叫吧!于是我发誓什么也不再相信了。但是这样也不行。人们弄得我晕头转向,不知东南西北了。

我去拉比那里求救。他说:"书上写着:当一辈子傻瓜也比做一小时恶人强。你不是傻瓜。他们才是傻瓜哩。凡是令邻人感到羞耻的人,自己就会失去天堂。"……

我想到别的镇上去。可是大伙儿又忙着给我说亲了,他们追着我,几乎把我的外套后摆都扯了下来。他们冲着我唠叨。唾沫星子都溅到我的耳朵上了。她根本不是什么贞洁的女子,但是他们对我说她是个纯洁的处女。她走路一瘸一瘸的,可是他们说那是故意的,是由于怕羞。她有个私生子,可是他们对我说,那是她的小弟弟。我嚷道:"你们是白费时间。我绝不会娶那个婊子。"于是他们勃然大怒道:"你怎么这样讲!难道你不感到可耻吗?我们可以把你带到拉比那里去,罚你的款,因为你败坏她的名声。"于是我意识到要逃出这些人的手心不是那么容易的,我心想,他们是决心拿我当靶子玩了。其实要是结了婚,丈夫就是主人了,如果她没有意见,我也可以同意嘛。再说,一辈子不吃一点苦头,那是不可能的,也不应抱这样的期望。

于是我就到了她土房,那房子是建立在沙地上的。那帮人追着我起哄,他们像耍狗熊似的耍弄我。走到井边时,他们终于停下来。他们不敢惹埃尔卡。她的嘴巴就像装上了铰链,会豁然打开,她的舌头可厉害呢。我走进了屋,屋里拉着绳子,上面凉着衣服。她打着赤脚站在洗衣盆旁洗东西呢。她穿一件估衣店买来的破旧长毛绒袍子,把头发向上编成辫子,用发卡卡到头顶上。屋里的臭味几乎使我喘不过气来。

显然她知道我是谁,她瞧了我一眼说:"瞧这是谁来了!是他来了,这个傻子。坐吧。"我都对她讲了,毫无保留。"老实告诉我吧,"我说,"你真是处女吗?那个淘气的叶齐尔真是你的小弟弟吗?别骗我,我是个孤儿。"

"我自己也是孤儿呀,"她回答说,"谁要是捉弄你,就叫谁的鼻子尖儿歪了。但是他们想占我的便宜,没门儿。我要五十盾的嫁妆,另外他们还必须募一笔现款给我。不然的话,就让他们来吻我的那个吧。"她倒是挺坦率的。我说:"给嫁妆的是新娘而不是新郎。"于是她说:"别跟我讨价还价了。要么干脆说'行',要么干脆说'不行',要不然,你从什么地方来还回到什么地方去吧。"——刘兴安、张镜译文

原译文注:

1 拉比(犹太教教士),负责主持宗教仪式,执掌犹太人的法律,并从事教学和精神治疗。
2 面条煮后加佐料,盘成团状放进炉中烤成布丁状食用。
3 弥赛亚:犹太人期望中的复国教主。据说当弥赛亚降临时,死人亦可复活。
4 犹太风俗,每遇重大庆典,都要奏乐,羊角号是所用乐器之一。

——刘兴安、张镜译文

译文三：

傻子金宝
艾萨克·巴什维斯·辛格
（节选）

  我是傻子金宝。我不认为我自己是傻子。其实我一点也不傻,但人家就爱这么称呼我。我还在学校时他们就给我起了那名字。我一共有七个浑号：白痴、驴子、傻头、笨蛋、哭丧脸、傻瓜、傻子。但流传最广的还是最后那个名字。我傻在哪里？容易受骗！他们说："金宝,牧师太太快临盆啦,你知不知道？"我就逃课去看她。唉,原来他们在骗我。我怎么知道的？因为她根本没有大肚子。但我从未看过她肚子。这是不是真的很笨呢？那群坏蛋乐得手舞足蹈,大笑大闹一番还不够,居然念起晚祷文来。而且,他们给我带去牧师太太产后吃的,不是葡萄干,而是羊屎。我不是个手无缚鸡之力,如果我掴任何人一记耳光,他就会给我打到西天去。但我天性不爱打人。我常这么对自己说：算了吧。他们因此就常常欺负我。

  一天我从学校回来,听到狗叫,我虽然不怕狗,但也犯不着先去惹它。因为说不定有一头是疯的,咬你一口,那你就完了。因此我转头就跑。后来我回头一看,看到整个菜市场的人都捧着肚子大笑起来。原来叫的不是狗,是饿狼神偷拉比。我又怎么知道是他呢？因为他叫得像头母狗。

  爱闹事,爱恶作剧的家伙知道我容易上当后,纷纷找我寻开心。"金宝,沙皇到法林堡了……金宝,月亮掉在土耳彬啦……金宝,何德那小子在浴室后面发现了宝藏……"而我这个笨蛋竟相信了他们。因为,一如经书所载（虽然怎样讲法我已忘记了）,凡事都有可能的。第二,全城人都这样说,你敢说个'不'字？如果你说,"呀,你们真会开我的玩笑！"那麻烦就来了。人们会生气,说："你是什么意思？你敢说我们骗你？"我还有什么办法？只好相信他了,最少我希望他们会因此快乐些。

  我是个孤儿。我祖父接养我时,他自己已有一条腿踏进棺材了。祖父死后,他们把我送到一个做面包的师傅去。唉,我在那里真够受的。任何一个女顾客,老的也好,年轻的也好,都最少骗我一次。"金宝,天堂里有个博览会呢……金宝,牧师在七个月里生下一条小牛……金宝,乌鸦飞过屋顶,生下了铜蛋。"一个神学院的学生有一次来买面包,就对我说："金宝,你在这里替老板刮着铲子时,救世主出现了。死者已从墓中复活。""那是什么话嘛,"我说,"我根本没听到羊角的号声。"他说："你聋了吗？"他们跟着就大叫道："我们都听见了！我们都听见了！"做蜡烛的丽施这时走来,用沙哑的声音说："金宝,你爸妈都从墓中走了出来,正四处找你呢。"

  说实在话,我心里知道哪有这种事,但他们还在说话时,我穿上了羊毛背心,出去了。说不定真有什么事情发生呢？反正出去走一次,也没有什么损失的。唉,不用说,我一出门口,他们马上就笑得嘴巴都合不拢。因此我发誓不再相信他们了,但这又没什么用处,他们实在把我搞糊涂了,使我真假不分。

  于是我跑去见牧师,求他指点。他说："经上载着,宁可一生做傻子,不可一刻做坏事。你不是傻子,他们才是傻子,因为凡令自己邻里蒙受羞辱的人,都会失去天国。"……

  我要离开这里,到第二个城去。但他们一知道这个,就忙着为我做媒,殷勤得几乎把我的大衣尾撕破。他们七嘴八舌的说个不停,说得我耳朵都积满他们的口涎了。她不是什么三贞九烈的女人,可是他们硬说她是个童贞女。她脚有点跛,可是他们却说这是她故意这样走的,因为她很怕羞。她生了个私生子,可是他们却说那是她弟弟。我大叫道："你们别浪费时间了,我怎样也不会娶那臭婆娘的。"但是他们气愤愤地说:"你怎可这样说话!你不觉得羞耻吗?你这样诋毁人家名誉,小心我们到牧师处告你。"这时我已知道他们不肯轻易地放过我的,因为我看出他们已决心作弄我到底。可是我想男人一结婚不就成了一家之主了么?如果她答应,我也无所谓。而且,一个人根本不能过一生而一点也不受到损害。我连想也不敢这么必想。

我到那间建在沙地上的泥屋去。他们高歌击鼓而来,好像是一群猎熊人。到了艾嘉的门口时,他们停下来了,因为他们实在怕惹她。她嘴巴好像上了铰链,轻轻一碰就开了,一开就不会饶人。我进了她的房子,里面在墙上挂满了晾衣的绳子,也挂满了衣服。她光着脚站在木盆旁边,正在洗衣服。她穿着一件破旧的(大概是从祖宗传下来的)丝绒长上衣。她把头发扎成许多小辫子,发夹夹得满头皆是。头上传出来的臭气,几乎闷得我窒息了。

看来她早已知道我是谁,她望了我一眼,说:"看谁来了!傻子来啦,找个椅子坐下吧。"

我把来意说了,什么也没瞒她。"告诉我实话吧,"我说,"你是不是处女,那么小顽皮耶奇儿真的是你的弟弟?别骗我,我是个孤儿。"

"我也是个孤儿,"她回答说:"谁骗你,谁就不得好死。他们最好不要以为我好欺负,占我便宜。本姑娘要五十基尔德(荷兰钱币名,译注)嫁妆,就让他们去募捐好了。若是没有这个钱,他们来舐本姑娘的屁股。"她话说得真坦白。我说:"嫁妆该是由新娘付的啊,哪里有由新郎付的?"她却说:"别跟我讨价还价,要就要,不要就拉倒——你请便吧。"——刘绍铭译文

评析:美国作家辛格的语言风格是:通俗生动、自然流畅、句子简短突兀、简洁朴素。《傻瓜吉姆佩尔》描写了圣人般的犹太人吉姆佩尔的痛苦遭遇。小说通过吉姆佩尔之口,叙述了自己苦难的一生。这是辛格小说采用的一种典型的叙述手法。我们比较的三种译文是:万紫《傻瓜吉姆佩尔》(万译);刘兴安、张镜《傻瓜吉姆佩尔》(安译);刘绍铭《傻子金宝》(简称刘译)。我们主要讨论该短篇小说第一章译文的部分典型译句。

小说开场白第一句的翻译,就显示不同译者的不同风格。

[1] I am Gimpel the Fool.

万译、安译:我是傻瓜吉姆佩尔。

刘译:我叫傻子金宝。

评析:原文用的是连系动词,第一种译文照译不误。译文在形式上和意义上与原文对等。译文达到了形式和意似。第二种译文,用了一个"叫"字来代替联系动词,形式上似乎没有对等,但意义上是对等的,且在一定程度上达到了风格上的对等。"叫"字比"是"字通俗,汉语口语中引出姓名时惯用"叫"字,因而译文更能反映原文通俗、口语化的风格,也更切合叙述者的口气,达到了意似和神似。

吉姆佩尔老是被人欺负,他自我排解道:

[2] If I slapped someone he'd *see all the way to Cracow*.

万译:要是我打人一拳,就会把他打到克拉科夫去。

安译:要是我扇谁一巴掌,准会把他扇到克拉科夫去。

刘译:如果我捆任何人一记耳光,他就会给我打到西天去。

评析:万译和安译直译了短语"see all the way to Cracow",这样的好处是保留了原文的地方色彩和民族特征。但是,"打到(或扇到)克拉科夫去",在汉语中没有什么引申含义,上述短语亦非固定词组或成语。它只是远离吉姆佩尔居住小镇的一座城市。因此,这一短语

离开小说的独特环境就失去了意义。刘译改成"西天"不失为一种方法,对中国读者来说,译文显得通俗易懂又合乎习惯,符合吉姆佩尔的口气。

吉姆佩尔整天听人讲假话,弄得晕头转向:

[3] They confused me so that *I didn't know the big end from the small*.

　　万译:……我<u>连粗细大小都分不清了</u>。
　　安译:……<u>不知东南西北了</u>。
　　刘译:……<u>使我真假不分</u>。

评析:若对这三种译文进行分析比较,不难发现,刘译在行文上最简练。例如小说中两次出现"another(man) in my place"的说法,万译和安译均照译成"换一个人处在我的地位",而刘译则是既简短又符合习惯的说法"换了别人"。由此可见,文学翻译仅仅达到形式对等或意义对等是不够的,最高的要求是风格的对等。善于发挥译文语言的优势,就能使译文达到神似,生动,有感染力。但是,有一点应该对初学翻译者提醒和告诫的是:初学翻译还是应该特别实事求是,"亦步亦趋",万万不可天马行空,然后语曰:"此乃活译也!"

吉姆佩尔被人们强拥着去与埃尔卡相亲。埃尔卡是一个凶悍泼辣的荡妇,接下来是她与吉姆佩尔之间的一段对话。她先赌咒发誓:

[4] ... and whoever tries to *twist* you *up*, may the end of his nose take a *twist*.

　　万译:谁要是想捉弄你,谁的<u>鼻子尖就会弄歪</u>。
　　安译:谁要是捉弄你,就叫谁的<u>鼻子尖儿歪了</u>。
　　刘译:谁骗你,谁就<u>不得好死</u>。

评析:原文用了两个"twist",体现了民间俗语的特色。但三种译文都无法表现两个 twist 的神韵,译文在形式上无法与原文对等。一、二种译文达到了意似,但不及第三种译文。第三种译文尽管在意思上似乎走了样,"鼻子尖弄歪"变成了"不得好死",然而却达到了神韵。因为不管"谁的鼻子尖就会弄歪"还是"就叫谁的鼻子尖儿歪了",在汉语中均不是什么强有力的诅咒语。刘译换用了汉语中习用的诅咒语:"谁骗你,谁就不得好死!"这就把埃尔卡赌咒发誓的口气译活了。

埃尔卡粗俗不堪,嘴巴很不干净,赌咒之后就口出污言:

[5] Otherwise *they can kiss my you-know-what*.

　　万译:否则,让他们来<u>吻我的那个玩意儿</u>。
　　安译:不然的话,就让他们来<u>吻我的那个</u>吧。
　　刘译:若是没有这个钱,他们来<u>舐本姑娘的屁股</u>。

评析:郭建中教授认为(1983),刘译的这个"舐"字,比万译和安译的"吻"字传神多了。"舐"字既粗又俗,加上"屁股"更觉其俗不可耐,恰恰表现了这个泼妇的口吻。相比之下,"吻"字就显得太"雅"了。不过,查阅汉语词典我们发现,"舐"字被明确标明是书面语,如果能改译成"舔",那才真正既粗又俗。至于"you-know-what"译成"那个"或"那个玩意儿",当然是较忠实的;但在这儿引申为"屁股"一词,出自这荡妇之口,非常恰当。但刘译的前半句"若是没有这个钱"略显拖沓,可改译成"没钱,就来舔老娘的屁股",更能传神。

埃尔卡在发过誓、骂过娘之后,就干脆下逐客令了:

[6] Either a flat "yes" or a flat "no"—*Go back where you came from*.

　　万译:要么干脆说"行",要么干脆说"不行",要不然,<u>你从什么地方来还回到什么地方去吧</u>。

安译：干脆说"行"或者"不行"——否则你哪里来就回哪里去。

刘译：要就要，不要就拉倒——你请便吧。

评析：前两种译文只做到了形似和意似，而第三种译文干脆利落，简洁有力，完全切合埃尔卡的性格，可以说达到了神似。破折号后面的一句逐客令，万译和安译显得拖泥带水，有气无力，不像是逐客令；刘译"你请便吧"行文简练，是句逐客令，但稍微雅些。似可译成"要就要，不要就拉倒——你滚好了！"

在该小说的其他部分，我们还可以看到这样精彩的译句：

小学徒与埃尔卡搞上关系后，在吉姆佩尔面前称赞埃尔卡。吉姆佩尔说大家都说他妻子的闲话，于是小学徒说：

[7] Ignore it as you ignore *the cold of last winter*.

万译：你别去理他，就像别理上一个冬天有多冷一样。

安译：别理睬它，就像你不理睬去年冬天的寒冷那样。

刘译：管他们干什么？他们的话，当作耳边风好了。

评析："耳边风"的表达非常贴切。

再如，吉姆佩尔指责妻子与其他男人鬼混，说：

[8] If my mother had known of it she'd *have died a second time*.

万译：如果我的母亲知道这件事，她会再死一次。

安译：我母亲要是有知，她会再一次死去。

刘译：如果我妈妈知道，她一定会气得从棺材里跳出来。

评析：万译和安译已经非常贴切了。刘译做了更大的发挥，渲染了气氛，使表达力进一步加强。

总结起来看，在体现原作风格方面，以"刘译"最佳，其成功的因素可以归纳为：对原文有深入透彻了解、大胆超越原文文字藩篱、充分发挥译文的归化优势，使得译文自然流畅、生龙活虎。万译和安译在尊重原文字面表达上做得较好，但为什么效果不佳？万译特别喜欢用数量词，其中，"一个"、"一次"、"一笔"等竟比安译多出二十次，与刘译更是相距更远。万译许多地方的衔接也不太到位，译文生硬。刘译则文笔流畅，但根据郭建中的分析(1983)，刘译的误译也不在少数，很多地方和原文的具体表达有较大出入，除开我们上面认可或欣赏的译文改造外。但即使如此，其文字依然神采飞扬，其胜在风格的传神再现，颇具文学翻译的辩证法思维。试想，如果译文既能在总体上体现原著风格，又能在具体语言细节的处理上力求正确，那么这样的译文将会多么完美。

例文[12]（人物描写）

At seventeen the promise of Noelle's early beauty had been more than fulfilled. She had matured into an exquisite woman. She had fine, delicate features, eyes a vivid violet color and soft ash-blond hair. Her skin was fresh and golden as though she had been dipped in honey. Her figure was stunning, with generous, firm, young breasts, a small waist, rounded hips and long shapely legs, with delicate ankles. Her voice was distinctive, soft and mellifluous. There was a strong, smoldering sensuality about Noelle, but that was not her magic. Her magic lay in the fact beneath the sensuality seemed to lie an untouched island of innocence, and the combination was irresistible. She could not walk down the streets without receiving propositions from passerby. They were not the casual offers that the prostitutes of Marseille received as their daily currency, for even the most obtuse men perceived something special in Noelle, something that they had never seen before and perhaps would never see again, and each was willing to pay as much as he could afford to try to make it a part of himself, however briefly. ——Sidney Sheldon: *The Other Side of Midnight*, 1973

译文一：

十七岁，萝爱拉就出落得更加尽善尽美了。一对动人的大眼睛，闪耀着紫罗兰色的光辉，灰黄色的长发，柔和地披散在浑圆的肩头，娇嫩白皙的皮肤，好象在蜜糖中泡过一样，光彩照人。她的身材苗条而丰满，令人神魂颠倒：坚挺的乳房、纤细的腰肢、滚圆的臀部，两条颀长匀称的大腿下面，是一双玲珑剔透的小脚。她的嗓音甜美，说起话来清脆而柔和。但她的女性魔力，主要还不在于身体上那种强烈的喷薄欲出的肉感，而是来自肉感下面隐藏的纯真，一种凛然不可冒犯的纯真。肉感与纯真的完美结合，使她更加魅力无穷。每当她在大街上行走，路人们纷纷向她注目、献殷勤。不过这一切，与马赛街头那些马路天使们随时都会遇到的肆意挑逗，是截然不同的。因为即使是最没有头脑的笨蛋，也看得出萝爱拉确实非同寻常。这种仙女，他们过去未曾见过，今后如能重睹芳颜，那真是祖上积德三生有幸。每个人都心甘情愿为她花掉最后的一分钱，哪怕只要能轻轻碰她一下。——汪村、工雨译文（《狰狞的夜》）（388字）

译文二：

十七岁了，诺拉果真长成美人，而且比人们预料的还要漂亮。一张动人的脸，水汪汪的眼睛闪烁着紫罗兰色的光辉，柔软的浅黄色头发显得夺目耀眼，鲜嫩的皮肤，宛如在蜜汁里浸泡过，细腻光亮。丰满坚实的胸脯，洋溢着青春的气息。柳腰、圆臀、颀长的大腿，还有一双精巧的小脚。如此苗条匀称的身材，确实令人神魂颠倒。她的嗓音清脆、温柔，使人感到甜美动听。她的魅力倒并不在于她身上那股外露的强烈性感，或者干脆可以称之为肉感，而在于隐匿在性感后面的纯真，在于这种凛然不可冒犯的纯真。性感与纯真糅为一体，使她更加魅力无穷。每当她出现在街头，就必然招来路人贪婪的目光，甚至挑逗性的言行。当然，诺拉所遭遇的，与流落在马赛街头的娼妓们每天都能碰上的猥亵逗乐，完全不能相提并论。因为，连最最愚蠢的家伙都能分辨出诺拉的非凡之处，分辨出这种非凡之处是他们从未领略过的，也是他们今后可能再也没有机会重睹的。于是，人们都愿意为了占有她而倾家荡产，哪怕只要能够挨近她也行。——李健、孔海云译文（《情与仇》）（412字）

译文三：

诺艾丽十七岁，早先便有的那种美丽就更加显得出类拔萃。她已经成为一个俊俏的女郎：身材苗条，一双媚人的紫色眼睛，加上柔软的淡黄色头发，标致极了。她的皮肤洁白细嫩，好象在蜜糖里浸过似的；胸脯饱满结实，其它各个部分也长得十分匀称；讲起话来清脆悦耳，甜滋滋的，谁见了都会动心。但是，从她身上散发出来的更重要的是天真无邪的气质。肌体上的完美加上少女的天真，使她无论在街上走到哪里，都要招来无数惊异的眼光：有的是属于爱慕的，有的是属于猥亵的。——丁振祺、戴天佑译文（《午夜情》）（214字）

译文四：

萝爱拉十七岁时果真长得俊美，出落得楚楚动人了。一双水汪汪的眼睛，闪耀着紫罗兰的光辉，淡黄色的秀发，柔和地披散在浑圆的肩头，洁白娇嫩的皮肤，宛如蜜糖泡过一样，细腻光亮。她的身材苗条而丰满，令人神魂颠倒：坚挺的乳房、纤细的腰肢、滚圆的臀部，两条修长匀称的大腿下面，是一双精巧的小脚。她的嗓音甜美，说起话来清脆而柔和。但她的女性魅力，主要还不在于身体上那种强烈的喷薄欲出的肉感，而是来自肉感下面隐藏的纯真，一种凛然不可冒犯的纯真。肉感与纯真的完美结合，使她更加魅力无穷。每当她在大街上行走时，就会招来路人爱慕的眼神和贪婪的目光。不过这一切，与马赛街头那些马路天使们随时都会遭遇到的肆意挑逗，是截然不同的。因为即使是最没有头脑的笨蛋，也看得出萝爱拉确实非同寻常。这种美女，他们过去未曾见过，今后如能重睹芳颜，那可是真见嫦娥下凡。每个人都心甘情愿为她花掉最后的一分钱，哪怕是只要能轻轻碰她一下。——华先发译文（《新编大学英译汉教程》）(392字)

评析： 译文一、二都是极佳的译文。译文一开头句中"出落"很好地使用了中国古典文学中的词语，按《辞海》，"出落"，为"长成"之意，犹言出挑。多赞美青年人的容貌、体态。《西厢记》第四本第二折："出落得精神，别样的风流"。译文二中译成"长成美人"，也是妙语，《长恨歌》中有"杨家有女初长成"。译文二中的"柳腰"运用了中国古典文学中对美女的形容词语，反映了译语文化的审美情趣常会不自觉地影响翻译的创作过程。译文四明显是在译文一基础上的修改，文字作了细微的调整，但改译文赫然出现"嫦娥下凡"，简直不可接受，比译文一的"柳腰"还不可取！从前三篇译文的字数上看，译文一为388字，译文二为412字，译文三为214字。很明显，译文三的译文出了问题。研究发现，译文三从"胸脯饱满结实"开始，译文变得很不严谨，漏译不少。最后的"有的是属于猥亵的"则属于误译。可见，光有语言水平还不够，还要有严谨的译风，否则就会粗制滥造，耽误作者，耽误读者。

本节练习

第五篇（写景）

Summer Sunrises on the Mississippi

(An excerpt from *Life on the Mississippi*)

Mark Twain

One can never see too many summer sunrises on the Mississippi. They are enchanting. First, there is the eloquence of silence; for a deep hush broods everywhere. Next, there is the haunting sense of loneliness, isolation, remoteness from the worry and bustle of the world. The dawn creeps in stealthily; the solid walls of the black forest soften to grey, and vast stretches of the river open up and reveal themselves; the water is smooth, gives off spectral little wreaths of white-mist, there is not the faintest breath of wind, nor stir of leaf; the tranquility is profound and infinitely satisfying. Then a bird pipes up, another follows, and soon the pipings develop into a jubilant riot of music. You see none of the birds, you simply move through an atmosphere of song which seems to sing itself. When the light has become a little stronger, you have one of the fairest and softest pictures imaginable. You have the intense green of the massed and crowded foliage near by; you see it paling shade by shade in front of you; upon the next projecting cape, a mile off or more, the tint has lightened to the tender young green of spring; the cape beyond that one has almost lost colour, and the furthest one, miles away under the horizon, sleeps upon the water a mere dim vapour, and hardly separable from the sky above it and about it. And all this stretch of river is a mirror, and you have shadowy reflections of the leafage and the curving shores and the receding capes pictured in it. Well, this is all beautiful; soft and rich and beautiful; and when the sun gets well up, and distributes a pink flush here and a powder of gold yonder and a purple haze where it will yield the best effect, you grant that you have something that is worth remembering.

翻译提示：本文描写的是密西西比河上夏天的日出的情景，通过融入作者的主观感受使读者如同身临其境，获得美的感受。就翻译而言，除了理解原文的内容意旨，还须把握原文的行文线索以及构段方式，才能使译文"言之有序"，再现原文的"意旨一贯"。

第六篇（状物）

It was the first rose of the year, big, red and heavy-scented. I had watched it grow from a bud, but somehow I had missed the final stage of the metamorphosis, so that it seemed to have changed from a bud to a full-blown rose overnight.

I had been waiting impatiently for this ultimate apparition of fully developed beauty, but now that it was actually here I was at a loss how to deal with it, overwhelmed by such perfection. I looked at the rose through the window, but I hesitated to go out into the garden and address it directly, although it was waiting there in evident expectation of a first act of homage.

When I finally plucked up the courage to go to it, I buried my face in its petals and inhaled its fragrance but could think of nothing to say beyond the trite words, "beautiful, beautiful." The rose seemed satisfied, however, and smiled at me warmly. A bee emerged from the heart of the rose, circled my head twice and flew off across the garden.

I felt that summer had begun.

(Michael Bullock, *The First Rose of the Summer*)

翻译提示：描写一朵玫瑰的花开，极其生动，如一股幽香拂面而来。

第七篇（幽默小品）

It is a fact that not once in my life have I gone out for a walk. I have been taken out for walks; but that is another matter. Even while I trotted prattling by my nurse's side I regretted the good old days when I had, and wasn't, a perambulator. When I grew up it seemed to me that the one advantage of living in London was that nobody ever wanted me to come out for a walk. London's very drawbacks— its endless noise and bustle, its smoky air, the squalor ambushed everywhere in it—assured this one immunity.

Whenever I was with friends in the country, I knew that at any moment, unless rain were actually falling, some man might suddenly say "Come out for a walk!" in that sharp imperative tone which he would not dream of using in any other connexion. People seem to think there is something inherently noble and virtuous in the desire to go for a walk. Any one thus desirous feels that he has a right to impose his will on whomever he sees comfortably settled in an arm chair, reading. It is easy to say simply "No" to an old friend. In the case of a mere acquaintance one wants some excuse. "I wish I could, but"— nothing ever occurs to me except "I have some letters to write." This formula is unsatisfactory in three ways. (1) It isn't believed. (2) It compels you to rise from your chair, go to the writing-table, and sit improvising a letter to somebody until the walkmonger (just not daring to call you liar and hypocrite) shall have lumbered out of the room. (3) It won't operate on Sunday mornings. "There's no post out till this evening" clinches the matter; and you may as well go quietly.

(Max Beerbohm, *Going Out for a Walk*)

翻译提示:极为精致的英国式幽默小品文,中国散文家梁实秋的作品堪与之比。翻译文字应灵活超脱。

第八篇(幽默小品)

The Freedom of the Fly

We can nowhere find a better type of a perfectly free creature than in the common house fly. Not free only, but brave. There is no courtesy in him; he does not care whether it is king or clown whom he tastes; and in every step of his swift, mechanical march, and in every pause of his resolute observation, there is one and the same expression of perfect egotism, perfect independence and self-confidence, and conviction of the world's having been made for flies.

Strike at him with your hand; and to him, the aspect of the matter is, what to you it would be, if an acre of red clay, ten feet thick, tore itself up from the ground and came crashing down with an aim. He steps out of the way of your hand, and alights on the back of it. You cannot terrify him, nor govern him, nor persuade him, nor convince him.

He has his own positive opinion on all matters; not an unwise one, usually, for his own ends; and will ask no advice of yours. He has no work to do—no tyrannical insects to obey. The earthworm has his digging; the bee her gathering and building; the spider her cunning network; the ant her treasury and accounts. All these are comparative slaves, or people of business. But your fly, free in the air, free in the chamber—black incarnation of caprice—wondering, investigating, flitting, flirting, feasting at his will, with rich variety of choice in feast, from the heaped sweets in the grocer's window to those of the butcher's back yard—what freedom is like this?

翻译提示:这是19世纪英国著名的作家和艺术评论家John Ruskin的不朽名篇,将一只苍蝇写得生动活泼,从庸俗中见奇趣。

第九篇(论说)

A Successful Old Age

As regards health, I have nothing useful to say since I have little experience of illness.

I eat and drink whatever I like, and sleep when I cannot keep awake. I never do anything whatever on the ground that it is good for health, though in actual fact the things I like doing are mostly wholesome.

Psychologically there are two dangers to be guarded against in old age. One of these is undue absorption in the past. It does not do to live in memories, in regrets for the good old days or in sadness about friends who are dead. One's thoughts must be directed to the future, and to things about which there is something to be done. This is not always easy; one's own past is a gradually increasing weight. It is easy to think to oneself that one's emotions used to be more vivid than they are, and one's mind more keen. If this is true it should be forgotten, and if it is forgotten it will probably not be true.

The other thing to be avoided is clinging to youth in the hope of sucking vigour from its vitality. When your children are grown up they want to live their own lives, and if you continue to be as interested in them as you were when they were young, you are likely to become a burden to them, unless they are unusually callous. I do not mean that one should be without interest in them, but one's interest should be contemplative and, if possible philanthropic, but not unduly emotional. Animals become indifferent to their young as soon as their young can look after themselves, but human beings, owing to the length of infancy, find this difficult.

I think that a successful old age is easiest for those who have strong impersonal interests involving appropriate activities. It is in this sphere that long experience is really fruitful, and it is in this sphere that the wisdom born of experience can be exercised without being oppressive. It is no use telling grown-up children not to make mistakes, both because they will not believe you, and because mistakes are an essential part of education. But if you are one of those who are incapable of impersonal interests, you may find that your life will be empty unless you concern yourself with your children and grandchildren. —Bertrand Russell

翻译提示：这是摘自 Bertrand Russell 的散文"How to Grow Old"中的一小段。表现作者超然看待人生的坦荡胸襟。

第十篇（论说）

Man's Youth

Thomas Wolfe

Man's youth is a wonderful thing: it is so full of anguish and of magic and he never comes to know it as it is, until it has gone from him forever. It is the thing he cannot bear to lose, it is the thing whose passing he watches with infinite sorrow and regret, it is the thing whose loss he must lament forever, and it is the thing whose loss he really welcomes with a sad and secret joy, the thing he would never willingly relive again, could it be restored to him by any magic.

Why is this? The reason is that the strange and bitter miracle of life is nowhere else so evident as in our youth. And what is the essence of that strange and bitter miracle of life which we feel so poignantly, so unutterably, with such a bitter pain and joy, when we are young? It is this: that being rich, we are so poor; that being mighty, we can yet have nothing; that seeing, breathing, smelling, tasting all around us the impossible wealth and glory of this earth, feeling with an intolerable certitude that the whole structure of the enchanted life—the most fortunate, wealthy, good, and happy life that any man has ever known—is ours—is ours at once, immediately and forever, the moment that we choose to take a step, or stretch a hand, or say a word—we yet know that we can really keep, hold, take, and possess forever—nothing. All passes; nothing lasts: the moment that we put our hand upon it, it melts away like smoke, is gone forever, and the snake is eating at our heart again; we see then what we are and what our lives must come to.

翻译提示：提供的参考译文非常精彩。译完请对照一下，看你能否达到这个水准。

第十一篇（论说）

Youth

Youth is not a time of life; it is a state of mind; it is not a matter of rosy cheeks, red lips and supple knees; it is a matter of the will, a quality of the imagination, a vigor of the emotions; it is the freshness of the deep springs of life.

Youth means a temperamental predominance of courage over timidity of the appetite, of the craving for adventure over the love of ease. This often exists in a man of 60 more than a boy of 20. Nobody grows old merely by a number of years. We grow old by deserting our ideals.

Years may wrinkle the skin, but to give up enthusiasm wrinkles the soul. Worry, fear self-distrust bows the heart and turns the spirit back to dust.

Whether 60 or 16, there is in every human being's heart the lure of wonder, the unfailing childlike appetite of what's next and the joy of the game of living. In the center of your heart and my heart there is a wireless station: so long as it receives messages of beauty, hope, cheer, courage and power from men and from the infinite, so long are you young.

When the aerials are down, and your spirit is covered with sorrow of cynicism and the ice of pessimism, then you are grown old, even at 20, but as long as your aerials are up, to catch waves of optimism, there is hope you may die young at 80.

翻译提示：本文美在文字，美在精神，由于美感共同性的作用，在翻译此文时，文中的许多亮点和美点，都要尽可能地移植到汉语中去。

第十二篇（论说）

Of Beauty

Virtue is like a rich stone, best plain set; and surely virtue is best in a body that is comely, thought not of delicate features; and that hath rather dignity of presence than beauty of aspect. Neither is it almost seen, that very beautiful persons are otherwise of great virtue; as if nature were rather busy not to err, than in labour to produce excellency. And therefore they prove accomplished, but not of great spirit; and study rather behavior than virtue. But this holds not always: for Augustus Caesar, Titus Vespasianus, Philip le Bel of France, Edward the Fourth of England, Alcibiades of Athens, Ismael the Sophy of Persia, were all high and great spirits; and yet the most beautiful men of their times. In beauty, that of favour is more than of colour; and that of decent and gracious motion more than that of favour. That is the best part of beauty, which a picture cannot express; no nor the first sight of the life. There is no excellent beauty that hath not some strangeness in the proportion. A man cannot tell whether Apelles or Albert Durer were the more trifler; whereof the one would make a personage by geometrical proportions; the other, by taking the best parts out of divers faces, to make one excellent. Such personages, I think, would please nobody but the painter that made them. Not but I think a painter may make a better face than ever was; but he must do it by a kind of felicity (as a musician that maketh an excellent air in music), and not by rule. A man shall see faces, that if you examine them part by part, you shall find never a good; and yet altogether do well. If it be true the principal part of beauty is in decent motion, certainly it is no marvel though persons in years seem many times more amiable; *pulchrorum autumnus pulcher* (beautiful persons have a beautiful autumn); for no youth can be comely but by pardon, and considering the youth as to make up the comeliness. Beauty is as summer fruits, which are easy to corrupt, and cannot last; and for the most part it makes a dissolute youth, and an age a little out of countenance; but yet certainly again, if it light well, it maketh virtue shine, and vices blush.

翻译提示：翻译前请仔细阅读王佐良翻译的《谈读书》，领会其特有的译笔。

第十三篇（论说）

The most complex lesson the literary point of view teaches—and it is not, to be sure, a lesson available to all, and is even difficult to keep in mind once acquired—is to allow the intellect to become subservient to the heart. What wide reading teaches is the richness, the complexity, the mystery of life. In the wider and longer view, I have come to believe, there is something deeply apolitical—something above politics—in literature, despite what feminist, Marxist, and other politicized literary critics may think. If at the end of a long life of reading the chief message you bring away is that women have had it lousy, or that capitalism stinks, or that attention must above all be paid to victims, then I'd say you just might have missed something crucial. Too bad, for there probably isn't time to go back to re-read your lifetime's allotment of five thousand or so books.

People who have read with love and respect understand that the larger message behind all books, great and good and even some not so good as they might be, is, finally, cultivate your sensibility so that you may trust your heart. The charmingly ironic point of vast reading, at least as I have come to understand it, is to distrust much of one's education. Unfortunately, the only way to know this is first to become educated, just as the only way properly to despise success is first to achieve it.

(Joseph Epstein, *Narcissus Leaves The Pool*)

翻译提示：这是一篇读书笔记，谈到了读书的方法和要旨，颇有启发意义。

第十四篇(论说)

The style of Dryden is capricious and varied, that of Pope is cautious and uniform; Dryden obeys the motions of his own mind, Pope constrains his mind to his own rules of composition. Dryden is sometimes vehement and rapid; Pope is always smooth, uniform, and gentle. Dryden's page is a natural field, rising into inequalities, and diversified by the varied exuberance of abundant vegetation; Pope's is a velvet lawn, shaven by the scythe, and levelled by the roller.

Of genius, that power which constitutes a poet; that quality without which judgment is cold, and knowledge is inert; that energy which collects, combines, amplifies, and animates; the superiority must, with some hesitation, be allowed to Dryden. It is not to be inferred, that of this poetical vigor Pope had only a little, because Dryden had more; for every other writer since Milton must give place to Pope; and even of Dryden it must be said, that, if he has brighter paragraphs, he has not better poems. Dryden's performances were always hasty, either excited by some external occasion, or extorted by domestic necessity; he composed without consideration, and published without correction. What his mind could supply at call, or gather in one excursion, was all that he sought, and all that he gave. The dilatory caution of Pope enabled him to condense his sentiments, to multiply his images, and to accumulate all that study might produce, or chance might supply. If the flights of Dryden therefore are higher, Pope continues longer on the wing. If of Dryden's fire the blaze is brighter, of Pope's the heat is more regular and constant. Dryden often surpasses expectation, and Pope never falls below it.

(Samuel Johnson, *Pope*)

翻译提示：这是就英国文坛上两个文豪文学风格的比较论述。译词当尽可华丽奔放。

第十五篇(演说)

Speech by President Nixon of the
United States at Welcoming Banquet

21 February 1972

Mr. Prime Minister and all of your distinguished guests this evening,

On behalf of all your American guests, I wish to thank you for the incomparable hospitality for which the Chinese people are justly famous throughout the world. I particularly want to pay tribute, not only to those who prepared the magnificent dinner, but also to those who have provided the splendid music. Never have I heard American music played better in a foreign land.

Mr. Prime Minister, I wish to thank you for your very gracious and eloquent remarks. At this very moment through the wonder of telecommunications, more people are seeing and hearing what we say than on any other such occasion in the whole history of the world. Yet, what we say here will not be long remembered. What we do here can change the world.

As you said in your toast, the Chinese people are a great people, the American people are a great people. If our two peoples are enemies the future of this world we share together is dark indeed. But if we can find common ground to work together, the chance for world peace is immeasurably increased.

In the spirit of frankness which I hope will characterize our talks this week, let us recognize at the outset these points: we have at times in the past been enemies. We have great differences today. What brings us together is that we have common interests which transcend those differences. As we discuss our differences, neither of us will compromise our principles. But while we cannot close the gulf between us, we can try to bridge it so that we may be able to talk across it.

So, let us, in these next five days, start a long march together, not in lockstep, but on different roads leading to the same goal, the goal of building a world structure of peace and justice in which all may stand together with equal dignity and in which each nation, large or small, has a right to determine its own form of government, free of outside interference or domination. The world watches. The world listens. The world awaits to see what we will do. What is the world? In a personal sense, I think of my daughter whose birthday is today. As I think of her, I think of all the children in the world, in Asia, in Africa, in Europe, in the Americas, most of whom were born since the date of the foundation of the People's Republic of China.

What legacy shall we leave our children? Are they destined to die for the hatreds which have plagued the old world, or are they destined to live because we had the vision to build a new world?

There is no reason for us to be enemies. Neither of us seeks the territory of the other; neither of us seeks domination over the other; neither of us seeks to stretch out our hands and rule the world.

Chairman Mao has written, "So many deeds cry out to be done, and always urgently; the world rolls on, time presses. Ten thousands years are too long, seize the day, seize the hour!"

This is the hour. This is the day for our two peoples to rise to the heights of greatness which can build a new and a better world.

In that spirit, I ask all of you present to join me in raising your glasses to Chairman Mao, to Prime Minister Chou, and to the friendship of the Chinese and American people which can lead to friendship and peace for all people in the world.

翻译提示：这是一篇非常精彩得体的演讲词。全篇文字浅显而语重心长。多处使用排比、重复等修辞手法，更是使得语篇恰当地传达出理性的感情、强烈的责任感和政治家的战略眼光。口语语汇，如"What is the world? In a personal sense, I think of my eldest daughter whose birthday is today,"或其他一些口语表达、听觉效果的修辞手法，如反诘等，以表示场面的亲切;尤其是对毛主席诗词的引用使得语篇在表意上很具有一种亲和力。

文学作品的翻译

第十六篇(人物对话)

<h3 style="text-align:center">Pride and Prejudice</h3>

Jane Austin

(An excerpt from Chapter One)

It is a truth universally acknowledged that a single man in possession of a good fortune must be in want of a wife.

However little known the feelings or views of such a man may be on his first entering a neighbourhood, this truth is so well fixed in the minds of the surrounding families, that he is considered as the rightful property of some one or other of their daughters.

"My dear Mr. Bennet," said his lady to him one day, "have you heard Netherfield Park is let at last?"

Mr. Bennet replied that he had not.

"But it is," returned she; "for Mrs. Long has just been here, and she told me all about it."

Mr. Bennet made no answer.

"Do you not want to know who has taken it?" cried his wife impatiently.

"You want to tell me, and I have no objection to hearing it."

This was invitation enough.

"Why, dear, you must know, Mrs. Long says that Netherfield is taken by a young man of large fortune from the north of England; that he came down on Monday in a chaise and four to see the place, and was so much delighted with it that he agreed with Mr. Morris immediately; that he is to take possession before Michaelmas, and some of his servants are to be in the house by the end of next week."

"What is his name?"

"Bingley."

"Is he married or single?"

"Oh! Single, my dear, to be sure! A single man of large fortune; four or five thousand a year. What a fine thing for our girls!"

"How so? How can it affect them?"

"My dear Mr. Bennet," replied his wife, "how can you be so tiresome! You must know that I am thinking of his marrying one of them."

"Is that his design in settling here?"

"Design! Nonsense, how can you talk so! But it is very likely that he may fall in love with one of them, and therefore you must visit him as soon as he comes."

"I see no occasion for that. You and the girls may go, or you may send them by themselves, which perhaps will be still better, for as you are as handsome as any of them, Mr. Bingley might like you the best of the party."

翻译提示：原文第一句为全文叙述定调，对话幽默俏皮，妙趣横生。译文应尽力传达这方面的韵味。

第十七篇（人物描写）

　　He was a man of fifty, and some, seeing that he had gone both bald and grey, thought he looked older. But the first physical impression was deceptive. He was tall and thick about the body, with something of a paunch, but he was also small-boned, active, light on his feet. In the same way, his head was massive, his forehead high and broad between the fringes of fair hair; but no one's face changed its expression quicker, and his smile was brilliant. Behind the thick lenses, his eyes were small and intensely bright, the eyes of a young and lively man. At a first glance, people might think he looked a senator. It did not take them long to discover how mercurial he was. His temper was as quick as his smile; in everything he did his nerves seemed on the surface. In fact, people forgot all about the senator and began to complain that sympathy and emotion flowed too easily. Many of them disliked his love of display. Yet they were affected by the depth of his feeling. Nearly everyone recognized that, though it took some insight to perceive that he was not only a man of deep feeling, but also one of passionate pride. (*The Masters*)

　　翻译提示：这一段足以代表作者的风格。句子不长，结构不复杂，用词也不艰深；可是一段之中包含许多矛盾，有些表达方式与汉语有差异，有些词语在文内的特殊意义很费推敲。译成汉语，在选词炼句两方面都要下工夫，否则有失原作的笔调。原作婉转曲折的，翻译时怕摸不透，不能达意。原作直抒胸臆的，翻译时怕情不切，流于浅薄。

第十八篇（人物描写）

Gone with the Wind
Margaret Mitchell
(An Excerpt from Chapter I)

　　Scarlet O'hara was not beautiful, but men seldom realized it when caught by her charms as the Tarleton twins were. In her face were too sharply blended the delicate features of her mother, a Coast aristocrat of French descent, and the heavy ones of her florid Irish father. But it was an arresting face, pointed of chin, square of jaw. Her eyes were pale green without a touch of hazel, starred with bristly black lashes and slightly tilted at the ends. Above them, her thick black brows slanted upward, cutting a startling oblique line in her magnolia-white skin—that skin so prized by Southern women and so carefully guarded with bonnets, veils and mittens against hot Georgia suns.

　　Seated with Stuart and Brent Tarleton in the cool shade of the porch of Tara, her father's plantation, that bright April afternoon of 1861, she made a pretty picture. Her new green flowered-muslin dress spread its twelve yards of billowing material over her hoops and exactly matched the flat-heeled green morocco slippers her father had recently brought her from Atlanta. The dress set off to perfection the seventeen-inch waist, the smallest in three counties, and tightly fitting basque showed breasts well matured for her sixteen years. But for all the modesty of her spreading skirts, the demureness of hair netted smoothly into a chignon and the quietness of small white hands folded in her lap, her true self was poorly concealed. The green eyes in the carefully sweet face were turbulent, willful, lusty with life, distinctly at variance with her decorous demeanour. Her manners had been imposed upon her by her mother's gentle admonitions and the sterner discipline of her mammy; her eyes were her own.

翻译提示：这是对女主人公的外表和性格的描写，生动活泼。译笔要求细腻。

第十九篇（人物描写）

Constantin Demiris was the ruler of an empire larger and more powerful than most countries. He had no title or official position, but he regularly bought and sold prime ministers, cardinals, ambassadors and kings. Demiris was one of the two or three wealthiest men in the world and his power was legendary. He owned the largest fleet of cargo ships afloat, and airline, newspapers, banks, steel mills, gold mines — his tentacles were everywhere, inextricably woven throughout the woof and warp of the economic fabric of dozens of countries.

He had one of the most important art collections in the world, a fleet of private planes and a dozen apartments and villas scattered around the globe.

Constantin Demiris was above medium height, with a barrel chest and broad shoulders. His features were swarthy, and he had a broad Greek nose and olive black eyes that blazed with intelligence. He was not interested in clothes, yet he was always on the list of best-dressed men and it was rumored that he owned over five hundred suits. He had his clothes made wherever he happened to be. His suits were tailored by Hawes and Curtis in London, his shirts by Bryony in Rome, shoes by Daliet Grande in Paris and ties from a dozen countries.

Demiris had about him a presence that was magnetic. When he walked into a room, people who did not know who he was would turn to stare. Newspapers and magazines all over the world had written an incessant spate of stories about Constantin Demiris and his activities, both business and social. (Sidney Sheldon: *The Other Side of Midnight*, 1973)

第二十篇（情节描写）

The only good part of his speech was right in the middle of it. He was telling us all about what a swell guy he was, what a hot-shot and all, then all of a sudden this guy sitting in the row in front of me, Edgar Marsalla, laid this terrific fart. It was a very crude thing to do, in chapel and all, but it was also quite amusing. Old Marsalla. He damn near blew the roof off. Hardly anybody laughed out loud, and old Ossenburger made out like he didn't even hear it, but old Thurmer, the headmaster, was sitting right next to him on the rostrum and all, and you could tell *he* heard it. *Boy*, was he sore. He didn't say anything then, but the next night he made us have compulsory study hall in the academic building and he came up and made a speech. He said that the boy that had carried the disturbance in chapel wasn't fit to go to Pency. We tried to get old Marsalla to rip off another one, right while old Thurmer was making his speech, but he wasn't in the right mood. (J. D. Salinger, *The Catcher in the Rye*)

翻译提示：本文风格属于幽默诙谐。要求译出其中的俏皮意味。

第二十一篇（情节描写）

All this while the Storm encreas'd, and the Sea, which I had never been upon before, went very high, tho'nothing like what I have seen many times since; no, nor like what I saw a few Days after: But it was enough to affect me then, who was but a young Sailor, and had never known any thing of the matter. I expected every Wave would have swallowed us up, and that every time the Ship fell down, as I thought, in the Trough or Hollow of the Sea, we should never rise more; and in this Agony of Mind, I made many Vows and Resolutions, that if it would please God here to spare my Life this one Voyage, if ever I got once my Foot upon dry Land again, I would go directly home to my Father, and never set it into a Ship again while I liv'd; that I would take his Advice, and never run my self into such Miseries as these any more. Now I saw plainly the Goodness of his Observations about the middle Station of Life, how easy, how comfortably he had liv'd all his Days, and never had been expos'd to Tempests at Sea, or Troubles on Shore; and I resolv'd that I would, like a true repenting Prodigal, go home to my Father.

These wise and sober Thoughts continued all the while the Storm continued, and indeed some time after; but the next Day the Wind was abated and the Sea calmer, and I began to be a little inur'd to it: However I was very grave for all that Day, being also a little Sea sick still; but towards Night the Weather clear'd up, the Wind was quite over, and a charming fine Evening follow'd; the Sun went down perfectly clear and rose so the next Morning; and having little or no Wind and a smooth Sea, the Sun shining upon it, the Sight was, as I thought, the most delightful that ever I saw.

翻译提示：本篇章描写了鲁宾逊初次出海遭遇风浪时的矛盾心态：是继续少年冒险，还是畏惧退缩。小说做了生动描写。

第二十二篇（电影对白）

Lord of the Rings—The Return of the King

Gandalf: Pippin saw in the Palantir a glimpse of the enemy's plan.
         Sauron moves to strike the city of Minas Tirith.
         His defeat at Helm's Deep showed our enemy one thing:
         He knows the heir of Elendil has come forth.
         Men are not as weak as he supposed, there is courage still. Strength enough perhaps to challenge Him.
         Sauron fears this.
         He will not risk the peoples of Middle-Earth uniting under one banner.
         He will raze Minas Tirith to the ground before he sees a King return to the

    throne of men.
    If the beacons of Gondor are lit, Rohan must be ready for war.
 Theoden: Tell me. Why should we ride to the aid of those who did not come to ours?
    What do we owe Gondor?
Aragorn: I will go.
Gandalf: No.
Aragorn: They must be warned.
Gandalf: They will be.
    You must come to Minas Tirith by another road.
    Follow the river and look to the black ships.
    Understand this:
    Things are now in motion that cannot be undone.
    I ride for Minas Tirith.

  翻译提示：这是电影《指环王》的精彩对白。在做此翻译前，须先播放影片，最好由学生直接将英文字幕抄写下来，在看完整部影片后进行翻译，然后再对照影片的中文字幕，教师加以讲评。这是最有趣味的翻译练习，相信学生会乐此不疲。教师尽可举一反三，挑选自己合意的英语影片进行观摩翻译。

第三节　科技语篇翻译

  科技语篇是传播自然科学和社会科学的知识和技术，包括理科、工科、医科、农科及社会等语域。科技题材英语的特点，就是大量使用科技词汇，每个学科都有专门的术语，语法上多用一般现在时态，多用被动语态、语句较长等。译者除了掌握好英汉语言知识和翻译技巧外，还必须对某一学科有研究。因此，最好的译文应该出自精通英汉语言知识和翻译技巧的所在学科专业工作者。

  例文[12]

  一、医学英语

Congestive Heart Disease

  This chapter emphasizes the special feature characterizing the diagnosis and treatment of congestive heart failure, whose high incidence in old age makes it an important problem of older people.

  Heart failure in the aged may result from any condition which interferes with the coronary blood flow, increases the work of the myocardium, or impairs myocardial function. Age-specific rates demonstrate a remarkable increase in congestive heart failure. Atherosclerotic heart disease and hypertensive heart disease separately or combined account for nearly 50 per cent of the reported cases of congestive heart failure.

Advances in treatments available to younger patients are equally valuable to older patients although treatment of congestive heart failure in older patients poses problems of greater magnitude than in younger persons and requires special consideration owing to the multiple pathological ailments and changes in pharmacological responses with age. For example, the elderly patient's extensive coronary artery disease and myocardial fibrosis impair heart action and decreased cerebral blood flow and hypoxia produce irrational behavior which makes the older person more difficult to manage and less capable of following directions. Chronic renal and liver impairments make older people more susceptible to digitalis toxicity, electrolyte disturbances, and hypoproteinemia. Although these changes tend to thwart therapeutic efforts and render management more difficult, attention to the diagnostic and therapeutic suggestions in this chapter should rectify and prevent recurrent congestive heart failure and provide more successful care in the hospital and at home.

The pathology of heart failure in the aged includes all form of heart disease in younger people and, in addition, the special entities found mainly in the elderly. The multiplicity of pathologic conditions increases with age and complicates the assessment of the pathologic basis for the heart failure. Heart failure in aged patients often has more than one cause and may be associated with numerous other disorders. (Raymond Harris, *The Management of Geriatric Cardiovascular Diseases*)

　　本章着重讨论在充血性心力衰竭的诊断与治疗中存在的特殊问题。由于充血性心力衰竭在老年人中的发病率颇高，因此该病便成为老年病中的一个重要课题。

　　老年人心力衰竭可由冠状动脉血流障碍、心肌负荷过重或心肌功能障碍造成。资料显示，充血性心力衰竭发生率随年龄增长而明显增高。动脉硬化性心脏病和高血压性心脏病单独或并存几乎占已报道的充血性心力衰竭病例的50%。

　　老年人心力衰竭的治疗比年轻心衰病人的治疗更加困难。由于年老，病人常有多种疾病并存，而且对药物反应也有改变，所以治疗时应顾及老年人的特殊性。不过，在年轻病人中采用的新治疗方法仍然适用于老年病人。老年人广泛的冠状动脉硬化以及心肌纤维变化影响心肌活动功能，而脑血流减少及缺氧又可引起非理性行为，结果，病人不能遵守医嘱接受治疗，致使病人更难处理。此外，在有慢性肝肾疾病的老年病人中更容易出现洋地黄中毒、电解质紊乱、低蛋白血症。虽然这些病理变化都可能影响有效的治疗，给治疗带来更多麻烦，但如果医生能注意本章中强调的诊断和治疗的建议，应能防止充血性心力衰竭的复发，并可使医院和家中的医护更成功。

　　老年心力衰竭的病理变化与年轻人的各类心脏病的病理变化相似。除此之外，在老年人还有其特殊性。由于年老，常有多种疾病并存的情况，致使对心力衰竭病理基础的评估更加复杂化。老年人心力衰竭病因众多，而且可能有各种其他疾病并存。——叶子南译文

　　评析：本篇选自一本有关老年心血管病的医学专著，内容主要是讨论老年人的充血性心力衰竭。翻译医学著作，最重要的是行文措辞必须符合医学专业的"行话"。在本篇中，"congestive heart failure"译成"充血性心脏衰弱"也可以，但医学文献里的说法是"充血性心力衰竭"。第二段中"condition which interferes with the coronary blood flow"普通译者会译成"干扰冠状动脉血流的状况"，意思虽然正确，但医生则将这个词组译成"冠状动脉血流障

碍"。不懂专业的人只能倚仗语言水平和翻译技巧来译,而懂专业的译者却能利用他自己的医学知识。"condition"译成"状况",但医学文献中"condition"常指病,如"heart condition"就是"心脏病"。第三段中"decreased cerebral blood flow"中的"decreased"被误认为是谓语动词,其实它是过去分词,起形容词作用。最后一段中的"disorders"有人译成"混乱",这个词在医学中应译成"疾病"。医学专业翻译是非常严谨的工作。正规的做法应该是译者在翻译完成后递交医学专家审校,使之符合专业行文规范。如果医学家亲自操笔翻译效果更佳。

二、学术论著的翻译

古庄(许国璋)在翻译罗素《西方哲学史》时,独创了一种独特的学术论著翻译文体。其特点表现在译文力求醒豁,不按词典译义,而按词的文化史涵义翻译。不按单句翻译,而按句段译出。用流水句法,不用三四十字的竹节句。避"词译"而用"阐译"。例如"feudal"不译"封建",译"拥据领地(之诸侯)";"anarchy"不译"无政府"(当时无中央政府),而译"诸侯纷争";"adventure"不译"冒险",或译"猎奇于远方",或译"探无涯之知",视上下文而定。再不然则用"释译"。例如"antiquity"不译"古代"而作"希腊罗马";"fame and beauty"在文艺复兴时期有特殊涵义,译成"享盛誉于邦国,创文艺之美";"asceticism"译"绝欲弃俗,攻苦食淡之说教";"prudential arguments"译"保身家保名誉之考虑"。凡词典译名之不能传意传神者,坚决避免之。罗素原文清丽可诵,译文至少应该明白畅晓。很明显,这是一种使译文意义显化的翻译法。它符合许国璋自己所言:"翻译目的,在于便利于不懂外文之读者,如不懂外文之读者读之不懂,翻译者不能说尽到责任。"(许国璋,1991:248)

例文[13]

During the 15th century, various other causes were added to the decline of the Papacy to produce a very rapid change, both political and cultural. Gunpowder strengthened central government at the expense of feudal nobility. In France and England, Louis XI and Edward IV allied themselves with the rich middle class, who helped them to quell aristocratic anarchy. Italy, until the last years of the century, was fairly free from Northern armies, and advanced rapidly both in wealth and culture. The new culture was essentially pagan, admiring Greece and Rome, and despising the Middle Ages. Architecture and literary style were adapted to ancient models. When Constantinople, the last survival of antiquity, was captured by the Turks, Greek refugees in Italy were welcomed by humanists. Vasco da Gama and Columbus enlarged the world, and Copernicus enlarged the heavens. The Donation of Constantine was rejected as a fable, and overwhelmed with scholarly derision. By the help of the Byzantines, Plato came to be known, not only in Neoplatonic and Augustinian versions, but at first hand. This sublunary sphere appeared no longer as a vale of tears, a place of painful pilgrimage to another world, but as affording opportunity for pagan delights, for fame and beauty and adventure. The long centuries of asceticism were forgotten in a riot of art and poetry and pleasure. Even in Italy, it is true, the Middle Ages did not die without a struggle; Savonarola and Leonardo were born in the same year. But in the main the old terrors had ceased to be terrifying and the new liberty of the spirit was found to be intoxicating. The intoxication could not last, but for the moment it shut out fear. In this moment of joyful liberation the modern world was born. ——B. Russel, *History of Western Philosophy*

教皇势力之衰落,始于15世纪以前。逮15世纪,更有多种原因,促其衰落,政治与文化,均呈急剧变化。火药用于争战,中央政府因之以强,拥据领地之公侯因之而弱。法王路易十一与英王爱德华四世,联富商以制诸侯,息纷争而致治。意大利于15世纪末,遭北方兵祸,然在此之前近百年间,实丰足昌盛文化发达之邦。此一新文化,崇希腊,法罗马,恶中古之僧侣,创人本主义之文明。凡建筑,凡文学风格,悉以古之巨作伟构为师。[15世纪]君士坦丁堡为土耳其所占。自希腊罗马之衰,古文化残存于世,仅君士坦丁堡一地。既陷,寓居于君士坦丁堡之希腊学人,相率流亡意大利,意大利倾慕希腊人文之学者,迎为上宾。达迦玛绕好望角抵印度,哥伦布西行发现新地,而世界为之扩大。哥白尼立日中心之说,而宇宙为之扩大。所谓君士坦丁大帝册封诏[注],学者证为数百年前赝物,儒林腾笑,教廷威信堕地。拜占庭学者西行,西方学者得读柏拉图原作,识其真谛,此与读僧侣纂疏之本,迥然不同。昔者,人间是烦恼悲泣之地,居尘世者,必升入天堂,始离苦海。今者,人间亦有乐趣:享盛誉于邦国,创文艺之美,猎奇于远方,皆人间乐事。雕刻绘事,诗歌词章,赏心悦目,奔进汹涌,美不胜数。几百年中绝欲弃智,攻苦食淡之说教,已置脑后。虽然,即在意大利,衰亡之中古思想仍有挣扎。萨方那罗拉,修身鄙世之僧人也;达·芬奇,无艺不精之大艺人也,而二人生于同年,同是本时代之人。大体言之,旧日之种种恐怖,今已失其恐怖;新获得之精神解放,使人陶醉,陶醉虽仅一时,然恐怖已驱除矣。此时也,精神解放,为之雀跃,为之欢庆,现代世界于焉诞生。——古庄译文

原译注:西罗马帝国于5世纪覆亡,正统东移。8世纪时,西罗马教皇以东罗马君士坦丁大帝诏书为根据,明其续承大统为合法。15世纪时,学者著文证明诏书为后世伪作,真相始白。

评析:古译文字明白晓畅、古朴典雅。古氏阐译的方法有下列几种:一是避免直译词的表层意思,而力求突出句段的深层含义,必要时还加以阐释。例如,首句"During the 15th century, various other causes were added to the decline of the Papacy to produce a very rapid change, both political and cultural",古译第一句是"教皇势力之衰落,始于15世纪以前"。从字面讲,原文并没有这一句;就全句涵义讲,却确实包含了这层意思。现在把它明白表示出来,不能谓之不信。二是不照搬字典定义,尽量参照上下文加以翻译:又如原文第二句"Gunpowder strengthened central government at the expense of feudal nobility",古氏阐译为"火药用于争战,中央政府因之以强,拥据领地之公侯因之而弱"。在"火药"后面加上"用于争战",将原文隐含的因果关系之意显化,表达更清楚。"at the expense of"分解译成"……因之以强,……因之而弱",意思更妥帖。三是不斤斤于"字比句次",而敢于"颠倒附益"(严复)。其中,"The long centuries of asceticism were forgotten in a riot of art and poetry and pleasure"一句,古氏先译后一部分"art and poetry and pleasure",并作了附益,译成"雕刻绘事,诗歌词章,赏心悦目",后译"in a riot",且加以发挥:"奔进汹涌,美不胜数。"最后才译头一部分"The long centuries of asceticism were forgotten"为:"几百年中绝欲弃智,攻苦食淡之说教,已置脑后。"这样译的好处是表达简明,不给人以滞涩之感。四是避免使用冗长的欧化句式,行文干净利落。原文第七句中,"the last survival of antiquity"阐译为"古文化残存于世,仅君士坦丁堡一地",使人明白残余指文化之残存。第八句"Vasco da Gama and Columbus enlarged the world, and Copernicus enlarged the heavens",古译做了具体的

补足:"达迦玛绕好望角抵印度,哥伦布西行发现新地,而世界为之扩大。"这是译文大胆的地方,也显出译者的胆识。这就是阐译之妙。又如第九句"The Donation of Constantine was rejected as a fable, and overwhelmed with scholarly derision",译成"所谓君士坦丁大帝册封诏[注],学者证为数百年前赝物,儒林腾笑,教廷威信堕地"。译者认为第十二句中的"asceticism"一词不但指"绝欲"、"攻苦食淡"这一方面,还兼指"弃智"的一面。又古氏把"riot"译成"奔迸汹涌,美不胜数",表达生动,与艺术、诗歌完全吻合。第十三句"Even in Italy, it is true, the Middle Ages did not die without a struggle; Savonarola and Leonardo were born in the same year",可以直译为:"当真,就在意大利,中世纪也还是经历了一场斗争才死去的;萨方那罗拉和列奥纳都两人是于同年才出生的。"古译做了补充:"虽然,即在意大利,衰亡之中古思想仍有挣扎。萨方那罗拉,修身鄙世之僧人也;达·芬奇,无艺不精之大艺人也,而二人生于同年,同是本时代之人。"古氏把"the Middle Ages"译为"中古思想",畅达多了。古译给人以深刻印象的另一点是,语句简短有力,文辞醒豁优美。一个例子是原文第五句"The new culture was essentially pagan, admiring Greece and Rome, and despising the Middle Ages"的译文:"此一新文化,崇希腊,法罗马,恶中古之僧侣,创人本主义之文明。"这一"崇"、一"法"、一"恶"、一"创",文约而旨博,读来痛快。本段最后一句也是佳译:"In this moment of joyful liberation the modern world was born"。"此时也,精神解放,为之雀跃,为之欢庆,现代世界于焉诞生。"意到神到,能使读者为文艺复兴的人文主义思想所陶醉、所感奋。整篇译文,畅快淋漓,真乃史书春秋笔法。(部分根据袁锦翔评论改写)

三、百科全书条目释文的翻译

1. 前言

百科全书翻译是一项讲究规范的工作,对于训练、培养学生的认真严谨的译风大有裨益。百科全书涉及的学科广泛,信息量大,翻译起来有相当大的难度。但由于其每个条目相对独立,各自成篇,反而比翻译长篇作品容易把握,因此,单卷本的《麦克米伦百科全书》(*The Macmillan Encyclopaedia*)(2002)曾大范围、多次性地被本书作者用作英语专业学生的翻译实践材料。

百科全书,根据《简明不列颠百科全书》(1986),其定性叙述是:用简明方式介绍各门类知识的工具书。该词来源于古希腊文 *enkyklopaideia*,原意为"全面的教育"或"完整的知识系统"。新版《辞海》(1999)对百科全书的释义是:"汇集各门学科或某一门类知识,按照辞典的形式分列条目,加以简要概述的工具书。具有查考和教育意义双重作用。"百科全书同其他种类的辞书一样,有严格的体例规范。从广义上讲,其体例规范包括选条、释文、图片、资料、学术名词和译名、书写格式、一般技术规格、目录系统、索引系统、参见系统、附录、编排等方面的规则,而狭义的体例仅指释文规则。本节以《麦克米伦百科全书》为蓝本,就条目释文的语体特征及翻译策略加以探讨。

2. 百科全书条目释文的语体特征分析

百科全书由组织在框架系统中的众多条目组成,是一有机整体。每一条目具有相对独立性。百科全书条目是一种权威性辞书的说明文字。介于专业论文和科普文章之间,具有一定的独立性。在介绍人物、事件等知识时,内容丰富、精确,引人入胜,有一定的完整体系。它把人类长期积累和经过历史考验已有定评的知识汇集起来,博采众长,不取一家之言。基本的事实须有确切的资料依据。语言严谨、朴实、简洁、通俗、流畅。

《麦克米伦百科全书》是一部单卷本综合性案头型百科全书,全书25,000余条,涵盖世界性的知识内容,尤以英国历史、地理、人物、文化的内容丰富详尽。该书的编写宗旨是"只重事实,不发表看法"(该书序言)。综观全书,其条目释文具有如下特点:

① 释文规范统一,编写体例严谨,具有相对固定的行文模式。例如,国家条目的模式为:国家的正式名称、地理位置、民族、经济、历史、政体、国家元首、语言、货币、面积、人口、首都等;城市条目的模式为:方位、隶属、交通、政治、经济、文化地位、历史沿革、建筑古迹、人口等;人物条目的模式为:生卒年月、身份和评价、简历、活动、著述、历史地位等;动物条目的模式为:拉丁学名、分类单位(门、纲、目、科、属)、分布地区、种类数量、体长、体征、价值或作用等。

② 篇幅短小,知识浓缩,简明扼要。由于本书是单卷本综合性百科全书,内容浓缩紧凑,平均条目合中文200字,千字以上的条目为数不多。因此,在理解和翻译释文时,译者较容易以条目为独立单元作整体把握。但由于汇集百科知识,有些专业性较强的条目翻译完还得请有关专家审读,以求术语表达符合专业规范。

③ 行文准确、明白、精炼。如前所述,它采用科学说明文体,使用规范化的现代英语书面语。语法现象相对容易分析,通常使用一般现在时和一般过去时,逻辑严谨,笔法平铺直叙而很少运用各种修辞技巧,客观阐述事实而罕有感情色彩强烈的各种语气和言外之意。其语言可称之为"百科全书语言"或"辞书语言"。作为本节要探讨的重点,兹列举该百科全书一条目和独立研编的《中国大百科全书》同一条目作比较,以示中英文在辞书语言表达上的同异:

[1] **aardvark** (Afrikaans: earth pig) A nocturnal African mammal, *Orycteropus afer*, also called ant bear. It is about 1.5m long, lives in grassland, and has a long snout, large ears, and a thick tail. Its strong claws are used to dig burrows and tear open the mounds of termites, which are picked up with its long sticky tongue. The aardvark is the only member of its order (*Tubulidentata*). (《麦克米伦百科全书》)

[2] 土豚(*Orycteropus afer*; aardvark) 哺乳纲管齿目土豚科的1种。是一种大型的食蚁兽。体型类似大袋鼠,但颇肥壮,体长150—180厘米,体重50—60千克;全身黄褐色,体毛稀疏,能延伸;耳长大而薄,类似驴耳;四肢粗强,趾端具强大而锐利的爪;尾呈圆柱形,尾肌很发达,基部粗,末端变细,长约70厘米。分布于撒哈拉沙漠以南的东非至南非。…栖息在丘陵和半草原地区。独自生活在较深的洞穴中。极善于挖土,掘进速度快。夜间活动以利爪抓破蚁丘,用长舌粘白蚁充食。……(《中国大百科全书》)。

从以上两个独立撰写的条目可以看出,英汉百科全书的行文都讲究言简意赅,两段文字尽管因不同辞书体例限制而长短不同外,在描写该动物属性、外观特征、习性、种类数量、分布地区的手法上相似。但他们又都遵循各自语言表达方式,英文开头使用一非完整定性叙述句,拉丁术语紧随其后,接着使用长句,一主语拖带一连串动词短语,主句和修饰性从句前后相连,分别使用了主动句和被动句。而中文条目则讲究短句,修饰词往往后置,句子干脆利落,用词严谨,有顿挫感,极不同于一般的白话语体。这就是典型的汉语辞书说明文的行文特点。这在具有百科辞典性质的中文《辞海》(1999)中也表现得非常明显。参照如下:

[3] 土豚(*Orycteropus capensis*)亦称"非洲食蚁兽"。哺乳纲,管齿目,土豚科。体长

90—140厘米,尾长48—60厘米。吻长,管状。无门齿和犬齿,颊齿圆柱形。舌细长,适于舐取食物。耳长大而尖。四肢短,前肢四指,后肢五趾,各具强爪。皮厚,红褐色或白色,被有稀疏的刚毛。昼伏夜出,以蚂蚁和白蚁为食。每胎一仔。产于非洲南部和中部。(《辞海》)

在这段中文释文中,从标点断句看,最短仅2字,最长不过9字。句子短促,多停顿。修饰词大部分后置,形成主谓结构。用词较正规,使用了辞书中专有的表述语言,如"亦称"、"具"、"被有"等等。由此可以看出,中文辞书的行文格式是相当固定的。在这一点上,英文百科全书的辞书文体特征远不如中文辞书明显。

因此,要将[1]英文条目翻译成中文,就得根据中文百科全书的行文格式来处理,以获取中文语体效果。现将[1]英文释文试译如下:

[4] 土豚 **aardvark**(南非荷兰语名:土猪 earth pig)一种非洲夜行哺乳动物,*Orycteropus afer*,又名大食蚁兽。体长约1.5米,栖居草原;长吻,大耳,粗尾巴。爪子锋利,用以挖地洞,扒白蚁穴;舌长,有黏性,用以舔食白蚁。属管齿目(*Tubulidentata*),是该目唯一的品种。

此译文打破了英语句法、词法的束缚,以简明扼要、短小精悍的断句,再现了原文的描写内容。这就是中译文力求顺应中文百科全书释文的语体特征而做出的调整。可见,语体并不是抽象的概念,它是通过具体的语句措辞来构筑的。辞书语言可以具体讲究到一个字,如用"其经历",而不说"他的经历";用"亦称",而不说"也叫做,也称作"等口语词。这一点在英语辞书语体里是难有区别的。另外,和英语百科全书不一样的是,中文译文可尽量避免在释文中重复条头及主语,英语在这一点上亦难做到,尽管英文释文也有自己的省略方式。我们还要看到,条目释文的翻译语体并非一成不变,科技、经贸题材的辞书语言又较文艺、历史、人物等题材的辞书语言不同,前者要求文从字顺,符合专业规范,注意术语词的使用,而后者专业术语性并不很强,但在辞书语言的遣词造句上有进一步发挥的空间,因而也就更能体现翻译技巧的灵活使用。本文将就此深入探讨。

首先,为了使中译文符合中文百科全书的行文规范,从语篇角度来考虑辞书条目的翻译是至关重要的。我们把单个条目或该条目释文的主要部分当作一个独立的翻译单位,翻译时,不做逐句逐句的迻译,而是将其融会贯通,彻底打破原文的结构,按汉语行文重新进行表述,使译文上下文自身连贯、完整。举例说明:

[5] **Schlieffen,Alfred,Graf von** (1833—1913) German general, who, as chief of the general staff(1891—1905), devised the Schlieffen Plan, on which German strategy at the outbreak of World War I was unsuccessfully based. The plan provided for a concentration of German forces on the Western Front, which would rapidly defeat France in a flanking movement through the Low Countries, while a smaller army held off Russian in the east (Schlieffen, Alfred, Graf von).

译文:施利芬 Schlieffen, Alfred, Graf von (1833—1913)德国将军。任参谋长时(1891—1905),制定了施利芬计划。该计划提出在西部前线集中德军主力,经低地国家从侧翼迅速击败法国,同时用一支较小的军队在东线牵制住俄军。在第一次世界大战爆发时,德军战略没有成功地按照该计划来制定(施利芬)。

评析:译文已将原文的句式彻底打散,另行重组。原文把制定计划(起因)和计划结果先作了交代,然后再回头详述计划的内容。译文则先把制定计划及计划内容表达完,再说明计划的结果。从句法上看,原文第一句的定语从句"on which German strategy at the outbreak of World War I was unsuccessfully based",跨越了原第二个完整句,被放到最后译出。这样编排更符合中文读者的阅读习惯。以上是作为整个条目释文在翻译中的处理,但翻译更多的是体现在句群(释文主要段落)的处理上。例如:

[6] By careful administration, skillful diplomacy, the selection of able generals, and the adoption of novel military tactics based on formations of infantry armed with the newly introduced arquebus, Nobunaga achieved domination between 1560 and 1582 over Kyoto and central Japan. He was treacherously assassinated (Oda Nobunaga).

译文:他精心治理,巧施外交策略,精选良将,采用新颖的军事战略,所组建的步兵团配备新引进的火绳枪,故其能从1560年至1582年统治京都和日本中部。后遭背叛被杀(织田信长)。

[7] Their skill as horsemen and archers halted Persian and Macedonian invasion but they remained a nomadic people until their disappearance during the Gothic onslaughts of the 3rd century AD (Scythians).

译文:他们(西徐亚人)善骑术,精弓箭,故能拒敌波斯人和马其顿人。他们一直是游牧民族。公元三世纪遭哥特人屠杀后消亡(西徐亚人)。

评析:上述二句译文都出现拆词、跨句、变更句型等译法,目的就是为了更符合中文辞书的表达方式,且略带中文史书笔法。[6]原文为极长的介词引导的状语分句,读者需读完28个词后才能接触到主句,按照一般的译法,势必译成"通过……他……",本译文将原从属分句化成主句,原名词性结构化成动词结构,以汉语"故其能"将原文主句连接起来,构成因果关系。[7]的主语"Their skill as horsemen and archers"译成两个动词句"他们善骑术,精弓箭",原文的谓语短语经翻译也和前面译句构成因果关系。另外,还可以通过下面一些译法来体现中文辞书的文体风格。

① 拆译:翻译,本身就意味着从拆解到重新组合的过程。这里所指的是具体到词组和句子的技术性拆译处理,这样可使译文轻松可读,摆脱原文的语法桎梏。

[8] Wenceslas' *unpopular* submission to the German king Henry the Fowler gave rise to a conspiracy of nobles, who incited Wenceslas's brother to assassinated him (Wenceslas, St).

译文:文策斯劳斯对德国国王亨利(捕鸟者)唯命是从,<u>令人反感</u>,导致贵族们密谋策划,煽动其弟去刺杀他(文策斯劳斯)。

[9] The main social division is between those engaged in agriculture and *the more prestigious* livestock farming(Turkmen).

译文:主要社会分工为从事农业和从事畜牧业人口,<u>而后者地位更高</u>(土库曼人)。

评析:[8]、[9]译文的共同特点是将修饰词抽出置后。拆译后的句子更符合汉语习惯,表达更加从容。

② 炼词:百科全书虽然属非文学类翻译,但同样讲究炼词。其目的是使译文在事实的基础上表达更到位。这符合中文百科全书的行文特点。

[10] Given command in the Baltic, he was *responsible* for the victory at Copenhagen (Nelson, Horatio).

译文:他受命指挥波罗的海战事,哥本哈根一役的胜利他功不可没(纳尔逊)。

[11] **Sandringham** 52 49N 0 30E A village in E England, in Norfolk. The Sandringham estate was bought by Queen Victoria for the Prince of Wales (later Edward VII) in 1861. Sandringham House, a 19th-century Tudor-style building, remains a royal residence. It was *the birthplace of George VI*, *who also died there* (Sandringham).

译文:桑德灵厄姆 Sandringham 东经0°30′,北纬52°49′。英格兰东部诺福克郡一村镇。1861年维克多利亚女皇为威尔士王子(后之爱德华七世)买下该处房地产。桑德灵厄姆宅邸是一座19世纪都铎风格的建筑,现仍是皇家行宫。乔治六世曾生于斯卒于斯(桑德灵厄姆)。

评析:[10]、[11]的划线部分的词语都根据上下文进行了锤炼,表达更简洁。例[11]的划线部分如果翻译成"这是乔治六世的出生地,他也在那里逝世",则显得太白,有节制地使用一些成语或文言词语不应当是辞书语言的忌讳。

③ 增补(阐译):不以增加原文多余信息为原则,而是为了使译文更显其义:

[12] He played a major part in the overthrow of the Tokugawa regime but was opposed to radical modernization and the complete abolition of feudalism. When his supporters clashed with the government in 1877, he *was torn between competing loyalties* but committed himself to the rebellion and was eventually forced to commit hara-kiri (Saigo Takamori).

译文:他在推翻德川幕府的运动中起主要作用,但反对激进的改革和彻底废除封建制度。1877年其部属和政府发生冲突,他既想效忠新政,又想维护旧制,左右为难,但还是参与了叛乱,最终被迫切腹自杀(西乡隆胜)。

[13] It was most used in antiquity, when silk was taken westwards and wool and precious metals eastwards, but was again travelled in the later middle ages, *notably by Marco Polo* (Silk Road).

译文:古时候最为通行。那时丝绸经此路西运,羊毛和贵金属经此路东运。中世纪后期再次成为旅行者之路。最著名者有马可·波罗之中国行(丝绸之路)。

评析:[12]中的"was torn between competing loyalties"要直译成中文几乎不可能,译者只好根据上下文加以阐译。[13]译文的补充使译文表达更醒豁。

以上我们对百科全书的文体特征做了充分分析,作者一再指出,辞书翻译对译文语言有特殊要求,要在准确的前提下,做到严谨、简洁、流畅,使译文具有汉语辞书语言的修辞特点。为此,译前的准备工作还应包括阅读、比较中英文百科条目,培养识别语体的语感和译感等,这样才能做到得心应手。

四、法律文件的翻译

法律英语是指法律界通用的书面英语(包括法律、法规、条例、协定等),尤其是指律师起草法律文件、合同惯常使用的语言。(孙万彪,2003:1)法律英语的文体属于"庄重(solemn)、刻板的(rigid)"文体。法律英语语句正规,结构严谨,有一定的程式。法律英语文词艰涩难懂,语句冗长复杂。可以说,法律英语翻译是翻译中难度最大的。译者在英语和汉语的功底和写作能力有较高的要求,同时还需要有一定的法律和经济方面的知识。

1. 法律英语的特点
使用正式(formal)的词语

在合同中,不用 before 而用 prior,不用 after 而用 subsequent,不用 if 而用 provided that。其他正式用语还有:construe (explain), deem (consider), operate, same, subject to (在……条件下), whereas(鉴于), without prejudice(不违背)。

使用不同意义的常用词

action(诉讼)、alienation(转让)、avoid(取消)、counterpart(有同等效力的副本)、execute(签署)、hand(签名)、instrument(法律文件)、negligence(过失)、party(一方)、prejudice(损害)、presents(本法律文件)、said(上述、该)、save(除了)、serve(送达)。

使用古英语和中古英语中常用但当代很少使用的词

主要是以 here, there 和 where 与介词合成的词:hereafter, herein, hereof, hereto, heretofore, hereunder, herewith; thereafter, thereat, thereby, therefore, therefrom, therein, thereof, thereon, thereto, theretofore, thereunder, therewith; whereas, whereby, wherein, whereof, aforesaid。

使用外来词语

ad hoc(专门的;专门地), *bona fide*(真诚地), *de facto*(事实上), *in re*(关于), *mutatis mutandis*(在细节上作适当修正后), *per se*(自身), *pro rata*(按比例)。

使用法律术语和行话、套话

alibi(不在犯罪现场)、appeal(上诉)、cause of action(案由)、damages(损失赔偿金)、defendant(被告)、due diligence(审慎调查)、letters patent(专利证书)、reasonable doubt(合理怀疑)、tort(侵权行为)。

为了使要表达的意思更为精确,常使用现成套话,如 and for no other purposes; shall not operate as a waiver(弃权声明书); shall not be deemed a consent(同意); including but not limited to; or other similar or dissimilar causes; without prejudice to。

词汇重复

词汇重复是法律英语中比较明显的特点。词汇重复是为了避免歧义,因此不使用首语重复法(anaphora)来联系句子。例如,

The servant's liability stems from the duty owed to a third person under the law requiring the servant to act as not to injure others.

句中重复了"servant",使关系清楚,一目了然。翻译中切忌以代词来翻译后面的重复词。

并列使用若干近义词

法律文件中有大量的词语并列现象,尤其是同义词或近义词并列使用,如:acknowledge and confess; act and deed; deem and consider; made and signed; fit and proper; terms and conditions; keep and maintain; pardon and forgive; able and willing; shun and avoid; aid and abet; cease and desist; fraud and deceit; null and void 等等。并列使用词语的主要目的是为了追求语义确切、论证严密和列举周详。这些近义词在英语中均有细微的区别和特定的含义,以相应的汉语进行翻译异常困难。例如,

Any payment to be made to the Lenders under this Agreement shall be free of and without any deduction or withholding of any tax, levy, impost, duty, or other charge of a similar nature...

句中的"tax，levy，impost，duty，charge"，译者很难译出其区别来，而且在我国的税法中也找不到对应的词，只能简略译成"各种税捐"。

2. 常用法律惯用表达语：

after prior notice to, and consultation with Party B　经事先通知乙方并与乙方协商后

any and all　任何和全部的

any breach of any of the terms, covenants or conditions contained in this Agreement
　　另一方违反本协议中的任何条款、规定或条件的行为

a reasonable person　有理性的人

as soon as reasonably possible　尽(可能)快地

bind them jointly and severally　各人共同和分别受其约束

cease and determine　终止

claim damages　要求得到损害赔偿

disclose or divulge　披露或泄露

except as herein provided　除本合同规定的外

for the purpose of this Agreement　在本协议中

hereinafter referred to as　以下简称

including, without limiting the generality of the foregoing　含，但不限于

in good standing　资格完备的

in contravention of　违反

in full force and effect　完全有效

in connection herewith(with this Agreement)　与本协议有关

in conformity with　遵从；符合

includes without limitation/includes but is not limited to　包括但不限于

in whole or in part of this Agreement　本协议的<u>全部或部分</u>

it is understood and agreed that...　双方理解并同意

liability for such damages shall not be waived　仍应给予损害赔偿

notwithstanding the above provision of this Clause...　尽管本条有上述规定

null and void　无效

on or about the date hereof　与本合同同日或稍后

one and the same　同一个；完全一样

pursuant to　根据本协议

require performance　要求另一方履行

save as described hereunder　除下文所述事项外

supplied or rendered　提供

the contract *to which Party A is a party*　以甲方为一方的合同

this Agreement is executed in Chinese　本协议以中文文本签署

under this Agreement　本协议项下的

under the relevant law　根据有关法律

unless otherwise provided for herein　除非本协议另有规定

unless otherwise specified herein　除非本合同另有规定
without prior written approval　未经事先书面批准
which shall not be unreasonably withheld　不应无理拒绝
with respect to　关于；就……而言
without prejudice to　不损害（权利、权益等），例如，
without prejudice to Sub-Article 2.1, …　在不违背第 2.1 款规定的情况下……
without prejudice to the Contractor's right to suspend/terminate this Agreement, …
　　在不影响承包商暂停/终止本协议的权力的情况下……

subject to
① 表示"遵照"、"遵循"：
Subject to paragraph 2 and 3, no reservation to this convention shall be permitted.
在遵循第二、第三两款的条件下，不允许对本公约作任何保留。
② 表示"须经"、"应受"：
The treaty is *subject to* ratification.
本条约须经批准。
…together with the total of any imports which otherwise are *subject to* quantitative restriction…
……连同本来应受数量限制的任何进口商品的总和……
③ 表示"以……为条件"、"在……的条件下"：
He shall acquire such rights *subject to* the payment of legal taxes and the fulfillment of other obligations.
在支付法律规定的税费和履行其他义务的条件下，他才能取得这些权利。
We shall go ahead, *subject to* your approval.
你一批准，我们就开始干。
④ 表示"可以"：
The schedule is *subject to* change without notice.
本时间表可随时更改，不另行通知。
…not *subject to* appeal.　不得上诉
⑤ 表示"受……的约束"、"受……的限制"：
The exceptions provided for in paragraph (a) are *subject to* the following additional provisions.
甲款的例外应受下列补充规定的约束。

3. 法律文件的句子结构
　　法律文件中的句子结构复杂、文词冗长、生涩费解，这与法律规定和合同条款的表述刻意追求精确、严密不无关系。拟定规定和条款，最主要的是确立主题事项，但有时候还必须顾及实施的依据、前提、条件、例外情况等，这就要借助相应的状语修饰语（短语和从句）缜密地表达规定和条款的完整意思。由此形成的英语复合句不可能不长。句子较少出现人称主语，更多的是被动语态和名词化结构。翻译时，必须对原文的篇章结构、辞法和句法认真加以分析，弄清各种修饰成分之间的关系。

[1] Upon successful completion of the tests the Purchaser shall sign a Plant Acceptance Certificate evidencing such completion and listing any agreed deficiencies to be corrected by CAE within such period as may be agreed with the Purchaser.

原译：如果这些试验均获成功，买方须在工厂验收合格证上签字，证明已完成这些试验，并注明双方一致认为并已被 CAE 校正的缺点。

改译：一旦顺利完成这些测试，买方须签署一张工厂验收证，证明测试已经完成，并列出将由 CAE 在买方同意的期限内校正的任何认可的缺陷。

评析：原译将"deficiencies to be corrected"误解为"deficiencies corrected"，前者表示将来时，后者表示完成时。上条规定的本意是在完成工厂验收后，设备如仍有缺陷，双方可协议在规定期限内予以校正，但应在验收证上注明。

[2] The "excepted risks" are war, hostilities, ... civil war, or unless solely restricted to employees of Contractor or of his subcontractors and arising from the conduct of the Works, riot, commotion or disorder, or...

原译："意外风险"包括战争、敌对……内战，或在工程进行中，由承包商的雇员、分包人制造的动乱、混乱……

改译："除外风险"包括战争、敌对状态……内战，或不纯粹是由总包商的或其分包商的雇员制造的和因施工而引起的暴动、骚乱或混乱……

评析："unless solely restricted to... of the Works"的本意是"只要不是纯粹由……所制造的以及不是因……而产生的"，由于结构混淆，译文正好与原意背道而驰。

[3] If, after the signing of this Agreement, the Chinese government either at the State, provincial, municipal or local level adopts any new law, regulation, decree or rule, amends or repeals any provision of any law, regulation, decree or rule, or adopts any different interpretation or method of implementation of any law, regulation, decree or rule, which contravenes this Agreement or which materially and adversely affects a Party's economic benefit under this Agreement, then upon written notice thereof from the affected party to the other Party, the Parties shall promptly consult and decide whether (i) to continue to implement this Agreement in accordance with the original provisions thereof as per the relevant provisions of the *Contract of Law of the People's Republic of China*; or (ii) to effectuate necessary adjustments in order to preserve each Party's economic benefit under this Agreement on a basis no less favourable than the economic benefit it would have received if such law, regulation, decree or rule had not been adopted, amended, repealed or so interpreted or implemented.

如果本协议签署之后，中国国家、省、市或地方政府通过任何新的法律、法规、法令或条例，修改或废除任何法律、法规、法令或条例的任何条款，或对任何法律、法规、法令或条例给予不同的解释或采取不同的实施办法，导致与本协议相冲突，或对一方在本协议项下的经济利益造成实质性的不利影响，受到影响的一方经书面通知另一方后，双方应立即协商并决定是否(i)根据《中华人民共和国合同法》的有关规定继续按照本协议的原条款执行本协议，或(ii)做出必要的调整，以保持各方在本协议项下的经济利益，使之不逊于各方在该等法律、法规、法令或条例未通过、未修改、未废除、未做出不同的解释或未采取不同的实施方法之前所能获得的经济利益。

评析： 翻译长句,首先要从语法分析入手理解句子的完整意思,而后在理解的基础上将其意思用通顺的汉语翻译出来。这个句子的主句(the Parties shall promptly consult and decide whether...)前面有一个很长的条件状语从句(If, after the signing of this Agreement, the Chinese government either at the State, provincial, municipal or local level adopts any new law, regulation, decree or rule, amends or repeals any provision of any law, regulation, decree or rule, or adopts any different interpretation or method of implementation of any law, regulation, decree or rule, which contravenes this Agreement or which materially and adversely affects a Party's economic benefit under this Agreement, then upon written notice thereof from the affected party to the other Party)和时间状语(then upon written notice thereof from the affected party to the other Party),在条件状语从句中,又夹带着一个时间状语(after the signing of this Agreement)和一个定语从句(which contravenes this Agreement or which materially and adversely affects a Party's economic benefit under this Agreement)。主句本身也相当复杂,除了有主语加两个并立的谓语和宾语的基本句子结构外,两个谓语动词还分别有方式状语(in accordance with the original provisions thereof as per the relevant provisions of the *Contract of Law of the People's Republic of China*)及目的状语(on a basis no less favourable than the economic benefit it would have received if such law, regulation, decree or rule had not been adopted, amended, repealed or so interpreted or implemented)修饰。就是在后一个方式状语中,也还有一个作定语的虚拟句(it would have received if such law, regulation, decree or rule had not been adopted, amended, repealed or so interpreted or implemented)。整个句子内有主句又有从句,修饰语套修饰语,环环相扣,构成了复杂的修饰和被修饰关系。只有弄清他们的相互关系,才能理解句子的完整意思。(根据孙万彪论述改写)

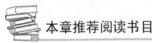

本章推荐阅读书目

郭建中、杨士焯等. 麦克米伦百科全书[Z]. 杭州：浙江人民出版社,2002.
孙万彪. 英汉法律翻译教程[M]. 上海：上海外语教育出版社,2003.
张今. 文学翻译原理[M]. 洛阳：河南大学出版社,1998.

本节练习

第二十三篇（医学）

Broken Heart

I had always assumed a broken heart was just a metaphor, a cliche of country music and romance novels. So I was as surprised as anyone to learn last week that doctors now consider it a real medical event, one that can kill.

The news comes from a report published in the *New England Journal of Medicine*, in which physicians at Johns Hopkins described a group of 18 mostly older women and one man who developed serious heart problems after experiencing a sudden emotional shock, such as the death of a loved one, or, in the case of one 60-year-old woman, a surprise birthday party.

What surprised the doctors who examined these patients was that none of them had actually suffered a heart attack. Indeed, few had any signs of heart disease at all. Yet at least five of the 19—and perhaps more—would have died without treatment, according to Dr. Ilan Wittstein, the cardiologist who led the study.

What was going on? To get to the bottom of it, Wittstein and his colleagues measured the levels of catecholamines—the family of stress hormones that includes adrenalin—that their patients were producing. In each case they found high levels of stress hormones—up to 34 times as great as normal levels and two to three times as great as those typically seen during severe heart attacks.

It's still unclear whether the hormones caused the cardiac problems or were caused by them. Nor can doctors explain why women's hearts seem more vulnerable than men's. "Men typically produce higher levels of catecholamines in response to a stressful event than women do," Wittstein says. "So if you had to guess, you'd guess that men would have this problem more than women."

The good news about the condition doctors are calling the broken-heart syndrome is that it's reversible—provided the initial shock isn't too great. And repeat occurrences appear to be uncommon no matter how many surprise birthday parties they throw you.

翻译提示：本文属科普性医学读物，请注意医学术语的翻译。

第二十四篇（医学）
Malpresentations, Malpositions, and Multiple Gestation
Steven H. Eisinger, M.D.

Objectives

At the end of this lecture/discussion and workstation, participants will be able to:
1. Define six types of malpresentations and methods for diagnosis.
2. List complications associated with each malpresentation.
3. Discuss the criteria for allowing vaginal delivery, and the management of vaginal delivery, when appropriate.
4. Discuss multiple gestation, with special attention to labor and delivery.
5. Perform safe, effective delivery of various malpositions and malpresentations using the maternal-fetal mannequin.

Definitions

Definitions are important to a discussion of malpresentations. *Lie* refers to the relationship of the long axis of the fetus to that of the mother, specified as *longitudinal*, *transverse*, or *oblique* (also referred to as *unstable*). *Presentation* refers to the portion of the fetus that is foremost or "presenting" in the birth canal. The fetus may present by its vertex, breech, face, brow, or shoulder. *Position* refers to a reference point on the presenting part, and how it relates to the maternal pelvis. For example, the reference point on the vertex is the occiput. When the fetal occiput is directed toward the mother's symphysis, or anteriorly, the fetus is in *occiput anterior* (*OA*) position. When the occiput is directed toward the maternal spine, the fetus is *occiput posterior* (*OP*). Intermediate positions around the compass are *left* and *right occiput anterior* (*LOA* and *ROA*), *left* and *right occiput transverse* (*LOT* and *ROT*), and *left* and *right occiput posterior* (*LOP* and *ROP*).

Methods of Diagnosis
There are three principal methods of determining fetal lie, presentation, and position. The first is Leopold's maneuvers or abdominal palpation. The second method is vaginal exam. The third method is imaging. Ultrasound is the preferred imaging method. Labor floor ultrasound examination is widely utilized in hospitals of all sizes, and every birth provider should have acquaintance with ultrasound skills in this setting to determine fetal lie, presentation, and position. Occasionally x-ray is necessary, particularly when fine detail is needed, such as the position of the limbs in a breech.

The Fetal Head and the Maternal Pelvis
Most fetal malpresentations (posterior, breech, face, brow) are clinically significant because the fetal head is not round, but rather ovoid or egg-shaped. The smallest of the fetal diameters is the *suboccipitobregmatic*; the largest is the *occipitomental*. The difference between them is three centimeters, or about 24 percent. When the head is in full flexion, the suboccipitobregmatic or smallest diameter presents to the pelvis. When the head is in full extension (or deflexion) the occipitomental or largest diameter presents. Delivery is much more likely to occur, and will be easier, if a smaller diameter presents. Therefore, the attitude of the fetal head (flexion versus extension) as it presents to the pelvis is of paramount importance. A degree of fetal extension of the head occurs with OP presentations, face and brow presentations, and some breeches.

Asynclitism also plays a major role in the mechanics of labor Asynclitism is lateral flexion of the head, such that the sagittal suture is not in the middle of the birth canal. Some degree of asynclitism is normal, and the fetal head may even shift back and forth from anterior to posterior asynclitism as the head accommodates more deeply into the pelvis. Extreme degrees of asynclitism may prevent labor from progressing. Asynclitism becomes a major factor in adequate forceps application.

The maternal pelvis also plays an important role in the cause of various malpresentations and prognosis for delivery. There are four pure types of pelves. Most women have a gynecoid or intermediate type:
- *Gynecoid* (round)
- *Anthropoid* (oval, with the long axis in the AP plane)
- *Platypelloid* (oval, with the long axis in the transverse plane)

• *Android* (triangular or heart-shaped, with the apex of the triangle anteriorly)

While a full discussion of pelvic types and pelvimetry is of limited clinical usefulness, it can be generalized that a narrow pelvis such as the anthropoid can cause persistent occiput posterior; the platypelloid pelvis can cause a transverse arrest; the android pelvis is prejudicial to delivery with all malpresentations; and an inadequate or small pelvis can be associated with most of the malpresentations, mainly based on the inability of the head to descend, engage, or rotate.

翻译提示：这是产科医学，请注意医学术语的翻译。英语专业学生的长处是语言基本功扎实，但对其他专业的知识，如医学专业知识自然不通，因此，翻译时会遇到不熟谙专业知识而产生的翻译困难。

第二十五篇（学术著作）
The authority of science vs. the authority of the Church

The period of history which is commonly called "period" has a mental outlook which differs from that of the mediaeval period in many ways. Of these, two are the most important: the diminishing authority of the Church and the increasing authority of science....

The authority of science, which is recognized by most philosophers of the modern epoch, is a very different thing from the authority of the Church, since it is intellectual, not governmental. No penalties fall upon those who reject is; no prudential arguments influence those who accept it. It prevails solely by its intrinsic appeal to reason. It is, moreover, a piecemeal and partial authority; it does not, like the body of Catholic dogma, lay down a complete system, covering human morality, human hopes, and the past and future history of the universe. It pronounces only on whatever, at the time, appears to have been scientifically ascertained, which is a small island in an ocean of nescience. There is yet another difference from ecclesiastical authority, which declares its pronouncements to be absolutely certain and eternally unalterable: the pronouncements of science are made tentatively, on a basis of probability, and are regarded as liable to modification. This produces a temper of mind very different from that of the medieval dogmatist.

The Renaissance encouraged the habit of regarding intellectual activity as a delightful social adventure

The Renaissance was not a period of great achievement in philosophy, but is did certain things which were essential preliminaries to the greatness of the 17th century. In the first place, it broke down the rigid scholastic system, which had become an intellectual strait jacket. It revived the study of Plato, and thereby demanded at least so much independent thought as was required for choosing between him and Aristotle. In regard to both, it promoted a genuine and first-hand knowledge, free from the glosses of Neo-platonists and Arabic commentators. More important still, it encouraged the habit of regarding intellectual activity as a delightful social adventure, not a cloistered meditation aiming at the preservation of a predetermined orthodoxy.

(B. Russell, *History of Western Philosophy*)

翻译提示：建议采用古庄的学术论著翻译文体。

第二十六篇（百科全书条目）

Nelson, Horatio, Viscount (1758—1805) British admiral. While serving in the West Indies, he married (1787) Mrs Frances Nisbet (1761—1831). At the outbreak of the French Revolutionary Wars he was given command of the Agamemnon in the Mediterranean. In 1794, at Calvi, he lost the sight in his right eye but went on to play an important part in the victory off Cape St Vincent (1797), for which he was knighted. Shortly afterwards he lost his right arm in action but in 1798 he destroyed France's naval, in the Mediterranean by his great victory in the battle of the Nile. Nelson spent the following year in Naples, where he fell in love with Emma, Lady Hamilton. Returning to England in 1800, Nelson, now Baron Nelson of the Nile, received a hero's welcome but his affair with Emma Hamilton, who gave birth to their daughter Horatia late in 1800, caused considerable scandal. Given command in the Baltic, he was responsible for the victory at Copenhagen (1801) and was created a viscount on his return. In 1803 he became commander in the Mediterranean. He blockaded Toulon for 18 months but in 1805 the French escaped, with Nelson hot in pursuit, and the ensuing chase culminated in the battle of Trafalgar (1805). Nelson directed this British triumph from aboard the *Victory* (ships) but was himself mortally wounded. He is buried in St Paul's.

翻译提示：注意百科全书翻译的格式，用辞书语言表达，力求准确。人物词条翻译。

第二十七篇（百科全书条目）

Nepal, Kingdom of A landlocked country in the Himalayas, between China (Tibet) and India. Most of the country consists of a series of mountain ranges and high fertile valleys, with some of the world's highest peaks, including Mount Everest, along its northern border and a region of plain and swamp in the S. Its predominantly Hindu population is of Mongoloid stock, the Gurkhas having been the dominant group since 1769. Economy: chiefly agricultural, the main crops are rice, maize, millet, and wheat. Forestry is also important Mineral resources are sparse, although some mica is being mined. Hydroelectricity is being developed on a large scale and some industry is being encouraged, including jute and sugar. Tourism is an important source of revenue. Exports, mainly to India, include grains, jute, and timber, as well as medicinal herbs from the mountains. History: the independent principalities that comprised the region in the middle ages were conquered by the Gurkhas in the 18th century and Nepal was subsequently ruled by the Shah family and then by the Rana, who continue to reign. In 1959 a new constitution provided for an elected parliament, but in 1960 the king dismissed the new government and in 1962 abolished the constitution. A pyramidal structure of local and national councils (*panchayat*) was set up, executive power lying with the king. Tension with India led to an economic "blockade" of Nepal by India in 1989. In 1990 unrest led to the restoration of parliamentary democracy. The Nepali Congress Party won multiparty elections in 1991. A Communist-led government was elected in 1994 but collapsed in 1996, when it was replaced by a coalition. Head of state: King Birendra Bir Bikam Shah Dev. Prime minister: Sher Bahadur Deuba. Official language: Nepali. Official currency: Nepalese rupee of 100 paisa. Area: 141 400 sq km (54 600 sq mi). Population(1994 est): 19 525 000. Capital: Kathmandu.

翻译提示：注意百科全书翻译的格式，用辞书语言表达。国家词条翻译。

第二十八篇（百科全书条目）

Spaniel One of several breeds of sporting dogs developed in Britain and thought to have originated in Spain. The English springer spaniel is typical, having a lean compact body, long muzzle, and long drooping ears. It is longer in the leg than the similar ∗ cocker spaniel but has the same flat wavy weather-resistant coat. It is generally black and white or liver and white, while the smaller Welsh springer spaniel is always red and white. The white Clumber spaniel, bred at Clumber Park, Nottinghamshire, England, is the heaviest breed. The Irish water spaniel has a distinctive curly dark-brown coat and is a strong swimmer. Height: 51cm (English springer); 53—61cm (Irish water spaniel); 46—48cm (Welsh springer). *See also* King Charles spaniel.

翻译提示：注意百科全书翻译的格式，用辞书语言表达。动物词条翻译。

第二十九篇（百科全书条目）

Scythians An Indo-European people who temporarily settled in Asia Minor before settling in what is now S Russia in the 6th century BC. The true Scythians, called Royal Scyths, established a kingdom N of the Black Sea and traded wheat for luxury goods with the Greek colonies there. Their skill as horsemen and archers halted Persian and Macedonian invasions but they remained a nomadic people until their disappearance during the Gothic onslaughts of the 3rd century AD. Objects recovered from their royal tombs demonstrate their metalworking skill and, especially in the animal designs that predominate as decorations, their artistry.

翻译提示：注意百科全书的翻译规范，用辞书语言表达。民族词条翻译。

第三十篇（法律文件）

(1) Neither Party may assign this Agreement, in whole or in part, without the other Party's prior written consent, except to (i) any corporation resulting from any merger, consolidation or other reorganization involving the assigning Party, and (ii) any entity to which the assigning Party may transfer all or substantially all of its assets; provided that the assignee agrees in writing to be bound by all the terms and conditions of this Agreement and provides documentation as evidence that the assignee has the ability and capability of meeting all of the obligations under this Agreement.

(2) Unless otherwise provided for herein, failure or delay on the part of any party to exercise any right, power or privilege under this Agreement shall not operate as a waiver thereof, nor shall any single or partial exercise of any right, power or privilege preclude

further exercise thereof or exercise of any other right, power or privilege. A waiver by one of the parties at any time of a breach of any term or provision of this Agreement committed by the other party shall not be construed as a waiver by such party of any subsequent breach to be committed by the other party, nor shall it be construed as a waiver by such party of its rights under such provision or any of its other rights under this Agreement.

翻译提示：注意法律文件的翻译规范。注意长句的翻译要求。

第三十一篇（法律文件）

Environmental Law
(An excerpt)

Today concern for the environment extends into such areas as chemical pollution of the air we breathe and the water we drink, strip mining, dam and road building, noise pollution, offshore oil drilling, nuclear energy, waste disposal, the use of aerosol cans and non-returnable beverage containers and a host of other issues. In fact, there is hardly a realm of national life that is not touched by the controversy that often pits those who style themselves environmentalists against proponents of economic growth in our energy-consuming society. The problem is to balance the needs of the environment against those of the economy or consumers trying to cope with the high cost of living without destroying the earth on which we all depend.

In the late 1960s both state and federal governments began enacting legislation and establishing new agencies to set and enforce open land from abuse by overzealous developers. The federal Clean Air Act of 1967, the Clean Air Act Amendment of 1970 and the 1972 amendments to the federal Water Pollution Control Act set new high standards for environment quality. In many cases states have followed suit by setting their own tough standards of air, water and land use. At every session of Congress and at most sessions of state legislatures new bills are brought forth, either to strengthen or weaken environmental standards, and hearings are held in which groups with different interests battle through private lobbies, industrial associations, labor unions and citizens' organizations to effect the legislation to their liking. Inevitably, tradeoffs are made—such as a lowering of mandated auto pollution standards for the immediate future against a raising of overall air quality requirements—and the degree to which long-term environmental considerations are taken into account ususlly depends upon the ability of environmental groups to bring their pressure to bear in the hearings.

翻译提示：熟悉了解英美法律。注意法律文件的翻译规范。

第七章　八级英译汉试卷评析篇

第一节　简　介

专业英语八级翻译考试是检测学生经过三、四年级翻译课训练后的一次考核,可称之为应试翻译。根据2004年《英语专业八级考试大纲》,翻译水平测试体现如下:

1. 测试要求:

(1) 能运用汉译英的理论和技巧,翻译我国报刊上的文章和一般文学作品。速度为每小时250至300个汉字。译文必须忠实原意,语言通顺、流畅。

(2) 能运用英译汉的理论和技巧,翻译英美报刊上的文章和文学原著。速度为每小时250至300个英文单词。译文要求忠实原意,语言通顺、流畅。

2. 测试形式:

本部分为主观试题,分两个项目:考试时间60分钟。

Section A: From Chinese to English

将一段150个汉字组成的段落译成英语。

Section B: From English to Chinese

将一段150个英语单词组成的段落译成汉语。

3. 测试目的:

按照《大纲》的要求测试学生的翻译能力。

4. 八级英译汉的评分标准分为五级,详见下表:

等级	分数	描述
5	10—9	优秀译文 译文忠实传达了原文的所有内容,充分传达了原文的风格和语气;只有1个或2个小的词汇错误;译文文雅(措辞恰当,句型多变)。
4	8—7	良好译文,出错很少 译文几乎传达了原文所有的内容;在理解单词、词组、句子或意思上出现的大错误相对很少;译文容易读通(整体清楚、流畅和连贯)。
3	6—5	尚可译文,有一些错误 译文充分传达了译文的大部分的内容;在理解单词、词组、句子或意思上偶尔出现错误;大部分译文容易读通。

续表

等级	分数	描述
2	4—3	不合格译文,经常出现错误 译文只传达了原文约一半的内容;在理解单词、词组、句子或意思上经常出现错误;译文的某些部分不容易读通。
1	2—1	拙劣译文 译文传达的内容少于原文的一半;几乎所有的句子都包含单词、词组、句子或意思上的错误;大部分译文无法读通。

(邹申,2005:414)

第二节 试卷评析

以下选取几篇英译汉试卷加以评析,由此发现八级英译汉试题的走向及应注意的问题。

例文[1]

TEM8(2000)英语专业八级英译汉试卷评析

If people mean anything at all by the expression "untimely death," they must believe that some deaths run on a better schedule than others. Death in old age is rarely called untimely—a long life is thought to be a full one. But with the passing of a young person, one assumes that the best years lay ahead and the measure of that life was still to be taken.

History denies this, of course. Among prominent summer deaths, one recalls those of Marilyn Monroe and James Dean, whose lives seemed equally brief and complete. Writers cannot bear the fact that poet John Keats died at 26, and only half playfully judge their own lives as failures when they pass that year. The idea that the life cut short is unfulfilled is illogical because lives are measured by the impressions they leave on the world and by their intensity and virtue.

译文一:

提起英年"早逝",人们或有所指。人们定会相信有些人死亡的时刻更为适宜。寿终正寝极少称为"早逝"。长寿即意味着生命之完整。但英年早逝常令人感到逝者美好时光尚未到来,一生之评说尚未做出。

然而,历史却否认这点,提起杰出的早逝者,人们定会忆起玛丽莲·梦露和詹姆士·迪恩。两人生命短暂,却完美无缺。诗人约翰·济慈26岁与世长辞,作家们对此难以接受。而他们自己过了26岁时却只能半开玩笑地认为今生今世无所作为。生命短暂即未成果——这观念荒谬无理。生命的价值取决于它留给世界的印象、它的贡献及它的美德。

译文二:

说起"早逝",人们或有所指,他们定然相信有些死亡更合天意。寿终正寝不能称作未尽天年——长寿即意味着生命的圆满。但英年早逝则会引发感慨：美好年华未竟，评说尚待时日。

然而历史并非如此。提及英年早逝，人们自会忆起玛丽莲·梦露与詹姆士·迪恩。两人的生命虽短，却照样圆满。诗人约翰·济慈年仅26岁便溘然长逝，作家们对此深感惋惜。过了26岁之后，他们便不无戏谑地叹息自己一生无所作为。"生命短暂即不圆满"，此种观点荒谬无理。生命的价值在其影响、在其勃发、在其立德于世。

评析：1. 短文的主题、语体把握不准

这是一篇议论文，前后两段共七句话150个词。此段文章虽短，但作者对"untimely death"（早逝）进行了明确的阐述。第一段是一般人对"untimely death"的看法，第二段则从历史角度举例说明"生命短暂即为不完整"的观点是不符合逻辑的，人生价值的高低并不取决于生命的长短，而是由生命的质量所决定的。许多考生把中心词"untimely death"译成"不及时的死亡"、"死亡之无常"、"死不瞑目"，甚至译成"死得很伟大"等，致使整篇译文与原文大相径庭（李淑琴，2001）。

另一个问题是语体表达不妥。原文为言简意赅的议论文，所以译文表达应尽量使用简洁的书面语言，尤其应避免口语化。但是不少考生只注意传达原文内容，对用词是否得体全然不顾。例如，开篇第一句：

If people mean anything at all by the expression "untimely death", they must believe that some deaths run on a better schedule than others.

误译：如果有人通过"死得太早了"这种说法来意味什么的话，那么，他一定认为一部分的死亡和另一些死亡相比，在时间上来得好。

这句译文拖沓、累赘，不符合议论文语体要求。

第二段第一句：History denies this, of course.

误译：历史当然不相信这一套啦！

显然，这句译文过于口语化，与原文的语体要求相去甚远。

语体得当是对译文水平的较高要求，满足这一要求绝非易事，译文的语体要尽量与原文语体保持一致，不可随意发挥。如有人还将上面一句译成"历史才不吃这一套呢，"或"历史老人对此说'不'！"等，都是非常不妥的。

2. 词的语境意义把握不准

词义误译主要是因为考生没有从搭配、语法、修辞及文化角度判断词义。"untimely"一词，根据 Longman Contemporary English-Chinese Dictionary，其概念意义有二：① not suitable for the time or occasion（不合时宜的）；② happening too soon（过早的）。从"untimely"与"death"的搭配关系看，应选择含义②，译为"早逝"，但有的考生译成"夭折"。而"夭折"在汉语中是指"未成年而死"。文中所举三个"早逝"的例子里，他们均不是未成年而死。这是汉语水平问题。另外，将"untimely death"译成"死的不是时候"、"死得太早了"，也都犯了措辞不严谨的错误。

第五句中的"summer death"被直译成"夏日死亡"、"中暑而死"等，也是没有意识到其特有的搭配和逻辑关系。在此"summer"应为"the best time (of a person's life)"，不正是"英年早逝"吗？

因一词多义误译的词还有第一段第三句中的"with the passing of a young person"，这个短语被误译为"看到一个年轻人擦肩而过"；第二段第一句中的"recall"被译成"召回、唤醒"。这都是因忽视上下文,望文生义,而导致的胡乱翻译。

由于语法判断错误而误译的地方也很多。如第一段第二句中的"death in old age"误译成"古时候的死亡",太可怕了。这是因为弄错了"age"的语法意义:"age"一词确有"时代"一义,但常用于专有名词,如"the Stone Age"(石器时代);此处的"age"是指"an advanced or old period of life"(老年),因此,该短语应译成"年老而终"。类似的错误还在第二段第二句中的"half"和"judge"二词上。有的考生没有分析"judge"在本句中的语法作用(谓语动词),将其当成名词,误译为"法官"。几乎有三分之一的学生把"half"看成谓语动词"judge"的主语,将"only half playfully judge their own lives as failures"译为"仅有半数的人(作家)开玩笑地说自己的一生"。在这里,"half"被看作名词,因此,有"一半"或"半数"的意思。但是,它用作主语时常与"of"连用。其实,"half"一词在此是副词,放在"playfully"前,作程度状语,含义为"partly, or completely"。因此,该部分可以译成:"他们只是半真半假地戏言自己的一生"。当然,说句良心话,上述这个短语的语法结构确实让人容易误解。

3. 译文表达欠妥帖

造成译文表达欠妥帖的最大障碍是翻译腔严重。从词法上看,考生不善把英语多名词化的动词转化为汉语中的多动词短语,过于拘泥于原文。从句法上看,考生不能打破原文语序,按汉语的习惯顺序表达;断句欠妥当。

4. 英语背景知识欠缺

背景知识欠缺集中表现在短文中三个人名的翻译上。考生不但对电影演员 Marilyn Monroe(玛丽莲·梦露)、James Deans(詹姆士·迪恩)不了解,似乎连 John Keats(约翰·济慈)如此重要的英国诗人都没有听过。不然,就不会将 Keats 译为"凯兹"、"凯茨"甚至译成"盖茨"!学生在参加八级考试前应该已经修过英国文学课才是。

例文[2]
TEM8(2002)英语专业八级英译汉试卷评析

The word "winner" and "loser" have many meanings. When we refer to a person as a winner, we do not mean one who makes someone else lose. To us, a winner is one who responds authentically by being credible, trustworthy, responsive, and genuine, both as an individual and as a member of a society.

Winners do not dedicate their lives to a concept of what they imagine they should be; rather, they are themselves and as such do not use their energy putting on a performance, maintaining pretence, and manipulating others. They are aware that there is a difference between being loving and acting loving, between being stupid and acting stupid, between being knowledgeable and acting knowledgeable. Winners do not need to hide behind a mask.

Winners are not afraid to do their own thinking and to use their own knowledge. They can separate facts from opinions and don't pretend to have all the answers. They listen to others, evaluate what they say, but come to their own conclusions. Although winners can admire and respect other people, they are not totally defined, demolished, bound, or awed by them.

Winners do not play "helpless," nor do they play the blaming game. Instead, they assume responsibility for their own lives.

译文一：

"胜者"与"败者"这两个字眼含有众多的意思。当我们将某人称作胜者时，我们并非指他是一个致使他人一败涂地的人。对我们来说，胜者乃这样一位君子，他无论是作为一个个人抑或是作为社会的一分子，一切反应均能由衷而发，做到诚信，可靠，乐善好施，且绝不伪善。

胜者不会穷其毕生之精力，去拘泥于某个他们所想像的为人之道；相反，他们会保持其真我本色，并且，作为这种追求真我的仁者，他们不会耗费精力来装腔作势，维持一种自命不凡的姿态，或去操纵他人。他们深知，在爱戴他人和装作爱戴他人之间，在愚顽不化和大智若愚之间，在学识渊博和佯装学富五车之间，实质上存在着天壤之别。胜者断无必要去藏匿于面具背后。

胜者无畏于独立的思维和运用其自己的知识。他们能够在事实与舆论之间明辨是非，不会僭称自己无所不晓。他们会倾听他人的见解，对他人所言作出鉴别，而最终所得出的却是其自己的结论。虽然胜者可能会钦佩并敬重他人，但他们不会受制于他人，惧怵于他人，为他人所囿，或被他人所摧垮。

胜者绝不耍"凄惨无助"之把戏，也决不玩"委过于人"之游戏。相反，他们会毅然肩负起对自身人生的责任(忍辱负重，无怨亦无悔)。

译文二：
……

成功者不会毕生致力于这样一种信念，即想像自己应该成为何种人。相反，他们即他们自己。因此，他们不会费神去装腔作势、故作姿态、摆布他人。他们明白，爱与装爱、傻与装傻、博学与装博学之间是有区别的。成功者无须躲藏在面具后面。

成功者敢于独立思考，敢于运用自己的知识。他们能够把事实从纷繁的意见中剥离出来，而又不会假装知晓一切。他们倾听别人的意见，评品他人的言论，却能得出自己的结论。虽然胜利者也能钦佩他人、尊敬他人，但是，他们不会完全被他人所规定、所摧垮、所束缚、所吓倒。

成功者不会佯装"无助"，也不会玩弄"推诿"，相反，他们承担起自己的生活责任。——毛荣贵译文

评析：这是篇论说文，就"胜者"加以议论，文章短小精悍，立意明了。两篇译文各有特色。从考生的翻译看，他们学习到了英语专业四年级，尚不能确定什么样的汉文化词语可以或不可以放进译文里。例如一些考生会把"They are aware that there is a difference between being loving and acting loving, between being stupid and acting stupid, between being knowledgeable and acting knowledgeable"译成了下面若干句：

(a)"成功者能意识到真诚与伪善、无知和表明愚蠢、孔子与南郭的区别"；

(b) 他们很清楚，惹人喜爱和博人敬爱，生而愚笨和行为鲁莽，满腹经纶和举止明智，这些都是截然不同的。

(c) 他们清楚地意识到装有爱心和真心付出爱心，表现出愚蠢和真的做出傻事，以及表现出学富五车之状和真正做出有才华的事之间的区别。

(d) 他们清楚地知道可爱和假装可爱，愚蠢和大智若愚，知识渊博和假装博学间是有区别的。

上面这些划线部分都是错误地滥用了汉语词语,有的还使用地方方言,这是很不合适的。当然,译文一也使用了"学富五车"、"大智若愚"的说法。它们的优劣,正好供我们评说!

Winners do not need to hide behind a mask.

(a) 智者不需隐居。
(b) 智者从不需遮遮掩掩的。
(c) 胜利者不需要伪装自己。
(d) 赢者不要装哭装笑,他们直面人生。

毛荣贵(2003:86)指出,"直译"的精髓是真正意义上的"翻译",而不是牵强的"释译",更不是糅合了译者主观想像和猜测的"演绎"。能直译尽量直译,上述数例把"mask"这个形象抛弃了,实属不必要。应老老实实地译成"成功者无须躲藏在面具后面"。这里顺便提及,在本书第六章"小说的翻译"一节《傻子金宝》的译文里,演绎成分也是很多的。只要处理得法,也未尝不可。

例文[3]

TEM8(2003)英语专业八级英译汉试卷评析

In his classic novel, "The Pioneer," James Fenimore Cooper has his hero, a land developer, take his cousin on a tour of the city he is building. He describes the broad streets, rows of houses, a teeming metropolis. But his cousin looks around bewildered. All she sees is a forest, "Where are the beauties and improvements which you were to show me?" she asks. He's astonished she can't see them. "Where! Why everywhere," he replies. For though they are not yet built on earth, he has built them in his mind, and they are as concrete to him as if they were already constructed and finished.

Cooper was illustrating a distinctly American trait, future-mindedness: the ability to see the present from the vantage point of the future; the freedom to feel unencumbered by the past and more emotionally attached to things to come. As Albert Einstein once said, "Life for the American is always becoming, never being."

译文一:

在其经典小说《开拓者》中,詹姆士·菲尼摩尔·库珀让主人公,一个土地开发商,带他的表妹参观正在由他承建的一座城市。他描述了宽阔的街道,林立的房屋,热闹的都市。他的表妹环顾四周,大惑不解。她所看见的只是一片树林。"你想让我看的那些美景和改造了的地方在哪儿啊?"她问道。他见表妹看不见那些东西,感到很惊讶。"哪儿?到处都是啊!"他答道。虽然那些东西还未建成在大地上,但他已在心中将它们建好了。对他来说,它们都是实实在在的,宛如已建成竣工一样。

库珀这里阐明的是一种典型的美国人特性:着眼于未来,即能够用未来的角度看待现在;可以自由地不为过去所羁绊,而在情感上更多地依附于未来的事物。正如阿尔伯特·爱因斯坦曾经说过的那样:"对美国人来说,生活总是在发展变化中,从来不会静止不变。"

译文二:

詹姆斯·费尼莫尔·库柏在其经典小说《拓荒者》中,记述了主人公——一位土地开发商——带着表妹游览一座他将要建造的城市的情景。他向表妹描绘了宽阔的街道,排排的房屋,俨然一座熙来攘往的大都市。然而,表妹环顾四周,却一脸迷茫,她所看到的只是一片树林。于是她问:"你要给我看的美景和改观在哪里啊?"他很惊讶,她居然还不能心领神会。便回答说:"还问哪里?这不到处都是嘛。"因为尽管他还没有把它们真正建成,他却早已在心中构想好了。它们对他来说是如此具体真实仿佛它们早已建成。

库柏在这里揭示了一种美国人独有的特征,即前瞻性:他们能够站在未来的高度来看现在的一切;摆脱过去束缚而更加亲近未来。正如艾尔伯特·爱因斯坦曾言:"对美国人来说,生活总是进取,而非守成。"

评析: 本篇原文大约160个词,题意较醒豁,文字流畅清晰,但有一些生词,如"teeming, trait, vantage, unencumbered"等。翻译考试中最怕碰上生词。考生此时也只好尽量根据上下文猜测词义了。而一些单词看似容易,其实也很费思量,如"cousin",有人将其译成"堂姐",到底是什么,确实很难确定,只好根据上下文,大致译成"表妹"。"improvements"也是无法确切表述,译文一将其译成:"改造了的地方",译文二译成:"改观"。"He's astonished she can't see them",绝大多数译文是"他很惊讶,她居然看不到",似乎不错,但如果细想,就会发现应该是"他很惊讶,她居然还不能心领神会"。因为那些楼房街道毕竟还没建成,那只是一张蓝图,此时表妹是听不明白他的规划而已。"are not yet built on earth"被许多考生译成"尚未在土地上建成",其实"on earth"在此表示"究竟、到底、真正"。"future-mindedness"也是不好译的简单词,可译成"前瞻性"、或更直接的"未来感"。在"Life for the American is always becoming, never being"中,"becoming"和"being"非常精炼,而且采用了尾韵的手法,翻译时应力求表达出来。

例文[4]

TEM8(2004)英语专业八级英译汉试卷评析

  For me the most interesting thing about a solitary life, and mine has been that for the last twenty years, is that it becomes increasingly rewarding. When I can wake up and watch the sun rise over the ocean, as I do most days, and know that I have an entire day ahead, uninterrupted, in which to write a few pages, take a walk with my dog, read and listen to music, I am flooded with happiness.

  I'm lonely only when I am overtired, when I have worked too long without a break, when for the time being I feel empty ad need filling up. And I am lonely sometimes when I come back home after a lecture trip, when I have seen a lot of people and talked a lot, and am full to the brim with experience that needs to be sorted out.

  Then for a little while the house feels huge and empty, and I wonder where my self is hiding. It has to be recaptured slowly by watering the plants and perhaps, by looking again at each one as though it were a person.

  It takes a while, as I watch the surf blowing up in fountains, but the moment comes when the worlds falls away, and the self emerges again from the deep unconscious, bringing back all I have recently experienced to be explored and slowly understood.

译文一:
  只有在我过于劳累,在我长时间无间断地工作,在我感到内心空虚,需要填补的时候,我才寂寞。而有时在我巡回演讲后回家时，在我见了许多人，讲了许多话，且经历多得需要清理时，我才寂寞。

于是有那么一小会儿感觉房子又大又空，我都不知道我的自我藏在哪儿了。于是我会给植物浇浇水，或者将它们再挨个儿瞅瞅，好像它们是人一样。这样我才慢慢地重新找回自我。好大一会儿，我看着水浪从喷泉中喷涌而出，但只有当世界在我身边逐渐消逝时，那一时刻才会到来，自我又从内心深处的无意识中冒出来，带来我最近的种种经历，让我探究，慢慢领会。

译文二：

只有在我疲劳过度的时候，在我长时间工作而没有休息的时候，或是在我感到心头空虚而需要充实的时候，我才感到孤独。有时，当外出讲学回家，见过许多人，讲了很多话，满脑子的感受，需要梳理的时候，我也会感到孤独。

屋子有一阵子显得既大又空，而我不知自我潜藏何处。只有去浇浇花草，或许，然后再注目每一株花草，将之视为活生生的知己，我才能渐渐找回失去的自我。

找回自我，需要一点时间。我看着浪花迸若喷泉，不过这样的时刻降临了，身边的世界渐次隐遁，自我，再次从深茫的无意识中浮现，带回了最近的经历，那等待探究、需要细想的经历。

评析：原文选自美国女作家 May Sarton（1912—1995）著的"The Rewards of Living a Solitary Life"。其作品常涉及日常生活、隐居、痛苦、疾病、欢乐等方面，语言精辟，内涵丰富，颇具哲理，令人深思。要求翻译的文字共 156 个单词。全文有 5 个独立句子，每句 2 分。在第一段中，"empty"和"filling up"是两个关键词。有人把"empty"理解为"饥饿"，因此要"吃饱"，但是，结合前面的"I am lonely"，就应该意识到是心灵"空虚"。在第二句中，"full to the brim"是一个形象的表达，其含义是："漫到边；溢；满"。形容"脑子里经历十分多"。"after a lecture trip"是"外出讲学后回家"。"recapture"是个难词，有考生误将其当作"capture"。其实作者用它来表示"找回自我"。

例文[5]

TEM8(2005)英语专业八级英译汉试卷评析

It is simple enough to say that since books have classes, fiction, biography, poetry—we should separate them and take from each what it is right that each should give us. Yet few people ask from books what books can give us. Most commonly we come to books with blurred and divided minds, asking of fiction that it shall be true, of poetry that it shall be false, of biography that it shall be flattering, of history that it shall enforce our own prejudices. If we could banish all such preconception when we read, that would be an admirable beginning. Do not dictate to your author; try to become him. Be his fellow worker and accomplice. If you hang back, and reserve and criticize at first, you are preventing yourself from getting the fullest possible value from what you read. But if you open your mind as widely as possible, then signs and hints of almost imperceptible fineness, from the twist and turn of the first sentences, will bring you into the presence of a human being unlike any other. Steep yourself in this, acquaint yourself with this, and soon you will find that your author is giving you, or attempting to give you, something far more definite.

译文一:

[书既然有小说、传记、诗歌之分,就应区别对待,从各类书中取其应该给予我们的东西。这话说来简单。]然而很少有人向书中索取它能给我们的东西,我们拿起书来往往怀着模糊而又杂乱的想法,要求小说是真实的,诗歌是虚假的,传记要吹捧,史书能加强我们自己的偏见。读书时如能抛开这些先入之见,便是极好的开端。不要对作者指手画脚,而要尽力与作者融为一体,共同创作,共同策划。如果你不参与、不投入,而且一开始就百般挑剔,那你就无缘从书中获得最大的益处。你若敞开心扉,虚怀若谷,那么,书中精细入微的寓意和暗示便会把你从一开头所碰上的那些像是山回水转般的句子中带出来,走到一个独特的人物面前。[钻进去熟悉它,你很快就会发现,作者展示给你的或想展示给你的是一些比原先要明确得多的东西。]

译文二:

[既然书籍有不同的门类,如小说、传记、诗歌等,我们就应该把它们区分开来,并从每种中汲取它应当给我们提供的正确的东西。这话说起来固然容易,]然而,很少有人要求从书籍中得到它所能提供的东西,通常我们总是三心二意地带着模糊的观念去看书:要求小说情节真实,要求诗歌内容虚构,要求传记阿谀奉承,要求历史能加深我们自己的偏见。如果我们读书时能抛弃所有这些成见,那将是一个极可贵的开端。我们对作者不要指手画脚,而应努力站在作者的立场上,设想自己在与作者共同创作。假如你退缩不前,有所保留并且一开始就批评指责,你就在妨碍自己从你所读的书中得到最大的益处,然而,如果你能尽量敞开思想,那么,书中开头几句迂回曲折的话里所包含的几乎难以觉察的细微的迹象和暗示,就会把你引到一个与众不同的人物的面前去。[如果你深入下去,如果你去认识这个人物,你很快就会领悟作者正在给你或试图给你某些明确得多的东西。]

译文三:

然而很少有人愿意接受书上告诉我们的东西。通常我们是带着一种不够明确和专一的目的来读书的。我们要求小说是真实的,诗歌是虚构的,传记是夸奖人的,历史是带有我们自己偏见的。如果我们读书时能够抛弃这种偏见,那将会是一个很好的开端。不要试图去改变作者的想法,跟随作者的思路,把自己当作他的一位合作伙伴吧。假如一开始你就犹豫不决,不愿接受作者观点,或者是不同意甚至抨击作者,你将给自己设置障碍,无法充分利用书本。另一方面,假如你尽量使思想开放,那么文章开头就可以给你一些暗示,由此一个与众不同的人物形象将跃然呈现于你面前。

译文四:

[既然书籍分门别类,有小说、传记、诗歌等,我们也应区别对待,从中汲取它们各自所能提供的——此话说起来再容易不过了。]然而,人们对书籍往往求非所予。开卷之时,我们常常思想模糊,思维割裂,苛求小说真实,认定诗歌造作,视传记为美化,期望史书认同一己之见。阅读之时,若能摒弃所有此类成见,那将是一个可喜的开端。不要对作者指指点点,而应尝试设身处地,做作者的同道和"同谋"。若是你一开始便故步自封,先入为主,求全责备,你就不可能最大限度地从所读的书中获益。但是,你若能大大敞开思想,那么,开篇的那几行曲径通幽的文字,那若明若暗的微妙表达和深意将把你带到一个独具特色的灵魂面前。投身其中,知晓此境,不用很久,你就会发现作者正在传递给你的,或试图传递给你的,原来如此显豁。——丁国旗译文

评析：本文原文标题为"About Reading Books"，作者是 Virginia Woolf。（弗吉尼亚·伍尔夫，1882—1941，英国小说家）。在译文一中，第一句被译成两句，先译"to say that..."，后译主句。表达的顺序正好倒过来，但在信息传达功能上是和原句等值的，在和下文的连贯上也是得体的。第二句中"come to"、"divided"、"ask of"、"true false"、"flattering"、"prejudices"等词语的意义看似不难，但实际翻译起来颇费思索，必须反复推敲其在上下文中的含义才能找到确切的对等词语。以上两句，译者是合在一起译的。"dictate"、"become him"、"fellow-worker"和 "accomplice"等词语都做了别致的处理。"open your mind as widely as possible"译成"敞开心扉，虚怀若谷"两个四字词语，词义贴切，也符合原文的语体特点。"steep"本义"浸泡"，译文根据汉语表达习惯译为"钻进去"，取"钻研"义。

第三节 亟待加强的几个问题

八级英译汉考试是典型的应试翻译。和普通的翻译训练与实践不同的是，它有严格的时间限制。学生必须在规定的时间里完成指定的翻译文字，他们不能查阅词典，也无暇考虑选词用字，翻译起来难免匆匆忙忙，碰到生词只好根据上下文揣猜，译文势必粗糙。根据分析（丁国旗，2006），发现在非考试环境下完成的译文中出现的错误显著比考试环境下的译文减少。因此可以判断，考试的压力在一定程度上影响了翻译的理解过程。真正的翻译，应该是精推细敲、甚至须经过"一名之立，旬月踯躅"的磨砺，我们怎好用这样的译文去苛求考生？但是，本着严格要求的精神，我们还是需要对考生试卷中的基本错误细加分析。兹列举如下。

1. 英语基本功不够扎实

英译汉中原文理解失误主要表现在缺乏语境和语篇意识，对英语词汇多义性认识不足，词义理解不透彻，词义掌握片面单一，断章取义。我们只举简单的例子：

We can choose to make opera, and other expensive forms of culture, accessible to those who cannot individually pay for it. (1997)

如果愿意，我们完全可以使歌剧或其他昂贵的文化形式面向那些个人没有支付能力的普通大众。

有些学生对总体语境缺乏把握，把句子读断了，将"make"（使）理解为"制作"，译成"让付不起钱的大众来制作戏剧或其他昂贵的文化形式"。这其实也是个语法问题，这些考生的语法没有过关！

2. 汉语基本功欠缺

汉语基本功欠缺导致英译汉中译文表达的失误，具体表现在：

用词不当："untimely death"（早逝）（2000）译成"夭折"（本指"未成年而死"）。

语体欠妥：八级英译汉试卷大多为言简意赅的议论文，译文表达应当尽量使用简洁的书面语言，避免累赘，避免口语化。但有些学生只注意传达原文内容，对语体是否恰当全然不顾，突出表现在译文过分口语化。如将"It should have been easy"（此事本来易如反掌，1996）译成"这本来是小菜一碟"；将"death in old age"（年迈而终，2000）译成"一大把年纪的时候过世"，这些错译都是太过散漫。

搭配不当：如将"untouched farmland"（尚未开发的农田，1995）译为"未触及的农田"；将"dazzling communication skills"（令人叹服的交际本领，1996）译为"耀眼的交流技巧"；将"improve marriage"（改善婚姻状况，1999）译为"提高婚姻"；将"whose lives seemed equally brief and complete"（他们俩的一生似乎同样都是短暂却又完满，2000）译为"他们的生命似乎同样简洁完整"等。

3. 背景知识缺乏

背景知识包括文学、政治、军事、历史、地理、社会等各方面。结果把"baby-sitter"（照看孩子的人，1995）译成"婴儿车"；或不恰当地使用了一些中国文化色彩浓厚的词语，如将"opera"（1997）译成"京剧"；将当时的美国总统"Ronald Reagan"（罗纳德·里根，1996）译成"雷诺·李根"等，反映出相当部分学生对英美政治人物的孤陋寡闻。而部分考生将英国文学史上著名的古典诗人"John Keats"（1795—1821）约定俗成的汉译名"约翰·济慈"分别译成"凯兹、凯茨、甚至"盖茨"；将美国著名影星"Marilyn Monroe"（1926—1962）约定俗成的汉译名"玛丽莲·梦露"译成五花八门的中文名字，都说明学生的相关背景知识的严重不足（陈小慰，2002）。

此外，根据行家的分析，许多翻译错误还由于误看误读、间歇性迷惑、精力不集中等因素，如把"cow"（牛）看成"crow"（乌鸦）、"Maximum"（最高的）看成"Marxism"（马克思主义）、"the Chin Dynasty"（秦朝）看成"the Ching Dynasty"（清朝）、"biography"（传记）当成了"biology"（生物），甚至当成"geography"（地理）！这样的翻译岂不南辕北辙、缘木求鱼？类似的错误不仅见于初学者，也见于高名家，如将divers faces（各种面容）译成"潜水夫的脸"、将dropping slow译成"落雪"（余光中，2002：2）。

从以上分析可见，凡是欠缺的地方就是需要我们改进的地方。我们要加强语言基本功的训练，加强文化与语言的认识。同时，在面对八级考试前，还要强化考前训练。

本章推荐阅读书目

高等学校英语专业高年级英语教学大纲[Z]. 外语教学与研究出版社，2000.
高校英语专业八级考试大纲[Z]. 上海外语教育出版社，2004.

本章练习
第一篇

TEM8(1996)英语专业八级英译汉试卷

Four months before the election day, five men gathered in a small conference room at the Reagan-Bush headquarters and reviewed an oversize calendar that marked the remaining days of the 1984 presidential campaign. It was the last Saturday in June and at ten o'clock in the morning the rest of the office was practically deserted. Even so, the men kept the door shut and the drapes carefully drawn. The three principals and their two deputies had come from around the country for a critical meeting. Their aim was to devise a strategy that would guarantee Ronald Reagan's resounding reelection to a second term in the White House.

It should have been easy. These were battle-tested veterans with long ties to Reagan and even longer ones to the Republican party, men who understood presidential politics as well as any in the country. The backdrop of the campaign was hospitable, with lots of good news to work with: America was at peace, and the nation's economy, a key factor in any election, was rebounding vigorously after recession. Furthermore, the campaign itself was lavishly financed, with plenty of money for a topflight staff, travel, and television commercials. And, most important, their candidate was Ronald Reagan, a president of tremendous personal popularity and dazzling communication skills. Reagan has succeeded more than any president since John. F. Kennedy in projecting a broad vision of America —a nation of renewed military strength, individual initiative, and smaller federal government.

第二篇

TEM8(1998)英语专业八级英译汉试卷

I agree to some extent with my imaginary English reader. American literary historians are perhaps prone to view their own national scene too narrowly, mistaking prominence for uniqueness. They do over-phrase their own literature, or certainly its minor figures. And Americans do swing from aggressive over phrase of their literature to an equally unfortunate, imitative deference. But then, the English themselves are somewhat insular in their literary appraisals. Moreover, in fields where they are not pre-eminent—e. g. in painting and music—they too alternate between boasting of native products and copying those of the Continent. How many English paintings try to look as though they were done in Paris; how many times have we read in articles that they really represent an "English tradition" after all.

To speak of American literature, then, is not to assert that it is completely unlike that of Europe. Broadly speaking, America and Europe have kept step. At any given moment the traveler could find examples in both of the same architecture, the same styles in dress, the same books on the shelves. Ideas have crossed the Atlantic as freely as men and merchandise, though sometimes more slowly. When I refer to American habit, thoughts, etc., I intend some sort of qualification to precede the word, for frequently the difference between America and Europe (especially England) will be one of degree, sometimes only of a small degree. The amount of divergence is a subtle affair, liable to perplex the Englishman when he looks at America. He is looking at a country which in important senses grew out of his own, which in several ways still resembles his own—and which is yet a foreign country. There are odd overlappings and abrupt unfamiliarities; kinship yields to a sudden alienation, as when we hail a person across the street, only to discover from his blank response that we have mistaken a stranger for a friend.

第三篇

TEM8(1999)英语专业八级英译汉试卷

In some societies people want children for what might be called familial reasons: to extend the family line or the family name, to propitiate the ancestors; to enable the proper functioning of religious rituals involving the family. Such reasons may seem thin in the modern, secularized society but they have been and are powerful indeed in other places.

In addition, one class of family reasons shares a border with the following category, namely, having children in order to maintain or improve a marriage: to hold the husband or occupy the wife; to repair or rejuvenate the marriage; to increase the number of children on the assumption that family happiness lies that way. The point is underlined by its converse: in some societies the failure to bear children (or males) is a threat to the marriage and a ready cause for divorce.

Beyond all that is the profound significance of children to the very institution of the family itself. To many people, husband and wife alone do not seem a proper family -they need children to enrich the circle, to validate its family character, to gather the redemptive influence of offspring. Children need the family, but the family seems also to need children, as the social institution uniquely available, at least in principle, for security, comfort, assurance, and direction in a changing, often hostile, world. To most people, such a home base, in the literal sense, needs more than one person for sustenance and in generational extension.

第四篇

TEM8(2001)英语专业八级英译汉试卷

Possession for its own sake or in competition with the rest of the neighborhood would have been Thoreau's idea of the low levels. The active discipline of heightening one's perception of what is enduring in nature would have been his idea of the high. What he saved from the low was time and effort he could spend on the high. Thoreau certainly disapproved of starvation, but he would put into feeding himself only as much effort as would keep him functioning for more important efforts.

Effort is the gist of it. There is no happiness except as we take on life-engaging difficulties. Short of the impossible, as Yeats put it, the satisfaction we get from a lifetime depends on how high we choose our difficulties. Robert Frost was thinking in something like the same terms when he spoke of "The pleasure of taking pains". The mortal flaw in the advertised version of happiness is in the fact that it purports to be effortless.

We demand difficulty even in our games. We demand it because without difficulty there can be no game. A game is a way of making something hard for the fun of it. The rules of the game are an arbitrary imposition of difficulty. When someone ruins the fun, he always does so by refusing to play by the roles. It is easier to win at chess if you are free, at your pleasure, to change the wholly arbitrary roles, but the fun is in winning within the rules. No difficulty, no fun.

第五篇

TEM8(2006)英语专业八级英译汉试卷

I have nothing to offer but blood, toil, tears and sweat. We have before us an ordeal of the most grievous kind. We have before us many, many months of struggle and suffering.

You ask, what is our policy? I say it is to wage war by land, sea and air. War with all our might and with all the strength God has given us, and to wage war against a monstrous tyranny never surpassed in the dark and lamentable catalogue of human crime. That is our policy.

You ask, what is our aim? I can answer in one word, It is victory. Victory at all costs—victory in spite of all terrors—victory, however long and hard the road may be, for without victory there is no survival.

Let that be realized. No survival for the British Empire, no survival for all that the British Empire has stood for, no survival for the urge, the impulse of the ages, that mankind shall move forward toward his goal.

第六篇

The thirty-second day out of Bombay began inauspiciously. In the morning a sea smashed one of the galley doors. We dashed in through lots of steam and found the cook very wet and indignant with the ship: "She's getting worse every day. She's trying to drown me in front of my own stove!" He was very angry. We pacified him, and the carpenter, though washed away twice from there, managed to repair the door. Through that accident our dinner was not ready till late, but it didn't matter in the end because Knowles, who went to fetch it, got knocked down by a sea and the dinner went over the side. The ship's captain, looking more hard and thin-lipped than ever, would not notice that the ship, asked to do too much, appeared to lose heart altogether for the first time since we knew her.

第七篇

Though fond of many acquaintances, I desire an intimacy only with a few. The Man in Black, whom I have often mentioned, is one whose friendship I could wish to acquire, because he possesses my esteem. His manners, it is true, are tinctured with some strange inconsistencies, and he may be justly termed a humorist in a nation of humorists. Though he is generous even to profusion, he affects to be thought a prodigy of parsimony and prudence; though his conversation be replete with the most sordid and selfish maxims, his heart is dilated with the most unbounded love. I have known him profess himself a man-hater, while his cheek was glowing with compassion; and, while his looks were softened into pity, I have heard him use the language of the most unbounded ill-nature. Some affect humanity and tenderness, others boast of having such dispositions from Nature; but he is the only man I ever knew who seemed ashamed of his natural benevolence. He takes as much pains to hide his feelings, as any hypocrite would to conceal his indifference; but on every unguarded moment the mask drops off, and reveals him to the most superficial observer.

第八章 翻译写作篇

正如我们在第四章"翻译的文采篇"所述,翻译即写作,翻译就是再创作。译者必须具有良好的中文修养,才能充分发挥译文优势,写出高质量的译句。然而,英汉笔译工作者往往只注重英语的学习,将中文学习放在无足轻重的地位或无暇去潜修中文。殊不知在英汉笔译工作中,中文程度的高低起着十分重要的作用。翻译家陈廷祐认为,译得出译不出,基本上看英文的根底;译得好不好,主要看中文的根底。对于一个句子,一段英文,有了准确的理解以后,译文的质量主要得看中文水平如何,这里面的高下优劣之差往往很大(陈廷祐,1981:229)。对许多文学翻译作品的研究表明,在译者理解表达水平大致相等的情况下,真正能流传久远的译本,如林纾、傅雷、杨必等译本,皆胜在其译文文字之优美。而这些学识修养又主要是通过译文写作表现出来的。因此,我们十分关切翻译中的译文写作能力的培养。

第一节 汉语的表达优势和行文特点

1. 精炼简约

汉语文章的这一特点,与汉语词汇的特点有关(徐振宗,1995:117)。首先,词本身没有形态变化,即它没有性、数、格、时态这些形式上的变化。如"你去"、"我去"、"今天去"、"明天去",都是一个"去",词的语音和书写都没有发生变化。单复数都一样。其次,语词具有一定的伸缩性。许多单音节和双音节的词一经重叠,即表示另外的意思,词性也可能发生变化。如"人—人人"、"说—说说"、"高兴—高高兴兴—高兴高兴"等。许多双音节词还可以在特定的语境下节缩,并不影响原来意思的表达。如"无(执)照经营"、"毫不利(自)己,专门利(他)人";"供(应)需(求)见面"等。再次,大量的成语、典故、俗语、谚语、格言等,以极少的文字包容了大量的信息。如"负荆请罪"、"叶公好龙"等。这些都为文章的简练精约提供了可能。

2. 富于意象

汉字独特的形声构成,是汉语富于意象的重要因素。汉语文章比任何语言写成的文章都更富有意象。所谓意象,即感情与形象的有机结合。如"木欣欣以向荣,风飘飘而吹衣"、

"无边落木萧萧下,不尽长江滚滚来",都能构成鲜明的意象美。

刘海涛在《文体创作中的母语思维》一文中也指出,无论叙事性话语、抒情性话语,还是议论性话语,母语思维的本质特征和结构要素都在它们的生成过程发生显在或潜在的影响,母语思维中的"象性原则"、"并置原则"、"对偶原则"、"殿后原则",能导致汉语文本独特的语言结构和形式要素。又有学者陈果安(2002:464)补充了三原则:"铺排原则"、"凝练原则"和"协律原则"。从翻译的角度看,直接对译文写作有影响的有:

并置原则

在汉语写作中,我们经常可以看到"叠言"、"叠句"、"叠章"的语言形式,作者通过"并置"的语句,创造意象纷呈、语义丰满、语势张扬的叙述话语。例如,

> 诚信是一个明净的窗口,将自己的内心敞露在大家的面前;诚信是一把钥匙,打开别人对你可能产生的种种疑虑;诚信是一首动人的歌……
>
> 诚信是一轮金赤朗耀的圆月,唯有与高处的皎洁对视,才能沉淀出对待生活的真正态度;诚信是一枚凝重的砝码,放上它,生命摇摆不定……

通过并置的句式,不仅有声有色地强化了文意,同时还把文意展示为一个细腻、立体的意脉网络,见出才华和文采。

对偶原则

对偶也是一种并置,它强调词性、词义的相反相成。中国古代把世界看做阴阳二气交感互动的哲学思维,非常深刻地影响着汉民族的生存方式和对偶性思维。表现在写作上,最典型的就是骈体文和近体诗的写作,它们都要求对仗,并形成了严格的规范。这种规范后来甚至在蒙学教材中给固定下来。试看《声律启蒙》中的一节:

> 云对雨,雪对风。来鸿对去燕,宿鸟对鸣虫。三尺剑,六钧弓,岭北寻江东。人间清暑殿,天上广寒宫。两岸晓烟杨柳绿,一园春雨杏花红。两鬓风霜途次早行之客,一蓑烟雨溪边晚钓之翁。

这种对偶句式积淀在民族文化心理结构中,在写作中我们有了上句,往往下意识地就生带出下一句来。翻译到顺手处,译者自然也会写出这种句式。

凝练原则

汉文本的写作是非常讲究凝练的。中国人讲究"炼字"、"炼句"、"炼篇"、"炼意",讲究"推敲",讲究"增之一字而不可,删之一字而不得",林语堂认为,汉语的单音节性"造就了极为凝练的风格"。

声律原则

与凝练原则相关的是它的"声律原则"。在汉语中,声律对诗自不用说,对散文创作也有非常大的影响。声律还包括节奏。梁实秋曾指出:"字的声音,句的长短,实在都是艺术上所不可忽略的问题。譬如仄声的字容易表示悲苦的情绪,响亮的声音容易显出欢乐的深情,长的句子表示温和弛缓,短的句子代表强硬急迫的态度"(梁实秋《论散文》)。

只要我们掌握了汉语的行文特征和神韵,我们就能在翻译过程中,自觉地在字里行间继承发扬这种文字传统,创造出灿烂的译文篇章。

第二节 翻译写作论

一、翻译写作的理论基础

翻译写作的基础理论具有如下特征：

1. 揭示翻译写作的基本规律

翻译写作是以另一种文字重新再现原文精神产品的活动和过程，是将一种文字的思维成果转化为另一种文字符号的能动过程。翻译写作理论，亦可称之为翻译写作学，其研究任务之一，就在于阐明翻译写作规律，指导翻译写作实践，去掉盲目性，增强自觉性。

2. 阐述"感知、运思、表述"的交互作用和运动过程，三者构成翻译写作内容的核心系统。

翻译写作不仅与译者的生活、经历、智力、素质有关，而且与读者的心理要求、资历、文化水平有关。"感知、运思、表述"原是写作理论中使用的表达。（周姬昌，1989）翻译写作，如同创作，也是一个从感知到运思再到表述，是一个系统的过程。感知、运思、表述是翻译写作过程中的三个重要环节，也是以思维活动为主线来重新制作精神产品的关键。感知是了解原作者的创作心理，洞悉其遣词造句的用心。运思是翻译写作的重要组成部分。所谓运思，就是揭示翻译写作中思路和思维运动的规律，了解信息和符号在译文孕育过程中的作用。运思，简单地说，就是运用心思，就是构思译文。它是一种高级思维活动。而表述就是将感知、运思的结果付诸文字，形成译文。

对于一篇译文来说，感知、运思、表述是相互联系的翻译写作行为，它们随着翻译过程发展，并以运思内容的文字符号化而同时终结。它又和"译者-感知-运思-表述-读者"，构成一个较大的翻译写作系统。翻译写作主体在翻译写作实践活动中，综合运用自身多方面的素质、修养和能力，去感知、运思、表述，最后构成译文的必然过程。这是翻译写作学努力探讨的又一领域。指导人们的翻译写作实践，增强人们的译写能力，提高人们的翻译写作水平，正是翻译写作学的宗旨。

3. 翻译写作应高度重视双语的修炼，尤其强调母语的修养。为了培养翻译人才，必须设立一个专门的翻译教学计划，除了不可少的外语课程外，必须设置母语课程，把汉语，尤其是古汉语经典著作的学习纳入其中，使译者浸润母语文化，并能通过译者的译文，将中西方文化加以弘扬光大。

翻译写作课是一门综合性、实践性很强的基础课，它强调翻译实践，强调翻译技巧的运用，强调不同译文的比较学习。翻译教学可从三个层面上进行：在初学（本科专业三年级）阶段，以传统的词法、句法流派翻译教材为主纲，完成语言基本功学习与翻译技巧学习的顺利过渡，进而在四年级或研究生阶段，辅之以功能流派和当代译论派教材教学。

二、翻译写作与写作的共性要求

翻译写作与写作的共性已经在前面讨论了很多。这里还要强调如下：

1. 翻译的具体操作是在两个层次上进行的。一是词句层，也就是像作文一样的遣词造句过程。译者在这一层次上所思考的主要是词义的定夺及句式的安排。同时译者还要在句以上的语篇层次上进行操作，不仅要考虑几个句子，整个段落，还要考虑整篇文章。这道理也正和作文一样，光遣词造句是不够的，还必须善于谋篇布局，保持意义的连贯和流畅。

再者，发挥译文的语言优势，并不只是追求文字的漂亮。文学翻译自然应该具有文采，尤其是名著，但这种文采应该是原文文采的再现，就是用译文特有的表达手段，准确而深刻地表达原文的各种功能。译文优势来源于对原文深刻的洞察理解，结果于译文的深刻的精确表达。原文优美，译文也优美；原文简练，译文也应简练。也就是说，要体现原文的风格。因此，技巧和文采是文学翻译写作的两个重要因素，他们与上述翻译写作系统有着密切的横向联系，并与上述系统共同构成一个完整的翻译写作系统。翻译写作活动的最终目的是准确、流畅地表达原文作者的思想，使读者发生兴趣，能够理解和接受。也就是说，译文要获得理想的传播效果，就必须讲究表达的技巧和方法。翻译写作技巧，是一种熟练而巧妙的技能。它是译者熟练而巧妙地运用各种翻译手法，完美地表达思想内容的技能。普通心理学认为，技能是在个体身上固定下来的自动化的行动方式，是一些巩固了的概括化的系统，它以操作训练的方式为人所掌握，是后天获得的东西。它可以在长期反复的"操作训练"中为人所掌握。

2. 文采来自译者较高的艺术修养，即译者的文才、才华，它包括译者运用译文语言的能力，掌握各种表达方式、表现技巧的能力，是从翻译主题的总体表达能力来说的。而狭义的文采，是指遣词造句、修辞达意的能力，是从译者驾驭语言文字这一单项能力来说的。须知，原文是有文采的作品，翻译应该还之以文采，而不是平淡、稀松。译文的语言经过修饰，能切当地、艺术地表达思想感情，富有美感，这就是文采。文采的主要特点是艺术表达力强，具有审美效应。它是增强译文感染力的重要因素。

三、译者的译写修养

翻译写作活动既是认识活动，又是表述活动，因此，既需要以理论为指导，知识为基础，又要以语言艺术为手段。译者的理论修养、知识修养以及艺术修养，必然地直接关系着翻译写作的质量。从对一篇原文的数篇译文的研究可以看出，随着译者的学养的不同，译文也会呈现品质高低之分。同时，任何译文不仅是原作者的精神产品，也是译作者的精神产品，那译文的字里行间，无不饱含、浸润着译者的一切学识、修养、气质。为了能担当好这个译者的重任，我们还要对译作者提出更高要求，要求能够创作，不一定是文学作品，写写小文章也是一种创作。虽然不能要求译者的写作水平达到作家那样，但起码要能写出流畅明白的文字来，能欣赏鉴别文字好坏。有了这种主创力、识别力，在翻译时，才能看出原文水平的高低，不至于被原文外在文字表达结构牵着鼻子走，写出依样画瓢的译文来。曾记否？协助林纾翻译外国小说的共有魏易、曾宗巩等十六君，他们外文虽通，但中文水平欠佳，或写作能力远不如林纾，所以大都只能口述而不能作，他们成就了林纾，而自己默默无闻，可为一叹。因此，我们必须向翻译前辈，如严复、林纾、鲁迅、林语堂、梁实秋等学习，做个能写善译的作家型译家。

总的看来，翻译写作活动要求译者所具备的知识修养应该有以下四个方面：

1. 文学知识

也就是人的文学教育水平知识。这是人的素质培养。《参考消息》(2005/4/19)上有一篇文章，谈到：外国书籍中译本质量严重下降，问题主要出在国内的翻译而不是国外的写作水平上。……中国的翻译艺术正在走向衰落。人民文学出版社的资深编辑苏福忠对朱生豪词汇的丰富赞叹不已，认为这是真实再现莎士比亚多种多样的表达方式的一个重要条件。不过最重要的还是他的文学素养。朱生豪之所以能够翻译出不朽的译著，在于他驾驭中文的能力，而不是作为语言学家理解英文的能力。

这真是一针见血、一语中的。文章还提到，翻译作品质量下降的问题归咎于书面语言水平整体的下降、对版权的不当保护以及为求快求省不惜牺牲质量的出版业现状。因此，提高翻译作品的质量，就需要改善文学教育现状，对中国文化给予更有力的保护。译者自身必须具有丰富的中外古今文学知识修养。

2. 一般知识

丰富的社会经验、生活常识、天文地理知识，是翻译写作不可缺少的辅助材料。这也是吕叔湘所称之的"杂学"，或谓"百科知识"。

3. 专业知识

要求译者熟悉和精通专业知识，掌握本领域、本学科、本行业的概念体系、理论基础、历史演变、行话术语，否则，就无法进行专业翻译写作。

4. 体裁知识

写作形式复杂多样，不同目的、不同要求、不同用途，可以采用不同的体裁形式。文学体裁包括诗歌、散文、小说、戏剧、报告文学等；非文学体裁包括书信、合同、文件、产品说明等。作为译者，要想样样通，殊为不易。

总而言之，作为培养未来翻译人才的本科翻译教学，我们应充分认识翻译教学的关键所在，认识到翻译写作能力在理解、技巧、表达中的重要地位。我们要认识到，这项工作是长期性的，因为从本科翻译教学的具体情况看，外语能力、理解力仍是一大问题。对许多学生来说，能把译文理解表达正确清楚已属不易，能力和时间都不允许他们去对译文精雕细刻。外译汉尚且不易，汉译外更加困难。但只要我们认识到翻译写作能力的重要性，就有了努力的目标。

第三节　译文写作的格式规范

1. 格式与标点符号

标点符号是书面语言的有机组成部分。标点符号共有 16 种，即句号（。）、问号（？）、叹号（！）、逗号（，）、顿号（、）、分号（；）、冒号（：）、引号（""）、括号（（））、破折号（——）、省略号（……）、着重号（.）、连接号（-）、间隔号（·）、书名号（《》）等。只有掌握了它们的用法，才能正确地加以使用。使用标点符号的常见毛病有一逗到底、引号有前无后、滥用省略号、标点不占格或书写位置不准确等。

行款格式

标题上下空一行，写在稿纸当中。

署名写在标题下面正中,与标题相隔空一行。

每自然段开头要空两格。

分类项时所用序码必须统一。

段中原话引文和人物对话要加引号。

关于人物对话的行款格式也有规范要求。夹在段中的对话和提行对话都要用引号标明。另外,一般说来,说话人在前,话在后,说的话前面要用冒号。话在前,人在后,要用句号煞住标明。话在两头,人在中间,前面的话收尾用逗号,后面的话前头收尾用逗号,后面的话前头要用逗号。例如:

他说:"生命在于运动,经常运动身体好!"

"生命在于运动,经常运动身体好!"他说。

"生命在于运动,"他说,"经常运动身体好!"

2. 英文斜体字的处理(陈廷祐,1981:205)

英文中常夹有斜体字,它除了用于书信开头的称谓、书刊名称、船舰名称以外,大致还有以下两种用途:一是表示强调用斜体字这一部分文字的重要意义;二是用于外来语。

整体用斜体字的:

Obviously timing is vital, and dependent upon what is the aggressive strength of the enemy in Bulgaria and Thrace. *The prize would be to get into the Black Sea with supplies for Russia, warships, and other forces.*

显然,不失时机是十分重要的,而时机则取决于保加利亚和色雷斯的敌军的进攻力量如何。<u>我们将要得到的好处是:我们给予俄国的补给、我们的战舰和其他军事力量将进入里海</u>。

一个词用斜体字的:

英语中如夹有法文、德文、拉丁文等外来语时常以斜体字表示,如"*coup d'etat*"(武装政变)、"*en route*"(在途中)、"*de facto*"(事实上),则不必使用其他字体表示。

3. 人名的翻译格式

G. D. Kerr G. D. 科尔

George D. Kerr 乔治·D·科尔

Julien-Philippe Lacheroy 朱利安-菲利普·拉歇鲁瓦

Sr. Arthur Meier Schlesinger 老阿瑟·迈耶·施莱辛格

评析:Sr. 是 Senior 的简写;Jr. 是 Junior 的简写。

Joseph Needham 李约瑟

Winston Churchill 丘吉尔

John King Fairbank 费正清

评析:一些历史人物已有定译,应保留,而不应按普通人的名字来翻译。

参考词典:《世界人名翻译大词典》上下卷(中国对外翻译出版公司)
《世界姓名译名手册》(化学工业出版社)

4. 地名的翻译

地名的翻译应严格查阅地名词典,如《世界地名译名手册》(商务印书馆),自己不应随便翻译。有些英文拼写的地名中间有个半字线,这仍是一个地方,如 Marri-Mengal(马里-门加尔),译成中文,中间也应用半字线。但是 London-Paris air line,中文应用一字线,译成"伦敦

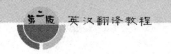

—巴黎航线"。(陈廷祐,1981:214)

5. 船名、军舰名的翻译

英文船名、军舰名一般用斜体,译成中文应加引号,并且把"号"放在引号内:

Eskimo　"爱斯基摩号"

Prince of Wales　"威尔士亲王号"

第四节　译文修改

修改,是译文写作的最后一个阶段,是译文制作必不可少的重要步骤。古今中外的大作家,无不高度重视修改,无不在精心修改方面下过很大的功夫。托尔斯泰的《战争与和平》曾七易其稿,曹雪芹的《红楼梦》也"增删五次"。写作如此,翻译何其不然? 一篇好译文,在很大程度上是靠修改而成的。

1. 推敲语言

译文在形成后,在与原文核对内容基本无误的情况下,最好能脱离原文对译文语言文字进行深入的推敲锤炼、加工润色。修改语言要注意修辞,讲究文采,对字、词、句反复琢磨,精益求精。推敲语言,就是把笼统的改明晰;把含混的改清楚;把沉闷的改生动;把抽象的改形象……语言的推敲,虽是修改程序中的最后一环,但很重要。修改一篇译文,往往要经过多次反复。完成初稿后趁热打铁,一鼓作气修改,能及时发现一些问题,但如果不是时间紧迫的话,不妨把译文暂时搁置一阵子,等到冷静下来,也许能发现更多问题。当然,如能请他人帮助修改,则能以另一种眼光看出更多的问题。

2. 检查文面

检查文面,是指在修改和抄写时检查文面是否符合规范要求。文面是译文的外表,它由文字书写、标点符号和行款格式组成。文面与准确表达内容有直接关系,写错一个字,用错一个标点,都会损害译文内容的准确表达。因此,我们必须重视文面问题。

文面主要是由文字构成的,抄写时首先要把字写好,无论标题、署名、行文,都要书写准确、清楚、整齐、美观。

书写准确,就是要写规范的字,不写错别字、自造字、异体字和繁体字。书写清楚,就是要笔画分明,结构准确,使人容易辨认,不要龙飞凤舞,拖泥带水,字迹潦草。书写整齐,就是要字体大小相称,不要忽大忽小,忽肥忽瘦,行与行做到横平竖齐,疏密得当。书写美观,就是要讲究书法工整,字体均称,字形美观。字迹不工整,在作业,尤其在考卷中会非常吃亏,你不认真写,怎能要求人家认真看?

3. 文章修改的符号

为了标明修改的情况,要使用习惯公认的修改符号。修改符号要求合乎习惯、清楚、美观。关于这方面的知识,详见 1981 年 12 月发布的《中华人民共和国专业标准校对符号及其用法》。

本章推荐阅读书目

陈廷祐.英文汉译技巧[M].北京：外语教学与研究出版社,1980.
陈果安.现代写作学引论[M].长沙：中南大学出版社,2002.
徐振宗、李保初.汉语写作学[M].北京：北京师范大学出版社,1995.
周姬昌.写作学高级教程[M].武汉：武汉大学出版社,1989.

练习答案

第二章 翻译的理解篇

第一节
[1] 她需要找个住的地方。
[2] 这些盘子通常放哪儿?
[3] 蜘蛛几天不吃食依然可存活。
[4] 我们看见了一条活生生的响尾蛇!
[5] 这个俱乐部大多数晚上有现场演奏的音乐。
[6] 那个端子有电。
[7] 这场演出正在实况直播。
[8] 污染仍然是目前非常让人关注的问题。
[9] 价格在上涨。
[10] 瞧,你流鼻涕了。
[11] 我的学校办了一个工厂。
[12] 他们冲破了敌人的封锁线。
[13] 昨天在城里他碰到了一位老朋友。
[14] 这出戏连演了一百个夜场。
[15] 我的表停了。

第二节

一、相似句
[1] 他幸免于死。
　　他郁闷而终。
[2] 她守在家里。
　　她操持家务。
[3] 这不是我该去的地方。
　　我没有地方好去。
[4] 他是世家子弟。
　　他是有家室的人。
[5] 我昨天说了他一顿。
　　我昨天和他交谈了很久。
[6] 她打扫了房间。
　　她很神气地走出房间。

[7] 他陪着她。
　　他和她交朋友。
[8] 此中有无困难呢？
　　此中有点困难吧？
　　注：句一是在完全不知有无困难时问的。句二是在认为有点困难时问的。
[9] 等我们吃饭的时候,我才来听取你的意见吧。
　　现在我们一面吃饭,我一面就来听取你的意见吧。
[10] 我们确知人是要死的。
　　我们确知那人是死了。
[11] 可惜你没有去。
　　幸亏你没有去。
[12] 我希望我有他那样富有。
　　我希望成为他那样的富人。
[13] 让我们修理房子。
　　让我们回家去吧。
　　注：repair 作及物动词用时,意为"修理",作不及物动词用时,意为"往(某处)"、"赴"＝"go".
[14] 他老是来干涉我的事。
　　他老是来妨碍我的事。
　　注："interfere in"意为"干涉","interfere with"意为"妨碍"。
[15] 我们租的船以时间计算。
　　我们只租了一小时的船。
[16] 明天会有一些客人来。
　　明天我要请一些客人来。
　　注：句一是无意志的,句二是有意志的。
[17] 他打算说什么？
　　他预定要说的是什么？
　　注："be about to"＝"be going to",为较文言的说法。"be to"意为"预定"。
[18] 他被视为天才。
　　他被崇为天才。
　　注："look upon as"＝"regard as"(视为)。"look up to as"＝"respect as"(作为……而崇仰)。
[19] 那岛环绕一圈五英里。
　　那岛直径五英里。
[20] 我没有注意到他。
　　我并未把他放在眼里。
　　注：句一是无意的,句二是有意的。

二、费解句
[1] 他随意自斟自酌。
[2] 他知道让孩子游荡下去是很不好的。
[3] 初生牛犊不怕虎。/无知者无畏。
[4] 无钱购买的东西,只好不要。
[5] 我知道他不是开玩笑的。
[6] 他向你致意。
[7] 那丢失的孩子很快就认明身份了。

247

[8] 说女人车技不好令人质疑。
[9] 那并不是因为他有很多钱。
[10] 我穿什么出去呢?
[11] 他继承了一大笔财产。
[12] 他一进房就整个儿跌倒在地板上。
[13] 他的英语完美无缺。
[14] 你的损失和我的比较起来真算不了什么。
[15] 她的丈夫死了至今不过半年。
[16] 他用钱豪爽。
[17] 当选的职员任期至1973年年底为止。
[18] 他刚在一星期前结了婚。
[19] 我的皮鞋穿破了。
[20] 奶奶是一名园艺能手。

三、修饰结构疑难句
[1] 质量好、品种多的消费品也供应充裕。
[2] 一天,医院里送来一位手臂严重烧伤的年轻女人。
[3] 科学家在好几年前说,有可能找到一种和玻璃性能一样好而又打不碎的物质。
[4] 我们的工作中经常出现新的矛盾,这些矛盾应正确予以处理。
[5] 一定有人提出反对,说这样一种看法完全歪曲了哲学的整个概念。
[6] 我们以后到其他星球去旅行时,将会经历各种强弱不一的引力。
[7] 已经拟就一张至今已教过的所有动词的表。
[8] 凡是成功的科学家常常把注意力集中在他发现尚未得到满意解答的问题上。
[9] 每天从全国各地传来各行各业取得伟大成就的消息。
[10] 以上说的就是艺术,也就是小说里确实具有的艺术,与诗歌、戏剧、绘画和音乐具有共通的性质,这一点我们大家都知道。

四、"多枝共干"式结构
[1] 他那时正在研究原始时期和古典时期的希腊雕塑。
[2] 滴滴涕喷射队和灭鼠队都出动了。
[3] 红军战士从中国的东南走到西北……越过亚洲一些最高的山脉和最大的河流。
[4] 爱克司光检查或死后检查表明有许多骨头已经折断。
[5] 1945年,他回到巴黎,仍在博物馆和学校任职。
[6] 民族解放运动的前途以及中国同第三世界国家之间关系的前景是怎样的呢?
[7] 但是他那巨大的决心、坚强的意志,对自己阶级使命和对党的崇高原则的坚贞不渝,使他克服了体力上的一切缺陷。
[8] 要是没有地心引力,你就根本不能讲话、叫喊和听到什么声音。
[9] 据我了解,李同志去买票了,约定我们和他在戏院里会面。
[10] 你写的句子应直截了当,开门见山,不要写得又长又复杂,让别人不好懂。

第三章 翻译的技巧篇

第一节 拆译

[1] 全城一片叹息,一片沉默。但是谁也没有故意流露出悲痛。

[2] 可是他们都成了沙漠里的牧民了,生活在苍天之下,大地之上。他们可也喜欢这种生活。
[3] 他们在你下榻的旅舍里安上窃听器,简直没有一点遮遮掩掩的样子。
[4] 斯派达尔后来说,希特勒的谈话"越说越远,越说越离奇,最后不知说到哪里去了"。
[5] 6月27日上午,天气晴朗,阳光明媚,鲜花盛开,绿草如茵,充满了盛夏之日的清新和温暖。
[6] 把他添上,名单就完备了。
[7] 她替我们泡茶,态度殷勤。
[8] 不流伤心泪,不是有情人。
[9] 世上无难事,只怕有心人。
[10] 滴滴香浓,意犹未尽。(广告语)

第二节 词类转译

[1] 读一点世界史对研究时事是有帮助的。
[2] 发明一样新菜要比发现一颗新星对人类幸福贡献更大。
[3] 景色之美,笔墨难以形容。
[4] 在城市和乡村,托儿所和幼儿园都在大量地增加。
[5] 从这所屋子可以看到西湖的景色。
[6] 他爱好中国画。
[7] 他倒是不抽烟的,可他爸爸却一支接一支不停地抽。
[8] 他演得比你所预期的要好得多。
[9] 我走进房间,看见他正在看书。
[10] 发展的道路是漫长的,但是我们已经坚定地走上这条道路。
[11] 我们不满足于我们现有的成就。
[12] 他们不信任他,讨厌他。
[13] 侯赛因茫然不解。
[14] 很抱歉,你打电话来时,我不在。
[15] 登陆的目的是要把该半岛一切为二。
[16] 他们那天和陪同人员去参观中国的长城。
[17] 一个穿着讲究的人上了车。他的外表和谈吐都像个美国人。
[18] 他们将为盲人和聋人修建一所学校。
[19] 全体伤员立即送进医院了。
[20] 他们对我们的问题表示同情和理解。
[21] 我认识到,通过中间人跟他们打交道是愚蠢的。
[22] 他看到那个陌生人的外表非常古怪,就更加惊讶了。
[23] 我们深信这一政策是正确的,并有坚定的决心继续奉行这一政策。
[24] 他是沉着果敢的人。
[25] 游园会真是圆满极了。
[26] 这音乐妙极了。
[27] 人们都说,我的故事乏味得很。
[28] 他们在关键时刻的行为给他留下了深刻的印象。
[29] "恐怕男孩子的想法与女孩子的想法是不一样的。"他说。
[30] 最后,他匆匆地向主人轻声道别,大步走向门口。
[31] 他好意地给我指路。
[32] 我幸运地遇到了他。
[33] 我们感到住房问题难以解决。

[34] 在苦难中,重返故园的念头始终在他心头萦绕着。
[35] 她脸上显露出愉快的表情。
[36] 由于人们应用电子计算机,因此促使劳动生产率突飞猛进。
[37] 他并不因为失败而放弃尝试。
[38] 听了他的话,我不禁打了一个寒战。

第三节　精简与增补

一、精简

[1] 快到村子时,他遇见了许多人。可是一个也不认识。这使他有点惊讶。
[2] 因为我们住在大路旁边,我们常邀请旅客或异乡人来访,品尝我们家酿的醋栗酒。
[3] 你所要的书籍,我已于昨日如数寄上,收到了没有?
[4] 人民犯了法,也要受处罚。
[5] 阅读时不要回头读。即使遇到生词也应继续读下去。
[6] 她睁圆眼睛听了一会儿。
[7] 他们成千上万地赶来了。
[8] 他穿一件落满灰尘的褴褛大衣,长仅及膝。
[9] 初秋时节,日子温暖迷人。
[10] 他神色黯然,心事重重。
[11] 他为人善良,见多识广。
[12] 她正是个理想的角色——秉性温和,聪明伶俐。
[13] 门开了,听众一拥而入。
[14] 他不诚实,不宜当出纳。
[15] 里边一定有人,我听见了人声。
[16] 祖母说,他们肯安静下来不争吵,就给讲个故事。
[17] 他就是在这里,我也没有工夫见他。
[18] 温度增高,水的体积就增大。
[19] 我们到戴维营过周末倒是更经常些。
[20] 他永远不必睡陌生的床。
[21] 为了不惊醒她,他轻轻推开房门,悄悄地溜了出去。
[22] 1984年秋天,我在莫斯科等待着去中国。
[23] 白宫里的生活是既活跃又紧张。
[24] 大街小巷早就传遍了各种流言蜚语。
[25] 仓库重地,禁止抽烟。
[26] 几个月之后我又渡海东去。
[27] 他领会了中国信息的微妙之处:言辞激烈,行事谨慎。
[28] 种瓜得瓜。
[29] 艾伦同纳赛尔进行了长时间的会商,但毫无结果。
[30] 八月中旬,修理组人员在骄阳下工作。
[31] 阅读时要有意识地把名词、代词和动词与别的词分开。
[32] 有志者事竟成。

二、增补

[1] 这是为取得革命事业胜利所必需的。
[2] 尽管昨天受了暴风雨的袭击,庄稼在晨曦中显得郁郁葱葱,茂盛异常。

[3] 纳赛尔以<u>政治家的手腕</u>和极大的耐心,说服了争执不休的兄弟们签订了一项协议。
[4] 人民的悲痛<u>情绪</u>失去了控制。
[5] 中国工业的发展仍然是政府的<u>首要课题之一</u>。
[6] 他们彼此的<u>亲密态度</u>使我吃惊。
[7] 他让法官的<u>职责战胜父子的私情</u>,而判决他儿子有罪。
[8] 一种新型的飞机正越来越引起人们的注意——这种飞机<u>体积不大</u>,<u>价格便宜</u>,<u>无人驾驶</u>。
[9] 他们不断地<u>反复玩味</u>着他的来信。
[10] 他在会上发表了讲话——<u>很动听</u>,<u>很有力</u>。
[11] 我就是带着这种心情进入外交界的,<u>满腔热情,但是知识肤浅得很</u>。
[12] 我们在工业、农业、商业、文化教育<u>各方面</u>都取得了迅速发展。
[13] 中美<u>两国</u>的社会制度根本不同。
[14] 轿车停在尼罗河希尔顿<u>饭店</u>的门口。
[15] 陈今年 32 岁,已经有了<u>两个孩子</u>。
[16] <u>一弯溪水</u>蜿蜒流过山谷,汇合到江河里去了。
[17] 我真替她万分担忧,但此时此地,既不宜<u>教训她一番</u>,也不宜<u>与她争论一通</u>。
[18] <u>一轮红日</u>从风平浪静的海面冉冉升起。
[19] 这纯粹是<u>一派</u>胡言。
[20] 狮是<u>百兽</u>之王。
[21] 大地都震动了,仿佛万马奔腾,<u>千夫</u>怒吼。
[22] 大部分是在<u>历代</u>沙皇统治下,通过殖民扩张而并入俄罗斯帝国的。
[23] 他们的主人切肉<u>啊</u>、倒酒<u>啊</u>、切面包<u>啊</u>、谈<u>啊</u>笑<u>啊</u>、敬酒<u>啊</u>,热情备至。
[24] 不要<u>认真嘛</u>!我不过开开玩笑<u>罢了</u>!
[25] 四月里,全世界听到中国"<u>乒</u>"的一声把球打了出去,到了七月,美国"<u>乓</u>"的一声把球打了回来。
[26] 一个人只要交上一次好运,今后,<u>幸运的大门</u>就会洞开。
[27] 天气闷热,所有人都好像热锅上的蚂蚁似的。
[28] 但是来人依旧络绎不绝,<u>有</u>的乘汽车,<u>有</u>的骑毛驴,<u>有</u>的步行。成千的人从别的阿拉伯国家赶来。

第四节 实译与虚译

[1] 对于绝大多数到厦门游玩的人,鼓浪屿是<u>必不可少的参观游览项目</u>(不游鼓浪屿,枉费厦门行)。
[2] 他刚满 22 岁的时候,生平第一次尝到了<u>做黑人的滋味</u>。
[3] 婴儿不会走路,不会说话,更不会自己吃饭洗澡,可是唯其无能反而<u>享尽了天下清福</u>。
[4] 越南战争成了他进入新政府的敲门砖。他担任政府的对外政策顾问,那是第三次了。
[5] 阿拉伯人和犹太人<u>生活在一起</u>,而且从这些地区最初有人来定居的时候就一直如此。
[6] 帝国主义者的性格既<u>残暴</u>,又<u>狡猾</u>。
[7] 每个人的生活都有<u>甜</u>有<u>苦</u>。
[8] 他选择<u>参军</u>而不<u>上大学</u>。

第五节 褒译与贬译

[1] 那个肥胖的<u>日本佬</u>!
[2] 我就说,我一想起你就<u>恶心</u>。你对我残酷到了可耻的地步。
[3] 然后,爱迪生把其创造天才转向另一项<u>宏大的</u>计划——发明用电来代替煤气以照明街道和建筑物的方法,即要设法制造电灯泡。
[4] 我们的会议最后确实制定了<u>进攻</u>的详细方案。进攻日期定在 1944 年 5 月 1 日。
[5] 他很聪明,有<u>抱负</u>。

[6] 他说:"对我们这一代人来说,尼克松有某种坏名声。我需要自己相信,他这个坏名声是不该有的。"
[7] 布朗先生接到作演讲的邀请时,感到非常荣幸。
[8] 汉斯说,这位先生是他所见到过的最有胆识的人。这种阿谀奉承未免过于露骨了。
[9] 我要让劳渥德人人都知道你是什么样的人,你干下了什么好事。
[10] 凡是忘掉过去的人注定要重蹈覆辙。

第六节 倒译与顺译

[1] 我相信,要不是他逼我埋头修改工作,本书就不可能像现在这个样子了。
[2] 这本霍金首次为普通人写的书,令外行读者获益良多。
[3] 本书内容包罗万象,读来兴趣盎然;但当读者在书中窥视作者的思维线索时,同样会感到兴致勃勃。
[4] 在这本书中,物理学、天文学和宇宙学的前沿,以及作者的勇气,都清晰地呈现在读者的面前。
[5] 正如霍金所明确声称的,他试图去理解上帝的意图。
[6] 尽管我们每天都生活在这个世界上,但对这个世界知之甚少。
[7] 我们对自己所赖以生存的一切,像太阳、重力和原子等,都很少思考。众所周知,有了太阳才有万物赖以生存的阳光;有了重力我们才能待在地球上,否则,地球旋转产生的离心力会把我们抛向太空;个体由原子组成,而我们的生存也依赖其稳定性。
[8] 在我们的社会里,家长或教师在回答上面提到的大部分问题时,往往会习惯性地耸耸肩膀,或者求助于模模糊糊回想起来的宗教格言。
[9] 但是,哲学和科学上的大部分进展,都是源于对上述这些问题探索。
[10] 他的努力,得出了迄今为止令人意想不到的结论:宇宙无边无际,时间无始无终,上帝无所作为。

第七节 反译

[1] 我不明白你的意思。
[2] 他故意不看杰西的脚。
[3] 你的两条腿还没有老得走不动呢。
[4] 这些日子叫人吃不消。
[5] 他们最好不要失信,因为目前一切的关键在此。
[6] 他太需要杰克的帮助,不好冒犯他。
[7] 我们刚想测量电压,但没测成。
[8] 所有这些问题尚无完整的答案。
[9] 他们不愉快地又坐了下来。
[10] 他不慌不忙地从信封里抽出信纸打开来。
[11] 他阅读没有什么困难。
[12] 老年人无忧无虑,在敬老院过着幸福的生活。
[13] 纯金属几乎没有可取的特性。
[14] 这似乎也只是很早就计划好的军事演习的准备工作而已,毫无恶意可言。
[15] 沙漠为不毛之地。
[16] 但计划尚未实现他即逝世,由他的儿子继位。
[17] 现在这里还有一个悬而未决的重大问题。
[18] 不过这种事情很不平常,似乎不符合自然规律。
[19] 他的回答文不对题。
[20] 如果对满洲的目标使用原子弹,那主要为了制造恐怖,而不是为了破坏。
[21] 我不叫你,不要进来。
[22] 他们只顾自己,不顾别人。

[23] 赫伯也许正在什么地方快死了。嘴里喊着爹妈,而周围连一个亲人也没有。
[24] 奥斯本是赛特立的干儿子。23 年来,这家子一向没有把他当外人。
[25] 一时全场寂静无声。
[26] 她那种心不在焉的神气,并不是因为那个茶会的缘故。
[27] 你应不失时机为我说说情。
[28] 林肯总统被刺的消息不胫而走。
[29] 拓荒者不避艰险。
[30] 费尔莉小姐终日足不出户。
[31] 欲速则不达。
[32] 我要大家都不吃亏。
[33] 他为伤风好了感到高兴。
[34] 我听到这样的事总要笑。
[35] 他常常生病。
[36] 机会难再。
[37] 许多人认为首相辞职实际上是很丢面子的。
[38] 他于 4 月 15 日一早顺利地进入该城。
[39] 然而,他们并没有得到多久的安宁。
[40] 他们指责他欺诈。
[41] 误解引起误译。
[42] 他的密探一直在监视我的行踪。

第八节　被动式翻译

[1] 这篇文章译成英语后失去了不少文采。
[2] 决定不能拖延了,一天也不能拖延。
[3] 他在青少年时期养成的自卑感还未完全消除。
[4] 世界各地比以往更感到中国的存在,感到它在世界政治形势中占有历史性的重要地位。
[5] 必须在适当的时候,用适当的方式处理这个问题。
[6] 据说,安排这次晚宴都是为了讨好劳伦斯。
[7] 大家普遍认为这样行事是不足取的。
[8] 人们相信,这么一次松松垮垮的会议是不大可能作出重大决定的。
[9] 希特勒也被历史风暴冲掉了。
[10] 罗伯特·芬恩被工厂老板开除了。
[11] 他到了两天就遭到了监视。
[12] 这个计划特别受到想更多地接触文学理论的人们的支持。
[13] 母亲是个多愁善感的女人,心地善良,容易为眼泪和柔弱所动。
[14] 庇护权不得为犯有反对和平罪、战争罪和违反人道罪的人们所用。
[15] 他为家境所迫,16 岁便辍学了。
[16] 她当众挨了一顿批评。
[17] 妻子的大多数来信都是由医院的护士念给他听的。
[18] 各国都将由总理代表。

第九节　数字和倍数翻译

1. 精确数字翻译

[1] 是去年的二倍

[2] 比 1965 年增加一倍以上。
[3] 比 1949 年增加了十多倍。
[4] 是去年的五倍。
[5] 是……的三倍。
[6] 农用柴油的产量增加了一倍多。
[7] 这时期它的领土扩大了九倍(为原来的十倍)。
[8] 化纤产量比 2000 年增加了两倍。
[9] 在 1999—2000 这段时间,小汽车产量增长了七倍(为原来的八倍)。
[10] 这些机器使生产率提高了两倍。
[11] 化肥产量增长了 1.5 倍多。
[12] 它有欧洲四倍大。
[13] A 轮转动比 B 轮快一倍。
[14] 集成电路的产量比去年增加了两倍。
[15] 氢原子的重量约为氧原子的 1/16(即比氧原子约轻 15/16)。
[16] 这种薄膜比普通纸张要薄一半(即是普通纸厚度的 1/2)。
[17] 新型晶体管的开关时间缩短到 1/3(即缩短了 2/3)。
[18] 电压升高 9 倍,电流强度便降低了 9/10(即 90%)。
[19] 该设备误差概率降低了 4/5。
[20] 这些产品的主要优点是重量减轻了 1/2。

2．模糊数字翻译

[21] 中午,天空像傍晚一样阴沉,我们许多人感到不耐烦,便走出帐篷,<u>三三两两</u>地谈论着天气。
[22] 尤格斯,身材魁伟,肩宽背阔,年轻力壮,干起活来,真是<u>百里挑一</u>的能人。
[23] 原来本是个管理得好好的企业,后来合股人内部发生分歧,现在搞得<u>乱七八糟</u>。
[24] "怎么啦? 你什么地方疼?"
"我的眼睛,疼得<u>很厉害</u>。"
[25] 她病情危急时,那位大夫好几天一直守护着她,只是在白天<u>打个盹儿</u>。

第四章　翻译的文采篇

第一节　巧用中国古代诗文典籍词语、句法

[1] 国之横祸莫过于老年暴君当政。
[2] 耕而后有所得;学然后知不足。
[3] 所见不真,犹不如盲,所言不实,不如缄默。
[4] 善未必美,美未必善也。
[5] 知其然者,任事;知其所以然者,任人。
[6] 授人以<u>鱼</u>,不如授人以<u>渔</u>。
[7] 无人能<u>望其项背</u>。
[8] 此机一失,大势去矣。
[9] 埃及果真<u>有朝一日</u>能从落后状态脱颖而出,海卡尔<u>功莫大焉</u>。

第二节　巧用汉语四字格词语

[1] 托马斯将军已于 1987 年<u>解甲归田</u>。
[2] 昨天体育场里观看比赛者<u>人山人海</u>。
[3] 他进入哈佛大学的机会<u>微乎其微</u>。

[4] 在那种场合该说什么话,实在是叫我一筹莫展。
[5] 不过我一旦做出决定,就大张旗鼓地去进行了。
[6] 我对这个消息半信半疑。
[7] 除非你有锦囊妙计,否则,我们是输定了。
[8] 她在这个问题上真是进退维谷。
[9] 他这是咎由自取。
[10] 她是个马马虎虎的女人,总是把忧愁抛至九霄云外。
[11] 那个家伙总是口蜜腹剑。
[12] 他看来像大发雷霆。
[13] 她找到了上个月她丢失的那些钥匙,真是喜出望外。
[14] 正如在战后各老牌帝国土崩瓦解一样,在我们开始生活的这个时代,新殖民主义也行将结束。
[15] 父母对子女是无微不至的。
[16] 英国没有这种天然的保护来阻挡好莱坞影片长驱直入。
[17] 因而,联合国在塞浦路斯维持和平的努力这个问题已开始使联合国陷入进退维谷的困境——确实,处处进退两难。
[18] 安理会本来可以避免一种冗长的高谈阔论。
[19] 他以自己对联合国工作驾轻就熟的稳健与机敏执行了安理会主席的职责。
[20] 她仪态万方地走进房子。
[21] 他身材修长,温文尔雅,风度翩翩。
[22] 他们只是在宴席上有一面之缘。
[23] 王宫四周,古木参天,蔚为壮观。
[24] 不过他是在废墟上重起炉灶。
[25] 他的声望会扶摇直上。
[26] 他是顺水推舟的专家。
[27] 可是艾登束手无策。
[28] 但是独裁者艾德礼,他犯了弥天大祸,却可以逍遥法外。
[29] 目前我们只看到这类影响在初露端倪。
[30] 这个理由是老生常谈。
[31] 她越来越六神无主。
[32] 他们想使他开口,但枉费心机。
[33] 他们衣着漂亮,花钱大方,来历不明。
[34] 汤姆一声不吭地离开了商店。
[35] 除了自己的意见以外,她对一切意见都不屑一顾。
[36] 天气好极了,令人心旷神怡。
[37] 我没有做什么一鸣惊人的事,只是工作罢了。
[38] 在我们整个危难期间,他始终忠心耿耿。
[39] 我很幸运,当时的情况真是千钧一发。
[40] 这奇怪的消息弄得我们目瞪口呆。

第三节 炼词用字

[1] 我们得到的是一个大零蛋。
[2] 卡特现在正拿石油开刀,下一个目标是谁呢?
[3] 一些人在吹这种风。
[4] 别此山看着那山高。

[5] 她对她丈夫的癖好只好<u>放任不管</u>。
[6] 舆论<u>为之哗然</u>,于是共和党发言人就举行了一次记者招待会对这件事进行解释<u>以求解脱</u>。
[7] 在台湾问题上,双方就没有<u>多少客气可讲了</u>,至于<u>让步就更说不上了</u>。
[8] 我的丈夫知道,要我只充当一名官场的<u>夫人</u>,我是不<u>甘心</u>的。
[9] 爱德华,也就是后来的温莎公爵,<u>喧宾夺主</u>地似乎成了书中的主角。
[10] 埃尔斯伯格回忆说,基辛格对尼克松"<u>极尽挑剔之能事</u>。"
[11] 别跟我<u>先生长,先生短</u>的。
[12] 他想远走高飞,免得心烦。
[13] 谁也没说过这里的日子<u>好过</u>。
[14] 我不是<u>三岁</u>的小孩子。
[15] 他这次来参观大学,使大学的三十周年纪念<u>生色不少</u>。
[16] 你可知道,我多么少不了他。
[17] 这个真理<u>放之四海而皆准</u>。
[18] 他<u>尝</u>过荣辱的滋味,过去<u>受人欢呼</u>,现在却<u>被人讥讽</u>。
[19] 切莫受他<u>花言巧语</u>之骗,那不是真话。
[20] 这张画画得比她本人漂亮。
[21] 我过去一直是吃<u>政治饭</u>的。但是,自从我从北京回来以后,我已成了一名政治家。
[22] 来自伦敦的报道更煽动了情绪,因为那些报道强调英国军队缺乏<u>进取</u>精神。
[23] 哈里曼最大的心愿就是希望阿夫里尔能<u>成名成家</u>。
[24] 可<u>不能小看她</u>,她是<u>有来头</u>的。
[25] 他有次说:"要是我们死了,我们希望大家能<u>等闲视之,不必惊慌</u>。"
[26] 由于<u>水土不服</u>,她只好回英国。
[27] 总统希望请一两名中国人来,以增加<u>四海之内皆兄弟</u>的气氛。
[28] 约翰是<u>天不怕地不怕</u>的。(反译)
[29] 外长伊斯曼·法赫米指责以色列人<u>不守信用</u>。
[30] 像我这样一个<u>走江湖卖唱的苦命人</u>,能做得出为了几个赏钱而去干通风报信的勾当?
[31] 我猜他准是<u>骄气凌人</u>,<u>不把我放在眼里</u>,我有什么办法呢?只能逆来顺受了。
[32] 她觉得她不能<u>打退堂鼓</u>,她必须继续过她那贫困而单调的生活。这是她犯了错误得到的惩罚,她要<u>自食其果</u>。
[33] 要我投票赞成给他们以援助,<u>除非太阳从西边出来</u>。
[34] 下学期你最好<u>加把油</u>。
[35] 她是属于<u>爱出风头</u>的女人。
[36] 尽管敌人<u>费了九牛二虎之力</u>,其阴谋却以失败告终。
[37] 既然人人的想法如出一辙,那么大家也都懒得多想。
[38] 22岁的时候,他生平第一次尝到了做黑人的<u>滋味</u>。
[39] 希特勒给德国人民带来了一场浩劫。
[40] 真是<u>乱翻了天</u>(×这真是一场大混乱)。

第六章　翻译的语篇类型

第一篇

联合国度过艰难的一年开始重整旗鼓

对联合国来说,过去的一年不堪回首。布什政府轻蔑地称它无足轻重,伊拉克的政权过度把它排除在外,去年8月驻巴格达办事处的大爆炸事件震惊了整个联合国。

256

联合国主管通信和新闻的副秘书长沙希·塔鲁尔说:"联合国的重要性受到各种攻击,情绪深受影响。另外,去年8月19日的袭击——我们称之为'我们的9·11'——使我们倍感痛心,因为我们失去了那么多朋友和同事。"

在那次爆炸事件中,共有22人丧生,包括办事处负责人塞尔吉奥·维埃拉·德梅洛。其后不久,联合国秘书长科菲·安南下令从伊拉克撤走所有联合国工作人员。

现在,联合国发现自己再次成为各种事务的中心,东河总部大厦弥漫的沮丧情绪逐渐消散。联合国开发计划署署长马克·马洛赫·布朗说:"(联合国)无疑开始恢复元气了。"

自年初以来,曾恶意批评联合国的布什政府官员恳请它重返伊拉克并为伊拉克的政治前途制定计划,联合国几十年来努力使塞浦路斯势不两立的土耳其族和希腊族实现统一的工作取得了突破,它还以非同寻常的敏捷迅速授权向海地派遣多国部队。

塔鲁尔先生描述了联合国从去年11月的低谷走向复苏的经过。去年11月,由美国斡旋达成的伊拉克权力移交协议只字未提联合国的作用。到了今年1月19日在此举行会议时,美国派驻伊拉克的最高文职行政长官保罗·布雷默三世和由美国任命的伊拉克临时管理委员会的成员请求联合国为巴格达的政治前途制定计划。

塔鲁尔先生说:"那项协议的主要支持者1月份来到纽约并说出'我们需要你们',这的确是一个重大转变。"

过去一年的对抗经历使联合国在重新插手伊拉克危机时非常谨慎。

通常被认为有可能接替安南职位的新加坡大使基肖尔·马赫布巴尼说,被排除在伊拉克之外只是"伊拉克带来的噩梦"之一。

他说:"另一个就是完全参与其中。"

"随着联合国越来越多地介入伊拉克事务,责任也将越来越多地由它来承担,我们必须小心谨慎,以免出现比如说伊拉克选举进程崩溃,所有人都到处宣扬'瞧,联合国又失败了'的情况。"

美国转而愿意与联合国合作对未来有什么意义,是一个有争议的话题。

哥伦比亚大学的法学和国际关系学教授迈克尔·W·多伊尔曾在2001年到2003年间担任安南的特别顾问。他说:"我认为,没有证据显示华盛顿对联合国的态度发生了根本性转变。这仍然是根据需要而定的多边主义。如果征求联合国的意见能让美国达到目的,那它就会这么做。反之,它就会把联合国晾在一边。"

马洛赫·布朗说,对美国与联合国的关系状况的评价总是走极端。

他说,"它从来就不像有些人想像的那么糟,也不像另外一些人认为的那么好。但是,较之上届政府而言,本届政府更多的时候是坏运占了上风。"

——许燕红译自美国《纽约时报》,转引自《参考消息》(2004/3/29)

第二篇
亚洲买主推动索思比艺术品热卖

对索思比拍卖行来说,2005年是至少15年来生意最好的一年:亚洲和俄罗斯买主是推动市场繁荣的新生力量。

索思比拍卖行昨天说,该公司去年卖掉价值27.5亿美元的艺术品,收入5.135亿美元,纯收益增加85%,达到6300万美元。今年的销售显示,艺术品的价格继续全面上涨。

索思比拍卖行称:"(今年)迄今为止,世界各地的销售情况都远远好于平均水平。"上个月,在伦敦举行的大型拍卖会上,索思比和克里斯蒂一共创下4.51亿美元的艺术品销售纪录。

艺术品——特别是当代艺术品市场的坚挺让人怀疑,这种增长能否持续下去。15年前艺术品市场也曾繁荣一时,但突然由盛转衰。某些作品的价格至今仍未恢复到应有水平。

索思比负责欧洲和亚洲市场的总经理罗宾·伍德黑德说:"上一次推动市场的是印象派作品,这一次则不同,各种门类的作品几乎都在热卖。"

他还说:"摄影作品和早期绘画大师的作品卖价极高。人们重新燃起对装饰派艺术的兴趣。对艺术品的购买潜力很强,拿到市场上销售的藏品也相当多。"

伍德黑德说,印象派和现代艺术这些传统领域增长强劲,但销售势头最旺的却是当代艺术品和非西方艺术品,特别是亚洲和俄罗斯的艺术作品。

他说,为了满足需求,索思比将在本月举办首次当代亚洲艺术品拍卖会;过去5年,索思比拍出的俄罗斯艺术品总价值增加了10倍。

他说:"随着中国、亚洲其他各国和俄罗斯经济的增长,这些国家都很关注流落到海外、具有历史价值和文化价值的本国艺术品,希望把它们买下来,运回祖国。"近来,富裕的中国家庭和俄罗斯家庭也开始购买西方作品。上个月,索思比伦敦拍卖会上售出的当代艺术品有11%被亚洲人买走。

——赵菲菲译自英国《金融时报》,转引自《参考消息》(2006/3/22)

第三篇

公众与曼德拉同展 DNA

南非人和外国游客受邀接受 DNA 检测,以确定自己的祖先。并且,他们的 DNA 检测结果还将与纳尔逊·曼德拉的检测结果放在一起展出。

这些检测是由在约翰内斯堡新落成的人类起源中心博物馆策划的,用以阐明它的一个主题:"所有人的基因都有联系,他们的根可追溯到曾经在非洲生活的同一个祖先。"

这些 DNA 样本将由南非国家卫生研究所检测,两周后出检测结果。接受检测的人可以选择匿名,或者在博物馆里展出自己的世系。

曼德拉的 DNA 检测结果来自几年前采集的一个样本,结果显示,他的祖先是非洲最早的居民——桑人。桑人的线粒体 DNA 中包含全人类最早的遗传印记,被称为 L1。曼德拉也是来自东非大湖地区一个非洲人族群的后裔。

南非的非洲人族群主要发祥于大湖地区,后来他们沿着东部海岸迁徙,最终定居在南非。

人类起源中心坐落在威特沃特斯兰德大学校园内,从下周二开始,每周6天对公众开放。

人类起源中心是根据姆贝基的想法成立的。5年前,他在乌卡赫兰巴——德拉肯斯贝赫山区散步时萌生了这种想法,并发现他对岩画的了解比自己的大多数向导还多。他希望展出令人惊叹的南非岩画收藏和研究,让广大公众受益。

该博物馆还将收藏相当数量的石器时代的工具和岩画,这些是人类早在260万年前就开始在南非定居的证据。

据人类起源中心的创作总监弗朗西斯·杰勒德称,只是到了后来,人们才离开非洲,迁徙到世界上其他地区。他说:"18000年前人类才到达美洲。"

——郭骏译自3月7日美联社,转引自《参考消息》(2006/3/15)

第四篇

欢迎客人

彼得·梅尔

旅游者有罪!我们经常听到有人历数旅游者的若干罪状:破坏珠穆朗玛峰的生态平衡;将口香糖留在博物馆和美术馆的长凳下面;穿着不合时宜的 T 恤衫进巴黎圣母院;带坏了当地农民;一天到晚,马不停蹄,走到哪里,哪里通常会变得意境萧然。很少有一群人受到如此大张挞伐,而我就是其中一分子。你也一样。作为游客,我在普罗旺斯大约有15年了,经常受到人们的口诛笔伐、冷嘲热讽,他们指责我的文章"毁了"这个地方。奇怪的是,这些有时是人身攻击且一向尖刻犀利的抱怨,并非来自普罗旺斯当地人,而是来自和我一样的游客。普罗旺斯人似乎认为我是个友善的怪人。

不论是来自伦敦、布鲁塞尔还是波士顿,从自己的角度出发,游客们对他们所谓的普罗旺斯的变化深感痛惜。在短暂的年度休假期间,他们从自己的所见所闻中知道普罗旺斯变了。市场拥挤,物价上涨,餐馆客满。咖啡馆阳光最好的桌子有主了,面包师的面包没了,服务员的耐心没了;无处停车,游泳池漏水也找不到人修。

普罗胜斯的大众旅游始于2600多年前,当时来自菲西的希腊人建立了马赛城。希腊人带来了文明之风。为当地人提供了工作;所以他们被认为是受欢迎的游客。罗马人也是如此,他们建造了我们至今还喜爱的纪念碑、高架桥以及圆形竞技场。之后,随着西哥特人、东哥特人和法兰克人的到来,普罗旺斯进入了衰败时期。那些人以恐吓当地居民、蹂躏乡里为乐。也许就是从那时起,旅游者背上了懒汉笨蛋的恶名。

经过多年亲身观察之后,我要为饱受非议的这类人说几句好话。绝大多数游客和蔼可亲,善解人意,他们不过是想要安然享受假期。他们到普罗旺斯来享受阳光美景,享用佳肴美酒,暂别尘嚣,以求闲适。当然,游客如织,尤其在七八月份,但拥挤的人群往往限于城镇和风景如画的村庄里。如果你想探幽寻静,开车不远就能到达美丽空寂的乡间。

就我个人看来,我从来都不觉得旅游季节有什么不可忍受之处;实际上,理应感谢旅游带来的一些影响。如果没有旅游收入,许多对公众开放的城堡和园林就会变得破败不堪;人们就会听任纪念碑残迹湮灭;很多餐馆单靠本地客源难以为继;音乐会和乡村节庆活动就不值得举办。乡村生活会变得更为贫乏。

显然,并非所有地方都是这样。世界上有些地方被过度开发,昔日的魅力不复存在。这通常是当地贪得无厌的结果,而游客却替贪婪成性的开发者担上了大部分罪名。

——刘跃骅译自美国《新闻周刊》,转引自《参考消息》2006/4/19

第五篇

密西西比河上夏天的日出

马克·吐温

密西西比河上夏天的日出真是百看不厌,令人神往。日出之前,万籁俱寂,静谧之趣笼罩四野,远离尘嚣的空灵之感不禁油然而生。曙色悄分,郁郁森森的树木绰约朦胧;泱泱涣涣的密西西比河依稀可辨;河面上水波不兴,白雾袅袅,紫纤迷幻;风闲而枝静,恬谧深沉,令人心旷神怡。晨光熹微,一鸟唱而百鸟和,继之,众鸟引吭,高歌一曲欢乐的颂歌。只闻其声而不见其鸟,人仿佛就优游在天籁的妙趣之中。等到昕昀烁夜,展现在眼前的便是一幅至柔至美的画卷:身前身后的树木枝繁叶茂、堆绿叠翠,浓黛浅消。放眼望去,一英里开外有一个河岬,河岬上的树木淡妆轻抹,仿佛春天般的娇嫩;远处的河岬则树色隐隐,微茫难辨;地平线尽头的河岬似乎枕在水面上,像一团迷蒙蒸腾的雾,融入浩渺的水天之中。广阔的河面好似一面巨大的镜子,淡淡地映着丛集的枝叶、曲折的河岸和渐行渐远的河岬,勾勒出一幅生动的画面,轻柔婉转,超逸绵邈。太阳慢慢爬上天空,或浅红横涂,或金粉竖抹,或紫霞漫洒,奇异曼妙,难以言传。这一切,能不令人怀想?

第六篇

译文一:

这是今年的第一支玫瑰,硕大,鲜红,芳香馥郁。它还是个小花苞时,我便开始关注它了,但我还是错过了花期变化的最后过程。于是,它好像昨天还是花蕾,一夜之间却已鲜花盛开。

我一直是迫不及待地盼望那最终花团锦簇的灿烂之美,但一旦它花枝招展地呈现在我眼前,我反倒手脚失措,震慑于如此绝美的姿色。我透过窗户看着玫瑰,犹豫着是否该走进花园里,直接与它相向,此时它早就等候在那里,期待着第一个致意。

我终于鼓起勇气走过去,将脸深埋在花瓣中,嗅着它的芳香。我脑子一点也想不出来话来,只有那句陈词滥调:"太美了,太美了。"玫瑰似乎已心满意足,对我温情地微笑着。一只蜜蜂从花心中冒出来,在我的头上绕了两圈,越过花园飞走了。

于是我觉得,夏日已经开始了。

(麦克尔·布洛克:《夏日的第一支玫瑰》)

译文二：

这是今年开的第一枝玫瑰。它花朵很大，颜色红艳，散发着浓郁的芬芳。从它是个小骨朵开始，我就密切关注着，但我终还是错过了绽放的瞬间。似乎它昨日还是花蕾，一夜之间却已鲜花盛开。

我一直在焦急等待它最终完全绽放的神奇美丽，但现在，它活生生地呈现在我面前，我却不知所措，深深震慑于它如此无暇的完美。我透过窗看着玫瑰，它仿佛一直等候在花园里，期待着我献上第一份殷勤，然而我却迟疑了，犹豫着是否要与它直接相向。

我终于鼓起勇气来到它的身旁。我把脸深埋于花瓣之中，贪婪地呼吸着它的芳香。除了那句陈词滥调"好美！好美！"我便想不出其他言语。玫瑰却似乎很满足，冲我暖暖地笑着。一只蜜蜂突然自花心里冒了出来，在我的头上绕了两圈，然后飞过花园，径自飞远了。

啊！我感觉到夏天来了！

（麦克尔·布洛克：《夏日里的第一枝玫瑰》）

第七篇

译文一：

说实在的，在我的一生中我一次也没出去散步过。我都是给带出去散步的。但那另当别论。即使当我跟在保姆身边蹒跚学步、咿呀学语的时候，就已经开始怀念坐在婴儿车中不用走路的美好时光了［我也仍然为过去那有手推车可坐、不必劳动两腿的好日子追悔莫及］。当我长大成人，我似乎觉得，住在伦敦的一大好处就是从没人会邀我出去散步。伦敦的特别坏处，是它的嘈杂喧哗之声完没了，烟尘弥漫，污秽四伏，［伦敦的最大缺陷——那没完没了的吵闹和喧嚣，那烟雾弥漫的空气，那四处蛰伏的污浊龌龊］这倒因此免去了我散步之劳。

每当我和朋友在乡间的时候，我知道随时随刻，除非雨真下到头上，某君必会突然说道［冷不丁对你叫一声］："散步去！"其口气之强硬，是其他任何情况下都见不到的［言者如此疾言厉色，他做梦也想不出这样的命令式口气还能在别的什么场合派上用场］。人们总以为，去散步的想法有着与生俱来的尊贵与高尚。有如此念头的人觉得，每当他看到有人舒舒服服坐在椅子上看书，他就有权力将散步的愿望加诸其身。对于一个老朋友，简单地说声"不"倒也省事，但对于一般相识，你就必须找出一个借口［寻点托辞］。"我很想去，但是——"我能找到的借口不外乎［我则什么借口也憋不出，除了诈称］"我要写些信"。这个老套式［但此招颇不令人满意］有三方面不能尽如人意：（1）人家不相信。（2）迫于情势，你不得不从椅子上起来，走向写字台，临时拼凑一封给某人的信［临时给某人胡诌起一封信］，直到那位暴走神［散步兜售者］磨磨蹭蹭地离开房间，他只是不敢当面发作，骂你是骗子或伪君子而已。（3）星期天早上行不通［这一招不管用］："今天晚上信才寄得出去［傍晚之前没有邮差］"，一句话就把你堵死了；于是你只好乖乖地跟着走［悄不吱声地跟着走吧］。

译文二：

老实说，我这一生中不曾散步过。我有被携带散步的经历；但那是另外一回事。甚至在我跟在保姆身边咿咿呀呀，路还没走稳之时，我便开始遗憾，那坐在手推车上的不用劳动双腿的好日子已经逝去不复返了。长大之后发现，伦敦生活之于我的一大好处就是从没有人要我出外散步。喧嚣嘈杂没完没了，烟尘污秽弥漫四伏，这是伦敦最糟糕的地方，倒正好免去我散步之苦。

当我和朋友呆在乡郊之时，我知道随时随刻，只要雨没有下下来，就会有人冷不丁地叫道："散步去！"。那种特有的专制霸道的口吻是他们做梦也不曾想到在其他情况下派上用场的。在人们看来，去散步的愿望里似乎隐含着某种高贵的内在。而且，每个爱去散步的人都觉得他们有义务把这种愿望加诸于一个舒舒服服在椅子上看书的人。拒绝一个老朋友是简单不过的，说"不"即可；拒绝一个一般相识的人则要编出些理由来。"我想去，可是——"我找不出其他的推脱之法，只能说"还有几封信要写"。但是这个老招式也有三点颇不令人满意。其一，它并不可信。其二，你不得不因此从椅子上起来，挪到写字台边上去，开始给某人胡诌起一封信来，直到那位热衷于散步的人悻悻然地离开；他只是不敢发作，不然一定骂你是骗子或者伪君子。其三，这招在星期天的早上不管用。"信到晚上才寄得出去"，一句话就把你堵死了。所以你还是乖乖地跟着去散步吧。

第八篇
苍蝇的自由
我们无论在什么地方都找不到像普通家蝇那样一种绝对自由的生物了。苍蝇不仅自由放任,而且勇敢无畏。它全然不讲什么谦恭礼让,不管是高贵的国土,还是贫贱的村夫,它都毫不在意,照样去吮舔;在它敏捷而机械地前进的每一步,或在它果断观察的每一间歇,总是露出一副自命不凡、无求于人、十分自信的神情,俨然认为世界是为苍蝇而创造的。

如果你用手去拍打它,其情其景好像一块一英亩大十英尺厚的红色黏土拔地而起,突然劈头盖脑的照直朝你猛砸下来。可是,苍蝇却振翅一飞,逃脱了你的一掌之击,接着又轻落在你的手背之上。你吓不倒它,制服不了它;既不能动之以情,也不能晓之以理。

苍蝇对一切事物都有自己的明确的见解,就其所要达到的目的而言,这些见解却也不失为睿智之见。它不会征求你的高见。苍蝇无需干活,在虫豸中没有统治它的暴君能使之俯首听命。蚯蚓要疏松土壤;蜜蜂要采花酿蜜和营造蜂房;蜘蛛要巧结迷网;蚂蚁也要聚财盘宝。相形之下,它们只是一群庸碌之辈。而我们的苍蝇却在户外逍遥自在,活像一位反复无常的黑色精灵鬼。它到处游荡,到处查访,东飞西荡,搔首弄姿,同时还能大饱口福,从食品店橱窗里陈列的糖果点心到肉铺后院存放的大堆肉食,诸般美味,任其挑选,还有何种自由堪与之媲美呢?

第九篇
译文一:
谈到健康,我讲不出金玉良言,因为自己少有病患。我这人吃喝随心,醒睡随意,虽然仔细论来个人爱好于健康多无大害,但却从不刻意去养生保健。

从心理学的角度讲,老年人有两忌。一忌过分怀旧。眷记忆,哀叹旧日、伤怀亡友,这些皆不足取。人要有意识地向前看,有意识地去想仍能有所为之事。当然,这也并非易事。过往的岁月,在我们肩上逐日加重着分量。我们总是认定情感已不复往昔纤细,头脑亦有欠敏锐。倘若真是如此,这话早该被忘记才对;而若人们连这话都记不起,想来话本身也就不会真有道理。

老年人第二忌:切忌抓住青年人不放,以求从其青春中汲取活力。儿女一旦长大,就想有自己的生活,如果此时做父母的好像关心小孩子一样对他们面面俱到,就有沦为负担之嫌。当然,特例也有,有的儿女对此就不以为意。我这里不是主张为人父母者不再去关心子女,而是建议父母应从思想上去关心子女,如果有能力的话从经济上去扶持子女。过分地在感情上去关心他们的做法并非上选。动物的幼崽一旦学会自理,母兽就听之任之;但人由于婴儿期长的缘故,父母往往很难对子女完全放手。

我认为有一种人最易将老年活得成功。这些人不拘泥于切身利害,而是依性之所好投入到适宜的活动之中。因为一个人只有在从事这些兴趣爱好时,长期积累的经验才真正得以结出果实,岁月的智慧也最终得以自由流淌。教训长成的子女不要犯错只是徒劳。一是他们不再听从,二是从错误中求教训本是学习之核心。但如若你没有个人爱好,就难免以一味顾念儿孙来填补生活的空虚寞落。——王巍译文

译文二:
谈到健康问题,我就没有什么可说的了,因为我没怎么生过病。我想吃什么就吃什么,想喝什么就喝什么,眼睛睁不开了就睡觉,从来不为对身体有益而搞什么活动,然而实际上我喜欢做的事大都是有助于增进身体健康的。

从心理方面来说,到了老年,有两种危险倾向需要注意防止,一是过分地怀念过去,老想着过去,总觉得过去怎么好怎么好,或者总是为已故的朋友而忧伤,这是不妥的。一个人应当考虑未来,考虑一些可以有所作为的事情。要做到这一点并非总是很容易的;自己过去的经历就是一个越来越沉重的包袱。人们往往会对自己说,我过去感情多么丰富,思想多么敏锐,现在不行了。如果真是这样的话,那就不要去想它,而如果

你不去想它,情形就很可能不是这样了。

另一件需要避免的事就是老想和年轻人呆在一起,希望从青年的活力中汲取力量。孩子们长大之后,就希望独立生活,如果你还像他们年幼时那样关心他们,你就会成为他们的累赘,除非他们特别麻木不仁。我不是说一个人不应当关心孩子,而是说这种关心主要应该是多为他们着想,可能的话,给他们一些接济,而不应该过分地动感情。动物,一旦它们的后代能够自己照顾自己,它们就不管了;但是人,由于抚养子女的时间长,是难以这样做的。

我认为,如果老年人对于个人以外的事情怀有强烈的兴趣,并参加适当的活动,他们的晚年是最容易过得好的。在这一方面,他们由于阅历深,是能够真正做得卓有成效的,也正是在这一方面,他们从经验中得出的智慧既可以发挥作用,又不致使人感到强加于人。告诫成年的子女不要犯错误,那是没有用的,一来他们不听你的,二来犯错误本身也是受教育的一个重要方面。但是如果你这个人对于个人以外的事情不发生兴趣,就会感到生活空虚,除非你老惦记着儿孙。——庄绎传译文

译文三:

提及健康这个话题,本人既少有病痛,故而并无忠告。饮食方面,我从不忌口;睡眠之道,惟"想睡就睡"一条。尽管本人爱做之事,大抵皆有益健康,但我从不刻意经营养生之道。

就心理层面而言,人届老年有两个危险,须得小心在意。一为沉湎过往。老是想当年、伤旧时、念亡友,根本于事无补。人一定要放眼未来,想想人生中尚得发挥之处。当然这并不容易;往昔的岁月是逐渐厚积的沉淀。与现时相较,人总自觉往日比较热情易感、灵敏便给,如所言确是,当便抛诸脑后;设若得以相忘,或便不尽属实。

另外尚有一危险,亦即纠缠年轻人不放,有似试图借由其生命力,返老还春。孩子大了,皆望自有一片天,如果父母还将其视若幼童,镇日价嘘寒问暖,那么除非子女麻木异常,否则这样的关心即形同负担。然此并不意味,为人父母当此际应对儿女不闻不问,而是谓关心应存乎内敛含蓄,其人尽可即之也温,其情但求适可而止。百兽一觉幼儿得以自立,总是放手令以自力更生,然人类因婴儿期较长之故,殊难割舍亲情。

个人深觉,若能超脱于上述儿女兴趣,积极从事合宜活动,晚年生活最易圆满。生命走到这里,长期经验真正称得上成果丰硕;也只有到此时,一个人从经验中累积的智慧,发挥起来才真如春阳融雪,不勉人以强。孩子大了,欲其不犯错根本无用,一来父母言语有如耳边风;二来教育之道本是"错中学"。设若不能自外于儿孙,自娱老怀,一颗心怕只有借着关注儿孙,方始有着落之处。

——李翠蓉译文

第十篇

青　春

托马斯·伍尔夫

青春奇妙无穷,充满着魅力,充满着痛楚。青春年少的时候不知青春为何物,老之将至才痛惜青春不再。谁都想让青春永驻,眼睁睁地看着青春流逝,心中会涌起无数的忧伤和追悔,都会充满难以排遣的哀怨,都会悲喜交集。即便有奇迹出现,令青春回头,谁也不会再去重温那蹉跎的岁月。

为什么?因为命途奇幻乖舛,青春的岁月难以名状,令人感怀不已。其根本原因又何在?青春年少的时候,虽然殷实富足,却两手空空;虽然气势恢宏,却一无长物。世间的富贵荣华触目皆是,心中的傲岸自信按捺不住,觉得人生妙不可言,唾手可得,非自己莫属。然而,当自己真的迈步向前、伸出手才知道,原以为可望可即伸手就能抓住的却是虚悬的梦幻。一切都如过眼云烟,飘然而逝,不复存在了。于是,心中泛起阵阵隐痛,依稀看到自己真实的面孔,看到自己无奈的未来。

第十一篇

译文一:

青　春

青春不是年华,而是心境;它不是桃面、朱唇、柔膝;它是坚定的意志、驰骋的想像、炽热的情感;它是生

命的深泉,汩汩地涌出。

青春意味着性情的优越,勇气驱走怯懦,冒险战胜苟安。二十岁有之,六十岁则更常见。岁月有加,并非垂老;理想泯灭,暮年即至。

岁月悠悠,容颜衰老;抛弃热忱,心灵受损。担忧、恐惧、自暴自弃,必然重创心灵,令心灵屈从、精神蒙尘。

无论年届花甲,还是二八芳龄,心中皆有奇迹的诱惑,永恒的童真,生命的快乐,你我心中皆有一台天线,只要接受来自人们和上帝的美丽、希望、快乐、勇敢的信息,就会青春永驻,风华正茂。

一旦天线倒下,心灵为愤世嫉俗和悲观厌世的冰雪所覆盖,你就有可能年方二十而衰;只要天线不倒,不断接受乐观的电波,你有望年届八十而终,年轻依旧。——毛荣贵译文

译文二:
青春不是生命的一段时光,不是指红润的脸颊、红扑扑的嘴唇和柔韧的双膝;它是一种精神状态,是指不懈的干劲、丰富的想像力和滚烫的情怀。它是生命春意正浓时的活力。

它是生命之源勃勃生机的涌泉。青春意味着战胜懦弱的那股大丈夫气概和摈弃安逸的那种冒险精神。往往一个60岁的老者比一个20岁的青年更多一点这种劲头。人老不仅仅是岁月流逝所致,更主要的是懒惰、不思进取的结果。

光阴可以在颜面上留下印记,而热情之火的熄灭则在心灵上刻下皱纹。忧虑、恐惧、缺乏自信,会扭曲人的灵魂,并将青春化为灰烬。

无论是60岁还是16岁,你需要保持永不衰竭的好奇心,永不熄灭的孩提求知的渴望和追求生活乐趣的热情。在你我的心底,都有一座无线电台:它能在多长时间里接收到人间万物传递来的美好、希望、欢乐、鼓舞和力量信息,你就会年轻多长时间。

当天线倒塌时,你的精神就被玩世不恭和悲观厌世的冰雪所覆盖,你就已经衰老了,即使你只是20岁;而你的天线巍然矗立着的时候,凭着高昂的乐观主义,你就有希望在80岁死去时仍然韶华不逝。

译文三:
青春,并非人生旅途中的一段时光,而是心灵中的一种状态;并非粉腮朱唇和矫健的身姿,而是头脑中的一个意念,思维中的一种潜能,情感世界中的一股灼灼生气,人生大好时光中蓬勃着的一抹新绿。

年轻,意味着乐于舍弃舒适的生活,四海闯荡,意味着具备超越羞怯和欲望的勇气。或许60岁的男人比20岁的小伙子更多地拥有这种勇气。人是不会仅仅因为时光的流逝而衰老的。放弃理想没有理想的人才是老人。

岁月可以在肌肤上留下道道皱纹,但丧失热情却会给灵魂刻下深深的痕迹。忧虑、恐惧、缺乏自信只会让人胸无大志,沦为尘土。

无论60岁还是16岁,人人都会受到好奇心得驱使,都会对未来对人生际遇中的欢乐怀着孩童般无尽的渴望。在你我心灵的深处都有一部无线电台,只要它从人群中、从无限的时空中永不间断地接受美好、希望、喝彩、勇气和力量的信息,你我就会永葆青春。

一旦这部电台坍塌,心灵就会被玩世不恭、悲观绝望的寒冰覆盖,即便只有20岁,但你已垂垂老矣!如果这部电台始终矗立在心中,去捕捉每一束乐观向上的电波,你便可望在80岁高龄甚至在撒手人寰的那一刻仍然拥有一颗年轻的心。
(《英汉翻译方法与试笔》)

译文四:
青春不是年华,而是心境;青春不是桃面、丹唇、柔膝,而是深沉的意志、宏伟的想象、炽热的感情;青春是生命的深泉在涌流。

青春气贯长虹,勇锐盖过怯弱,进取压倒苟安,如此锐气,二十后生有之,六旬男子则更多见。年年有加,并非垂老;理想丢弃,方堕暮年。

岁月悠悠,衰微只及肌肤;热忱抛却,颓唐必至灵魂。烦忧、惶恐、丧失自信,定使心灵扭曲,意气如灰。

无论年届花甲,抑或二八芳龄,心中皆有生命之欢乐,奇迹之诱惑,孩童般天真久盛不衰。人人心中皆有一台天线,只要你从天上人间接受美好、希望、欢乐、勇气和力量的信号,你就青春永驻,风华长存。

一旦天线倒塌,锐气被冰雪覆盖,玩世不恭、自暴自弃油然而生,即使年方二十,实已垂老矣;然则只要竖起天线,捕捉乐观的信号,你就有望在八十高龄告别尘寰时仍觉得年轻。

第十二篇

谈　美

德行犹如宝石,朴素最美;其于人也:则有德者但须形体悦目,不必面貌俊秀,与其貌美,不若气度恢弘。人不尽知:绝色无大德也;一如自然劳碌终日,但求无过,而无力制成上品。因此美男子有才而无壮志,重行而不重德。但亦不尽然。罗马大帝奥古斯提与泰特思,法王菲律浦,英王爱德华四世,古雅典之亚西拜提斯,波斯之伊斯迈帝,皆有宏图壮志而又为当时最美之人也。美不在颜色艳丽而在面目端正,又不尽在面目端正而在举止文雅合度。美之极致,非图画所能表,乍见所能识。举凡最美之人,其部位比例,必有异于常人之处。阿贝尔与杜勒皆画家也,其画人像也,一则按照几何学之比例,一则集众脸形之长于一身,二者谁更不智,实难断言。窃以为此等画像出画家本人外,恐无人喜爱也。余不否认画像之美可以超绝尘寰,但此美必为神笔,而非可依规矩得之者,乐师之谱成名曲亦莫不皆然。人面如逐部细察,往往一无是处,观其整体则光彩夺目。美之要素既在于举止,则年长美过年少亦无足怪。古人云:"美者秋日亦美。"年少而著美名,率由宽假,盖鉴其年事之少,而补其形体之不足也。美者犹如夏日蔬果,易腐难存;要之,年少而美者常无行,年长而美者不免面有惭色。虽然,但须托体得人,则德行因美而益彰,恶行见美而愈愧。

第十三篇

译文一:

文学观带给我们的最深刻的启示是使理智随心而动。当然这一启示并非人人都能领悟,一旦领悟,要铭记在心亦殊为困难。博览群书让我们感受到生命的丰美、复杂和神秘,而我也逐渐认识到,从更为广阔和深远的角度来看,文学的某些东西其深层里是非政治的——超乎政治之上。不管女权主义者、马克思主义者和其他有政治倾向的文学批评家会怎么想。如果你穷其一生读书,最终领悟到的要旨却是女人悲惨,资本主义腐败,或者应首先关注受害者,那么我得说你或许错过了最关键的东西。糟糕的是,你大概再没有时间把一辈子看过的五千多本书重读一遍了。

读书带着爱意与敬意,无论这些书有多伟大,多有益,哪怕不是那么的好,方能解出群书背后传递出的更大信息,无非就是陶冶你的感性,使你能够信任你的心灵。至少我是这么理解的:大量阅读导致人们质疑自己所受到的许多教育,这一点既十分有趣又颇具讽刺意味。不幸的是,要明白这一点,首先要接受教育,这好比要藐视成功,就必须先取得成功一样。

译文二:

文学观点传授给人的最玄奥的教训——可以肯定,该教训绝非人皆有效,一旦获得,要想牢记心头更是勉为其难——是让智识臣服于心灵。广泛的阅读教人知晓,生活是丰富多彩,错综复杂,也是神秘莫测的。从一个更宽广、更长远的眼光来看,我相信,文学中含有某种深刻的非政治化的东西——某种高于政治的东西,尽管女权主义者、马克思主义者,以及其他具政治倾向性的文学批评家可能另作他想。如果在你漫长的阅读生涯的尽头,你能带走的首要信息是,妇女的命运糟臭透顶,资本主义制度腐臭难当,或者对受害者的关注该高于一切,那么,我要说,你也许已经失去了某种最核心的东西。可惜,很可能已经没有时间重拾老路,把一生读过的四五千本书再重读一遍了。

怀着爱与敬佩去读书的人都知道,在一切书籍背后,无论是伟大的、优秀的,甚或一些并非那么精彩的书背后,都含有一则更宏大的信息,即最终都为了培养你的敏感,使你能信任自己的心灵。广泛的阅读具有这么一种迷人的反讽性:对我们所受的大部分教育表示不信任。至少就我个人的理解来看是如此。遗憾的是,能认识到这一点的唯一渠道是,首先接受教育,正如对成功表示正当轻蔑的唯一方式是先去取得成功。

译文三:
文学观最玄奥的一堂课是如何让智识服从心灵之驱遣。可以确定,这堂课不是每个人都可以学会;即使一时学会,要牢记心头也很难。博览群书则让我们感受生命的丰满,复杂和神秘。从一个更宽广更深远的角度来看,我相信,文学中含有某种深刻的与政治无关的东西——某种超乎政治之上的东西,尽管那些女权主义者,马克思主义者以及其他具有政治倾向的文学批评家可能会另做他想。如果终其一生,你在阅读中领略到的要旨只是妇女命运悲惨,资本主义腐败或者应给予受害者第一关注,那么,我要说,你也许已经错过了最核心的内容。可惜的是,你很可能已经没有时间把一生读过的五千多本书重读一番了。

怀着爱与敬仰的心情去阅读的人们明白,每本书——不管这些书是伟大的、优秀的抑或不是那么好的——背后都有更深的主旨,其最终将陶冶你的感性,让你能够相信自己的心灵。在我个人看来,广泛的阅读十分有趣也颇为讽刺的一点则是,它让我们对自己受过的大部分教育产生怀疑;而非常不幸,接受教育是明白这点的唯一途径,这就像要藐视成功,必须先取得成功一样。

第十四篇

译文一:
德莱顿的文风可谓变化多端,而蒲柏的文风则严谨一致;德莱顿的思想恣意奔放,心到笔到;而蒲柏的思想却固守他自己的写作规则。德莱顿时而激荡狂野如万马奔腾,而蒲柏却始终流畅平稳,始终如一,温文尔雅。德莱顿的篇章是一块高低起伏,各种繁盛的花草争奇斗艳的天然原野;蒲柏的文章则更像一块用镰刀修割过、用滚轧机压过,如天鹅绒般柔软平整的草坪。[德莱顿的篇章是自然的原野,高低起伏,草木丰茂,姿态万千;蒲柏的文章则是天鹅绒似的草坪,修剪刈刘之后,又碾整得一平如展。]

天赋,乃成就诗人之力量;没有天赋的素质,判断将索然无味,知识也将缺乏活力;天赋是一种能量,能聚、能合、能增、能兴。我们有点不情愿地说,德莱顿略胜一筹。但是,说他更富诗才,并不意味着蒲柏就诗才平庸。遍观弥尔顿身后诸位作家,莫不让位于蒲柏,即使是德莱顿,尽管其文更为华丽明快,可诗篇则略逊蒲柏一筹。德莱顿的作品受外因所激,为内情所迫,总是一蹴而就;他不假思索就写成文章,一字未改便付诸出版。他的心灵在召唤之下所能奉献的,或在一次远足中感悟的,正是他所追求、所给予的。而蒲柏却谨慎从容,所以能够浓缩情感、驰骋想像,或厚积薄发,或巧借机缘。因此,如果德莱顿飞得更高,蒲柏则飞得更远;若比之以火,德莱顿火焰更加明亮,而蒲柏的热量则更稳定持久。德莱顿往往出人意料,蒲柏则从不令人失望。

译文二:
德莱顿的文风变幻多姿,蒲柏的文风严谨一致;前者天马行空,心随意走,后者则侧重章法,以痂其心。德莱顿之文有时激荡迅猛;蒲柏则始终平顺温婉。德莱顿的篇章好比一片起伏不平的原野,草木丰茂,姿态万千;蒲柏则有如光滑如绸的草地,修剪艾刘,一平如展。

天赋,是一种成就诗人的伟大力量;一种若缺乏它判断了无新意,学问毫无生气的优秀品质;一种能聚,能合,能增,能兴的无限能量。虽然有点迟疑,我们可以说德莱顿在这方面略胜一筹。但是说德莱顿富于诗才,并不意味着蒲柏就缺乏诗才。蒲柏并不亚于自弥尔顿以来的其他一切作家。即使是说到德莱顿,他虽然有更精彩的段落,诗篇却不如蒲柏完美。德莱顿或受外因所逼又或为家用所迫,写文章多过于匆忙急躁;下笔不加思索,未及修改便付之出版。在需要时他的脑子里可以瞬时反应出来的,或者在一次远足中他所感悟的,既是他所追寻的,也是他所给予的。蒲柏的谨慎从容则让他能不断提炼其情感之精华,丰富他笔下的形象,把握一切机缘,厚积薄发。如果比之一次飞翔,德莱顿飞得更高,蒲柏则飞得更久;如果比之一团火焰,德莱顿拥有更亮丽的火焰,蒲柏则拥有更持久的热力。德莱顿常常出人意表,蒲柏从不令人失望。

第十五篇
美国总统尼克松在欢迎宴会上的讲话

1972年2月21日

总理先生,今天晚上在座的诸位贵宾:

我谨代表你们的所有美国客人向你们表示感谢,感谢你们的无可比拟的盛情款待。中国人民以这种盛情款待而闻名世界。我们不仅要特别赞扬那些准备了这次盛大晚宴的人,而且还要赞扬那些为我们演奏美好音乐的人。我在外国从来没有听到过演奏这么好的美国音乐。

总理先生,我要感谢你的非常盛情和雄辩的讲话。此时此刻,通过电讯的奇迹,看到和听到我们讲话的人比在整个世界上任何其他这样的场合都要多。不过,我们在这里所讲的话,人们不会长久地记住,但我们在这里所做的事却能改变世界。

正如你在祝酒时讲的那样,中国人民是伟大的人民,美国人民是伟大的人民。如果我们两国人民互相为敌,那么我们共同居住的这个世界的前途的确很暗淡。但是,如果我们能够找到进行合作的共同点,那么实现世界和平的机会就将无可估量地大大增加。

我希望我们这个星期的会谈将是坦率的。本着这种坦率的精神,让我们在一开始就认识到这样几点:过去一些时候我们曾是敌人。今天我们有巨大的分歧。使我们走到一起的,是我们有超越这些分歧的共同利益。在我们讨论我们的分歧时,我们哪一方都不会在自己的原则上妥协。但是,虽然我们不能弥合双方之间的鸿沟,我们却能够设法搭一座桥,以便我们能够越过它进行会谈。

因此,让我们在今后的五天里一起开始一次长征吧,不是在一起迈步,而是在不同的道路上向同一个目标前进。这个目标就是建立一个和平和正义的世界结构,在这个世界结构中,所有的人都可以一起享有同等的尊严;每个国家,不论大小,都有权利决定它自己政府的形式,而不受外来的干涉或统治。全世界在注视着。全世界在倾听着。全世界在等待着我们将做些什么。这个世界是怎样的呢?就我个人来讲,我想到我的女儿,今天是她的生日。当我想到她的时候,我就想到全世界所有的儿童,亚洲、非洲、欧洲以及美洲的儿童,他们大多数都是在中华人民共和国成立后出生的。

我们将给我们的孩子们留下什么遗产呢?他们的命运是要为那些使旧世界蒙受苦难的仇恨而死亡呢,还是由于我们有缔造一个新世界的远见而活下去呢?

我们没有理由要成为敌人。我们哪一方都不企图取得对方的领土;我们哪一方都不企图统治对方。我们哪一方都不企图伸出手去统治世界。

毛主席写过:"多少事,从来急;天地转,光阴迫。一万年太久,只争朝夕。"

现在就是只争朝夕的时候了,是我们两国人民攀登那种可以缔造一个新的、更美好的世界的伟大境界的高峰的时候了。

本着这种精神,我请求诸位同我一起举杯,为毛主席,为周总理,为能够导致全世界所有人民的友谊与和平的中国人民同美国人民之间的友谊,干杯。

——张培基译文

第十六篇

译文一:

凡是有钱的单身汉,总想娶位太太,这已经成了一条举世公认的真理。

这样的单身汉,每逢新搬到一个地方,四邻八舍虽然完全不了解他的性情如何,见解如何,可是,既然这样的一条真理早已在人们心目中根深蒂固,因此人们总是把他看作自己某一个女儿理所应得的一笔财产。

有一天,班纳特太太对她的丈夫说:"我的好老爷,尼日斐花园终于租出去了,你听说过没有?"

班纳特先生回答道,他没有听说过。

"的确租出去了,"她说,"郎格太太刚刚上这儿来过,她把这件事的底细,一五一十都告诉了我。"

班纳特先生没有理睬她。

"你难道不想知道是谁租去的吗?"太太不耐烦地嚷起来了。

"既是你要说给我听,我听听也无妨。"

这句话足够鼓励她讲下去了。

"哦,亲爱的,你得知道,郎格太太说,租尼日斐花园的是个阔少爷,他是英格兰北部的人;听说他星期一那天,乘着一辆驷马大轿车来看房子,看得非常中意,当场就和莫理斯先生谈妥了;他要在'米迦勒节'以前搬进来,打算下个周末先叫几个佣人来住。"

"这人叫什么名字?"

"彬格莱。"

"有太太的呢,还是个单身汉?"

"噢!是个单身汉,亲爱的,确确实实是个单身汉!一个有钱的单身汉;每年有四五千镑的收入。真是女儿们的福气!"

"这怎么说?关女儿们什么事?"

"我的好老爷,"太太回答道,"你怎么这么叫人讨厌!告诉你吧,我正在盘算,他要是挑中我们的一个女儿做老婆,可多好!"

"他住在这儿来,就是为了这个打算吗?"

"打算!胡扯,这是哪儿的话!不过,他倒作兴看中我们的某一个女儿呢。他一搬来,你就得去拜访拜访他。"

"我不用去。你带着女儿们去就得啦,要不你干脆打发她们自己去,那或许倒更好些,因为你跟女儿们比起来,她们哪一个都不能胜过你的美貌,你去了,彬格莱先生倒可能挑中你呢。"

——王科一译文

译文二:

有钱的单身汉总要娶位太太,这是一条举世公认的真理。

这条真理还真够深入人心的,每逢这样的单身汉新搬到一个地方,四邻八舍的人家尽管对他的性情见识一无所知,却把他视为自己某一个女儿的合法财产。

"亲爱的贝内特先生,"一天,贝内特太太对丈夫说道,"你有没有听说内瑟菲尔德庄园终于租出去了?"

贝内特先生回答道,没有听说。

"的确租出去了,"太太说道。"朗太太刚刚来过,她把这事一五一十地全告诉我了。"

贝内特先生没有答话。

"难道你不想知道是谁租去的吗?"太太不耐烦地嚷道。

"既然你想告诉我,我听听也无妨。"

这句话足以逗引太太讲下去了。

"哦,亲爱的,你应该知道,朗太太说,内瑟菲尔德让英格兰北部的一个阔少爷租去了;他星期一那天乘坐驷马马车来看房子,看得非常中意,当下就和莫理斯先生讲妥了;他打算赶在米迦勒节以前搬进新居,下周末以前打发几个佣人先住进来。"

"他姓什么?"

"宾利。"

"成亲了还是单身?"

"哦!单身,亲爱的,千真万确!一个有钱的单身汉,每年有四五千镑的收入。真是女儿们的好福气!"

"这是怎么说?跟女儿们有什么关系?"

"亲爱的贝内特先生,"太太答道,"你怎么这么令人讨厌!告诉你吧,我正在思谋他娶我们中的一个做太太呢。"

"他搬到这里就是为了这个打算?"

"打算!胡扯,你怎么能这么说话!他兴许会看中她们中的哪一个,因此,他一来你就得去拜访他。"

"我看没有那个必要。你带着女儿们去就行啦,要不你索性打发她们自己去,这样或许更好些,因为你的姿色并不亚于她们中的任何一个,你一去,宾利先生倒作兴看中你呢。"

——孙致礼译文

译文三：

饶有家资的单身男子必定想要娶妻室，这是举世公认的真情实理。

正是因为这个真情实理家喻户晓深入人心，这种人一搬到什么地方，尽管他的感觉见解如何街坊四邻毫不了解，他就被人当成了自己这个或那个女儿一笔应得的财产。

"我亲爱的本内特先生，"本内特太太有一天对丈夫说，"你听说了吗？内瑟菲德庄园到底还是租出去了。"

本内特先生回答他没听说。

"可确是租出去了，"她又说道，"朗太太刚才来过，她把这件事通通都告诉我了。"

本内特先生没答腔。

"难道你不想知道，是谁租下的吗？"他太太急得直喊。

"既然你想告诉我，我岂能不洗耳恭听？"

这就足以逗得太太接着讲了。

"嗨，亲爱的，你可要知道，朗太太说，租内瑟菲德庄园的是英格兰北边来的一个年轻人，有大笔家当；说他星期一坐了一辆驷马轿车来看了房子，一看就十分中意，马上跟莫理斯先生租妥，说要在米迦勒节以前就搬进去，而且他的几个用人下个周末就要先住进去了。"

"他姓什么？"

"宾利。"

"他成亲了，还是单身？"

"哦！单身，我亲爱的，一点儿不错！一个有大笔家产的单身汉；每年四五千镑，这对咱们的几个姑娘是件多好的事呀！"

"怎么个好法儿？这和她们有什么关系？"

"我亲爱的本内特先生，"太太回答说，"你怎么这么烦人！你要知道，我这是在捉摸着他会娶她们中的哪一个呢。"

"他住到这儿来就是打这个主意吗？"

"打主意！瞎胡说，亏你说得出口！不过，倒是很有可能他兴许看上她们中的哪一个呢，所以他一来你就得去拜访他。"

"我看没那个必要。你跟姑娘们可以去，要不然你就打发她们自己去；这样或许倒更好，因为你那么标致，比她们谁都不差，你一去，宾利先生也许倒先看上你了。"

——张玲、张扬译文

评析：原文文字幽默俏皮，妙趣横生。三个译文都尽力传达这方面的韵味。三篇文字都译文老道，充分展示了重译文学作品的精彩。

第十七篇

他行年五十，头顶已经秃了，鬓丝也斑白了，所以有些人觉得他看起来不止那个岁数。然而，初次接触，外貌给人的印象未必正确。他身材高大，肚子有点凸出，而骨骼却并不粗笨，倒是动作敏捷，步履轻快。同样，他的头很雄伟，淡淡的两鬓之间，眉宇高敞，而神情变化却比谁都快，笑起来风采絜然。厚厚的眼镜后面，一双小眼炯炯如电，仿佛他还是青春年少，充满活力。乍一看，人们也许会认为他俨然有元老风度，可是不久就察觉他很不稳重。忽而笑容可掬，忽而火冒三丈，无论做什么事，他似乎总是神经紧张，形于颜色。于是，人们不再觉得他像个元老，而且开始对他不满，说他太容易表同情，太容易冲动。许多人不喜欢他那样爱自我表现，可是，看他的感情如此深切，又不能无动于衷。他感情深切这一点，几乎人人都看得出来，但要洞察他不仅感情深切，而且傲岸愤激，可要有点知人之明。

第十八篇

译文一：

那郝思嘉小姐长得并不美，可是极富魅力，男人见了她，往往要着迷，就像汤家那一对双胞胎兄弟似的。

原来这位小姐脸上显然混杂着两种特质：一种是母亲给她的娇柔，一种是父亲给她的豪爽。因为她母亲是个法兰西血统的海滨贵族，父亲是个肤色深浓的爱尔兰人，所以遗传给她的质地难免不调和。可是质地虽然不调和，她那一张脸蛋儿实在迷人得很，下巴颏儿尖尖的，牙床骨儿方方的。她的眼珠子是一味的淡绿色，不杂一丝儿的茶褐，周围竖着一圈儿粗黑的睫毛，眼角微微有点翘，上面斜竖着两撇墨黑的鹅眉，在她那木兰花一般白的皮肤上，划出两条异常惹眼的斜线。就是她那一身皮肤，也正是南方女人最最喜爱的，谁要长着这样的皮肤，就要拿帽子、面罩之类当心保护着，舍不得让那大热的阳光晒黑。

1861年4月一个晴朗的下午，思嘉小姐在淘乐垦植场的住宅，陪着汤家那一对双胞胎兄弟———一个叫汤司徒，一个叫汤伯伦的——坐在一个阴凉的走廊里。这时春意正浓，景物如绣，她也显得特别的标致。她身上穿着一件新制的绿色花布春衫，从弹簧箍上撑出波浪纹的长裙，配着脚上一双也是绿色的低跟鞋，是她父亲新近从饿狼陀买来给她的。她的腰围不过十七英寸，穿着那窄窄的春衫，显得十分合身。里面紧紧绷着一件小马甲，使得她胸部特别隆起。她的年纪虽只十六岁，乳房却已十分成熟了。可是不管她那散开的长裙显得多么端庄，不管她那梳得光滑的后鬐显得多么老实，也不管她那叠在膝头上的一双雪白的小手显得多么安静，总都掩饰不了她的真性情。她那双绿色的眼睛虽然嵌在一张矜持的面孔上，却是骚动不宁的，慧黠多端的，洋溢着生命的，跟她那一副装饰起来的仪态截然不能相称。原来她平日受了母亲的温和训诲和嬷嬷的严厉管教，这才把这副姿态勉强造成的，至于那一双眼睛，那是天生给她的，绝不是人工改造得了的。

——傅东华译文

译文二：

斯佳丽·奥哈拉长得并不美，但是男人一旦像塔尔顿家孪生兄弟那样给她的魅力迷住往往就不大理会这点。她脸蛋上极其明显地融合了父母的容貌特征，既有母亲那种沿海地区法国贵族后裔的优雅，也有父亲那种肤色红润的爱尔兰人的粗野。不过这张脸还是挺引人注目，尖尖的下巴颏儿，方方的牙床骨儿。眼睛纯粹是淡绿色的，不带一点儿淡褐色，眼眶缀着浓密乌黑的睫毛，稍稍有点吊眼梢。上面是两道又浓又黑的剑眉，在木兰花似的洁白皮肤上勾画出两条触目惊心的斜线。那种皮肤深受南方妇女珍视，而且她们总是戴上帽子、面纱和手套，小心翼翼地保护好，免得给佐治亚的烈日晒黑。

1861年4月，有一天下午阳光明媚，她在父亲的塔拉庄园宅前门廊的荫处，同塔尔顿家两兄弟斯图特和布伦特坐在一起，那模样真宛如画中人。她穿着那件绿花布的新衣，裙箍把用料十二码波浪形裙幅铺展开来，跟她父亲刚从亚特兰大给她捎来的平跟摩洛哥羊皮绿舞鞋正好相配。她的腰围只有十七英寸，三个县里就数她腰身最细，那身衣服把她腰肢衬托得更见纤细。虽说年方十六岁，乳房却长得非常成熟。熨帖的紧身上衣把她乳房裹得格外显眼。尽管她长裙舒展，显得仪态端庄，一头乌丝光溜溜地用发网拢成一个发髻，显得风度娴雅，一双雪白的纤手交叉搁在膝上，显得举止文静，但真正的本性却难以掩饰。精心故作娇憨的脸上那绿眼睛爱动、任性、生气勃勃，和她那份端庄的态度截然不同。原来她一贯受到母亲的谆谆告诫和黑妈妈的严格管教才勉强养成这副礼貌；她那双眼睛才显出她的本色呢。

——陈廷良译文

译文三：

思嘉·奥哈拉长得并不漂亮，但是男人们一旦像塔尔顿家那对孪生兄弟为她的魅力所迷住时，便看不到这一点了。她脸上混杂着两种特征，一种是她母亲的娇柔，一种是她父亲的粗犷，前者属于法兰西血统的海滨贵族，后者来自浮华俗气的爱尔兰人，这两种特征显得太不调和了。不过这张脸，连同那尖尖的下巴和四四方方牙床骨，是很引人注目的。她那双淡绿色的眼睛纯净得不带一丝褐色，配上刚硬乌黑的睫毛和稍稍翘起的眼角，显得别具风韵。上头是两撇墨黑的浓眉斜竖在那里，给木兰花一般白皙的皮肤划了一条十分惹眼的斜线。这样白皙的皮肤对南方妇女是极其珍贵的，她们常常用帽子、面纱和手套把皮肤保护起来，不让受到佐治亚炎热太阳的暴晒。

1861年4月一个晴朗的下午，思嘉同塔尔顿家的孪生兄弟斯图尔特和布伦特坐在她父亲的塔拉农场阴凉的走廊里,她标致的模样使四周的一派春光更明媚如画了。她穿一件新做的绿花布衣裳,长长的裙子在裙箍上波翻浪涌般地飘展着,配上她父亲新近从亚特兰大给她带来的绿色山羊皮便鞋,显得分外相称。她的腰围不过十七英寸,是附近三个县里最细小的了,而这身衣裳更把腰肢衬托得恰到好处,再加上里面那件绷得紧紧的小马甲,她虽然只有十六岁但已成熟了的乳房便跃然显露了。不过,无论她散开的长裙显得多么朴实,发髻梳在后面的发型显得多么端庄,那双交叠在膝头上白生生的小手显得多么文静,她的本来面目终归是掩藏不住的。那双绿色的眼睛尽管生在一张故作娇媚的脸上,却仍然是骚动的、任性的、生意盎然的,与她的装束仪表很不相同。她的举止是她母亲的谆谆训诫和嬷嬷的严厉管教强加给她的,但她的眼睛属于自己。

——戴侃、李野光译文

第十九篇

译文一:

康斯坦丁·德米力斯的王国比世界上的许多国家更辽阔、更强大。他一无官职、二无头衔,却是权力无上的风云人物,当代世界上屈指可数的巨头之一。他不仅拥有世界上最大的商船队以及航空公司、报纸、银行、钢厂、金矿,掌握着十多个国家的经济命脉,甚至他经常做买卖部长、宰相、外交官、亲王等职衔的交易。此外,他也是著名的艺术珍品收藏家,拥有一个私人飞行队,十多座别墅、庄园遍布全球各个风景胜地。

康斯坦丁·德米力斯身材较高,膀乍腰圆,胸膛宽阔,黑黝黝的皮肤油光发亮。他虽不讲究衣着,但从服饰上一望而知他是属于上流社会的。

他黑色的眸子中闪耀着机智的光辉,外表具有极强的吸引力。只要他一走进大厅,不相识的人也不由自主地朝他转过脸来。世界各地的报刊杂志争相报道有关他的种种消息,从实业、社交生活到风流艳事,都是记者的秃笔写之不尽的好题材。(《狰狞的夜》)

译文二:

康斯坦丁·戴米里斯主宰的帝国比大部分国家还要强盛,还要疆域辽阔。他既无爵位,又无官职,然而他经常对一个个总理、红衣主教、大使,乃至国王进行收买、出卖。戴米里斯是天下最富有的二、三位巨阔之一。他的势力之大,达到了神奇的地步。他拥有全球最庞大的货船队,拥有一家航空公司、报社、银行,还拥有钢铁厂、金矿,他的触角遍及世界各地,紧紧地与几十个国家的经济命脉缠绕在一起。

他是世界最重要的艺术收藏馆的主人,有一大群私人飞机,并在世界各地买下了十几幢公寓、别墅。

康斯坦丁·戴米里斯身材中等偏高,宽肩膀,胸部阔得同身高极不相称。他脸色黝黑,长着一只宽大的希腊种鼻子,一双深橄榄绿的眼睛闪烁着智慧的光芒。虽然他对衣着不感兴趣,但是在穿戴最时髦的男子的名单上,他总是榜上有名。据传,他有五百多套西装。他到一处,就在一处做衣服。他的西装是伦敦霍斯柯蒂斯公司裁制的,衬衫是罗马布里欧尼公司定做的。鞋子是巴黎达里艾特·格兰德的,而领带则来自十几个国家。

戴米里斯的外表有一股磁力。他一迈进一间屋子,不认识的人都会调过脸来对他注目而视。各国的报纸、杂志连篇累牍地介绍康斯坦丁·戴米里斯其人,他的生意买卖,以及他的社交活动。(《情与仇》)

译文三:

康斯坦丁·德米里斯统治的帝国比大多数国家更为辽阔,更为强大。他并没有头衔或官方的职位,但是他定期地收买和出卖首相、红衣主教、大使和国王。德米里斯是世界上最富有的两、三个人中的一个,他象传说中的人物那样,权力大得令人难以置信。他拥有当时世界上最大的商船队,一家航空公司,还有好几家报纸、银行、钢厂和几座金矿——他的触须伸向四面八方,同几十个国家所组成的错综复杂的经济网不可分割地联系在一起。

他珍藏的艺术品在世界上占有十分重要的地位,他有若干架私人飞机,有十几幢公寓和别墅分布在世界各地。

康斯坦丁·德米里斯的身材中等偏高,胸部显得过份地宽厚,肩膀也很宽阔。他的肤色黝黑,希腊式的鼻子十分宽大,一双深橄榄绿的眼睛闪射着智慧的光芒。虽然他对服装并不感兴趣,然而在人们的心目中总是属于那种穿着最考究的人。人们谣传他有五百多套衣服。他无论到了什么地方就顺便在那儿做衣服。他的西装是由伦敦的霍维斯一柯蒂斯服装店裁制的,他的衬衫是在罗马的布里奥尼内衣厂定做的,他的鞋是请巴黎的达利艾——格朗特鞋店特制的,他的领带是从十几个不同的国家购买的。

德米里斯举止不凡,很有吸引力。当他走进一个房间时,那些不知道他是谁的人都会转过脸来盯着他看。世界各地的报纸和杂志连续不断地刊载了大量的报道,来描绘康斯坦丁·德米里斯这个人,以及他的商业活动和社会活动。(《午夜情》)

第二十篇

译文一:

他演说中的高潮发生在他讲到正当中的时候。他正在讲给我们听,他是怎样一个漂亮的人物,怎样地吃得开,讲得眉飞色舞,得意洋洋,于是突然一下,坐在我前排那个名叫艾德加·马沙拉的家伙,放了一个奇臭无比的屁。在礼堂大庭广众之中大放其屁,确是一件尴尬不堪的事,不过也很有趣。老马那个家伙,可真厉害,一屁放出,几乎把屋顶都轰掉了。没有一个人敢笑,欧森白那家伙装作没有听见的样子,但是就在讲坛上欧森白旁边的塞默校长,大家都知道他确是听到了的。

你说他没有生气吗?他当时虽则一句话也没有说,可是到了第二天晚上,他把我们全部赶进教室强迫用功,后来他跑过来,对我们大训其话。他说昨天在礼堂惹起骚动的学生,没有进宾夕预校的资格。我们很想要老马在校长训话的时候,再放么一个响屁,可惜他那时没有那种雅兴。

——钱歌川译文

译文二:

他演讲最精彩的部分是在半当中。他正在告诉我们他自己有多么了不起,多么出人头地,坐在我们前面一排的那个家伙,爱德迦·马萨拉,突然放了个响屁。干这种事确实很不雅,尤其是在教堂里,可也十分有趣。老马萨拉,他差点儿没掀掉屋顶。可以说几乎没一个人笑出声来,老奥森贝格还装出压根儿没听见的样子,可是校长老绥摩也在台上,正好坐在他旁边,你看得出他已经听见了。嘿,他该多难受。他当时没说什么,可是第二天晚上他让我们到办公大楼上必修课的大教室里集合,他自己就登台演讲。他说那个在教堂里扰乱秩序的学生不配在潘西念书。我们想叫老马萨拉趁老绥摩正在演讲时照样再来一个响屁,可他心境不好,放不出来。

——施咸荣译文

评析:译文一和译文二都是很精彩的。相比之下,译文一似更见功夫,戏谑嘲讽的口吻通过一些译词充分表现出来,如,"漂亮的人物"、"吃得开"、"眉飞色舞,得意洋洋"、"大放其屁"等。

第二十一篇

译文一:

而风飙亦遒增其势,海波益恣,实为余放舟时所不经见者。余晕益不能支。余初意但一观巨浸,不料艰险一至于此。但虞巨浪更来者,舟且立覆,沈殁浪纹之内,更无履岸之时。方余悲戚时,深自怨艾咎怨,谓上帝赦余,得免于死,重践乾土者则愿趋庭长侍老亲,不更于探险之事。毋论年命何若,誓不更睹风帆,长作守成之子。安有自寻灾害,掷此身于海若。眩晕中乃益信中庸之言,为计至得,为生亦易,安有以七尺之躯,随飙母而旋转。嗟乎浪子,今日回头矣。

此种知识,及悔过之深衷,不期乃逐风飙,与相上下,飙盛而余思亦弗弱,至于明日。风乃小止,水波略平,余于颠簸中亦稍习,惟长日弗适,以余眩尚在也。是晚天朗气清,飙力全息,暮景澄然,斜日红如火齐,落于海波尽处。明日天气仍佳,微飙不动,日光穿射,一色纯绿,海中眼界,为余生平第一次窥涉者。

——林纾译文(注:文中标点为编者所加)

译文二：

　　这时风势愈来愈大，只见我所从来没有到过的海面上，波浪翻天，汹涌异常，虽然还没有像我后来几次以及过了几天所见到的那样凶，但也能够让我触目惊心，因为我这时只是一个初出茅庐的水手，对于海上的事完全没有知识。我觉得每一个浪花都仿佛要把我们吞下去；我们的船每次降落到浪涡里的时候，我都以为它是浮不起来了。在这种痛苦心情下，我发了许多誓，下了几次决心，说假使上帝在这次航行中留下我的性命，假使我有日再踏上陆地，我一定一直跑到我父亲身边，一辈子不再坐船了；说我一定听从他的忠告，不再自寻这种烦恼了。我觉得他关于中等生活的看法，句句真实；我觉得他一辈子实在过得安闲自在，既没有碰到过海上的风雨，也没有碰到过陆地上的种种艰难困苦。我决定要像一个真正的回头浪子，回到我父亲跟前去。

　　这些明智而清醒的想法，在暴风雨发作着的当儿，甚至在它停止以后的某一短时间内，一直盘踞在我的头脑里。但到了第二天，风也停了，浪也静了，我就开始对海上生活习以为常了。不过那天我还是整天无精打采，因为我还有点晕船。到了傍晚，天气完全晴了，风也完全停止了，继之而来的是一个美丽可爱的黄昏。当晚的落日和第二天早晨的日出都非常清朗。此时风平浪静，太阳的光线照在上面，那种景致，真是我从来没见过的。

——徐霞村译文

译文三：

　　这时风暴越刮越猛，海面汹涌澎湃，波浪滔天。我以前从未见过这种情景。但比起我后来多次见到过的咆哮的大海，那真是大巫见小巫了；就是与我过几天后见到的情景，也不能相比。可是，在当时，对我这个初次航海的年轻人来说，足以令我胆战心惊，因为我对航海的事一无所知。我感到，海浪随时会将我们吞没。每次我们的船跌入浪涡时，我想我们会随时倾覆沉入海底再也浮不起来了。在这种惶恐不安的心情下，我一次又一次地发誓，下了无数次决心，说如果上帝在这次航行中能够留我一命，只要让我双脚一踏上陆地，我就马上回到我父亲身边，今生今世再也不乘船了。我将听从父亲的劝告，再也不自寻烦恼了。同时，我也醒悟到，我父亲关于中间阶层生活的看法，确实句句在理。就拿我父亲来说吧，他一生平安舒适，既没有遇到过海上的狂风恶浪，也没有遭到过陆上的艰难苦困。我决心，我要像一个真正回头的浪子，回到家里，回到我父亲的身边。

　　这些明智而清醒的思想，在暴风雨肆虐期间，乃至停止后的短时间内，一直在我脑子里盘旋。到了第二天，暴风雨过去了，海面平静多了，我对海上生活开始有点习惯了。但我整天仍是愁眉苦脸的；再加上有些晕船，更是打不起精神来。到了傍晚，天气完全晴了，风也完全停了，继之而来的是一个美丽可爱的黄昏。当晚和第二天清晨天气晴朗，落日和日出显得异常清丽。此时，阳光照在风平浪静的海面上，令人心旷神怡。那是我以前从未见过的美景。

——郭建中译文

译文四：

　　就在这当儿，但见我从未见过的海面上，狂风刮得更加凶猛，浪头涌得很高。当然，这还不如我后来所经历的以及我以后几天所见到的那样凶猛；但这对我来说，已够让我心惊胆战的了，因为我不过是个第一次出海的水手，对海上的事情一无所知。我觉得，每个浪头打来都会把我们吞噬掉；每次我们的船落入浪谷，我都以为，再无升起之希望。这在痛苦的折磨中，我起了许多誓，发了许多狠，倘若上帝保佑，让我这回死里逃生，重新回到岸上，我一定会立刻回到家中，回到父亲身边，今生今世不再坐船；我肯定会听取他的忠告，绝不再把自己送进这样的灾难。现在，我终于茅塞顿开，明白了他所说的关于中等状态生活的真谛；想起来，他这辈子活得多么悠闲，多么舒服啊，从未经受过海上的风暴以及陆上的烦恼；所以我决心回到家中，回到父亲身边，做个名副其实的回头浪子。

　　在风暴平息之前，我的脑子里一直萦绕着这些明智且冷静的想法，甚至在风暴平定之后的一段时间里，我也有这样的想法。可是，第二天，风平了，浪也静了，我对大海又适应起来。当然，这一整天，我的情绪仍很低沉,况且还有点晕船。不过,到了晚上,天空晴朗起来,风也早已停息,一个迷人的、美丽的黄昏将临了;太阳浑圆地落下,次日清晨又圆圆地升起,简直没有一丝气息,海面平滑如镜,阳光洒满了海面。我想,这真是我所见到的最宜人的美景。

——义海译文

译文五:

风越刮越猛,我从没到过的海上波涛汹涌——但是,同我后来看到的几次相比,都还算不了什么。然而,对于当时我这样一个毫无航海知识的年轻生手,这景象已足以叫我胆战心惊了。每个浪头打来,我都觉得会把我们船吞没;每一次船落在波谷,我都以为要直沉海底,再也起不来了;在这种惶惶不安、战战兢兢的心情下,我多次发誓又几回痛下决心,说是只要上帝在这次航行中饶我一命,只要让我的脚仍能踏上陆地,我就马上直奔老家,回到父亲的身边,今生今世再也不上船了;而且,我要听从父亲的劝告,再也不干这类自讨苦吃的事了。到了这时,我才真正认识到我父亲的远见卓识,认识到他处世上那种中庸之道的妙处;他这一辈子过得轻松自如、安闲舒适,既没去海上蒙受狂风暴雨之苦,也没在陆地上遭受艰难困苦的折磨。我决意要做个回头的浪子,一旦上岸,便回到我父亲的身边。

在狂风大作的当儿,甚至在风停以后的一段时间里,这些冷静清醒的想法总盘旋在我脑海中;第二天风浪小了些,我也就稍稍习惯了一些。但整整一天里,我打不起精神来,因为我仍然有点晕船;时近黄昏,天开始放晴,风也完全停了,随之而来的是个风光无限的晴朗傍晚;只见轮廓格外分明的太阳落了下去后第二天早晨又原样升了起来,照耀在风平浪静的海面上;我觉得,在我见到过的景象中,这是最叫我看得满心喜欢的。

——黄杲炘译文

译文六:

这时风势越来越大,我从未到过的海面上,波涛汹涌,海浪滔天。虽说这海浪还没有像我后来几次以及过了几天所见到的那样汹涌澎湃,但对我这个头次出海且对大海一无所知的年轻生手来说,足以令我胆战心惊了。我觉得每一个巨浪都仿佛要把我们吞下去。每次我们的船跌落到浪谷,我都以为我们浮不起来了。在这极度的痛苦中,我发了许多誓,并多次下决心,假如上帝在这次航行中留下我的性命,假如我有一天再踏上坚实的陆地,我要径直回家,跑到父亲身边,一辈子不再坐船了。以后我一定听从他的忠告,再也不自讨这种苦吃了。我现在觉得他关于中间阶层生活的看法非常正确。我觉得他一辈子实在过得舒适惬意,既没有碰到过海上的狂风巨浪,也没有遇到过陆地上的艰难困苦。我决定要像一个真正的回头浪子,回到父亲身边去。

这些明智而清醒的想法在暴风雨发作的时候,甚至在它停止后的一小段时间内,一直盘踞在我的脑海里。但到了第二天,一切都风平浪静时,我就又开始有点习惯这海上生活了。不过我还是整天没精打采的,因为我还有点晕船。到了傍晚,天气完全晴了,风也完全住了,继之而来的是一个美丽可爱的傍晚。傍晚的落日是那样清晰,第二天早晨的日出也同样明朗。此时风平浪静,阳光明媚,海面上的这种美景,真是我从未见过的。

——范纯海、夏旻译文

第二十二篇

《指环王》字幕译文

甘道夫:皮平从水晶球里窥见敌人的行动计划。
   萨龙移师去攻打米纳斯提瑞斯了。
   他在圣盔谷的战败使我们的敌人明白:
   他知道埃兰迪的继承者已经降临。

人类不是他想像的那么不堪一击。他们勇气依旧。也许还强大到足以挑战他。
萨龙就怕这个。
他不敢冒险进犯在一面旗帜下众志成城的中土各族民众。
他要赶在王者重登人类王位之前,将米纳斯提瑞斯夷为平地。
一旦刚多的烽火燃起,罗翰国必须整装待战。

西尔登:且慢。为什么我们要跑去支援那些曾对我们见死不救的人?
我们有何亏欠刚多?
阿拉贡:我愿前往。
甘道夫:不可。
阿拉贡:必须有人给他们报警。
甘道夫:会有人的。
你必须抄另一条路去米纳斯提瑞斯。
沿河边走,要提防那些乌帆船。
要明白:
势态正在发展,已经无法扭转。
我要赶赴米纳斯提瑞斯。

第二十三篇

心　碎

　　我本来一直以为心碎只是一种比喻,是乡村音乐和浪漫的爱情小说惯用的手法。所以当我上周得知,医生们现在认为心碎真的是一个医学问题,一个能致人死亡的问题时,我感到无比吃惊。

　　这个消息来自《新英格兰医学杂志》的一篇报道。在这篇报道中,约翰斯·霍普金斯医疗中心的医生们说,18名大多年岁较大的女性和1名男性因遭受突然的情感冲击而出现了严重的心脏问题。这种情感冲击可以是亲人的死亡,而对一名60岁的女性而言则是一个意想不到的生日聚会。

　　给这些病人做检查的医生们感到奇怪的是,这些病人竟然没有一个以前得过心脏病。实际上,几乎没有人带有任何罹患心脏病的体征。然而领导这项研究的心脏病专家伊兰·维特斯坦医生说,如果没有得到治疗的话,在这19人中至少有5人——可能更多——已经死亡。

　　这到底是怎么回事?为了追根溯源,维特斯坦及其同事测量了这些病人体内儿茶酚胺的浓度。儿茶酚胺是一种包括肾上腺素的应激激素,他们发现每一个病人的应激激素的浓度都很高——最高达到正常水平的34倍,为突发严重心脏病时的两到三倍。

　　现在还不清楚是应激激素造成了心脏问题还是心脏问题造成了应激激素浓度的升高。医生们也无法解释为什么女性的心脏好像要比男性脆弱。维特斯坦说:"在遇到紧张的情况时,男性释放的儿茶酚胺往往高于女性。所以如果一定要猜的话,人们会认为男性出现这个问题的几率多于女性。"

　　医生们将这种疾病称为心碎综合征,好在只要最初的情感冲击不是太大,这种疾病是可以治愈的。复发看来并不常见,不管别人为你举办多少次意想不到的生日聚会。

　　　　　　　　　　　　　　　　　　——殷欣译自美国《时代》周刊,转引自《参考消息》(2005/4/6)

第二十四篇

胎先露异常、胎方位异常以及多胎妊娠

斯蒂芬·H·艾辛格　医学博士

目标

通过本章的学习和培训,应掌握:

1. 确定六种异常胎先露及其诊断方法。
2. 列举与各种异常胎先露有关的并发症。

3. 讨论允许阴道分娩的标准及阴道分娩的适当处理。
4. 讨论多胎妊娠,尤其关注临产和分娩。
5. 利用母—胎人体模型对各种异常胎方位和异常胎先露实施安全、有效的分娩。

定义

讨论胎先露异常时,定义非常重要。**产式**表示胎儿的长轴和母体长轴间的关系,具体表现为**纵产式**、**横产式**或**斜产式**(**不稳定产式**)。**胎先露**表示在产道里,胎儿的最前面部分,即"先露"。胎儿的先露部分可以是头顶、臀部、面部、额部或肩部。**胎方位**表示先露部分的某一参照点以及它和母体骨盆的关系。例如,头颅的参照点是枕骨部。当胎儿枕骨部朝向母体的耻骨联合,即前位时,胎儿处于**枕前位**。当枕骨部朝向母体的脊柱时,则胎儿处于**枕后位**。根据枕骨在骨盆所处的位置分**左枕前位**和**右枕前位**、**左枕横位**和**右枕横位**、**左枕后位**和**右枕后位**。

诊断的方法

确定胎产式、胎先露和胳方位有三个主要方法。第一种是里奥波得法,或腹部触诊。第二种是阴道检查。第三种是影像检查。超声波是首选的影像检查法。产时超声波检查在各级医院中广泛运用。每个接生人员必须熟练运用超声技术以利于时确定胎产式、胎先露和胳方位。偶尔也有必要使用 X 线透视,特别是当需要了解细节,如臀先露时肢体的位置时。

胎头与母骨盆

大多数胎儿先露异常(枕后位、臀位、面先露、额先露)在临床上很重要,因为胎头不是圆形的,而呈椭圆形或卵圆形。最小的胎头间径是**枕下前囟径**;最大的胎头间径是**枕额径**。他们之间的差别是3cm,即约24%。当胎头完全俯曲时,枕下前囟径,即最小的胎头间径通过骨盆。当胎头完全仰伸时,则枕额径,即最大的胎头间径通过骨盆。如果先露为最小的胎头间径通过时,则阴道分娩的可能性较大,且更为容易。因此,胎头通过骨盆时,胎头的姿势(俯曲或仰伸)至关重要。一定程度的胎头仰伸,可出现于枕后位、面先露与额先露。还有某些为臀先露。

产式不均倾在分娩动力学中亦起重要的作用。不均倾产工以头的侧边屈曲,这样矢状缝不在产道的正中线。一定程度的不均倾是正常的。随着胎头进一步调整着进入骨盆,它能前后移动,甚至由前不均倾改为后均倾。极其严重的不均倾会使产程停滞。不均倾产式是产钳助产的主要原因。

母体骨盆在各种先露异常的产生和产程进展中也起重要作用。骨盆有四种类型。大多数妇女是女性型,即中间型:

女性型(圆形)

类人猿型(椭圆形,长轴位于前后平面上)

扁平型(椭圆形长轴位于左右平面上)

男性型(三角形,或心型,三角形的在前面)

充分讨论骨盆类型和骨盆测量法临床意义有限,我们可以总结出,骨盆狭窄,如类人猿型,会导致持续枕后位;扁平型骨盆会导致枕横位嵌顿;男性型骨盆不利于分娩,会发生各种各样先露异常;狭小骨盆可伴有多种先露异常,主要是因为胎头不能下降、衔接或旋转。

——陈琼华译文

第二十五篇

科学的权威与教会的权威

吾人所谓"现代",其思想观点,实大异于中古。其中,主要区别有二,一曰教会之权威日衰,二曰科学之权威日增。……

科学的权威,已为近世多数哲学家所承认。此一权威,殊不同于教会的权威。科学权威,理智的力量也;教会权威,统治的力量也。人于科学权威,可以拒绝,可以接受。拒绝,无须受惩罚。接受,无须出于保身家保名誉之考虑。科学所以有权威,唯一原因,是科学有内在的足以令人折服的力量。再者,科学的权威,明一理有一理之权威,明二理有二理之权威。科学的权威,止于已明之理:不若天主教义,乃包罗万象之体系,道德准则,人生理想,甚至世界之过去与未来,无一不在此体系之内。科学如有所见,仅以此时此物已有科学实证者为限。知识,海洋也;科学之所知,一小岛耳。科学的权威,尚有一点不同于教会的权威。教会每有宣示,必曰此千真万确,万事不移。科学作出的判断,曰此是暂时的结论,此有盖然性,科学的结论可加以修正,此是科学家共有的见解。科学家之思想,截然不同于中古时期固执教义之士,盖在于此。

——古庄译文

文艺复兴,以读书论学为乐事,成为风尚

　　文艺复兴的哲学成就,殊不足道。但十七世纪之伟大成就,文艺复兴实开其先河。中古世纪,僵化的经院学派统治学术,学者头上,套有紧箍。文艺复兴破其成法,是其功绩,此其一。中古之时,不读柏拉图之书。及文艺复兴,柏拉图之学又兴,柏拉图与亚里士多德二人之间,何去何从,必须有充分的独立思考,方能作出判断。于是,相率读二氏之原作,究其立言之本,中古柏拉图学派的章句注释,阿拉伯学者之笺疏,悉加屏弃。尤有进者,以读书论学为乐事,成为社会风尚,与经院中秘室冥思大异其趣。前者,探无涯之知,后者,不过神道设教冀其不堕而已。

——古庄译文

第二十六篇

　　Nelson, Horatio, Viscount　纳尔逊(1758—1805)　英国海军上将。1787年在印度群岛服役时,与尼斯贝特夫人(1761—1831)结婚。法国革命战争爆发时,奉命在地中海指挥"阿伽门农"号战舰。1794年在卡尔维一役中右眼失明,但他继续指挥作战,在圣维森特角附近的胜利中起到重要作用,因而获得爵士称号。不久在海战中失去右臂。1798年在地中海。尼罗河战役(Nile, Battle of)中全歼法国舰队。随后几年他在那不勒斯度过,在那里他爱上了＊汉密尔顿夫人(Lady Hamilton)。1800年回到英格兰,受到英雄般的欢迎。此时他已是尼罗男爵纳尔逊,但与汉密尔顿夫人的私情酿成大丑闻。汉密尔顿夫人在1800年生下了他们的女儿霍雷希娅。他受命统领波罗的海战事,哥本哈根一役的胜利他功不可没。归国后即晋封于爵。1803年任地中海舰队司令,封锁法国土伦港达18个月之久。1805年法军逃脱,纳尔逊穷追不舍,最终演化成＊特拉法尔加战役(Trafalgar, the battle of)(1805)。纳尔逊在"胜利"号战舰(船舶 ships)上指挥这场英军大胜仗。是役他身负致命重伤,后葬于圣保罗大教堂。

第二十七篇

　　Nepal, Kingdom of　尼泊尔王国　南亚内陆国。位于中国西藏和印度之间。大部分国土由连绵的山脉和高耸肥沃的谷地组成。沿北部国界及南部平原和沼泽区,有世界最高山峰(包括珠穆朗玛峰)。占人口多数的印度教徒为蒙古人种,从1769年起廓尔喀人建立王朝至今。经济:以农业为主。主要作物有水稻、玉米、小米和小麦。林业亦重要。除云母外,矿产资源稀少。正大规模发展水力发电。政府鼓励发展工业,如麻纺和制糖。旅游业是重要的岁入来源。外贸主要出口印度,包括谷物、典麻、木材及山中草药。历史:中世纪时期该地区由独立公国组成。到18世纪为廓尔喀人所征服,后由沙阿家族统治,再接着拉纳政权上台,统治至今。1959年通过新宪法,产生第一届民选政府。1960年尼泊尔国王解散新政府,并于1962年废除该宪法。后建立金字塔结构的地方性和中央事务委员会(panchayat),国王掌有行政权。1989年与印度一度关系紧张,遭至印度对其实施经济封锁。1990年的骚乱使议会民主政体得以恢复。1991年尼泊尔国民大会党赢得多党选举的胜利。1994年大选共产党获胜,1996年垮台,为联合政府所取代。国家元首:国王比兰德拉·比尔·比克拉姆·沙阿·德夫。首相:谢尔·巴哈杜尔·多伊巴。官方语言:尼泊尔语。官方货币:尼泊尔卢布(=100派沙)。面积:141,400平方公里(54,600平方英里)。人口(1994估计):19,525,000。首都:加德满都。

练习答案

第二十八篇

Spaniel　西班牙猎狗　英国培育的运动狗中的一种。一般认为源于西班牙。英国跳猎是典型的一种,身体瘦而结实,口鼻长,耳长而长垂,腿比相似的科克猎(cocker)长,其皮毛同样呈平伏卷曲状,耐寒,

通常黑白相间或深暗红色或白色相间,而小型的威尔士跳猎都是红白相间。白色的克伦伯长毛垂耳狗,培育于英国诺丁汉郡的克伦动物园,是最大型的品种。爱尔兰泅水猎狗有明显的暗棕色卷毛,擅长泅水。体高:51厘米(英国跳猎)。参见"查理王猎"(King Charles spaniel)。

第二十九篇

Scythians　西徐亚人　一支印欧语系的民族,曾短暂居住于小亚细亚,后于公元前6世纪定居于现俄罗斯南部。真正的西徐亚人被称作"正宗西徐人"。他们在黑海北部建立王国并用小麦和那里的希腊殖民地交换奢侈品。西徐亚人善骑术,精弓箭,故能拒敌波斯人和马其顿人。他们一直是游牧民族。公元前3世纪经过哥特人屠杀后消失。从他们的皇家陵墓中发掘的物品表明他们具有冶炼技术,尤其是作为装饰的动物图案更显示了他们的艺术技巧。

第三十篇

(1) 任何一方未经另一方事先书面同意,不得转让本协议的全部或部分,除非转让给(i)涉及转让方的因兼并、合并或其他重组而产生的任何公司,(ii) 转让方可以向其转让全部或绝大部分资产的实体;但受让方须书面同意受本协议所有条款和条件约束,并提供文件证明受让方有资格、有能力履行本协议项下的全部义务。

(2) 除非本协议另有规定,任何一方未能或延迟行使其在本协议下的任何权利、权力或特权,不应视为其放弃该权利、权力或特权;单项或部分行使任何权利、权力或特权,亦不妨碍其进一步行使该权利、权力或特权或行使其他权利、权力或特权。一方在任何时候放弃追究另一方违反本协议任何条款或规定的行为,不应被视为该一方放弃追究另一方以后的违约行为,亦不应被视为该一方放弃其在该规定下的权利或其在本协议项下的其他权利。

——孙万彪译文

第三十一篇

环境保护法
(摘录)

今天,环境问题已扩大到了下列领域:人们呼吸的空气和饮用的水之化学污染、露天采矿、堤坝和道路之修建、噪声污染、近海石油钻探、核能、三废处理、溶胶罐和不回收容器之利用和一系列其他问题。事实上,国民生活的任何一个方面都没有不涉及这样一种争议一这种争议往往使以环境论者自居的人同美国耗能社会经济增长主张者对立起来。问题在于把保护环境的需要同经济需要和试图既能应付昂贵的生活费用而又不致破坏人们所赖以为生的地球的消费者的需要平衡起来。

60年代末,各州政府和联邦政府都曾开始立法建立新的机构,来制定并执行保持空气和水洁净的标准,来保护美国现有的尚未开发的土地免受过分积极的开发商的糟蹋。1967年联邦《空气洁净法》、1970年《修正空气洁净法》和1972年联邦《水污染防治法》修正条款都给环境质量规定了新的标准。在许多情况下,各州也追随效尤,纷纷提出其对利用空气、水和土地的严格标准。美国国会的每次会议和各州州议分的大多数会议上,都提出了许多不是要提高便是要降低环境标准的新议案;还举行了听证会,会上不同利益的集团通过私人院外集团、工业联合会、工会和分民组织,使立法合自己的胃口。(利益不同的各方)必然要互相作出让步才能取得进展一如,以在不久的将来降低强制规定的汽车污染标准来换取提高空气质量的整体要求;而照顾到长期环境考虑的程度如何,则一般取决于各环境利益集团对听证会施加有效压力的能耐了。

(原文及译文均选自《英汉翻译简明教程》)

第七章 八级英译汉试卷评析篇

第一篇

译文一：

要谋求再次当选理应轻而易举。这是一些久经沙场的退伍老兵，与里根有着千丝万缕的漫长联系，与共和党的联系甚至更为久远。这些人深谙总统政治，一如他们熟知这个国家中的所有政治事务那样。竞选的背景十分宜人，可供大做文章的好消息俯拾皆是：美国正置身于太平盛世之中；作为选举的一个关键因素，整个国家的经济在步出萧条期之后正强劲反弹。此外，竞选本身所筹得的款项更是不计其数。用于支付一流水平的竞争班子工作人员工资、进行巡回造势，以及制作播放电视广告的钱款绰绰有余。最为重要的是，他们所推介的总统候选人是罗纳尔德·里根，一位风度翩翩，魅力无穷，又极具迷人沟通技巧的执政总统。与约翰·F·肯尼迪以来的任何一位历届总统相比，里根更成功地勾勒出了一幅广阔的关于美国未来的前景——美国将成了一个重振军事雄风、民众富于个人进取心、联邦政府更加精简高效的国家。

译文二：

这应该不是件难事。这都是些跟着里根多年、久经沙场的老将，他们跟共和党则有更深厚的渊源，是这个国家里最熟悉总统政治的人。竞选的背景也很有利，也很多好消息可供炒作。例如，美国上下一片和平，美国经济这一竞选要素也在经过一段时间的衰退之后开始强劲反弹。此外，这次竞选本身得到了慷慨资助，因此有充裕的资本用于组织一流的竞选班子、支付巡回演讲和电视广告的费用。而最重要的一点是，他们的候选人是罗纳德·里根，他可是位极具个人魅力和沟通技巧的总统。自约翰·F·肯尼迪总统以来，里根是最成功地勾勒出美国蓝图的总统：一个军事力量复兴、富有个人进取心、联邦政府得以精简的国家。

第二篇

译文一：

那么，要谈论美国文学，倒并非意欲断言，它与欧洲文学全然大相径庭。广而言之，美国与欧洲一直同步发展，协调一致。在任何一个特定的时刻，旅行者在两地均能目睹同一样式的建筑实例，相同款式的服饰，书架上相同的书籍。在大西洋两岸，思想如同人员与货物往来一样自由交流，尽管有时会略显迟缓。当我提及美国式的习惯、思想等概念时，我意欲在《美国式的》这一词汇之前加上某种限定，因为欧美（尤其是英美）之间的差异往往只是程度上的差异而已，并且有时候仅仅只是微乎其微的一点程度差异而已。差异的多寡是件极为微妙的事务，这极容易使一个英国人在审视美国时大感不解。他所审视的那个国家，从某些重要的意义上来说，诞生于他自己的国家，并在某些方面仍与他自己的国家相差无几——然而，它却实实在在是一个异邦。两者间存在着某些古怪的交替重叠，以及令人甚感突兀的陌生感；亲缘关系已让位于一种突如其来的异化与疏远，这种情景仿佛就像我们隔着马路向另一个人打招呼，结果却从这个人漠无表情的反应中发现，我们原来竟将一个陌生人误认为我们的熟人。

译文二：

〔在某种程度上，我赞同我那假想中的英国读者的观点。美国文学史家或许惯于过分狭隘地看待其本国文坛，误将卓著当作独特。他们确实会用过多的笔墨来渲染其本国文学，至少，对其次要作家他们肯定会这样做。此外，美国人确实会走极端，要么咄咄逼人地大肆渲染其文学，要么进行着同样不幸的亦步亦趋式的顶礼膜拜。但反过来说，英国人自己在其文学鉴赏中也显得有些狭隘愚陋。此外，在他们并无上乘表现的领域——例如绘画与音乐，他们也会走极端，不是吹嘘他们本国的作品，就是大肆模仿欧洲大陆的作品。有多少幅英国绘画试图看上去仿佛是在巴黎完成的；但我们又有多少次曾在文章中读到它们真正代表着一种"英国式的传统"呢？〕

那么，要谈论美国文学，倒并非意欲断言，它与欧洲文学全然大相径庭。广而言之，美国与欧洲一直同步发展，协调一致。在任何一个特定的时刻，旅行者在两地均能目睹同一样式的建筑实例，相同款式的服饰,书架上相同的书籍。在大西洋两岸,思想如同人员与货物往来一样自由交流,尽管有时会略显迟缓。当我提及美国式的习惯、思想等概念时,我意欲在"美国式的"这一词汇之前加上某种限定,因为欧美(尤其是英美)之间的差异往往只是程度上的差异而已,并且有时候仅仅只是微乎其微的一点程度差异而已。差异的多寡是件极为微妙的事务,这极容易使一个英国人在审视美国时大感不解。他所审视的那个国家,从某些重要的意义上来说,诞生于他自己的国家,并在某些方面仍与他自己的国家相差无几——然而,它却实实在在是一个异邦。两者间存在着某些古怪的交替重迭,以及令人甚感突兀的陌生感;亲缘关系已让位于一种突如其来的异化与疏远,这种情景仿佛就像我们隔着马路向另一个人打招呼,结果却从这个人漠无表情的反应中发现,我们原来竟然错将生人当成了熟人。

第三篇

译文一:

在某些社会中,人们希望拥有孩子是出于所谓的家庭原因:传宗接代,光宗耀祖,讨好祖辈,使那些涉及到家庭的宗教仪式得以正常进行。此类原因在现代世俗化的社会中似显苍白,但它们在其他地方曾一度构成并确实仍在构成强有力的理由。

此外,有一类家庭原因与下列类别不无共通之处,这便是:生儿育女是为了维系或改善婚姻:能拴住丈夫或者使妻子不致于无所事事;修复或重振婚姻;多子多孙,以为家庭幸福唯有此法。这一点更可以由其反面得到昭示:在某些社会中,无法生儿育女(或无法生育男孩)对婚姻而言是一种威胁,还可作为离婚的现成借口。

后代对于家庭这一体制本身所具有的深远意义远非如此。对许多人来说,夫妻两人尚不足以构成一个真正意义上的家庭——夫妻需要孩子来丰富其两人小天地,赋予该小天地以真正意义上的家庭性质,并从子孙后代身上获取某种回报。

孩子需要家庭,但家庭似乎也需要孩子。家庭作为一种社会机构,以其特有的方式,至少从原则上说,可在一个变幻莫测、常常是充满敌意的世界中让人从中获取某种安全、慰藉、保障,以及价值取向。

译文二:

在某些社会中,人们希望拥有孩子是出于所谓的家庭原因:传宗接代,光宗耀祖,博取祖辈的欢心,使那些涉及到整个家族的宗教仪式得以发挥其应有的作用。此类原因在现代世俗化的社会中似显苍白,但它们在其他地方曾一度构成并确实仍在构成强有力的理由。此外,有一类家庭原因与下列类别不无共通之处,这便是:生儿育女是为着维系或改善婚姻:能拴住丈夫或者使妻子不至于无所事事;修复婚姻或为婚姻注入新的活力;多子多孙,以为家庭幸福,唯系于此。这一点更可因其相反情形而得以凸现:在某些社会中,无法生儿育女(或无法生育男孩)于婚姻而言可构成一种威胁,并可作为离婚的一个顺理成章的(或现成的)缘由。

除了所有这一切以外,还有一个原因,那就是后代对于家庭这一体制本身所具有的深远意义。对许多人来说,夫妇两人尚不足以构成一个真正意义上的家庭——夫妻需要孩子来丰富其两人小天地,赋予该小天地以真正意义上的家庭性质,并从子孙后代身上获取某种回报。

孩子需要家庭,但家庭似乎也需要孩子。作为一种社会体制,家庭以其特有的方式,至少从原则上说,可在一个变幻莫测、常常是充满敌意的世界中让人从中获取某种安全、慰藉、保障,以及价值取向。于大多数人而言,这样的一个家庭基础,即使从其表层意义上来讲,也需要不至一人来维持其存在,并使其世代相传,生生不息。

第四篇

译文一:

梭罗所理解的"低层次",即为了拥有而去拥有,或与所有的邻居明争暗斗而致拥有。他心目中的"高层次",则是这样一种积极的人生戒律,即要使自己对自然界永恒之物的感悟臻于完美。对于他从低层次上节省下来的时间和精力,他可将其致力于对高层次的追求。毋庸置疑,梭罗不赞成忍饥挨饿,但他在膳食方面所投入的精力仅果腹而已,只要可确保他能去从事更为重要的事务,他便别无所求。

付出努力才是其本质所在,除非我们终生与困难为伴,否则就无幸福可谈。正如济慈所言,除去不可能做之事,我们一生获得的满足有多大,取决于我们选择的困难有多强。罗伯特·福罗斯特谈到"苦中求乐"时,也有异曲同工之理。就通常宣传的幸福而言,其致命弱点在于声称不用付出努力即可获得幸福。

我们甚至在竞赛中寻求困难。我们需要困难,因为没有困难也就无所谓竞赛,竞赛是制造困难以求得乐趣之道。竞赛规则就是任意强加的困难。违犯竞赛规则就是破坏乐趣。下棋时,随心所欲,肆意更改强制之规更易获胜。然而乐趣源于获胜而又遵守规则。没有困难就没有乐趣。

译文二:

梭罗所理解的"低层次",即为了拥有而去拥有,或与所有的邻居明争暗斗而致拥有。他心目中的"高层次",则是这样一种积极的人生戒律,即要使自己对自然界永恒之物的感悟臻于完美。对于他从低层次上节省下来的时间和精力,他可将其致力于对高层次的追求。勿庸置疑,梭罗不赞成忍饥挨饿,但他在膳食方面所投入的精力仅果腹而已,只要可确保他能去从事更为重要的事务,他便别无所求。

殚精竭虑,全力以赴,便是其精髓所在。除非我们愿意直面那些需要我们全身心投入的艰难困苦,否则便不会有幸福可言。正如叶芝所言,除却某些不可能的情形,我们于人生中所获取的满足皆取决于我们在多高的境界中选择我们所愿意面对的艰难困苦。当罗伯特·弗罗斯特言及"以苦为乐"时,他内心所思,大体如此。商业广告中所宣扬的那种幸福观,其致命的缺陷就在于这样一个事实,即它宣称,一切幸福皆唾手可得,不费吹灰之力。

即便于游戏之中,我们也需要有艰难困苦。我们之所以需要它,因为设若没有困难,便断无游戏可言。游戏即是这样一种方式,为了享受其中的情趣而人为地使事情变得不那么轻而易举。游戏中的种种规则,便是将困难武断地强加于人。当有人将情趣摧毁殆尽时,他总是因为拒不按游戏规则行事而使然。这犹如下棋;如果你随心所欲、心血来潮地去更改那些全然武断的游戏规则,这样去赢棋当然会更加容易。但下棋的情趣则在于,应在规则的限定范围内赢取胜利。一言以蔽之,没有艰难,断无情趣。

第五篇

译文一:

我所能奉献的没有其他,只有热血、辛劳、眼泪和汗水。摆在我们面前的,是极为严峻的考验。等待着我们的是漫长的斗争和艰苦的岁月。

要问我们的政策是什么?回答是:战斗。陆海空全面战斗。竭尽全力,用上帝赋予我们的一切力量作战,同人类罪恶史上最为黑暗、最为凶残的暴政作战争:这就是我们的政策。

要问我们的目标是什么?那就是两个字:胜利!不惜一切代价,去赢得胜利!无论道路多么崎岖,也要夺取胜利。唯有胜利,才能生存。

大家必须认识到这一点,没有胜利,就没有英帝国的存在,就没有英帝国所代表的一切,就没有推动人类朝着目标奋进的时代脉搏和动力。

译文二:

我所能奉献的唯有热血、辛劳、眼泪和汗水。我们所面临的将是一场极其严酷的考验,将是旷日持久的斗争和苦难。

若问我们的政策是什么?我的回答是:在陆上、海上、空中作战。尽我们的全力,尽上帝赋予我们的全部力量去作战,对人类黑暗、可悲的罪恶史上空前凶残的暴政作战。这就是我们的政策。

若问我们的目标是什么?我可以用一个词来回答,那就是胜利。不惜一切代价,去夺取胜利——不惧一切恐怖,去夺取胜利——不论前路如何漫长、如何艰苦,去夺取胜利。因为没有胜利就不能生存。

我们务必认识到,没有胜利就不复有大英帝国,没有胜利就不复有大英帝国所象征的一切,没有胜利就不复有多少世纪以来的强烈要求和冲动：人类应当向自己的目标迈进。

第六篇

　　出孟买湾之后的第 32 天开始就透着些许的不祥。清晨，海浪先是将一扇船门砸坏。我们冒着浓浓的雾气冲了进去，发现厨师浑身湿透，正在对这条船大发牢骚。"它变得一天比一天不中用了。它愣是要想法子把我淹死在这炉灶前。"他显得异常的愤怒。我们设法让他平静下来，而木工尽管被海水冲走过两次，但还是努力把门修好。由于发生了这一变故，我们的晚饭直到很晚才弄好，但这一点最终也变得无关紧要，因为前去厨房端饭菜的纽莱斯被汹涌的波涛掀倒在地，饭菜顺着船舷全都撒入海中。船长脸上的表情变得愈发严峻，双唇紧咬。他全然没能意识到，整条船由于被要求去完成许多它力所能及的任务，打从我们认识它以来，首次出现了力不从心的迹象。

第七篇

　　尽管我喜欢广交朋友，但我只愿与为数不多的几人成为至交。我所提及的那位黑衣男士，就是那样一个我希冀与其成为莫逆之交的人，因为他深得我的景仰。诚然，其行为举止不乏某些怪异的出尔反尔，他全然可被称为幽默家王国中的幽默大师。虽然他慷慨大方，乃至奢靡无度，但他仍假惺惺地希望人们将其视作节俭与审慎之奇才。尽管其言谈之中满是污秽和自私的格言，其内心却充盈着最博大无际的爱心。据我所知，他常宣称自己是人类憎恶者；然而，他的脸庞上却总洋溢着怜悯之情。虽然其神情会柔化为一片慈悲，我却听到过他使用最为恶劣的言辞，其恶劣程度可谓无以复加。有些人佯装人道与柔情，也有一些人则夸耀说这样的秉性乃天性使然。但在我所有认识的人当中，唯有他羞耻于其与生俱有的慈悲之心。他会竭力掩饰其真情，一如任何一个伪君子会掩饰其冷漠那样。然则，在每一个毫无防范的瞬间，那戴着的假面具便会脱落下来，使其毕露于哪怕是最为肤浅的观察者。

参考书目

包惠南.文化语境与语言翻译[M].北京：中国对外翻译出版公司,2001.
柴梅萍.电影翻译中文化意象的重构、修润与转换.www.hjenglish.com.
陈德鸿、张南峰.西方翻译理论精选[C].香港：香港城市大学出版社,2000.
陈果安.现代写作学引论[M].长沙：中南大学出版社,2002.
陈廷祐.英文汉译技巧[M].北京：外语教学与研究出版社,1980.
陈小慰.从八级翻译测试看学生亟待加强的几个方面[J].中国翻译,2002(1).
范仲英.实用翻译教程[M].北京：外语教学与研究出版社,1994.
冯树鉴.实用英汉翻译技巧[M].上海：同济大学出版社,1995.
冯庆华.实用翻译教程[M].上海：上海外语教育出版社,1997.
冯庆华、吴群.英译汉别裁[M].北京：外文出版社,2001.
傅仲选.实用翻译美学[M].上海：上海外语教育出版社,1993.
高克毅.一块肉、五香味：谈 David Copperfield 的中文翻译[A].外文中译研究与探讨[C].
　　香港中文大学翻译系,1998.
辜正坤.中西诗比较鉴赏与翻译理论[M].北京：清华大学出版社,2003.
郭著章、李庆生.英汉互译实用教程[M].武汉：武汉大学出版社,1988.
郭建中.科普与科幻翻译[M].北京：中国对外翻译出版公司,2004.
郭建中、杨士焯等.麦克米伦百科全书[Z].杭州：浙江人民出版社,2002.
郭建中.译文如何重现原著风格[J].中国翻译,1983(11)38—42.
郭建中.比较一部小说的三种译文[J].中国翻译,1993(5)41—45.
黄邦杰.译艺谭[M].北京：中国对外翻译出版公司,2003.
柯飞.翻译中的隐与显[J].外语教学与研究,2005(4).
柯平.英汉与汉英翻译教程[M].北京：北京大学出版社,2002.
勒梅琳.英汉翻译概要[M].天津：南开大学出版社,2001.
李鲁、李霄翔.英译汉练习：Feeling is believing[J].中国翻译,2000(5),71—74.
李树德.英语辅导报大学教师版 04～05 学年第 23 期.
李淑琴.语境——正确翻译的基础[J].中国翻译,2001(1).
李文革.西方翻译理论流派研究[M].北京：中国社会科学出版社,2004.
李文阳.浅论法律英语的语言特点及翻译[J].中国翻译,1994(2),13—16.
李运兴.英汉语篇翻译[M].北京：清华大学出版社,1998.
连淑能.英译汉教程[M].北京：高等教育出版社,2006.
林纪熹.英语形似句辨异[M].福州：福建人民出版社,1982.

林相周.英语理解与翻译讲话[M].上海：上海译文出版社,1985.
刘天民.英文翻译方法和实例[M].香港：香港宏业书局,1976.
陆国强.英汉和汉英语义结构对比[M].上海：复旦大学出版社,1999.
罗新璋.翻译论集[M].北京：商务印书馆,1984.
马红军.翻译批评散论[M].北京：中国对外翻译出版公司,2002.
毛荣贵.翻译美学[M].上海：上海交通大学出版社,2005.
钱伯城.古文观止新编[M].上海：上海古籍出版社,2000.
钱歌川.翻译的技巧[M].北京：商务印书馆,1982.
钱歌川.翻译的基本知识[M].长沙：湖南科学技术出版社,1981.
邵志洪.翻译理论·实践与评析[M].上海：华东理工大学出版社,2003.
思果.译道探微[M].北京：中国对外翻译出版公司,2002.
思果.翻译研究[M].北京：中国对外翻译出版公司,2002.
思果.翻译新究[M].北京：中国对外翻译出版公司,2002.
思果.名师译评丛书[Z].北京：中国对外翻译出版公司,2004.
苏福忠.译事余墨[M].北京：生活·读书·新知三联书店,2006.
孙万彪.英汉法律翻译教程[M].上海：上海外语教育出版社,2003.
孙致礼.新编英汉翻译教程[M].上海：上海外语教育出版社,2003.
谭载喜.奈达论翻译[Z].北京：中国对外翻译出版公司,1999.
偶西、董乐山、张今.英译汉理论与实例[M].北京：北京出版社,1984.
汪榕培.实用英语词汇学[M].沈阳：辽宁人民出版社,1983.
汪涛.实用英汉互译技巧[M].武汉：武汉大学出版社,2001.
王寅.英译汉：句法结构比较[J].中国翻译,1993(5),10—13.
翁显良.文学翻译丛谈[M].北京：中国对外翻译出版公司,1983.
魏志成.英汉比较翻译教程[M].北京：清华大学出版社,2004.
伍铁平.模糊语言学[M].上海：上海外语教育出版社,1999.
许渊冲.翻译的艺术[C].北京：中国对外翻译出版公司,1984.
许渊冲.文学与翻译[C].北京：北京大学出版社,2003.
徐振宗、李保初.汉语写作学[M].北京：北京师范大学出版社,1995.
杨茂勋.普通语言学[M].厦门：厦门大学出版社,1993.
杨士焯.简析彼得·纽马克的语义翻译和交际翻译理论[J].福建外语,1989(3—4).
杨士焯.翻译原则种种[Z].(译文),外国语 1990(3).
杨士焯.On the Distinction between Languge and Dialect [J]. The Linguist (U.K), 1996(5).
杨士焯.彼得·纽马克翻译新观念概述[J].中国翻译,1998(1).
杨士焯.An Interpretation of Cultural Translation[J]. The Linguist (U.K), 1998(4).
杨士焯.从一篇翻译看英语专业三年级学生的翻译问题[J].中国翻译,2000(3).
杨士焯.发挥译文的语言优势[J].上海科技翻译,2002(1),23—26.
杨士焯.英语专业三年级学生如何提高英汉翻译技能[J].中国翻译,2002(11).
杨士焯.论英语部分亲属词的模糊性及汉译处理[J].集美大学学报,2003(3).
杨士焯.百科全书条目释文的语体特征及翻译策略[J].山东外语教学,2003(6).

杨士焯.从重译文学作品看译语文化的介入[J].集美大学学报,2004(3).
杨士焯.简论翻译写作学的建构[J].写作,2008(3).
杨士焯.翻译教材编写方法探索[J],厦门大学学报(哲社)教学研究专辑,2008.
杨士焯.英汉翻译写作学[M].北京:中国对外翻译出版公司,2012.
杨志才.一篇精彩的译文[J].中国翻译,1983(10)40—42.
余光中.余光中谈翻译[M].北京:中国对外翻译出版公司,2002.
喻云根.英译汉教程[M].北京:北京工业大学出版社,1998.
袁锦翔.一种新的翻译文体[J].外语教学与研究,1987(3).
张今.文学翻译原理[M].开封:河南大学出版社,1987.
郑玉琪、王晓冬.小议电影片名的英汉翻译原则[J].中国翻译,2006(2):66—68.
周姬昌.写作学高级教程[M].武汉:武汉大学出版社,1989.
邹申.语言测试[M].上海:上海外语教育出版社,2005.
祝吉芳.英汉翻译方法与试笔[M].北京:北京大学出版社,2004.
庄绎传.英汉翻译简明教程[M].北京:外语教学与研究出版社,2002.
中国翻译1990—2005.

Bassnett, S. *Translation Studies*[M]. Shanghai: Shanghai Foreign Language Education Press, 2004.

Bell, R. *Translation and Translating*[M]. Longman Group UK Limited, 1991.

Hatim, B. *Discourse and the Translator*[M]. Shanghai: Shanghai Foreign Language Education Press, 2004.

Jakobson, R. On Linguistic Aspects of Translation[A]. Reuben, A. B. *On Translation*[C]. Cambridge: Havard University Press, 1959.

Lefevere, A. *Translation, Rewriting and the Manipulation of Literary Fame*. London: Routledge, 1992.

Newmark, P. *Approaches to Translation*[M]. Oxford: Pergamon, 1981.

Newmark, P. *A Textbook of Translation*[M]. Hemel Hemstead: Prentice Hall International, 1988.

Nida, E. A. *Language, Culture and Translating*[M]. Shanghai: Shanghai Foreign Language Education Press, 1993.

Savory, T. *The Art of Translation*[M]. London: Cape, 1957.